3rd Edition

Advanced

MARKET LEADER

Business English Teacher's Resource Book

Bill Mascull

Course components

FOR STUDENTS

Course Book with DVD-ROM

The key course component, comprising 12 units, four Working across cultures sections and four Revision units.

DVD-ROM

Included with the Course Book, the DVD-ROM includes the i-Glossary, extra self-study exercises, Course Book audio and scripts, interview videos and Case study commentaries and Grammar references.

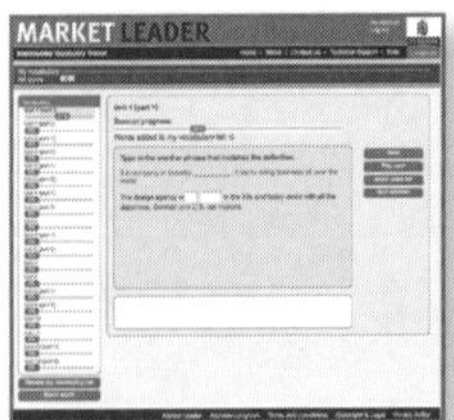

Vocabulary Trainer

www.marketleader.vocabtrainer.net

A personalised, interactive online tool which allows students to practise using target language from the Course Book in a variety of ways.

Practice File

A self-study workbook which provides extra practice for vocabulary, grammar and writing from every unit. Also includes activities to improve pronunciation and fluency through day-to-day functional English.

Business Grammar and Usage

Provides clear explanations and targeted practice to strengthen any weak points your students may have.

FOR TEACHERS

Teacher's Resource Book with Test Master CD-ROM

Includes step-by-step lesson notes and a photocopiable Resource bank of further practice exercises.

Test Master CD-ROM

Included with the Teacher's Resource Book, this CD-ROM contains digital, customisable versions of the Test File tests, the audio for these tests and 12 further unit tests.

Test File

Six photocopiable tests including four Progress tests linked closely to the Course Book, an Entry test and an Exit test.

Active Teach

The digital version of the Course Book, with interactive activities and accompanying audiovisual resources for use in class with interactive whiteboards or on a computer.

Subscription website

www.market-leader.net

A source of information and extra resources for teachers to supplement their lessons, including exclusive FT content-based lessons.

Introduction

Market Leader is an extensive business English course designed to bring the real world of international business into the language-teaching classroom. It has been developed in association with the *Financial Times*, one of the world's leading sources of professional information, to ensure the maximum range and authenticity of international business content.

1 Course aims

In addition to new authentic reading texts and listening material, the Third Edition features a number of exciting new resources:

- specially filmed interviews with business practitioners for each unit
- *Case study commentaries* on DVD-ROM, with expert views on each case
- *Working across cultures* – regular input and tasks to develop students' intercultural awareness and skills
- four *Revision* units, one after every three main units
- an interactive *i-Glossary* on DVD-ROM
- additional photocopiable tasks in this Teacher's Resource Book
- *Active Teach* software to deliver the course digitally, through an interactive whiteboard or computer.

This course is intended for use either by students preparing for a career in business or by those already working who want to improve their English communication skills. *Market Leader* combines some of the most stimulating recent ideas from the world of business with a strongly task-based approach. Role plays and case studies are regular features of each unit. Throughout the course, students are encouraged to use their own experience and opinions in order to maximise involvement and learning.

2 The main course components

Course Book

This provides the main part of the teaching material, divided into 12 topic-based units. The topics have been chosen following research among teachers to establish which are the areas of widest possible interest to the majority of their students. The Course Book provides input in reading, speaking and listening, with guidance for writing tasks, too. Every unit contains vocabulary-development activities and a rapid review of essential grammar. There is a regular focus on key business functions, and each unit ends with a motivating case study to allow students to practise language they have worked on during the unit. For more details on the Course Book units, see *Overview of a Course Book unit*. After every three units is a spread called *Working across cultures*. Here, students are introduced to key intercultural concepts, developing their awareness and skills in order to function effectively in international business situations. There are also four Revision units in the Course Book that revise and consolidate the work done in the main units and culture spreads.

Audio and DVD-ROM materials

All the listening material from the Course Book is available on the audio CD. A number of these tracks provide students with exposure to non-native English accents which they may find challenging to understand, but which will help them build confidence in their own speaking. All of the audio files are also provided in fully downloadable MP3 format on the DVD-ROM, allowing transfer to personal computers and portable audio players. The DVD-ROM is an integral part of the course. All 12 interviews from the Course Book can be viewed on the DVD-ROM, with the option of subtitles, depending on the user's preference. The interviews are accompanied by 12 video commentaries on the *Case studies*, delivered by experienced business consultants. The interviews (which form the main listening focus of each unit) and commentaries provide an opportunity for students to get expert perspectives on the latest business practice through English. None of the videos are scripted and, as such, expose students to authentic examples of natural speech. In addition, the DVD-ROM provides the students with interactive, self-study practice activities. These allow them to revisit problem areas and reinforce work done in class in their own time. The activities provide further listening practice, opportunities for task repetition and instant, personalised feedback.

The DVD-ROM also includes the *i-Glossary*, an interactive mini-dictionary which provides definitions and pronunciation of all the key vocabulary from the Course Book and which encourages further self-study.

Vocabulary Trainer

This is an online, self-study tool that lets students take control of their own learning. Once students have created a personal account, the Vocabulary Trainer tests them on the meaning, spelling, collocation and use of vocabulary learned in class. Their development is automatically recorded so they can chart their own progress outside the classroom.

Practice File

This gives extra practice in the areas of grammar and vocabulary, together with a complete syllabus in business writing. In each unit, students work with text models and useful language, then do a writing task to consolidate the learning. Additionally, the Practice File provides regular self-study pronunciation work (with an audio CD and exercises).

Teacher's Resource Book

This book provides teachers with an overview of the whole course, together with detailed teaching notes, background briefings on business content, the *Text bank* and the *Resource bank*.

The Text bank provides two extra *FT* reading texts per unit, followed up with comprehension and vocabulary exercises. The Resource bank provides photocopiable worksheet-based communication activities linked to particular sections of the Course Book units:

- *Listening bank*: extra activities based on each Course Book *Listening* interview
- *Speaking bank*: extra activities based on each *Skills* section
- *Writing bank*: a model answer to the Course Book *Writing* task, together with an additional writing exercise

Test File
Six photocopiable tests are available to teachers and course planners to monitor students' progress during the course. There is an *Entry test*, four *Progress tests*, which test both skills and language knowledge, and an *Exit test*, which reviews the work done throughout the course.

Test Master CD-ROM
Included in the Teacher's Resource Book, the Test Master CD-ROM is a useful assessment resource to accompany the course. It includes digital, editable versions of the Test File tests, enabling valid, tailored assessment. It also contains the accompanying audio files and a further 12 unit tests. Full keys and audio scripts are also provided to make marking the tests as straightforward as possible.

***Market Leader* Active Teach**
The Active Teach software provides digital access to a range of course components via an interactive whiteboard or computer. Components include the Course Book, video and audio with printable scripts, interactive activities based on the Course Book content, editable tests, the Teacher's Resource Book and the phonetic chart. It also includes the *Writing file*, which provides good models for product writing, and *Help* videos to make using the software as easy as possible. Using Active Teach facilitates student engagement and enables clear giving of instructions and valuable feedback. It is also ideal for use on a laptop in one-to-one classes.

3 Overview of a Course Book unit

Listening and discussion
Students have the opportunity to think about the unit topic and to exchange ideas and opinions with each other and with the teacher. There is a variety of stimulating activities, such as listening to short extracts, expressing personal preferences and answering questions. Throughout, students are encouraged to draw upon their life and business experience.

The authentic listening texts are based on interviews with businesspeople and experts in their field. Students develop listening skills such as prediction, listening for specific information, ordering facts, note-taking and correcting summaries.

Essential vocabulary related to the listening topic is presented and practised in each of these sections, through a variety of creative and engaging exercises. Students learn new words, phrases and collocations, and are given tasks which help to activate the vocabulary they already know or have just learned. There is further vocabulary practice in the Practice File.

There are a number of discussion activities throughout the book. Their purpose is to activate students' world knowledge, improve their fluency in English and provide them with opportunities to respond to the content of the recordings and texts.

Reading and language
Students read interesting and relevant authentic texts from the *Financial Times* and other business sources. They develop their reading skills through a variety of tasks, such as matching headings and text, ordering items, completing summaries and pairwork information exchange. They also practise useful business lexis from the texts.

The texts provide a context for the language work and discussion in this section. The language work develops students' awareness of common problem areas at advanced level. The focus is on accuracy and knowledge of key areas of grammar, text cohesion and idioms. In some units, more than one language area is presented, and there are extra practice exercises in the Language reference section at the end of the Course Book.

Business skills
This section helps students to develop their spoken and written communication skills in the key business areas, such as presentations, meetings, negotiations, telephoning, problem-solving, social English, business correspondence and report writing.

Each section contains a Useful language box, which provides students with the support and phrases they need to carry out the business tasks in the regular role-play activities. The Writing file at the end of the Course Book also provides students with useful model texts and writing guidelines.

Case study
Each unit ends with a case study linked to the unit's business topic. The case studies are based on realistic business problems or situations and are designed to motivate and actively engage students. They use the language and communication skills which they have acquired while working through the unit. Typically, students will be involved in discussing business problems and recommending solutions through active group work.

All of the case studies have been developed and tested with students in class and are designed to be easy to present and use. No special knowledge or extra materials are required. For teaching tips on making the best use of the case studies, see *Case studies that work* on page 5.

Each case study ends with a realistic writing task. These tasks reflect the real world of business correspondence and will also help those students preparing for business English exams. Models of writing text types are given in the Writing file at the end of the Course Book.

4 Using the course

Accessibility for teachers
Less-experienced teachers can sometimes find teaching business English a daunting experience. *Market Leader* sets out to provide the maximum support for teachers. The *Business brief* section at the beginning of each unit in the Teacher's Resource Book gives an overview of the business topic, covering key terms (given in bold, and which can be checked in the *Longman Dictionary of Business English*) and suggesting a list of titles for further reading and information.

Authenticity of content
One of the principles of the course is that students should deal with as much authentic content as their language level allows. Authentic reading and listening

texts are motivating for students and bring the real world of business into the classroom, increasing students' knowledge of business practice and concepts. Due to its international coverage, the *Financial Times* has been a rich source of text, video and business information for the course. The case studies present realistic business situations and problems, and the communication activities based on them – group discussions, simulations and role plays – serve to enhance the authenticity of the course.

Flexibility of use

An essential requirement of business English materials is that they cater for the wide range of needs which students have, including different areas of interest and specialisation, different skills needs and varying amounts of time available to study. *Market Leader* offers teachers and course planners a unique range of flexible materials to help meet these needs. There are suggestions in this book on how to use the unit material extensively or intensively, with fast-track routes through the units focusing mainly on speaking and listening skills. The lesson notes include suggestions on extending the classwork through the DVD-ROM and photocopiable materials in the Text bank and Resource bank sections of this book. In addition, this book gives suggestions on how to extend the course using components including the Practice File, the *Business Grammar and Usage* book, and the *Market Leader* specialist series, which develops vocabulary and reading skills (see *Extending the course*).

5 Case studies that work

The following teaching tips will help when using case studies:

1 Involve all the students at every stage of the class. Encourage everyone to participate.
2 Draw on the students' knowledge of business and the world.
3 Be very careful how you present the case study at the beginning. Make sure your instructions are clear and that the task is understood. (See individual units in the Teacher's Resource Book for detailed suggestions on introducing the case study.)
4 Ensure that all students have understood the case and the key vocabulary.
5 Encourage the students to use the language and business skills they have acquired in the rest of the unit. A short review of the key language will help.
6 Focus on communication and fluency during the case-study activities. Language errors can be dealt with at the end. Make a record of important errors and give students feedback at the end in a sympathetic and constructive way.
7 If the activity is developing slowly or you have a group of students who are a little reticent, you could intervene by asking questions or making helpful suggestions.
8 Allow students to reach their own conclusions. Many students expect there to be a correct answer. You can give your own opinion, but should stress that there usually is no single 'right' answer.
9 Encourage creative and imaginative solutions to the problems expressed.
10 Encourage students to use people-management skills, such as working in teams, leading teams, delegating and interacting effectively with each other.
11 Allocate sufficient time for the major tasks such as negotiating. At the same time, do not allow activities to drag on too long. You want the students to have enough time to perform the task, and yet the lesson needs to have pace.
12 Students should identify the key issues of the case and discuss all the options before reaching a decision.
13 Encourage students to actively listen to each other. This is essential for both language practice and effective teamwork!

6 Extending the course

Some students will require more input or practice in certain areas, either in terms of subject matter or skills, than is provided in the Course Book. In order to meet their needs, *Market Leader* provides a wide range of optional extra materials and components to choose from.

***Business Grammar and Usage* New Edition**

For students needing more work on their grammar, this book provides reference and practice in all the most important areas of business English usage. It is organised into structural and functional sections. The book has been revised and updated for the Third Edition and complements the *Language review* sections of the Course Book.

***Market Leader* specialist titles**

Many students will need to learn the language of more specialised areas of business English. To provide them with authentic and engaging material, *Market Leader* includes a range of special-subject books which focus on reading skills and vocabulary development. Each book includes two tests and a glossary of specialised language.

***Longman Dictionary of Business English* New Edition**

This is the most up-to-date source of reference in business English today. Compiled from a wide range of text sources, it allows students and teachers rapid access to clear, straightforward definitions of the latest international business terminology. The fully updated New Edition includes an interactive CD-ROM with 35,000 key words pronounced in both British and American English, together with practice material for both the BEC and BULATS exams, and is now available as an iPhone or iPod Touch app to download from the Pearson Longman website.

***Market Leader* website www.market-leader.net**

The *Market Leader* companion website provides up-to-date information about the Course Books and specialist titles and offers a wide range of materials teachers can use to supplement and enrich their lessons. In addition to tests for each level, the website provides links to websites relevant to units and topics in the Course Book and also downloadable glossaries of business terms. The *Premier Lessons* subscription area of the website has a bank of ready-made lessons with authentic texts from the *Financial Times* that have student worksheets and answers. These lessons are regularly updated and can be searched in order to find relevant texts for the unit, topic and level that students are studying. *Premier Lessons* can be used in the classroom or for self-study.

Contents

Notes on units

(including *At a glance*, *Business brief* and *Lesson notes*)

Text bank

Resource bank

Speaking

Listening

Writing

(Case study model answers and writing tasks)

UNIT 1

First impressions

AT A GLANCE

	Classwork – Course Book	Further work
Lesson 1 *Each lesson is about 60–75 minutes. This time does not include administration and time spent going through homework in any lessons.*	**Listening and discussion: First impressions in presentations** Students discuss some of the techniques for making effective and even inspirational presentations, and listen to an expert in this area, Anneliese Guérin-LeTendre, who works with Communicaid, a culture and communication-skills consultancy. They also work on vocabulary related to presentations.	**Practice File** Word power (pages 4–5) **Resource bank: Listening** (page 189) **i-Glossary** (DVD-ROM)
Lesson 2	**Reading and language:** ***It's not what you know*** Students discuss the importance of networking in different professions, and read an article about it. They then look at the use of adverbs.	**Text bank** (pages 118–121) **Practice File** Text and grammar (pages 6–7) **ML Grammar and Usage**
Lesson 3	**Business skills: Networking** Students discuss tips for communicating with people they don't know or don't know very well. They listen to some delegates meeting for the first time and networking at a conference, and then introduce themselves to another participant at an international conference. **Writing: formal and informal register** Students complete a formal e-mail invitation and write a reply, accepting the invitation.	**Resource bank: Speaking** (page 177) **Practice File** Skills and pronunciation (pages 8–9)
Lesson 4 *Each case study is about $1\frac{1}{2}$ to 2 hours.*	**Case study: Movers and shakers** Logistaid, a non-governmental organisation, is trying to raise its profile by holding a charity dinner. Students work on organising the event and on follow-up activities promoted at the dinner to support the organisation's work in developing countries.	**Case study commentary** (DVD-ROM) **Resource bank: Writing** (page 204)

For a fast route through the unit, focusing mainly on speaking skills, just use the underlined sections.

For one-to-one situations, most parts of the unit lend themselves, with minimal adaptation, to use with individual students. Where this is not the case, alternative procedures are given.

BUSINESS BRIEF

First impressions are important in business, of course, and most important in the highly stressful situations of **presentations** and **job interviews**. They are also key in **networking** and **business negotiations**. Here we look at presentations and networking/business negotiations in particular.

Presentations

Public speaking is perhaps the most nerve-racking of business skills, but it's said that if even experienced speakers don't feel the **adrenalin** flowing and **nervousness** building before a presentation, there's something wrong. **Preparation** and **rehearsal** are important, but cannot totally prepare a speaker for a roomful of perhaps sceptical people, or equipment that fails just as one is getting into full flow.

Structure is very important, of course, and the advice to **say what you're going to say, say it and then say what you said** can be useful. However, advanced students should be able to analyse and discuss very effective presentations that they have seen where the speaker does not follow this model at all. That said, less-experienced presenters should probably stick to it.

Some experts say that speakers should learn the **opening section** of their presentation by heart, and get off to a good start that way, perhaps with a **surprising fact or figure**. But presenters should learn how to sound as if they are saying this **spontaneously**, as even a short **rote-learned** section can sound insincere. Using **anecdotes** and **humour** inappropriately can be dangerous in some cultures. If in doubt, leave them out. Be aware of your **body language**.

PowerPoint is now widespread everywhere in the developed world, and using **overhead transparencies** would not make a good first impression. Don't overcrowd the slides with information, don't use too many, and speak to the audience, making **eye contact** with them, not the screen. Speakers are now so used to relying on PowerPoint that it's becoming hard to have a realistic **back-up plan** if the equipment fails, but it would be good to have one, perhaps using **handouts**.

The **question-and-answer session** at the end of a presentation has the potential to ruin a good impression created earlier. The speaker should, where possible, walk towards each questioner and repeat the question so that the whole audience can hear it. This also has the advantage of giving you time to think about the answer. If you don't know the answer, **don't bluff** – tell the questioner that you or a more qualified person from among your colleagues can deal with it later, perhaps by e-mail. Don't allow the session to ramble on, and mark the end of it clearly. (See more on Q&A sessions in Unit 10.)

The impressions created during the first two or three minutes of a presentation are important, but it's hard to imagine a presentation that cannot be 'saved' after a disastrous start if the rest of it goes relatively smoothly. Part of your job is to work on techniques that will allow your students to **recover** in this way.

Networking and business negotiations

Getting to know people with whom you may do business later is very important in some industries. Industry events like trade fairs are designed to do this. The **etiquette of business cards** is central in some cultures, for example in Asia. The amount of **eye contact**, the ratio of **talking time** to **listening time**, and **appropriate subjects** to talk about are all key.

Some cultures expect potential **business contacts** to go through a series of social situations after the initial contact: business lunches, karaoke evenings, golf games, to name a few. All these are used as a way of getting to know people in cultures where the first impression is just the first step in sizing up a person and deciding whether they are someone to do business with.

First impressions and your students

Everyone should be able to relate to this subject. In-work students will have stories to tell about the effect that they made at job interviews or with clients. Pre-work students can talk about how they will approach and prepare for their first job interviews.

Read on

Ann Demarais and Valerie White: *First impressions: What you don't know about how others see you*, Hodder Mobius, 2004

Gerd Gigerenzer: *Gut feelings: The intelligence of the unconscious*, Penguin, 2008

Malcolm Gladwell: *Blink: The power of thinking without thinking*, Penguin, 2006

Gert Hofstede: *Cultures and organisations: Software of the mind – intercultural cooperation and its importance for survival*, McGraw Hill, 1996

Tom Leech: *How to prepare, stage and deliver winning presentations*, 3rd edition, AMACOM, 2004

Steve Shipside: *Perfect your presentations*, Dorling Kindersley, 2006

Ros Taylor: *Develop confidence*, Dorling Kindersley, 2006

Fons Trompenaars: *Managing people across cultures*, Capstone, 2004

LESSON NOTES

Warmer

- Ask students what they would do to create a good impression in these situations:
  - at a job interview;
  - when giving a presentation;
  - at a drinks reception as part of a professional event, such as a conference;
  - at the beginning of a sales negotiation.
- Don't pre-empt the rest of the unit too much; hopefully students will start to think about issues such as what/how much you say, how much you listen, body language, appropriate dress, etc. in the different contexts.

Overview

- Tell the students that they will be looking at communication, especially in the context of organisations.
- Ask students to look at the Overview section on page 6. Tell them a little about the things on the list, using the table on page 8 of this book as a guide. Tell them which points you will be covering in the current lesson and in later lessons.

Quotation

- Get students to look at the quotation and ask them what they think about it. (It's hard to argue with it.)

Listening and discussion: First impressions in presentations

Students discuss some of the techniques for making effective and even inspirational presentations, and listen to an expert in this area, Anneliese Guérin-LeTendre, who works with Communicaid, a culture and communication-skills consultancy. They also work on vocabulary related to presentations.

A

- Discuss question 1 with the whole class as a quick-fire activity. Get students to discuss the remaining questions in pairs or small groups, then go through the answers with the whole class.

Sample answers

1 Possibilities are endless: concentrate on presentations in a business context. Get students to distinguish between internal presentations (i.e. to colleagues) and external ones (e.g. sales presentations to clients).

2 Many will say that it's the beginning. But holding an audience's attention in the middle, and wrapping up effectively without letting the question-and-answer session run out of control, can also be problematic.

3 Ask a rhetorical question or a real question that requires a response from the audience; state an amazing fact or figure; tell a joke (but beware of potential cultural pitfalls); tell a relevant anecdote; use a quotation; make an emphatic statement – be enthusiastic. Students will no doubt come up with others – you could compile a 'top five' by collecting them all on the board and then getting students to vote for each one.

4/5 One in which the speaker uses humour (but be aware of cultures where seriousness is prized), personal anecdotes, state-of-the-art visual aids, and ad-libs (teach this expression); interacts with and involves the audience if appropriate; and knows whether to talk for a long time or keeps it short and simple. People in some cultures (e.g. France and Germany) have quite long attention spans; others (English-speaking ones, for example) probably prefer it short(ish) and sweet.

6 These issues are usually culturally focused, e.g. open arms in some cultures suggest a person is open and honest, whereas crossing your arms might suggest you are unapproachable. Standing upright shows confidence, whereas slouching might make you look lazy. Making eye contact with your audience shows you are talking to them and that you are not shy.

B CD1.1

- Prepare students for what they are going to hear, play the recording once and ask students to answer the two questions.

1 Between 60% and 90%

2 From their voice, facial expression, posture and other factors, such as the way they use the room/space and the way they dress

C CD1.2

- Play the second part of the recording and elicit the answers.

She talks about the way you stand (posture), eye contact, voice (modulation and intonation) and controlling gestures which can distract an audience.

D CD1.2

- Read through the tips with students before you play the recording again, explaining any difficulties. Play the recording and do the exercise as a quick-fire whole-class activity, and then discuss the tips with the whole class.

1 posture **2** upright **3** charge **4** lectern
5 scan **6** modulation **7** shades **8** distraction

i-Glossary

Resource bank: Listening (page 189)

Students can watch the interview with Anneliese Guérin-LeTendre on the DVD-ROM.

E – F

- Do these as quick-fire whole-class activities. Work on stress of words, e.g. *mannerism* and *adjustment*, if necessary.

Exercise E

1 c **2** d **3** a **4** b

flicking the hair
nervous fidgeting with a bracelet or a ring
constant adjustment of a suit jacket
nervous cough

Exercise F

Sample answers

Fidgeting with a pen or papers, jangling coins in a pocket, pacing around, 'um-ing' and 'er-ing' a lot when speaking

G – H

- Go through the pronunciation and meaning of words in the box with the whole class.
- Get students to do the exercise in pairs.
- Circulate, monitor and assist where necessary.
- Then with the whole class get students to call out the answers.

1 nodding 2 nodding off 3 leaning towards 4 leaning 5 slouching/slouched 6 wander 7 staring

- Work on any other difficulties, for example the stress and pronunciation of misinterpretation.
- Get individual students quickly to enact some of these 'silent signals' for the whole class. This should lead to some hilarity!
- Ask if these things, and related things, are particularly badly thought of in their own cultures. (Running fingers through one's hair is very bad in many places, for example.)
- Get students to give other examples relevant to their own cultures. Be tactful if they mention things which would seem quite innocuous elsewhere.

I – J

- Tell students that the idea here is to concentrate on making a good impression during the first two minutes of the presentation – they don't have to prepare more than those two minutes.
- You can ask students to include an interesting fact or anecdote about themselves, a list of three, e.g. three things they like doing, and a rhetorical question to make it more memorable. You can start with your own presentation to give them an idea.
- Afterwards, check what students remember about each other.
- To avoid wasting time, allocate the subjects to different students around the class, then get them to prepare their presentations individually.
- Circulate, monitor and assist where necessary.
- Explain the task in Exercise J.
- Divide the class into four groups, and get individual students to stand up and deliver the beginning of their presentations to other members of the group. This could be done in parallel, with each of the four groups using a different corner of the classroom.
- Members of the group make notes about each presenter in their group in turn. Limit the number of presentations to about two or three in each group, depending on the time available.
- Circulate and monitor.
- Call the class to order and get students to say what some of the positive effects and the distractions were, without identifying individual presenters. (Concentrate on this and do not try to deal with language mistakes as well.)
- Then get two or three students to stand up in front of the class and give the introductions to their presentations, trying to put positive aspects into practice, and trying to avoid the possible distractions.
- If this is your first lesson with students, they might be quite nervous, so reassure them as much as possible. (Don't confuse an advanced level of English with having a good level of presentation skills.) Treat any distractions tactfully. (It's probably best not to discuss them with the whole class.)
- You could then get other students to be ready to give their presentation introductions in later lessons. (Two or three per lesson is probably enough.)
- To end the activity on a positive note, get students to put away their notes and give three items of information about the people who gave presentations.

Reading and language: *It's not what you know*

Students discuss the importance of networking in different professions, and read an article about it. They then look at the use of adverbs.

- To ease students into this section, discuss Exercise A with the whole class, asking some leading questions about students' own professions, or ones they hope to enter. (In-work students will find this easier than pre-work ones. You could talk about the importance of networking in professions where there are a lot of freelancers, e.g. media. Try to avoid too much cynicism about politics, but some students may say that this is a networking profession par excellence.)

In 2009, a study by the UK government into social mobility found that, despite accounting for only 7% of the population, people who were privately educated represent 75% of judges, 70% of finance directors and 45% of top civil servants. It also states that employers need to change their internship policies, because internships are frequently allocated on the basis of nepotism and favouritism, giving people from a privileged background an unfair boost onto the career ladder.

B

- Work on the meaning and pronunciation of difficult words, e.g. *insincere* and *manipulative*. Then get students to do the exercise in parallel pairs. Circulate, monitor and assist where necessary. At this point in the lesson, start to concentrate more on language accuracy, noting points that need work on the board, and coming back to them at the end of the exercise, getting students to say the right thing.
- With the whole class, get students to say what they came up with in their pairs, getting them to justify their answers.

C

- Get students to focus on the task before they start reading the article, which they can do individually or in pairs.
- Circulate and assist where necessary, bearing in mind that advanced learners should only have occasional problems of understanding.
- With the whole class, get students to discuss the answers.

1 The writer appears to agree with this statement. He argues shy people just need to invite people they like to dinner and later suggests that the best-connected people concentrate their efforts on people they like.

2 The writer disagrees. Building personal networks and finding contacts is useful for recent graduates. However, most people already have lots of contacts. The dilemma is how to make the most of our existing network.

3 The writer's view is that the best-connected people don't appear to be manipulative, because they concentrate their efforts on people they like and don't have any specific business goals in mind when they network.

4 The writer partially agrees here. He says online tools accelerate the process, but that high-level networking is primarily a face-to-face activity.

5 The writer partially agrees with this statement. He adds that it's about forming a network on a mutually beneficial basis and returning favours.

D

- Get students to look through the article again on their own, looking for the expressions.
- Then call the class to order and get students to call out the answers.
- Work on stress and pronunciation of words such as *re<u>ferr</u>al* and *altru<u>is</u>tic*.
- Point out that the s of apropos is silent. (You could even joke that this is a French lesson, not an English lesson.)

1 bumped into **2** leverage **3** sleazy **4** apropos of nothing **5** (provide a) referral **6** flow **7** selfless; altruistic

E

- Briefly recap what adverbs are with students before doing the exercise. (Remind them that not all words ending *-ly* are adverbs, e.g. *friendly*, and that there are also exceptions like *hard* and *fast*.)
- Do the exercise as a quick-fire whole-class activity, not forgetting to discuss those where there are two or three possibilities (most of them – point out that item 8 is different as the adverb is qualifying an adjective). Grammar purists may say that the first possibility for item 3 is wrong as it 'splits' the infinitive. If this comes up, just say that it sounds much more natural than The *dilemma is how, successfully, to leverage existing contacts*.

1. We already have enough friends and contacts.
   We have enough friends and contacts already.
2. You probably have more than 150 close contacts.
   Probably you have more than 150 close contacts.
   You have more than 150 close contacts, probably.
3. The dilemma is how to successfully leverage existing contacts.
   The dilemma is how to leverage existing contacts successfully.
4. It is important also to determine how well your contacts understand what you do.
   It is also important to determine how well your contacts understand what you do.
   It is important to determine how well your contacts also understand what you do.
5. One investment bank merely had a system for asking for two referrals.
   One investment bank had a system for merely asking for two referrals.
   One investment bank had a system for asking for merely two referrals.
6. The chances of receiving a referral are greatly increased if they understand exactly what you do.
7. High-level networking is primarily a face-to-face activity.
   High-level networking is a face-to-face activity primarily.
8. If you connect with your network on this mutually beneficial basis, the financial rewards will flow.

F

- With the whole class, get students to discuss this in relation to their own industries or ones that they would like to join.

➡ Text bank (pages 118–121)

Business skills: Networking

Students discuss tips for communicating with people they don't know or don't know very well. They listen to some delegates meeting for the first time and networking at a conference, and then introduce themselves to another participant at an international conference.

A

- As a lead-in to the section, ask students:
  - What do you understand by the term *networking*?
  - When do you network? Where? Who with? In what situations have you / do you network in English? Do you enjoy networking? Why (not)? How is it useful? (Don't spend too long on this if students never network.)
- Get students to discuss the points in pairs and then report back to the whole class. Get them to specify what sort of networking occasions they are thinking of. Go through reactions with the whole class.

Students may well say 'It depends,' but in British culture it's:

- probably not a good idea to bang on (teach this expression) about one's own products or services, without asking questions about those of the other person's organisation;
- probably best to avoid comments about clothes, appearance, etc. Compliments about a talk can be expressed by saying *That was very interesting*, etc.;
- probably good to ask the other person a few questions about him/herself, but don't overdo it;
- possible to arrange to go for a drink or for a business lunch (but lunch is much less important in the UK than some other places). Don't bring the bosses unless there's a very good reason.
- good to introduce him/her to someone you know before moving away. In any case, say something before moving away, e.g. *It was nice talking to you*. Don't just walk off.

B 🔊 CD1.3, 1.4

- Go through the points 1–8 with students. You could get them to anticipate the language that they might hear in relation to each one.
- Play the recording and elicit the answers.

	Conversation 1	Conversation 2
1 Introduce yourself.	✓	✓
2 Compliment someone.	✓	✓
3 Ask for an opinion.		
4 Agree with someone.	✓	✓
5 Check the	✓	✓
pronunciation of	–	✓
someone's name.		
6 Swap business cards.		
7 Refer to future contact.	–	✓
8 Introduce someone to	–	✓
someone else.		
	–	✓

- Don't forget to ask students about other possibilities for ice-breaking – see what they come up with and treat any incongruous suggestions tactfully.

C CD1.3, 1.4

- Get students to anticipate what they might hear in the gaps.
- Play the recordings again, allowing time for students to write in the missing words.
- Then do a round-up with the whole class, talking about the appropriacy of each question in different places.
- Question 4 might be appropriate in India and other Asian countries, but not in English-speaking and European countries. Best to be avoided, on the whole.

1 What **do you think** of the conference so far? *Conversation 1*
2 **How's business** in your part of the world? *Conversation 2*
3 **What do you like** most about living in your city? *neither**
4 **Excuse/Pardon me** for asking, but how much do you earn, by the way? *neither**
5 **I don't suppose you know** of any good places to eat near here, do you? *Conversation 2*
6 **Do you mind me** asking where you are from? *Conversation 1*
7 I didn't enjoy the dinner very much last night. **Did you**? *Conversation 2*
8 I don't think you've met (name of person), **have you**? *Conversation 2*

* Note that questions 3 and 4 are not in either conversation, so students will have to guess at the missing words.

D

- Do this as a quick-fire whole-class activity.

Sample answers

I think we've met before, haven't we?

What's business / the economic situation / the weather like in your country these days?

What do you like most about working in (*city/company*)?

What do you recommend I go and see in (*city/company*)?

What did you think of the last talk / his/ her presentation / the conference last year / the dinner last night?

Have you seen their latest model? Great, isn't it?

Advanced students should be able to come up with some good possibilities of their own.

Question 4 in Exercise C is unadvisable, of course. Some might also say that the negativity of question 7 is best avoided.

E CD1.3

- Play the recording again or get students to look at the script on page 167 of the Course Book.
- Get students to call out the answers.

- They use open questions:
  So, what did you think of the last presentation?
  And what do you think of the conference so far?
- They use question tags and agree with each other:
  Great, wasn't it? I always enjoy her talks, don't you?
  Yes, she really knows how to captivate an audience, doesn't she?
  Not bad. Fewer people than last year, aren't there?
  Yes, it must be the venue. Copenhagen isn't exactly the cheapest city to get to.
  No, that's true.
- Yasmin also asks a direct question politely:
  Do you mind me asking where you are from?
- Yasmin compliments Erik:
  You speak excellent English.

F CD1.4

- Go through the expressions in the Useful language box, working on stress and friendly intonation.
- Play the recording of Conversation 2 again, or get students to look at the script on page 167 of the Course Book.
- Elicit the answers.

1 That's a great calling card, if you don't mind me saying.
I thought your face looked familiar!
I know what you mean. Neither am I.
It's funny you should say that, ...
I don't think you've met (*name*), have you?
Good talking to you.
I'm afraid I have to make a quick call.
2 Get students to say which they prefer.
3 The last two expressions in 1 above.
You could also say:
I'm sorry, I think the next session is starting.
I'm just going to get something from the buffet / get another coffee. See you later.
I'm just going outside for a cigarette.
Sorry, but I've just seen a friend. Please excuse me. (It's been) great talking to you.

G

- Prepare students for this simple role play. Get them to turn to the relevant pages and prepare what they are going to say.
- Circulate, monitor and assist if necessary, but don't interrupt the pairs if they don't need help.
- When the pairs are ready, start the role plays. Note good points of language use, as well as half a dozen points that need further work, and add these on one side of the board.
- When the pairs have finished, call the class to order. Ask one or two pairs to 'perform' their role play for the whole class.
- Praise good use of networking language that you heard in the role plays. Then go over points that need more work, getting individual students to say the right thing.

Resource bank: Speaking (page 177)

Writing: formal and informal register

Students complete a formal e-mail invitation and write a reply, accepting the invitation.

H

- Introduce the idea of writing practice. Say that this is one of many exercises in *Market Leader* to practise writing. This might be a good time to mention the Writing file in the Course Book (pages 142–148) and the Writing section of the Resource bank in this TRB (pages 204–215).
- Point out that this particular exercise is about formal and informal register. Explain that register is using the correct type of language for particular situations, and that the register of this e-mail is quite formal.
- Explain that although this is an e-mail, it's a formal invitation from a Chamber of Commerce. It's similar in style and language to a formal letter, with the exception perhaps of the ending. Ask students how the correspondence might end if it was a letter, not an e-mail. (A letter would probably end in *Yours sincerely*, but this is not usually used in e-mails.)
- In some gaps, all three choices are possible from the grammatical point of view, but only one is possible to maintain its formal register.
- Go through the exercise with the whole class, discussing why they choose particular items, rather than just ploughing through it.

1 b **2** c **3** a **4** b **5** c **6** a **7** c **8** c **9** b **10** c

- Get students to do this for homework. Students have to write a reply accepting the invitation, but requesting more information, e.g. ask about the event details. Use formal or semi-formal language.
- Give these additional instructions:
  - Accept the invitation, thanking them politely.
  - Say you need more time to think about it and request some more information.
  - Ask about the event details, e.g. the number of attendees, the type of audience, how long the talk should be, the date/time of the dinner, etc.
  - Remember, as you do not know the sender personally, you should use appropriately formal or semi-formal language.
- If possible, get students to e-mail their work to you. Don't forget to go over it in the next class, concentrating on register and on any items that are causing difficulty to several students.

Sample answer

From: ......

To: Gloria Patterson,
Metropolitan Chamber of Commerce

Date: 19 October

Subject: Re: 'Business Today' event

Dear Ms Patterson

I am writing with reference to your e-mail of 18 October. First of all, I would like to thank you for inviting me to speak at the event 'Business Today' as organised by the Chamber of Commerce. I am considering your request, but would be grateful if you could send me further details regarding the event.

I would be very interested to know the type of audience you are expecting and whether they are local dignitaries, experienced professionals or business students and so on. Could you please let me know how many people you expect to attend the talks? I would also like to know how long my talk should be, for example, 30 minutes or one hour?

Finally, could you please confirm the date, time and venue of the conference dinner as mentioned in your letter.

Many thanks.

I look forward to hearing from you soon.

Best regards,

[Name
Position
Company]

(149 words)

Writing file (Course Book page 142)

CASE STUDY

Movers and shakers

Logistaid, a non-governmental organisation, is trying to raise its profile by holding a charity dinner. Students work on organising the event and on follow-up activities promoted at the dinner to support the organisation's work in developing countries.

- If this is the first case study you have done with the class, be sure to prepare it carefully beforehand. Read the information in the introduction of this Teacher's Resource Book (pages 4–5).
- In class, pay particular attention to clearly breaking down the case study into the different tasks and making sure that students understand and follow the structure of what you are doing, giving clear instructions for each step before starting it.

Stage 1: Background and planning meeting

- Get students to focus on the photo of the lorries. As a lead-in to the case study, ask students the following questions:
  - What do you understand by the term *NGO*?
  - What are some of the NGOs you are familiar with in your country?
  - Would you be interested in working for an NGO? Why? / Why not?
- Read the background information aloud (or ask a student to read it). Explain that Logistaid is a fictitious organisation. Deal with any other questions students may have.
- Write the headings from the left-hand column of this table on the board and elicit information from students to complete the right-hand column.

Organisation	Logistaid
Purpose of organisation	Provides emergency assistance in more than 50 countries
Type of emergency situations dealt with	Natural disasters, conflict
Main promotional event	Charity gala dinner with well-known movers and shakers (teach this expression)
Purpose of dinner	To raise the profile of the organisation

- Go through the invitation and explain any difficulties. Explain the task, which is to finalise details of the invitation in appropriate ways. Bring students' attention especially to points 4 and 5, which are not mentioned in the draft letter. (Re. point 4, say that the entertainers would be sympathetic to the charity, and would perform for free.)
- Divide the class into parallel groups of four or five and start the activity.
- Circulate, monitor and assist if necessary, but don't interrupt the groups if they are functioning acceptably. Note good points of language use, as well as half a dozen points that need further work, and add these on one side of the board.
- When the groups have finished, ask a representative of each to say what their choices were. (Get them to explain to the rest of the class who their chosen businesspeople are if they are only famous in the students' own countries.)
- Ask them also to explain how they arrived at the ticket price that they selected.
- Don't forget to ask students about the question of who will provide entertainment at the event, and, most importantly, what the follow-up will be, in relation to the movers and shakers that they selected and the work they might do.

- Praise the good uses of language that you heard, especially in relation to the topic of this unit, and work on five or six points that need improvement, getting individual students to say the right thing.

Stage 2: Listening CD1.5

- Explain to students that they are now at the event, and about to listen to a speech by Logistaid's MD, Ed Kaminski.
- Before you play the recording, ask students what they might expect to hear in a speech like this.
- Then get students to focus on the questions and play the recording once or twice.
- Explain any difficulties and elicit the answers.

Sample answers

Ed Kaminski first got involved with Logistaid when he was a student of engineering. He took a gap year, or a year out, and travelled the world. The reason why he got involved with the NGO is because he realised that although people had a great ability to design and build magnificent monuments and beautiful cities, there were still many people in the world without a roof over their heads, sick people without a hospital and children without a school. So he decided to do something about it.

He doesn't talk about facts and figures about the organisation's work, e.g. *I'd like to tell you about the number of refugees we've helped to re-house, or the number of vaccinations we've managed to give, or the number of teachers we've managed to send out to remote areas to educate enthusiastic kids, but I won't.*

The speech is quite effective, as it is inspirational. The speaker uses rhetorical questions, repetition, contrast of ideas (*I'd like to … but I won't*), emphasises his point, and uses lists of three, e.g. *people in the world without a roof over their heads, sick people without a local hospital, and children without a school.* The speech should encourage the audience to contribute or make a donation to Logistaid.

Stage 3: Task

- Explain the activity and get a student to read out Student A's role.
- Divide the class into parallel groups of six and hand out the roles. If there is room, students could stand, each group in a different corner of the classroom.
- When students have absorbed the information, the networking can begin.
- Circulate, monitor and assist if necessary, but don't interrupt if the groups are functioning acceptably. Note good points of language use, as well as half a dozen points that need further work, and add these on one side of the board.
- Get representatives of each group to explain what happened in it from a networking point of view.
- Praise the good uses of language that you heard, especially in relation to the topic of this case study, and work on five or six points that need improvement, getting individual students to say the right thing.

Stage 4: What happens next?

- Go through the task and give a few ideas if you feel that students need some inspiration.
- Then get students to re-form the groups that they were in for the previous role play, but tell them that this time they are Logistaid staff deciding on the different ways of raising the organisation's profile.
- Get the groups to start their discussion in parallel. Circulate, monitor and assist if necessary, but don't interrupt the groups if they are functioning acceptably.
- Note good points of language use, as well as half a dozen points that need further work, and add these on one side of the board.
- When the groups have finished, bring the class to order.
- Get a representative of each group to summarise the ideas that they came up with.
- Praise the good uses of language that you heard, especially in relation to the topic of this case study, and work on five or six points that need improvement, getting individual students to say the right thing.

One-to-one

Go through the case study in a similar way to the above. In the task, you and your student can take different pairs of roles successively.

During the different activities, monitor the language that your student is using. Note down any good examples of language and points that need correction or improvement. Come back to these at the end of each activity. Don't forget to praise any good examples of language use and point out some of the language that you chose to use.

 DVD-ROM: Case study commentary

Stage 5: Writing

- Make sure students understand that they must include the three different points in the letter. Get them to do it for homework.
- If possible, get them to e-mail their work to you. Don't forget to go over it in the next class, concentrating on register and on any items that are causing difficulty to several of the students.

Writing file (Course Book page 142)

Resource bank: Writing (page 204)

UNIT 2 Training

AT A GLANCE

	Classwork – Course Book	Further work
Lesson 1 *Each lesson is about 60–75 minutes. This time does not include administration and time spent going through homework in any lessons.*	**<u>Listening and discussion: Apprenticeships</u>** Students discuss training they have had and listen to Dr Bernd Atenstaedt, Chief Executive of German Industry-UK, talking about the apprenticeship system in Germany. They then listen to four people talking about their training experiences and work on training-related vocabulary.	**Practice File** Word power (pages 10–11) **Resource bank: Listening** (page 190) **i-Glossary** (DVD-ROM)
Lesson 2	**Reading and language:** ***Training leaders to connect the dots*** Students read about a Chinese manufacturing company and how its boss transformed quality through training. They then work on vocabulary from the article and discuss whether the training methods in the article could be used in the contexts that they deal with. Students then look at language used for emphasis in business communication.	**Text bank** (pages 122–125) **Practice File** Text and grammar (pages 12–13)
Lesson 3	**<u>Business skills: Clarifying and confirming</u>** Students listen to two telephone conversations where people need to clarify and confirm information, and work on related language. **Writing: effective e-mails** Students look at tips for writing e-mails, analyse a sample e-mail and practise writing more and less formal e-mails.	**Resource bank: Speaking** (page 178)) **Practice File** Skills and pronunciation (pages 14–15)
Lesson 4	**<u>Case study: Training at Carter & Randall</u>** Students come up with some solutions for a large multinational that is looking for a fast and efficient way of training its staff based in different locations around the world.	**Case study commentary** (DVD-ROM) **Resource bank: Writing** (page 205)

For a fast route through the unit, focusing mainly on speaking skills, just use the underlined sections.

For one-to-one situations, most parts of the unit lend themselves, with minimal adaptation, to use with individual students. Where this is not the case, alternative procedures are given.

BUSINESS BRIEF

Some cultures take training more seriously than others. Anyone who has stood in a slow supermarket queue in the UK while a checkout operative 'trains' a new recruit using the 'just-watch-me' method will understand this. Other organisations will have a more methodical approach to the **induction** and training of new employees.

With **in-service training**, organisations are concerned that the immediate costs will be high and the long-term **return on investment** hard to assess, and also the disruption caused by people being away from their jobs, even for a few hours. They are also worried that staff with new-found skills might leave for better jobs or that competitors might **poach** them.

For a long time, companies have had a role in the **technical education** of their employees with **apprenticeship schemes**, where apprentices often combine **on-the-job training** with more theoretical classes in a technical institution. Apprenticeships usually last several years. In many places, companies have to repair deficiencies in the school system, providing basic courses in **literacy** and **numeracy** for some young employees. But in some cases, they are also giving training at **tertiary level**: think, for example, of McDonald's Hamburger University, which provides technical and management courses to the chain's employees and, in the UK, has even started awarding nationally recognised degrees.

Distance learning courses provide a solution to managers who do not want employees to be away from their desks but, for many, the benefits of **human interaction** in the training classroom are hard, if not impossible, to replicate in other ways. **Blended learning**, combining **face-to-face** classes with **online materials**, may be the way forward. In some areas, the social element is key: some companies organise **awaydays** involving sports activities such as whitewater rafting or paintball 'battles', ostensibly to inculcate team-building and leadership skills, but some employees dislike these 'days out for the boys'.

It can be difficult to evaluate the immediate benefits of **soft-skills** training such as **effective communication**, **leadership skills**, **team building**, **assertiveness training** and **conflict management**. Skills in these areas can be difficult to measure, whereas in **hard skills**, **can-do statements** about what people are capable of are a useful yardstick of whether **specific learning objectives** have been reached. For example, as language trainers, we assess the ability of learners to perform particular tasks in English, rather than just their mastery of grammatical structures.

Mentoring and **coaching** are currently fashionable forms of one-to-one, personal development in business, particularly for senior executives, and for **high flyers** who are being groomed for jobs at that level. **Mentoring programmes** tend to be long term and allow a lower-ranking manager to be mentored by a more experienced executive who is not their immediate boss – someone who can bring another perspective. The **mentor** offers personal training and advice as the junior employee – the **mentee** or **mentoree** – rises through the organisation. **Reverse mentoring** is also becoming common, with junior employees tutoring more senior ones in the latest technologies and social trends, so that senior managers can keep up with new factors affecting their business, such as social networking.

In the past, many companies could offer employees a **job for life**. Today, people are more aware of the need to keep their **skills updated** with **continuous** and **self-directed learning**, knowing that their organisation may let them go at any time. Many companies function with a core of in-house salaried employees, some of whom may later become contractors or **freelancers**, with their former employer as their first client. The company in effect serves as a training organisation for this cadre of freelancers, but the freelancers have to be sure that their **professional development** continues: that they are keeping their skills and knowledge up to date after they leave.

Training and your students

Pre-work students will have opinions about the training or education they have been through and that they are currently in, and hopefully will be encouraged by this unit to think about the role of training in their future careers. In-work students will have opinions about their previous training experiences and future training needs.

Read on

Russell L. Ackoff, Herbert J. Addison, and Sally Bibb: *Management f-laws: How organizations really work*, Triarchy, 2007

P. Nick Blanchard, James W. Thacker and Andrew Stull: *Effective training – systems, strategies and practices*, Pearson, 2006 edition

Marcia L. Conner: *Learn more now – 10 simple steps to learning better, smarter and faster*, Wiley, 2004

Robert Harvey, Paul Stokes, David Megginson: *Coaching and mentoring: Theory and practice*, Sage, 2008

Gavin Ingham: *Motivate people: Get the best from yourself and others*, Dorling Kindersley, 2007

David Kay and Roger Hinds: *A practical guide to mentoring*, How To Books, 2009 edition

Henry Mintzberg: Managers not MBAs: *a hard look at the soft practice of managing and management development*, Berrett-Koehler, 2005

Donald Sull, with Yong Wang: *Made in China: What Western managers can learn from trailblazing Chinese entrepreneurs*, Harvard Business School Press, 2005

LESSON NOTES

Warmer

- Ask students to brainstorm, in small groups, the types of training they would like to have (apart from English-language training, of course) and why – this could range from training in other languages, through lessons to play an instrument, to business skills like accounting or leadership training.
- Don't let this run on too long. After about three minutes, get a representative of each group to call out the subjects that the different members of their group came up with, and why they chose them.

Overview

- Tell students they will be looking at different types of training and professional development.
- Go through the overview panel at the beginning of the unit, pointing out the sections that students will be looking at.

Quotation

- Ask students what the quote means and what they think of it. You could ask what a training course for a monarch might consist of. Treat tactfully, of course.

Listening and discussion: Apprenticeships

Students discuss training they have had and listen to Dr Bernd Atenstaedt, Chief Executive of German Industry-UK, talking about the apprenticeship system in Germany. They then listen to four people talking about their training experiences and work on training-related vocabulary.

A

- Students work in pairs to discuss the three questions. At this point, do not intervene too much, except to help students with the names of different types of training courses in English where necessary.
- Then, with the whole class, get feedback from each pair. Start to work on correct use of words like *train, coach, educate*, etc. In relation to question 1, you could get students to come up with other words that people use about training, e.g. *challenging, enjoyable, stimulating, practical.*
- Discuss the questions and get students to talk especially about work placements as a way of leading in to the next section.

B CD1.6

- Get individual students to say what they understand by *apprenticeship*, and if it exists in their own countries as an officially recognised form of training, but don't pre-empt Exercise D too much. Get students to practise the stress of *apprenticeship.*
- Say that Dr Atenstaedt is based in London and that the organisation he works for 'is the voice of German industry in the UK'. (If students want to know more, they can go to http://www.gi-uk.co.uk.)
- Get students to focus on the question and play the recording.
- Elicit the answers.

a) Benefits of apprenticeships for the apprentice: it gives a young person a focus in life; apprentices also get a monthly allowance. (They also get on-the-job training.)

b) Benefits of apprenticeships for the employer: apprentices become permanent employees who will show loyalty to a company because they have been trained by the company.

C CD1.7

- Get students to read the statements and predict some of the answers.
- Play the second part of the recording and elicit the answers.

1. About **60 per cent** of school leavers **go into apprenticeship programmes / become apprentices.**
2. The majority of apprentices like to work for **well-known companies**, e.g. **BMW, Mercedes** and **Siemens.**
3. Apprenticeship programmes in Germany usually last **between two and** three and a half years, and apprentices **sign a contract / sign an employment contract** at the start.
4. Apprentices tend to work **three to four days** and spend **one to two days** doing their vocational training.
5. Apprenticeships are well established in Germany: there even exists a **Training Act** including various **recognised skills** for different kinds of professions.
6. Germany is proud of the two expressions: **Trained in Germany** and **Made in Germany.**
7. They have been in talks with the (**British**) **government** to set up a similar (**dual**) **training system** in the UK.

D

- Do as a whole class activity. In a multinational class, get students to compare and contrast the options in different countries.

E CD1.8–1.11

- Explain the task and get students to focus on the four people they are going to hear.
- Play the recording and elicit the answers.
- With the whole class go through the answers, asking students for their reactions, rather than just ploughing through the exercise.

1. B: electronics technician; F: aeronautics technician
2. R: degree in Business Studies and French; M: degree in Linguistics, specialising in German
3. F: they were worried he would be missing out on a decent education
4. F: because he saw an ad in an aeronautical magazine about apprenticeships with Rolls Royce; he would be going to college, getting qualifications and spending time working on planes, all while being paid.
5. B: Technical Service, Parts, Marketing, Sales, and the Product department
6. M: Because she's just graduated / finished her degree
7. R: Zurich
8. F: The satisfaction of knowing that you've fixed something. He also loves working in development and testing because it's innovative and hi-tech.

F

- Work on the questions with the class and elicit the answers.

Suggested answers

Brendan says don't be afraid to take risks and do something you will enjoy and believe in.

Falak says you have to aim high and go for it and being enthusiastic is important.

Rachel says you need to have passion for what you do, as well as having a good understanding of what's going on in the marketplace. She also says you need to do lots of research to find out what options are available.

Marieke asks for advice as she has no work experience – get your students to give their suggestions.

G

- Get students to work on this exercise in pairs. Circulate, monitor and assist if necessary, but don't interrupt the pairs if they are functioning acceptably.
- Bring the class to order and elicit the answers.
- Work on stress and pronunciation (e.g. *qualify* v. *qualification*, *graduate* (the person) v. *graduate* (the verb)) and highlight word stress on the board.

1 training **2** trainer/trainee **3** employment **4** employer/employee **5** apprentice **6** allowance **7** educate **8** educator **9** internship **10** qualification **11** placement **12** advice **13** advisor/adviser **14** graduate **15** graduate

H

- Do as a quick-fire whole-class activity, working on any remaining difficulties.

1 internship **2** technician **3** development **4** advisor/adviser **5** qualifications **6** training **7** placement **8** industry **9** allowance **10** graduate **11** employment

I

- Students can discuss these questions in small groups or pairs.
- Circulate, monitor and assist if necessary, but don't interrupt the groups if they are functioning acceptably.
- With the whole class, get representatives of different groups to give their reactions, and compare and contrast them.

i-Glossary

Resource bank: Listening (page 190)

Students can watch the interview with Dr Bernd Atenstaedt on the DVD-ROM.

Reading and language: *Training leaders to connect the dots*

Students read about a Chinese manufacturing company and how its boss transformed quality through training. They then work on vocabulary from the article and discuss whether the training methods in the article could be used in the contexts that they deal with.

Students then look at language used for emphasis in business communication.

A

- Tell students the subject of the anecdote (teach this word if they don't know it) and get them to focus on the two pre-questions before reading it.
- With the whole class, elicit the answer to question 1 and ask students to talk about the situation in question 2, getting them to compare and contrast their organisations. http://www.gi-uk.co.uk.)http://www.gi-uk.co.uk.)

1 The lesson the boss at Haier wanted the employees to learn was one of 'creative destruction': to do things well, or to be more creative, it is sometimes better to destroy what you have done and start all over again.

B

- Get students to focus on the two questions here, and to read the main article in pairs or individually.
- Circulate, monitor and assist if necessary, but don't interrupt unnecessarily.
- Call the class to order and elicit the answers.

1 Haier's approach to executive education is very practical and involves executives working in teams, discussing problems across the company, learning about other departments, trying out ideas for possible solutions and then reporting back to colleagues in class.

2 The possible benefits to this approach are that managers learn about the company as a whole as they learn how to 'connect the dots' and stop seeing things only from their position in the organisation, which makes them more versatile as managers. They also learn to improve their general management skills in a very practical way, putting ideas into practice at work. Haier therefore gets an immediate 'return on investment' from the training.

- Don't just plough on with the next exercise. Get students' reactions to the article and talk about any lessons that could be applied to their own organisations.

C – F

- Get students to work on these exercises in small groups, discussing the possible alternatives. Circulate, monitor and assist if necessary, but don't interrupt the groups if they are functioning acceptably.
- Bring the class to order after each exercise and compare different groups' answers.

Exercise C

Sample answers

1 Haier's executive education involves training general managers to deal with **a range of threats and opportunities/challenges/problems**.

2 The writer of the article interviewed **the staff that run Haier's training centre and executives who did the training**.

3 More than 70 of Haier's senior managers take part **in weekly sessions on Saturday mornings**.

4 Executives on the programme discuss possible solutions to problems and then **try them out at work; later they report back to colleagues and perhaps refine their action plan**.

5 Executive teams are mixed up regularly on the course to **keep them fresh**.

6 Two of the main outcomes are that managers can better understand **various parts/departments of the organisation and how to 'connect the dots'; to understand Haier's situation as a whole**. (Other possible outcomes: how to spot opportunities for productive collaboration and build general management skills. (See paragraph 5 and question 7.))

7 Participants become more versatile as they learn to face different challenges **and improve their general management skills**.

8 The coaches think of ways to check progress; they provide correction and **help executives to refine their action plan**.

Exercise D

1 d **2** f **3** g **4** c **5** j **6** a **7** i **8** h **9** e **10** b

Exercise E

Get representatives of different groups to say what their conclusions were, and discuss with the class as a whole.

Exercise F

It is important because one of the key skills that employers are looking for is good communication skills, both in speaking and writing. It's essential to be able to communicate well, and knowing how to emphasise your point is particularly useful in these situations: when writing e-mails, reports, proposals, as well as when working in a team, leading a team, negotiating or giving presentations.

1 *... to discuss their individual challenges, explore possible solutions and discuss how best to implement proposed changes.* (lines 38–42)
Faculty mixes executives from different functions, business units and provinces ... (lines 42–44)
First, ... Second, ... Third ... (lines 54–65)
They also help the executives refine their action plan, devise practical ways to track progress and facilitate mid-course correction. (lines 76–79)

2 *One of the most daunting, however, is ...* (lines 2–3)
... one of the most successful companies in China. (lines 14–15)
... get the most value for their investment ... (lines 82–83)

3 *... Haier has risen from a nearly bankrupt collective enterprise 25 years ago to one of the most successful companies in China.* (lines 12–15)
... discuss what worked and did not ... (lines 50–51)
... understand Haier's situation as a whole, rather than looking at the market through the window of their own silo. (lines 62–65)

4 *turbulent markets* (lines 1–2), *volatile markets* (line 7), *versatile general managers* (lines 19–20), *in the pejorative sense* (line 71)

5 *... discuss what worked and [what] did not...* (lines 50–51)
These courses are anything but 'academic' ... (lines 70–71)

G

- Get students to do this for homework and if possible e-mail it to you before the next lesson. Don't forget to give feedback then.

Sample answer

Are you fed up with hum-drum departmental meetings? Do you ever wonder why the meeting was called in the first place? Have you ever thought you could keep the meeting on track more effectively than the Chair?

Even for the most cynical of you, I'd strongly recommend our inspiring in-house training, Managing meetings successfully. Not only is it right on topic, but it is one of the most enjoyable courses I've attended for a long time. Why? Firstly, it's practical; secondly, the trainer manages to make the deathly topic of meetings fun; and thirdly, it gave our department the best value for our modest training budget.

Experienced trainer Carolina Modesti facilitates various role-plays, including the standing-up meeting for project updates, the Zen-style meeting as an antidote to confrontational meetings and the videoconference meeting for non-techie managers.

Carolina's training company has other courses on offer – I've already requested one on coaching for our department.

Sign up now: you'll experience meetings as you've never experienced them before!

Contact Adam Koehler in HR – places are limited.

(173 words)

 Text bank (pages 122-125)

Business skills: *Clarifying and confirming*

Students listen to two telephone conversations where people need to clarify and confirm information, and work on related language.

A CD1.12, CD1.13

- Tell students about the subject of this whole section (see above) and get them to focus on the two questions.
- Play both recordings once or twice and elicit the answers, getting students to explain their reasoning.

The first conversation between Mel Van Der Horst and Naomi Taylor is more formal than Mel's conversation with the receptionist, Pierre. That's because Mel and Pierre are clearly work colleagues who know each other quite well. Mel and Naomi have apparently never met, so they are more polite and formal with each other.

B

- Go through the expressions in the Useful language box, working on stress and intonation, getting individual students to say the different utterances.

You'd use the more formal-sounding expressions with people you know less well, e.g.

Would you mind repeating that / going over that again for me?

Sorry, could I ask you to give me those details again?

Could you explain/clarify what you meant by / when you said ...?

Let me see if / make sure I understood you correctly. You're saying ...

Is that right/correct?

Can I just check that?

I'd just like to confirm that.

No, I meant to say that / what I meant was ...

Not quite, it's ....

Well, actually, what I said/meant was ...

Not exactly, I said/meant that ...

With people we know well we tend to be more direct, e.g.

And the date was ...?

So that's nine o'clock on Thursday, then.

It's also common for native English speakers in the UK to say *sorry* when asking someone to repeat details and when correcting a misunderstanding, e.g. *Sorry, not quite, it's ...; Sorry, no, I meant to say that / what I meant was ...*

C – **D** CD1.12, CD1.13

- Play the recordings again and elicit the answers.

Exercise C

1 d **2** a, c, e **3** b, f

Exercise D

The speakers use a more direct style to check and confirm information, e.g.

M: *You mean we can't have that room at all?*
P: *No, what I meant was ...*
M: *C2's the one next to the vending machines on the third floor? Right?*
P: *OK, I'll put you in B13 from nine to midday, ...*

E

- Explain the situation. Read out Student A's role, and the role information.
- Then divide the class into pairs and allocate the roles; get Student Bs to turn to page 149 and give them time to absorb their information.
- Get the pairs to start their conversations when they are ready, sitting back to back, or, better still, using telephone equipment.
- Circulate, monitor and assist if necessary, but don't interrupt the pairs if they are functioning acceptably.
- When most pairs have finished, bring the class to order. Ask one or two of the pairs how their conversations went.
- Praise good language points that you heard and go over half a dozen expressions that have been causing problems, especially in the area of clarifying and confirming, getting individual students to say the right thing.

 Resource bank: Speaking (page 178)

Writing: *effective e-mails*

Students look at tips for writing e-mails, analyse a sample e-mail and practise writing more and less formal e-mails.

F

- Ask students to work in groups of three or four. Start with a discussion of students' use of e-mail. Who do they write to? How often do they use e-mail? Does their writing style vary according to the recipient of the e-mail (how and why)? Do they ever have to write in English? How often do they write e-mails in English, and who to?
- Circulate, monitor and assist with the discussions. Make a note of any useful vocabulary students use relating to the topic of e-mail, and three or four common errors for correction with the whole group. Write these on the board, in two separate sections, while students are completing the task. Earlier finishers can be referred to the board to see if they know all the words and if they can correct the errors.
- Go through the language points for praise and correction on the board with the whole class.
- As a round-up of the discussion, ask students who writes the most e-mails in English in each group and find out more details about this.
- Ask students to work in the same groups of three or four. Brainstorm five tips for writing effective e-mails. Tell all students to write down the tips, as they will need to refer to these later. Set a five-minute time limit for this. Circulate and monitor what students are writing.
- Regroup students, so that they now have a partner from a different group. Get them, in pairs, to compare ideas.
- Ask students to read the tips and see if their ideas were mentioned. Go through any difficult words and phrases (e.g. *subject header, recipient, proofread*) with the whole class.

G

- In pairs, ask students to decide if the e-mail follows the tips. What things are good about it? What could be better?

Sample answers

It is one very long paragraph, which could be edited down and split up.

Essential information like the time and date of the first session are missing.

The *FYI* in the subject line could be misleading, as the readers might think they don't have to do anything except read the e-mail, when in fact they are asked to reply at the end of the message.

On the positive side:

It gives important information at the top.

There are no spelling or grammatical errors.

The semi-formal register is appropriate for the readers.

It doesn't overuse abbreviations.

It asks for action.

H

- Get students to do this for homework, incorporating what they have learnt in this section, and if possible e-mail it to you before the next lesson. Don't forget to give feedback then.

Sample answers

1

To: Pat Fischer

Subject: Staff Development Day

Hi Pat

This is just to ask you about the Staff Development Day on 14 May. It sounds interesting, and I'm thinking about coming along. Could you give me some more details about the event?

What is the focus of the day, and what types of activity will be involved? When are the start and finish times, and what time's lunch? Who else is going to be there, and who's running the event? Also, is it going to be held here in the company offices or at an off-site location? If so, where?

Is it necessary for me to attend the entire day? I ask because I have a meeting scheduled for that morning, but I can probably re-arrange it if I have to. Let me know what you think.

All the best

2

To: Development Team

Subject: Staff appraisals

Attachment: Feedback form

Hello everyone

I'm writing to arrange an appraisal interview with each of you next month. The main aim of the interview is to discuss your performance and professional development.

In preparation for the appraisal, I have attached a feedback form. I'd be very grateful if you could complete and return this within the next 14 days.

Could you also e-mail me with three possible dates and times – in order of preference – when you would be available for your appraisal next month? It should take about 90 minutes.

Let me know if you have any queries about the appraisals.

Many thanks

 Writing file (Course Book page 143)

CASE STUDY

Training at Carter & Randall

Students come up with some solutions for a large multinational that is looking for a fast and efficient way of training its staff based in different locations around the world.

Stage 1: Background and listening CD1.14–1.17

- Get students to study the background information in the Course Book.
- Write the headings on the left-hand side of the table and elicit information from students to complete the right-hand side.

LESSON NOTES / CASE STUDY

Company	Carter & Randall
Based in	Cleveland, Ohio
Industry	Consumer goods – 100s of household names
Key success criteria	Excellent customer service Role of sales force to provide timely info about sales, customer buying habits and competitors' activities

- Explain the task. Ask students to give some ideas about what salespeople might say about their training needs.
- Students listen to each recording once or twice – you could get them to write short summaries in pairs. Go through points with the whole class, asking them if they can relate to these ideas from their own experience. (Whether they do will depend largely on whether they are pre-work or in-work students, and their experience of sales.)

- Speaker 1 (Amy Cheng, the graduate recruit) says the training stopped after the training programme for new graduates in the first year. She mentions that there are training modules on the intranet, but she wants to 'take some ownership' of her learning and develop particular skills. She's interested in a leadership course.
- Speaker 2 (Charlie Turner, the veteran Sales Rep) says there's nothing he can learn about selling. And he's got a good relationship with his customers. He also comments that with a full-time job and a family, it's hard to find the time for training. His main concerns are all the new applications and software, for which the training is ad-hoc and informal. He also can't keep up with all the new products, and prefers to sell 'the old favourites'.
- Speaker 3 (Kamal Satinder, the first Regional Manager) says he wants some help with his merged sales team, which is not integrating well and creating tension and rivalry in the team. He wants to make them 'externally competitive but internally cooperative'.
- Speaker 4 (Jessica Armstrong, the second Regional Manager) says the Sales Reps have to be able to familiarise themselves quickly with new products without losing too much valuable time in the field. Some of her experienced Sales Reps could do with updating their skills in customer awareness training to become better listeners, more responsive to customers needs, and 'pro-active' in their approach to selling.

Stage 2: Press release

- Get students to read the press release quickly and get them to say what the implications for the UK Director of Sales are – the sales force will have to be trained in using the new system.
- Ask which of the people above would probably be most resistant to it (probably the veteran Sales Rep).

Stage 3: Tasks

- Read through Task 1 and explain any difficulties. When the situation is clear, allocate the roles and make sure that the Student Bs turn to the correct page.

If you think your students will need further input, here are some suggestions they might consider. Otherwise, you could give them these ideas after the task, and compare them with what the ones that they came up with.

- The training could probably be a combination of face-to-face instructor-led training on day 1, and hands-on in-store coaching and assessment on day 2.
- The company will probably need to consider hiring an external training company to deal with such a large-scale training programme that needs to be done in a short space of time.
- One option for post-training support is to make some sales people 'power users' and give them extra training. The 'power users' can be future troubleshooters for their colleagues before referring problems to the IT help desk.
- A training manual that will fit in the glove-compartment of a car would be useful for sales reps.

- When students are ready, get them to start the activity. Circulate, monitor and assist if necessary, but don't interrupt the groups if they are functioning acceptably. Note language points for praise and correction later.
- When pairs have finished, bring the class to order. Ask one or two of the pairs to say what happened in their meeting and the ideas that they came up with, but don't pre-empt Task 2 too much.
- Praise good language points that you heard and work on half a dozen that need it.
- Then move on to Task 2. 'Separate' the pairs and get students to work in groups of three to six, with one or two representatives from each of the three departments. Appoint a chair for each group and tell the chairs that they will be presiding over their group, leading the discussion, but trying not to dominate it.
- Explain the task and deal with any difficulties; when groups are ready, get them to begin.
- As before, circulate, monitor and assist if necessary, but don't interrupt the groups if they are functioning acceptably. Note language points for praise and correction later.
- When pairs have finished, bring the class to order. Ask one or two of the groups to say what happened in their meeting and some of the ideas that they came up with.
- Praise good language points that you heard and work on half a dozen that need it, getting individual students to say the right thing.

One-to-one

Go through the first two stages as above. For Task 1, take one of the roles and get your student to take the other.

Monitor the language that you both use. After the discussion, draw attention to some key language that your student used correctly and give praise. Also work on five or six points for correction, e.g. pronunciation, vocabulary, structural errors.

If there is time and interest, do the role play again, this time swapping roles.

Repeat the procedure for Task 2.

It's also well worth recording activities such as role plays, summaries and presentations with a one-to-one class for intensive correction work from time to time.

 DVD-ROM: Case study commentary

Stage 4: Writing

- Point out the breaking news on page 149 of the Course Book. Tell students that their writing task has to take this into account.
- Brainstorm the information that should go in the e-mail and put these points on the board. All this information should have come up in the role plays in Tasks 1 and 2.
- Ask students to look at the writing tips in the Business skills section again and the model e-mail in the Writing file (Course Book page 145).
- Get students to write the final e-mail for homework. If possible, get them to e-mail it to you so that you can give feedback in the next class.

➡ Writing file (Course Book page 145)

➡ Resource bank: Writing (page 205)

UNIT 3

Energy

AT A GLANCE

	Classwork – Course Book	Further work
Lesson 1 *Each lesson is about 60–75 minutes. This time does not include administration and time spent going through homework in any lessons.*	**Listening and discussion: Clean energy** Students discuss sources of energy and ways of saving energy. They then listen to an energy expert talking about alternative energy and learn and practise some energy-related language.	**Practice File** Word power (pages 16–17) **Resource bank: Listening** (page 191) **i-Glossary** (DVD-ROM)
Lesson 2	**Reading and language:** ***The danger of losing touch with reality*** Students read an article about the head of a Norwegian oil company and his views on how the world economy should respond to the need to limit greenhouse gases.	**Text bank** (pages 126–129) **Practice File** Text and grammar (pages 18–19)
Lesson 3	**Business skills: Decision-making** Students look at meetings where decisions are made and the language that is used for this. **Writing: layout and structure of reports** Students look at the structure and layout of reports.	**Resource bank: Speaking** (page 179) **Practice File** Skills and pronunciation (pages 20–21)
Lesson 4	**Case study: Energy saving at Tumalet Software** Students look at the problems of energy cost at a software company and make proposals for savings.	**Case study commentary** (DVD-ROM) **Resource bank: Writing** (page 206)

For a fast route through the unit, focusing mainly on speaking skills, just use the underlined sections.

For one-to-one situations, most parts of the unit lend themselves, with minimal adaptation, to use with individual students. Where this is not the case, alternative procedures are given.

BUSINESS BRIEF

The debate on current energy use is dominated by oil. Many experts predict that we are reaching **peak oil**, the point at which production will reach its highest point, as no more reserves will be found to replace those that have been **depleted**. Others say that new oil reserves will be found and exploited, especially as the rising price of oil will make it worthwhile to **exploit** reserves that were not previously **economically viable**. Oil is of course key to the car industry, but is also used to fire **power stations** and is the raw material for many **plastics**. The **volatility** of many of the countries that produce oil is one of the key issues in **geopolitics**.

Another **fossil fuel** is **natural gas**, often transported in refrigerated, liquid form as **liquefied natural gas** (LNG). Most of the new **power stations** developed around the world are **gas fired**. Again, the political dimension is acutely important with, for example, Russia able to cut off its supplies to its southern (and potentially western) neighbours at will.

But the fossil fuel that was so important in the Industrial Revolution, **coal**, is still key to many **developing-world economies**. A new coal-fired power station opens in China every week, and the booming economies of Asia in general are causing a fast rise in **carbon emissions**, even as emissions are rising less slowly, or even falling, in other parts of the world.

Emissions from using these **hydrocarbons** of **carbon dioxide (CO_2)** and other **greenhouse gases** cause **global warming**, and limiting them was the key goal of the **Kyoto Agreement** in the 1990s. A system of **carbon trading**, where emitters of carbon who did not use their **quota** could sell it to others who were exceeding theirs, was instituted. But following the world **economic crisis** of 2007–2009, increasing sniping from **climate sceptics**, the failure of the **Copenhagen summit** in 2009 and the relatively modest objectives for **carbon reduction** agreed at **Cancún** in 2010, progress in confronting **climate change** has been very slow.

Oil, gas and coal are, of course, **non-renewable** or **unsustainable** energy sources. Despite the lack of political will at Copenhagen and Cancún, oil-based economies such as the US are looking at **renewables** as a way of becoming less dependent on oil, quite independently of the debate on global warming. In Texas, the world's biggest **wind farms**, with their **wind turbines**, can be found next to oil wells. **Wave power** is being developed off the stormy coasts of Scotland, **tidal power** already exists in estuaries with large tidal differences, such as La Rance in Brittany, and **solar panels** are to be found in the deserts of Spain. **Hydroelectric power** has been around for a long time. But all these renewables together contribute only about four per cent of the world's **energy requirements**.

Of course, the most controversial renewable is **nuclear energy**. Some countries, such as France, depend heavily on it – nearly 80 per cent of electricity there is generated by nuclear power stations. **Green lobbyists** are opposed to **nuclear power** because of the potential risks. However, some of its erstwhile opponents have come round to the view that it is the answer to global warming.

And **alternative energy sources** (other than renewables mentioned above) are slowly emerging. Cars powered by **hydrogen fuel cells**, whose only emission is water vapour, have started to appear, and this form of energy could one day have many other applications – however, development lead-times for this are extremely long.

Energy and your students

Both pre-work and in-work students should be able to talk about energy sources and energy costs as consumers and be aware of the environmental issues and the dwindling supply of **fossil fuels**. They may also have opinions on the merger of energy companies, nuclear power and their governments' energy policies. **Energy conservation** is an important area, and students should be able to talk about what they have done in their own homes and lifestyles to reduce energy consumption.

Read on

Nancy Birdsall and Arvind Subramanian: *'Forget emissions, focus on research'*, Financial Times, November 17 2009.

Gwyneth Cravens: *Power to save the world: The truth about nuclear energy*, Vintage, 2008

David MacKay (editor): *Sustainable energy – without the hot air*, UIT, 2008

Ron Pernick: *The clean tech revolution: Discover the top technologies and companies to watch*, Collins, 2008

Paul Roberts: *The end of oil*, Bloomsbury, 2005

For further reading see also:

http://en.wikipedia.org/wiki/Renewable_energy

http://en.wikipedia.org/wiki/Chernobyl_disaster

http://en.wikipedia.org/wiki/Deepwater_Horizon_oil_spill#FRTG

http://www.ft.com/cms/s/0/2cc64f26-d3b6-11de-8caf-00144feabdc0.html

LESSON NOTES

Warmer

- Ask students how energy-conscious they are. Get them to give a show of hands for each of these questions, and briefly discuss each one without pre-empting the rest of the unit.

  Do they ...
  - consistently switch off lights and turn down heating when leaving a room at home?
  - use energy-saving light-bulbs?
  - pay attention to energy loss from their house/flat, installing double- or triple-glazing, insulating the loft, etc.?
  - recycle newspaper, cardboard and glass?
  - pay attention to fuel economy when buying a car?
  - pay attention to fuel economy when driving?
  - look forward to being able to own an electric or hybrid car?
- You could add more questions of your own.

Overview

- Tell students they will be looking at developments in the energy industry.
- Go through the overview panel at the beginning of the unit, pointing out the sections that students will be looking at.

Quotation

- Ask students to say what Paul Ehrlich meant by this. (Energy use causes damage to the environment, so unlimited low-cost energy would cause unlimited damage.)
- Tell interested students that they can find out more about him at: http://en.wikipedia.org/wiki/Paul_R._Ehrlich.

Listening and discussion: Clean energy

Students discuss sources of energy and ways of saving energy. They then listen to an energy expert talking about alternative energy and learn and practise some energy-related language.

A

- Students work in small groups of three or four to discuss the four questions. Circulate and help students by providing any vocabulary they need. (Even for advanced-level students, some of the vocabulary might be difficult.)
- Circulate, monitor and assist if necessary, but don't interrupt the groups if they are functioning acceptably.
- Bring the class to order. Work on the word stress of any vocabulary relating to energy which students might have had difficulties with, e.g. *nuclear, environment, electricity, fossil fuels, petrol, renewables*, etc.
- Get students' feedback on their ideas as a whole class.

2 Suggested answers

a) Some of the 'cleaner' energies include renewable energy such as wind power, solar (or photovoltaic) power, marine (wave/tidal) power, gases such as hydrogen and oxygen, fuel-cell power, bio-fuels, also liquid gas and low-carbon technologies generally.

b) 'Dirtier' energies include fossil fuels such as oil and coal: oil because of the danger of oil spills such as the Deepwater Horizon disaster, also known as the BP oil spill, in the Gulf of Mexico in 2010; whilst carbon is considered to be a 'dirtier' energy, because CO_2 emissions are thought to be one of the main causes of global warming.

Some might argue that gas is a relatively clean energy, although drilling for gas, e.g. in the Arctic, or building gas pipelines can damage the environment. Others may argue that nuclear energy is a relatively clean energy compared to oil and coal, but nuclear waste is hazardous, and the effect of radioactivity can last up to 100 years. The effects of a nuclear accident are catastrophic on both the environment and the human population, as was seen with the Chernobyl disaster in northern Ukraine in 1986 that affected Ukraine, Belarus and Russia.

B – D CD1.18, CD1.19

- Introduce Angus McCrone and ask students if they watch Bloomberg business news on television and the Internet. Explain that Bloomberg New Energy Finance is a publication specialising in new forms of energy.
- Get students to read through the text and predict what might be in the gaps, before they hear the recording.
- Then play the recording, stopping at appropriate points and elicit the answers.

Exercise B

1 wind **2** low-carbon **3** carbon prices
4 clean energy **5** renewable

- Get students to discuss the question in Exercise C in pairs and report back to the class. Make sure that they give coherent reasons for their choices.

Exercise C

Students' own answers, possibly wind power or solar energy

- Get students to look at the points in Exercise D. Work on the stress and/or meaning of *-able* if necessary and play the recording again.
- Elicit the answers.

Exercise D

1, 2, 4, 6

Resource bank: Listening (page 191)

Students can watch the interview with Angus McCrone on the DVD-ROM.

E

- Ensure students understand that the idea is to spot the impossible word in each case.
- Get them to call out the answers as a whole-class activity.
- Work on any difficulties, for example the meaning and stress of photovoltaic. (Point out that this describes the principle behind solar panels.)

1 carbon **2** consumption **3** reduction **4** turbine
5 renewable **6** photovoltaic

F CD1.20

- Tell students that they are going to hear three experts talk about clean energy and reductions in carbon emissions.
- Play the recordings one by one and elicit the answers after each recording.

1 b **2** c **3** a

G CD1.21

- Get students to look through the statements, then play the recording.
- Elicit the answers and work on any remaining difficulties.

LESSON NOTES

1. Speaker 1 thinks **manufacturing companies** should make donations to offset their carbon emissions.
2. Speaker 2 says paying a carbon tax would only work **if taxes were reduced elsewhere.**
3. Speaker 3 insists that wealthier countries should stop **making demands on** developing countries.
4. Speaker 3 points out that many people in developing countries still don't have **(piped) gas and electricity**.
5. Speaker 2 wouldn't mind living near a wind farm because it would **bring employment (and services) to the area.**
6. Speaker 3 says having wind turbines is better than living next to a **nuclear plant / nuclear power station.**

H

- If there is time and interest, get students to discuss these points in pairs and then report their 'findings' to the whole class.
- Otherwise, do as quick-fire whole-class activity.
- In either case, insist on correct use of energy-related language.

i-Glossary

Reading and language: *The danger of losing touch with reality*

Students read an article about the head of a Norwegian oil company and his views on how the world economy should respond to the need to limit greenhouse gases.

A – C

- Tell students about the subject of the article and do Exercise A as a quick-fire whole-class activity. Then get students to read the article in pairs and compare their answers with Helge Lund's views.
- Circulate, monitor and assist if necessary, but don't interrupt the pairs if they are functioning acceptably.
- Round up the answers with the whole class, getting students to compare their views with Lund's, e.g. *We originally said that we thought it was true that a carbon tax on industry could help reduce greenhouse gases, and Helge Lund says this in the article.*

Exercise B

1. Helge Lund believes this to be true, and Norway has a good record for 'curbing' greenhouse gas emissions by being one the first countries to impose a carbon tax.
2. He warns that this is unrealistic, given that fact that our world is built on hydrocarbons. He says it'll be harder to change than politicians and people realise.
3. He says this is a reality – the world's population will grow from 6.8 billion today to 9 billion by 2050, and economic development means that more people will need energy for their cars and domestic appliances.
4. He argues this is not the case. Oil and gas are far easier to extract, transport, store and use than the alternative energies currently available.
5. He doesn't believe private companies need government support to make technological advances. He thinks competition between companies and the market is what drives technological advances, not political initiatives.
6. He says oil and gas will get more expensive, the supply will decrease and people will need to consume less.

- With the whole class, get students to call out the answers to Exercise C.

Exercise C

1 moving away (from) **2** die-hard **3** engage with
4 curbing **5** weaning ... off **6** set to **7** watchdog
8 deny **9** highlights **10** stifle **11** setting
12 come up with

D

- Get students to discuss the four questions in pairs.
- Circulate, monitor and assist if necessary, but don't interrupt the pairs if they are functioning acceptably.
- Note good points of language use, as well as half a dozen points that need further work, and add these on one side of the board.
- Call the class to order and get some of the individual pairs to say what their findings were.
- Praise good language points that you heard and work on half a dozen that need it, referring to notes you made on the board, getting individual students to say the right thing.

Sample answers

1. Helge Lund is a pioneer in that he, as an oil-industry representative, wants to get involved with the transition from high-carbon to low-carbon energy. His company, Statoil, is a pioneer in storing carbon dioxide underground in order to reduce its harmful effects.
2. He thinks carbon taxes or, preferably, an emissions trading scheme set by governments, will encourage companies to find profitable solutions. However, he objects to what he sees as political support and funding for particular alternative energies, which stops companies from being more innovative in their search for solutions.
3. Increase energy prices, reduce demand for new consumer goods, etc.
4. Students' own answers. Some might argue that oil companies form a 'strategic' industry in which the state needs to be directly involved. Others might say that even if they are strategic, they are best run by businesspeople rather than politicians, who would be better off having an 'arm's length' relationship with these companies. Politicians can influence companies' approach to climate change, for example, through legislation, rather than through government ownership.

E

- Do this with the whole class if there is time. Otherwise, ask your students to look at the Language reference section for homework and report back in the next class. (Don't forget to do this in the next class if this is what you have asked them to do.)

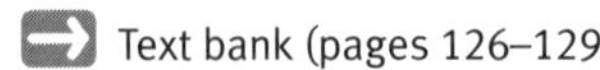
Text bank (pages 126–129)

Business skills: Decision-making

Students look at meetings where decisions are made and the language that is used for this.

A – B

- Discuss the questions in Exercise A with the whole class. Be tactful – especially where managers are present with employees who work under them. (Pre-work students will have more difficulty relating to this topic, so introduce it quickly – you could make a joke about the pleasures of the meetings that await them in their working lives!)

- Read through the eight statements in Exercise B and deal with any vocabulary difficulties, e.g. *reluctant*.
- Give students time to discuss the statements in pairs. If there are any students with little or no experience of business meetings, try to pair them with students who do. If no student has experience of meetings, ask them to predict which statements might be true of a 'good' meeting.

Exercise B

Students' own answers here. One point to note is that 'good' arguing does not threaten anyone's prestige, but promotes solution-oriented discussions. Another point is that people are sometimes not aware that they stop themselves from contributing ideas at meetings, because they don't feel confident about their language level when arguing a point, or they worry that people will not take their ideas seriously.

- With the whole class, you could get students to vote on each of the points in Exercise B and write the results on the board. Discuss each point just after students have voted. (This could be very interesting – it might give you the chance to find out about the decision-making culture of the organisations whose employees you teach, and about attitudes to decision-making in different cultures.)

C – E CD1.22

- Get students to listen to the recording 'cold', then elicit the answers for Exercise C.

Exercise C

There has been a petrol spill (leak) at a refinery in the Philippines. They decide to hold an investigation into the refinery but not stop production at this stage.

- Get students to look at the expressions in the Useful language box. Work on the stress and intonation of the expressions, getting individual students to read them with feeling. (Ensure, especially at this level, that students do not say *I am agree with you*. Though, if this comes up, you could mention that *We're all agreed, then* is possible.)
- Play the recording again, and elicit the answers for Exercise D.

Exercise D

1 be an idea (*Putting forward proposals*)
2 entirely sure; stage (*Disagreeing indirectly*)
3 do have to (*Emphasising a point)*
4 don't think; rush into (*Avoiding making decisions)*.
5 suggestion: we could set up (Putting forward proposals)
6 really concerned; minor. (*Emphasising a point)*

- With the whole class or with students working in pairs, elicits students' ideas about the answers to the questions in Exercise E.

Exercise E

Sample answers

By phrasing the proposal as a question rather than expressing it more directly, Tony does not reveal whether or not he wants the action to take place. Tony's commitment to the proposal is therefore weaker than if he'd said something more direct. It also makes it easier for other people to reject the proposal without loss of face for the person who made the suggestion.

Alain clearly doesn't think Tony's proposal is a good idea, but he avoids disagreeing directly with Tony, presumably because he wants to maintain a good working relationship, and a more direct expression could create embarrassment for Tony.

F

- Tell students that they are going to participate in three different and unrelated meetings. Divide the class into groups of three and allocate the roles.
- Tell them they should just look at the information for the first role for the moment and get them to turn to the correct page.
- Circulate, monitor and assist if necessary, with instructions for the first role play: Meeting 1. When groups are ready, they can begin.
- Circulate, monitor and assist if necessary, but don't interrupt the groups if they are functioning acceptably.
- Note good points of language use, as well as half a dozen points that need further work, and add these on one side of the board.
- When most groups have finished, call the class to order and ask one or two of the groups what happened in their role play.
- Praise good use of meetings language that you heard in the role plays. Then go over points that need more work, getting individual students to say the right thing. Tell them that you will be listening out for the correct/improved forms in the next role play.
- Repeat the above procedure for Meetings 2 and 3, trying to ensure that they integrate the corrections you made for Meeting 2 into the role play for Meeting 3, if and where relevant.

➡ Resource bank: Speaking (page 179)

Writing: layout and structure of reports

Students look at the structure and layout of reports.

G

- You could start by getting students to look at this area on pages 146–147 of the Writing file in the Course Book, working on the ideas that may not be familiar to them, e.g. register – the appropriate style for the context in which one is writing.
- Do the exercise as a quick-fire whole-class activity.

1 plan **2** draft **3** readers **4** register **5** errors
6 layout **7** headings **8** rewrite

H

- Get students to work on this in pairs, books closed. Then, with the whole class, go over the answers.
- Work on any remaining difficulties by going back to the Writing file if necessary.

I

- Get students to start this in pairs in class and then finish it for homework. Don't forget to go over it in the next class.

Correct order of report: D, B, A, G, C, H, F, E

Suggested improvements required: Give the report a title and add headings and sub-headings: Introduction, Findings, Conclusions and Recommendations. And possibly add an executive summary, if this were a longer report. Also number sub-sections in findings and recommendations.

Sample answer

Relocating staff to Sunnydale Business Park

Introduction

Given the high cost of office space in the city centre, the company will be relocated to the new Sunnydale Business Park on the outskirts of the city in January next year. This move will provide more spacious facilities.

Despite these benefits, a major issue is the lack of public transport links to the business park. Therefore, I was requested by senior management to investigate this issue.

The main aims of the report are to find out how many staff will be adversely affected by the relocation; investigate transport links to the new premises; and make recommendations in order to help staff get to and from Sunnydale Business Park.

Findings

1 **Transport options to the new location**
This data is based on my experience travelling from the city in my car, and on online research and telephone interviews with the local council and train and bus companies.

- **Car and private transport**
  The Sunnydale Business Park is approximately 30 kilometres from the city centre. The location has easy access by motorway to the city centre, although there is heavy traffic in rush hours.
- **Train services**
  The nearest train stations are in Havington and Patchett. Havington is six kilometres away. Mainline trains run every 30 minutes to this station in peak hours and every hour off-peak and at weekends. Patchett is only four kilometres away, but the service is less frequent, with trains stopping once an hour.
- **Bus services**
  There are currently no bus services from the city centre to the new premises.

2 **How staff plan to travel**
The date for this research was gathered by way of a written survey. Follow-up interviews were conducted with staff who did not know how they will travel to the new location. A total of 310 staff will be based at the new premises. The following chart is a summary of the findings. More details are provided in Appendix 1.

Travel to existing premises

Walk or cycle	Bus	Train	Car, motorbike or car share	Total
70	101	64	75	310

Travel to Sunnydale Business Park

Walk or cycle	Train and cycle	Car, motorbike or car share	Don't know	Total
20	20	172	98	310

The research indicates that more staff will be using private vehicles to get to work at the new location: 172 as opposed to the current figure of 75. The main reason for this is that the public transport options are very limited. There is no bus service and the nearest train stations, Havington and Patchett, are six and four kilometres away, respectively. Furthermore, the train services are not very frequent.

The findings also show that almost a third of staff (98) at all levels in the company do not know yet how they will travel to the new location. The main reasons for this were that they did not have use of a private vehicle (26) or did not know how they would travel between the train station and the business park (72). For more details see Appendix 2.

Conclusions

The fact that almost a third of staff (98) do not know how they will travel to the new location is a major concern for them and the company. It can be concluded that the company will need to help staff with transport arrangements. To do nothing would adversely affected staff morale, and there is a risk that some staff would leave the company due to the relocation.

Recommendations

In light of these findings, these are my recommendations:

1 **Taxi or shuttle bus service at Havington station**
Given the distance from the train stations to the business park, the company could provide a morning and evening shuttle bus or taxi service to and from Havington train station. The timetable would be integrated with the train times from the station. A similar service at Patchett station would be less useful, as the train service is less frequent.

2 **Car-sharing scheme**
Due to the fact many staff will now be using their cars to get to work, I would also recommend that the company provides staff with some incentives to set up a car-sharing scheme. This would be a very cost-effective, flexible option for many staff.

Both these solutions should be closely monitored and reviewed after three months in order to evaluate their effectiveness.

Writing file (Course Book pages 146–147)

CASE STUDY

Energy saving at Tumalet Software

Students look at the problems of energy cost at a software company and make proposals for savings.

Stage 1: Background

- Tell students briefly the subject of the case study (see summary just above.)
- Get students to look at the pie chart showing energy consumption in office buildings. Get one or two students to present it as if in a presentation, e.g. *The three main uses of energy in office buildings are heating, cooling and office equipment. Heating represents 27 per cent of energy use in office buildings, just ahead of cooling on 25 per cent, and office equipment, also on 25 per cent*, etc.
- Ask students if they are surprised by any of the above figures, and if so, why.
- Get students to study the background information in the Course Book. If you think it's useful, read it aloud or ask a student to read it aloud. Deal with any vocabulary questions they may have.
- Write the headings from the left-hand column of this table on the board and elicit information from students to complete the right-hand column.

Company/ organisation	Tumalet
Based in	Silicon Valley, California
Office space	Four buildings over 90,000 square metres
Energy-saving goals	Reducing CO_2 emissions as part of its sustainable business strategy
Investment	\$500k over the past five years
Energy savings	\$600k
ROI*	120 per cent
Latest developments	Downturn in business Fluctuating gas and electricity prices
Result of above	Company wants to find new ways to reduce energy costs

* Teach this abbreviation for return on investment, i.e. the profit from an investment, usually expressed as a percentage of the amount invested, as here.

Stage 2: Reading and listening CD1.23

- Get students to read the article entitled *Green business makes sense* individually, then ask some quick-fire questions about it.
- Get individual students to summarise the article as a whole, under these headings.

Office buildings: proportion of US energy consumption	33%
Office buildings: proportion of US CO_2 emissions.	38%
Proportion of energy wasted	30%
Green initiatives affordable?	Yes, good for the bottom line*
Possible retro-fits**	Low-energy bulbs Dimming of hallway lighting during day Turn things off/down Keep up with cleaning and maintenance
Result	Significant savings

*Teach this expression: it's the final result for a company's profit or loss in a particular period.

**Improvements made to an existing building, etc.

- Tell students they are going to hear part of a meeting between Tumalet's Sustainable Business Manager, Joanne Hopper, and the Energy Project Team.
- Play the whole recording and ask students to make a list of the tasks the new Energy Project Team will have to work on.
- Students listen again. In pairs, they compare ideas. If necessary, replay the recording. Go through points with the whole class.

Suggested answers

1 Make proposals for energy savings and possible investment in new equipment/technologies.
2 Think of ways to get staff involved in the energy-efficiency drive.
3 Investigate the availability of renewable energies.

- Then get students to quickly read the article entitled *California utility expands rebates* individually or in pairs.
- Circulate, monitor and assist if necessary, but don't interrupt the groups if they are functioning acceptably.
- You may have to explain *rebate*, *dole out* and *offset the cost*.
- With the whole class, elicit the answer.

Tumalet Software could receive rebates from the utility company, which would help them to fund more energy-efficiency initiatives.

Stage 3: Task

- Tell students they are now part of the Energy Project Team at Tumalet. One of their duties is to collect information about ways to save energy and report back to the group.
- Divide the class into groups of three and allocate the roles in each group. Get students to read and absorb their information. Circulate, monitor and assist if necessary, but don't interrupt students' reading if this is not necessary.
- Call the class together, say which student (A, B or C) will be chairing each meeting. Get all students to look at the agenda for the meeting.
- When they are ready, and there are no further questions, tell them to begin their role plays. Circulate, monitor and assist if necessary, but don't interrupt the groups if they are functioning acceptably.
- Note good points of language use, especially in relation to meetings language, as well as half a dozen points that need further work, and add these on one side of the board.
- When most groups have finished, call the class to order and ask one or two of the groups what happened in their discussion. Try to draw some common threads together.
- Praise good use of energy vocabulary and meetings language that you heard in the role plays. Then go over points that need more work, getting individual students to say the right thing.

One-to-one

Go through the information in the Course Book with your student. Explain any difficulties. In the Task, get the student to prepare one of the roles and you take one of the others. At the same time, monitor the language that your student is using. Note down any good examples of language and points for error correction or improvement. Come back to these later. Praise any good examples of language used and go over any errors, including pronunciation.

Do Task 2 together. Don't dominate the conversation in this task, but say enough to keep it going and allow your student to ask and answer questions. You could record the discussion on audio or video, if the student agrees, and use it for intensive correction.

 DVD-ROM: Case study commentary

Stage 4: Writing

- Tell students that they should write a report based on the outcome of the role-play meeting that they participated in. Remind them about the points that are important for reports and tell them that they should refer to the information in the Writing file for guidance. Get students to do this task for homework and e-mail it to you for correction before the next class. Don't forget to give feedback in the next class if you ask them to do this.

Writing file (Course Book pages 146–147)

Resource bank: Writing (page 206)

WORKING ACROSS CULTURES 1

International presentations

As this is probably the first Working across cultures unit that you are doing with students, explain what cultural awareness is: the idea that people should be aware of different attitudes, ways of behaving, taking decisions, using time, etc. that other cultures may have, and how these attitudes must taken into account in doing business in different cultures.

A

- Get students to discuss the statements in pairs.
- Circulate, monitor and assist if necessary, but don't interrupt the groups if they are functioning acceptably.
- Ask different pairs for their opinions, and compare and contrast the answers with the whole class.

B

- Get students to rewrite the statements in pairs, then contrast the different rewritings with the whole class – it may not be possible to reach a consensus for each one.

C CD1.24–1.26

- Tell students that they are about to hear three people talking about their experiences of giving presentations multinationally.
- Focus specifically on the two questions.
- Play each recording once or twice and get individual students to answer the questions.
- Talk about the implications of each answer for a few minutes – don't just plough on with the next recording.

Speaker 1

Talks about the language used in presentations. The speaker has learned that, as a native speaker, it's important to adapt the language you use for non-native speakers in the audience who won't necessarily understand idioms, slang and colloquial expressions.

Speaker 2

Talks about audience response and interaction. The speaker has learned that audiences react and interact differently around the world.

Speaker 3

Talks about the figures and pronunciation. The speaker has learned that non-native English speakers need more time to digest numbers and figures. Using visuals can help compensate for these sorts of language problems, e.g. pronunciation. Also, before using any foreign names, do some research on the pronunciation.

D

- Get students to work on the stress and intonation of *self-deprecating*, *privacy* (point out the two possible pronunciations – with the i as in *river* or as in *hive*), *gestures*, etc. and explain the meaning of *thumbs up* if necessary.
- Get them to work on the exercise. Circulate, monitor and assist if necessary, but don't interrupt the pairs if they are functioning acceptably.
- When pairs have finished, elicit the answers. Discuss the answers for each text, seeing if students agree with them. Don't just plough on to the next exercise.

1 self-deprecating **2** punch lines **3** Q&A sessions
4 non-verbal signals **5** unnerving
6 hand gestures **7** thumbs up **8** privacy

E – F CD1.27

- Tell students that they are going to hear Anneliese Guérin-LeTendre talk about the training course that she runs. (Remind students that they already heard her speaking in Unit 1.)
- Get students to look through the four sentences in Exercise E.
- It's quite a long recording, so stop in convenient places to allow students to make notes and to explain any difficulties.
- Play the recording again, again stopping at appropriate points, and elicit the answers.
- Get students to look through the questions in Exercise F and anticipate the answers – they will already have some ideas after their first hearing.
- Play the recording again, stopping at appropriate points, and elicit the answers, discussing each one briefly before playing the next part of the recording.

Exercise E

1 culture **2** cultural difference **3** expectations
4 particular audience **5** presenter **6** English
7 typical presentation style **8** adapted/modified

Exercise F

1. The difference between what we can see and what is underlying
2. The presenter's expertise (in order to gain credibility)
3. The spoken word, the visual or even the written word
4. It might be considered appropriate for business. Sometimes it can be interpreted as being quite frivolous, even cynical sometimes. Alternatively, it can create a relaxed atmosphere and diffuse tensions.
5. 'Context' refers to the level of detail the audience expect. Some cultures prefer to have a lot of detail (known as 'high context', e.g. Germany, France). Others, e.g. the Anglo-Saxon nations, appreciate more concise presentations.

G

- Get students to discuss the question in pairs, bearing in mind some of the points that have already come up in this unit. Go round the class and assist where necessary.
- Bring the class to order and get representatives of each pair to talk about their ideas, and compare them.

Sample answers

On the surface: dress style, age, greeting styles

More underlying: attitudes to authority, body language, attitude to time, emotion shown in public, physical gestures, directness of speech, humour

(You could draw an iceberg on the board, with nine-tenths of it underwater, and put the answers on the appropriate part of the iceberg – above water or below.)

If you think students are ready to go further, you could point out that intercultural experts suggest there are actually three levels: what you can see (e.g. dress code), what is just below the surface (e.g. body language) and what is much deeper and harder to detect (e.g. social class, attitudes to authority).

Task 1

- Get students to prepare the task in pairs or small groups. If you are concerned that the presentation may be too repetitive in content, assign each group topics to talk about from the list so that they don't all choose the same items.
- Go round the class and assist where necessary.
- Bring the class to order and get a representative of some of the pairs to give a mini-presentation about these points. Keep this short and sweet, so as to allow as many speakers as possible to present their ideas. Monitor the language being used, especially in relation to intercultural issues.
- After all the presentations, praise good use of intercultural language that you heard in the presentations. Then go over points that need more work, getting individual students to say the right thing.

Task 2

- Get students to do this for homework and report back in the next lesson. Tell them that YouTube is a good source of presentations. You could also get them to talk about the presentation styles of reporters on TV in different countries.
- Some useful web links:
  - Present Like Steve Jobs (http://www.youtube.com/watch?v=2-ntLGOyHw4)
  - Deliver a Presentation like Steve Jobs (http://www.businessweek.com/smallbiz/content/jan2008/sb20080125_269732.htm)
  - Apple iPad – Steve Jobs Presentation (http://en.vidivodo.com/348417/apple-ipad-_-steve-jobs-presentation)
  - Procter & Gamble: Bob McDonald addresses employees as incoming CEO (http://www.youtube.com/watch?v=w6j6qd6oqdA)
  - Bob McDonald: Values Based Leadership (http://www.youtube.com/watch?v=yY6vzvFOqxU&NR=1)
  - Mike Southon, entrepreneur and FT journalist (http://www.youtube.com/watch?v=DGOeK2HF_sA)
  - Henry Stewart, founder and CEO, Happy Computers (http://www.youtube.com/watch?v=VpcotzZ-woY)
  - TED Talks homepage (http://www.ted.com/talks)
  - TED talk by 'child prodigy' Adora Svitak (http://www.ted.com/talks/adora_svitak.html)
- And here are some ideas for other presentations that you might want to get students to give at different points in the course:

Presentation 1
Speaker: Film director
Topic: Your latest film
Audience: Film distributors
Event: An international film festival
Place: Rio de Janeiro, Brazil
Time: 10 minutes

Presentation 2
Speaker: Company CEO
Topic: Why it is a sound investment to buy shares in your company.
Audience: potential investors
Event: a roadshow tour organised by the management to raise its profile in key financial centres across Europe.
Time: 10 minutes

Presentation 3
Speaker: University rector
Topic: Advantages of studying in this country
Audience: Erasmus students
Event: An education fair
Place: Brussels, Belgium
Time: 10 minutes

Presentation 4
Speaker: An Olympic champion in (choose a sport)
Topic: Why my city/country is the best place for the summer/winter Olympic Games in six years' time
Audience: the members of International Olympic Committee (IOC)
Event: a visit of the IOC Evaluation Commission
Place: your country
Time: 10 minutes

UNIT **A** # Revision

This unit revises and reinforces some of the key language points from Units 1–3 and from Working across cultures 1, and links with those units are clearly shown. This revision unit, like Revision units B, C and D, concentrates on reading and writing activities.

For more speaking practice, see the Resource bank section of this book, beginning on page 171. The exercises in this unit can be done in class, individually or collaboratively, or for homework.

1 First impressions

Vocabulary

- This exercise gives students further practice in the vocabulary of body language in presentations on page 7.

1 gestures **2** nodding **3** contact **4** mannerisms **5** staring **6** scanning **7** fidgeting **8** Posture **9** upright **10** slouching

Adverbs

- Students are given further practice in using adverbs, following on from Exercise E on page 8.

1 I would **strongly** recommend that you rehearse your presentation several times.
2 Don't rely **heavily** on PowerPoint. People come to see you, not the slides.
3 It's **hugely** important that your own personality comes across in the presentation.
4 Check that all the multimedia equipment is working **properly** beforehand.
5 Try to breathe **deeply** – it'll help you to relax.
6 It's **utterly** impossible to do the perfect presentation, so don't put too much pressure on yourself.

Skills

- This exercise gives students practice in the language of networking, from pages 10 and 11.

1 do; favour **2** mind me **3** looked familiar **4** coincidence **5** business **6** mean **7** excuse me

2 Training

Vocabulary

- This exercise develops the training- and career-related vocabulary on page 15.

1 developed **2** apprentices **3** qualification **4** graduate **5** training **6** internship **7** employer **8** intern **9** employees

Emphasising your point

- This develops the language of clarifying and confirming on page 17.

1 was anything but **2** Not only was; (but) it was also **3** What; was **4** It was; that got her **5** are anything but **6** Not only do; (but) they also

Writing 1–2

- These two exercises practise the language of formal e-mails.

Exercise 1 – Sample answers

1 warmly / am writing to / write to **2** take part in / join **3** is to / will be to **4** attached **5** held **6** (please) let **7** do / take part in **8** any queries / any further questions **9** (please) feel free / do not hesitate / you are welcome **10** forward

Exercise 2 – Sample answer

Dear Annabel

Thank you for the invitation to do this training session. It certainly looks like it will be very useful for me.

Unfortunately, I will not be able to attend on September 1st as I will be away on a business trip that week. Could you please let me know when the next session will be held?

I'd also like to know what the technical requirements are in order to participate in the online training. For instance, do I need to have a webcam?

Best wishes

3 Energy

Vocabulary

- This practises energy-related vocabulary from this unit.

1 solar panels **2** greenhouse gas emissions **3** carbon tax **4** wind farms **5** fossil-fuel **6** renewable-energy **7** wind turbines **8** energy efficiency

Articles

- Students get further practice in this area, as seen on page 24, which is tricky for even advanced learners.

1 a **2** the **3** a **4** the **5** an **6** the **7** the **8** – **9** the **10** a **11** an **12** the **13** – **14** – **15** the **16** the **17** a **18** the **19** the **20** –

Skills 1–2

- Further work on decision-making language is given here.

Exercise 1

1 I know I keep going **on** about this, but it is important.
2 The best **course** of action is to call another meeting.
3 I'm not so **sure** I agree with you there.
4 **Would** it be an idea to issue a press release?
5 I'm in two **minds** about this proposal.
6 I don't think we should make any **hasty/rash/sudden** decisions.
7 I see things a **little/bit** differently from you.
8 Let's not **rush** into a decision until we have all the facts.

Exercise 2

1 c **2** a/d **3** h **4** a **5** b/d **6** d **7** b **8** d

Cultures 1: International presentations

- Students get to work further on presentations-related vocabulary from this section.

1 underlying **2** self-deprecating **3** dress code **4** establish credibility **5** take it for granted **6** get straight to the point **7** go down well **8** get the message across **9** delivery technique **10** personal touch

UNIT 4

Marketing

AT A GLANCE

	Classwork – Course Book	Further work
Lesson 1 *Each lesson is about 60–75 minutes. This time does not include administration and time spent going through homework in any lessons.*	**Listening and discussion: Customer relationship management** Students discuss some statements about marketing, some of them controversial, and listen to Dr Jonathan Reynolds, a marketing academic, talking about customer relationship management (CRM). They then discuss some of the issues that Dr Reynolds raises.	**Practice File** Word power (pages 22–23) **Resource bank: Listening** (page 192) **i-Glossary** (DVD-ROM)
Lesson 2	**Reading and language:** ***'Is the customer always right? Yes, she is.' / What women really want!*** Students read two articles on women as consumers, discuss the information in them and work further on marketing language.	**Text bank** (pages 130–133) **Practice File** Text and grammar (pages 24–25)
Lesson 3	**Business skills: Making an impact in presentations** This section continues work on presentations at an advanced level. Students look at adapting presentations to particular audiences, listen to a presentation that illustrates this, and work on presentation language. **Writing: presentation slides** Students look at this area by commenting on some examples of slides and designing their own.	**Resource bank: Speaking** (page 180) **Practice File** Skills and pronunciation (pages 26–27)
Lesson 4	**Case study: Relaunching Home2u** Students work on a new marketing campaign to attract young Hispanic customers to a chain of home-improvement stores.	**Case study commentary** (DVD-ROM) **Resource bank: Writing** (page 207)

For a fast route through the unit, focusing mainly on speaking skills, just use the underlined sections.

For one-to-one situations, most parts of the unit lend themselves, with minimal adaptation, to use with individual students. Where this is not the case, alternative procedures are given.

BUSINESS BRIEF

In marketing, as in other areas, the Internet is changing everything. Amazon, Google and Facebook have emerged as extremely **strong brands** in **e-commerce, searching** and **social networking** respectively. But there is also great **interplay** between these different types of site. In terms of leading people to the **e-commerce sites,** the influence of the **rankings** of Google and other search engines, and the advertising on them, is enormous. Companies are also having to build and protect the **presence** of their brands on **social networking** sites – a brand can have **'friends'** on Facebook. The brand's marketers would often prefer that presence to be maintained and enhanced mainly by the company (or its **web-hosting agency**) rather than by consumers, even friendly ones. **Reputation management** has become an issue. A social-networking site where travellers detail their experiences of airlines and hotels has been threatened with legal action by hotel owners, who say that some users' comments are unjustified and even **libellous**. (See the Business brief for Unit 10 for more on the issues and vocabulary of e-commerce.)

Another area where information technology is having a massive impact is in **customer relationship management (CRM)**. Previously, **segmentation** – identifying **prospective customers** with **homogenous characteristics** – had been based on broad **breakdowns** of customers by **region, social class** and, in some cases where a more detailed approach was possible, **psychometric analysis** of **personality**. It is on this broad analysis that many **global brands** have been and continue to be based. However, in **retailing**, using the tools of CRM such as **data mining** – the study of data collected through **loyalty cards** – allows marketers to identify individual patterns of **consumer behaviour** and model **offers** of particular interest to them as individuals, sometimes referred to in this context as **segments of one**. Data-mining software allows vast amounts of information to be **analysed**: this is a prime example of how information can be **exploited** to produce **intelligence**. With increasing corporate access to this intimate knowledge, as with the knowledge gained through **profiling** the Internet use of individual users, issues of **privacy** are becoming key.

Marketing and your students

Both pre-work and in-work students should have lots to say about marketing as consumers. Get younger ones (and even some older ones) to talk about their social-networking habits in relation to their behaviour as consumers.

In-work students not involved in sales or marketing may say that marketing does not directly concern them. However, the ideal of **market orientation** is one that most organisations subscribe to, in theory at least – the idea that marketing does not exist to foist the company's products on buyers, but to identify what customers want in the first place, and to satisfy those needs with products designed to meet them. Students may be lucky enough to work for companies at the leading edge of technology, that not only strive to identify customer needs but **anticipate** them; or even more than that, in the sense that consumers did not know they needed a particular product until it appeared – think of Apple's iPad.

Read on

Philip Kotler et al.: *Marketing management*, Prentice Hall, 2009

Dave Chaffey et al.: *Internet marketing: Strategy, implementation and practice*, Prentice Hall, 2008

Malcolm McDonald, Ian Dunbar: *Segmentation: How to do it, how to profit from it*, Butterworth/Heinemann, 2004

Francis Buttle: *Customer relationship management*, Butterworth/Heinemann, 2008

Jon Reed: *Get up to speed with online marketing: How to use websites, blogs, social networking and much more*, FT/Prentice Hall, 2010

LESSON NOTES

Warmer

- Ask students to randomly brainstorm expressions they think of when they hear the word *marketing*. Do this as a quick-fire whole-class activity and write words and short expressions on the board, for example:

  salespeople *advertising* *slick commercials*
  creating needs *conspicuous consumption*
  e-commerce

  sales with a college education *clever communication*
  Mad Men (US television series about the advertising industry in New York in the 1960s)

Overview

- Tell students that they are going to look at some key marketing issues. Go through the overview panel at the beginning of the unit in the Course Book, pointing out the sections that your students will be looking at.

Quotation

- John Sculley was President of Pepsi-Cola, and then later CEO of Apple from 1983 to 1993, before Steve Jobs retook control of the company that he had founded. (Pepsi and Apple are today both seen as market-oriented organisations *par excellence*, but Apple's sales were falling fast at the end of Sculley's tenure, forcing him to leave.)
- Ask students what they think of the quotation. It could be argued that market share and sales volume are still important in many industries but that, even there, marketers have to think increasingly in terms of 'personal' relationships with individual consumers, for example with messages to them that are increasingly customised. Ask students to what extent they think this is possible/desirable. (You could give the example of the information collected by Amazon that presents you with selections of books or music 'you might be interested in', based on your previous purchases.)

Listening and discussion: Customer relationship management

Students discuss some statements about marketing, some of them controversial, and listen to Dr Jonathan Reynolds, a marketing academic, talking about customer relationship management (CRM). They then discuss some of the issues that Dr Reynolds raises.

A

- Tell students that they are going to look at some statements about marketing, and explain any difficult vocabulary, e.g. *referral*.
- Get students to discuss the points in pairs. Circulate, monitor and assist if necessary, but don't interrupt the groups if they are functioning acceptably.
- Bring the class to order and ask pairs for their 'findings', comparing those of different pairs.
- Correct any mistakes that you heard, especially in relation to marketing language, getting individual students to say and use the expressions correctly.

B CD1.28

- Tell students that they are about to hear a marketing lecturer talk about customer relationship management. Ask if any of them have come across this expression before and if so, in what context.
- With the whole class, get students to look through the summary and anticipate what might be in the gaps.
- Play the recording, stopping at convenient points, and elicit the answers.

1 interact with customers **2** telesales calling
3 customer-centric / customer centric **4** at the hear
5 differences and preferences **6** consistent service

C

- With the whole class, get individual students to say the words in the box with the correct stress and pronunciation, e.g. *in<u>tru</u>sive*.
- Then get them to work on the article in pairs. Circulate, monitor and assist if necessary, but don't interrupt the groups if they are functioning acceptably.
- When most pairs have finished, call the class to order and elicit the answers.
- Don't just plough through the answers without discussing them. After each paragraph, ask some related questions. For example, after paragraph 1, you could ask students if they have experienced increased personal resistance to unsolicited e-mails (junk e-mail).

1 intrusive marketing **2** direct mail
3 customer experience **4** multichannel relationship
5 customer loyalty **6** word-of-mouth referrals
7 long-term customers **8** market share

D

- Get students to discuss the points in pairs. Circulate, monitor and assist if necessary, but don't interrupt the groups if they are functioning acceptably.
- Bring the class to order and ask pairs for their 'findings', comparing those of different pairs.
- Correct any mistakes that you heard, especially in relation to marketing language, getting individual students to say or use the expression correctly.

E CD1.29

- Prepare students for what they about to hear by getting them to focus on the questions.
- Play the recording and elicit the answers.
- Again, personalise the activity by asking questions, for example about students' attitudes as consumers to loyalty cards like Tesco's – do they like them? (But don't pre-empt question 3 in Exercise G below too much.)

He mentions three methods:
- loyalty marketing schemes (e.g. Tesco supermarket's Clubcard);
- companies investing in the customer value to find out why customers are using their brand;
- price promotion activity.

He says investing in the customer value, in the longer term, is a 'better bet' because companies then have a better chance of retaining customers over the longer term. He feels that price promotion activity has the biggest drawbacks because this retains customers whilst the price is low, but raises the question as to whether those companies can retain that low-cost position in the marketplace.

F CD1.30

- Move on to the final part of the interview. Get students to focus on the questions and work on their preferred pronunciation of *privacy* (/ˈpraɪvəsi/ in AmE but /ˈprɪvəsi/ in BrE).
- Play the recording and elicit the answers.

LESSON NOTES

1. The 'glass consumer' means that people are now more transparent to companies. (*Companies can see through us and know exactly how we behave and how we think.*)
2. He describes three different attitudes to privacy:
   - 'privacy fundamentalists': people who are concerned about the amount and quality of information that is held about them by companies, and want that to be legislated against;
   - 'privacy pragmatists': those who accept the reality that companies collect data about us, and think it may even help us in terms of getting better offers in the long term;
   - 'privacy indifferents': people who couldn't care less about what information is collected about them, and are often very unaware of what is collected.

G

- Go through the questions. Depending on time and interest, discuss them with the whole class or in small groups, comparing and contrasting students' attitudes.
- Insist on correct use of marketing language and work on any difficulties.

Resource bank: Listening (page 192)

Students can watch the interview with Jonathan Reynolds on the DVD-ROM.

i-Glossary

Reading and language: *'Is the customer always right? Yes, she is.' / What women really want!*

Students read two articles on women as consumers, discuss the information in them and work further on marketing language.

A

- Tell students that they are going to work in pairs and each one in the pair is going to read a different article about women as consumers. Allocate the articles to each pair and circulate, monitor and assist if necessary, but don't interrupt the pairs if they are functioning acceptably.
- When most of the pairs have finished, call the class to order and elicit the answers.

Suggested answers

1. ... women control 72 per cent of purchasing and consumer spending in the US ... (Article 1, lines 5–7)
2. And the earnings gap with men is expected to narrow further as the number of women being educated grows at a faster rate than men. (Article 1, lines 9–13)
3. Electronics: Best Buy, which is a seller of electronic toys for children, has been promoting more female staff and trying to make stores more appealing to women and girls. (Article 1, lines 28–32)
   Home improvement/DIY: Home Depot [...] the über-male DIY store has launched a range of home products by a woman designer. (Article 1, lines 32–37)
   Harley-Davidson, long a symbol of male pride ... (Article 2, lines 34–35)
4. Marketing Director at Barclays Local Business [...] comments: 'We know that women small business customers are less risky and more profitable for us ... (Article 2, lines 48–52), but he doesn't say why.
5. Barbara K's 30-piece tool kit is designed to help. These tools are not only better looking but are also made for a woman's hand and strength, and weigh a little less than regular tools. (Article 2, lines 28–33)
   Harley-Davidson, long a symbol of male pride, has added a section on its website dedicated to women motorcyclists ... (Article 2, lines 34–37)

Suggested answers (not mentioned in articles): iPod offers players in different colours; top fashion houses like Burberry's have designed carry cases.

- As ever, personalise the exercise here by asking students what they think of these ideas.

B

- Get students to quickly read the other article, then complete the exercises as a quick-fire whole-class activity. Work on any difficulties, for example the pronunciation and stress of *viral*.

1 consumer **2** appealing **3** launched **4** study **5** influenced; ads **6** word-of-mouth; viral **7** hook; target **8** individual requirements

C

- Get students to discuss these questions in pairs or as a quick-fire whole-class activity. (Treat tactfully, as ever.)
- Correct any mistakes in the use of marketing language, getting individual students to say the correct form.

D – E

- These terms are quite technical, so get students to look at the Language reference section in the Course Book, pages 130–131.
- Write some of the examples quickly on the board if necessary, pointing out the finer details. Get different students to recap different parts of the explanations.
- With the whole class, get students to identify the four examples in the articles, getting them to explain why they are defining or non-defining.
- Then get students to work on Exercise E in pairs. Circulate, monitor and assist if necessary, but don't interrupt the pairs if they are functioning acceptably.
- Call the class to order, get students to give their answers, and, above all, explain them.

Exercise D
Suggested answers

Article 1

- *... some companies have worked out where the money is.* (lines 24–25) (defining relative clause)
- *Ikea, the Swedish home furnishing retailer, provides a child-minding room. Best Buy, which is a seller of electronics toys for children, has been promoting more female staff ...* (lines 26–30) (both non-defining relative clauses that provide additional information)

Article 2

- *It is time to design products and marketing campaigns that actually appeal to the buying needs and habits of women.* (lines 1–4) (defining relative clause)
- *Women now buy 10% of all Harleys sold, which is a stark contrast to a mere 2% in 1985.* (lines 38–41) (non-defining relative clause)

There are more examples in Exercise E.

Exercise E

1 who is **2** that/who are **3** which/that is **4** which are **5** which has (long) been; which/that is **6** which/that are **7** which/that are

These words can be omitted because they are either defining relative clauses, where the main clause and the relative clause have different subjects, or non-defining relative clauses with participle phrases.

- Go through the questions. Depending on time, discuss them with the whole class or in small groups, comparing and contrasting students' attitudes.
- Students may choose to talk about their buying/consumer habits and those of family and friends if they prefer. You could photocopy the following questions and hand them out, or prepare them on PowerPoint if you have the facilities. Don't waste time writing them on the board.
  – How often do you normally go shopping? Where do you usually shop? Why do you not go to alternative retailers?
  – If money was no object, what luxury product would you buy? Choose only one. What factors might influence your choice of retailer? What goods would you definitely not buy?
  – If you hate shopping, or know someone who does, how would you improve the store to cater for those waiting for a friend or partner?
- Insist on correct use of marketing language and work on any difficulties.

Text bank (pages 130–133)

Business skills: Making an impact in presentations

This section continues work on presentations at an advanced level. Students look at adapting presentations to particular audiences, listen to a presentation that illustrates this, and work on presentations language.

A

- Talk about formal and informal language – something that advanced-level students should be familiar with. Elicit ideas from students, too, about non-linguistic aspects, e.g. in their countries, how presenters would be expected to dress in particular formal contexts, e.g. at conferences.

B – C CD1.31, 1.32

- Explain the task, play the recordings and elicit the answers to questions in Exercise B.
- Play the recordings again and elicit the answers to questions in Exercise C.

Exercise B

Presenter 1: a university lecturer teaching marketing to a group of students

Presenter 2: a marketing manager presenting a new campaign to some colleagues

Exercise C

Presenter 1: 1, 3, 5, 6, 10

Presenter 2: 2, 4, 7, 8, 9

- Discuss any issues, comments, etc. as they arise.

D – E CD1.33, 1.34

- Get students to anticipate what might go in the gaps before they listen to the recording. (You could get them to 'hide' the Useful language box at the bottom of the page with a piece of paper.)
- Play recording 1.33 and elicit the answers for Exercise D. Then do the same for recording 1.34.

Exercise D

1 what I was saying **2** let's just go back
3 up the key points **4** that's all we have
5 take another look at **6** quote the words of
7 one thing I'd like **8** finally, I'd like to

- Get students to look at the Useful language box now. Have them underline six expressions that they would like to learn, and practise saying them to their partner in simultaneous pairs.
- With books closed, get two or three individual students to say some of their expressions.
- Then, with the whole class, get students to categorise the expressions, as in Exercise E.

Exercise E

a) 2, 5, 8 (and possibly 6)
b) 1, 2
c) 6
d) 3, 4, 7, 8

F – G

- Get students to look at the techniques in the box, then work in pairs – Student A looks at the script for Presenter 1 and B for Presenter 2.
- Then, with the whole class, get students to categorise the expressions in the Useful language box under the two headings in Exercise G.

Exercise F

Suggested answers

Presenter 1

1. Use of repetition, e.g. ... *the Axe campaign, is taking **the same old** ideas and just adding new technology. ...* Marketers are pushing ***the same old buttons ...***
2. Referring to a surprising fact, e.g. *Marketing is too often confused with selling.* (a bold statement)
3. Asking 'real' or rhetorical questions, e.g. *But what is marketing? Now, you're probably wondering, what's the significance of all of this?*
4. Quoting someone, e.g. *According to marketing guru Philip Kotler, there are five key processes in marketing.*
5. Emphasising key words, e.g. *What is **unseen** is the extensive market research and development of products, ...*
   *But what **is** marketing?*
   *But a company that **fails** at any one of these processes will not survive.*
   *Marketers are pushing the **same** old buttons to sell more variations of the same old products.*
   *And that's what I'd like you to do for your next assignment: **innovate**.*
   *Think about a product that will make **your** life easier.*
6. Building rapport with the audience, e.g. *So, you know, 'Houston, we have an innovation problem'.* (using humour and informal language)
   Clearly, we've got to do something different here. (involving the audience)
   Oh, sorry, folks, but that's all we have time for today. (informal)
7. Listing points in threes or fives, e.g. ... *five key processes in marketing. First, there's ...*
8. Calling for action, e.g. *And that's what I'd like **you** to do for your next assignment: innovate.* (asking the audience to do something)
   *Think about a product that will make **your** life easier.* (asking the audience to reflect)

Presenter 2

1 Use of repetition, e.g. ***It may look like an Armani, it may feel like an Armani****, but if you look at the price tag, you'll see it costs a fraction of the price of* ***an Armani****.*

2 Referring to a surprising fact or figure, e.g. ... *did you know that China's fashion market will probably grow to around 12.4 billion US dollars over the next two years?*

3 Asking 'real' or rhetorical questions, e.g. *Have you seen this coat?* (It could be either here.)

4 Quoting someone, e.g. *I'd like to quote the words of a journalist from the* FT *here ...*

5 Emphasising key words and/or figures, e.g. *It may* ***look*** *like an Armani, it may* ***feel*** *like an Armani, ...*
... you'll see we're talking about over ***five billion*** *euros.*
If there's just ***one thing*** *I'd like you all to remember, it's...*

6 Building rapport with the audience, e.g. *You know, a funny thing happened to me the other day.* (telling an anecdote)
Well, of course, she gave me a list ...
I bet you didn't know that, did you?
That's a huge increase in growth, isn't it? (using informal language and question tags to invite the audience to agree with him)
But if you can't beat them, join them! (using humour)

8 Calling for action, e.g. *If there's just one thing I'd like you all to remember, it's focus on our customer base.* (asking the audience to reflect on something)

(Presenter 2 also uses two contrasting ideas e.g. *Anyway, I'm not here to tell you about my wife's new coat. ... I'm here to tell you how this new campaign is going to give us a competitive advantage.*)

Exercise G

Students' own answers. There may be no hard-and-fast answers here – ask students about their own cultures and what would be acceptable in each context there. Then compare this with what would be acceptable in the English-speaking world in each case.

Resource bank: Speaking (page 180)

Writing: presentation slides

Students look at this area by commenting on some examples of slides and designing their own.

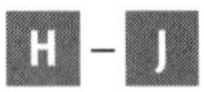

- Do this as a whole-class activity to get students into the subject. Get students to comment on the slides before looking at the tips in Exercise I.
- Then get students to give other tips, as in Exercise J. (Adjust your expectations to the students' backgrounds. Pre-work students who have rarely or never used PowerPoint will, naturally, have fewer ideas than an executive with 10 years' experience of giving presentations.)

Exercise I

a) Tip 2 (punctuation): don't use more than one question mark.

b) Tip 1 (type size): the font is too small to read, especially at the back of a large room.

c) Tip 3 (use bullet points / lists of three): this list would look more effective with three bullet points.

d) Tip 1 (too much text; type size); tip 3 (use bullet points).

e) Tip 1 (font): the font is hard to read; tip 2 (spelling): should read *successful*.

Exercise J

Students' answers might include:

- Avoid using too many different fonts and typefaces – two or three is probably enough
- Use a corporate or university logo on each slide when presenting to people from outside the organisation.
- Don't use combinations of text in colours on backgrounds that make them hard to read, e.g. yellow on orange.
- Don't go crazy with all the different animation schemes in PowerPoint for transition between slides – one or two different types of transition is enough.

Experienced students should come up with others.

- For homework you could give further proof-reading practice by asking students to look out for five or six effective slogans in adverts in newspapers and magazines, or TV ads, posters, fliers and other publicity material in their own language, then translate them into English. Students then compare their ideas in the next class.
- Alternately, you could find errors in local tourist information leaflets or posters for international events or other advertising material in English and get students to correct them in class e.g. *Womans' volleyball championship*. (You could encourage students by pointing out that, these days, many native speakers, even at graduate level, would have trouble with this one – the correct version, by the way, is *Women's volleyball championship*.)
- Students can also proof-read the slides of a presentation in English for a classmate or colleague. What are their most common errors? But do this only where appropriate and deal with it tactfully. If there are managers and the people that they manage in the same class, it's probably not a good idea to get the subordinates to correct the managers' English (or even, perhaps, vice-versa)!

K

- Get students to prepare these mini presentations for homework. This will also give them more time to prepare, so as to be able to include an anecdote or news story, a memorable quote, surprising fact or figure and/or image with a caption (teach this word), etc. Where possible, they should prepare PowerPoint slides that exemplify the principles above.
- Get students to give presentations over the classes that follow – one or two per class over two classes will probably be enough on this subject. Maintain an element of surprise by only telling students at the beginning of each class who will be presenting during that class. This way they will all hopefully be motivated to prepare something.

CASE STUDY

Relaunching Home2u

Students work on a new marketing campaign to attract young Hispanic customers to a chain of home-improvement stores.

Stage 1: Background, Customer survey and Task 1

- Tell students briefly the subject of the case study (see summary just above.)
- Get students to look at the information in both the background and the customer survey in pairs. Meanwhile, write the headings on the left of the box below on the board.
- Call the class to order and elicit the information from the class to complete the right-hand side of the box, inserting information from the customer survey too, using 'approximate' phrases like the ones shown, rather than just repeating the exact figures from the survey.
- Get one or two students to present the information quickly in their own words, e.g. Home2u is a chain of more than 2,000 stores in North America and Puerto Rico. It sells ... . Its main customers are ... etc.

Company	Home2u
Business	Home-improvement retailer
Stores	2,000 in US (including Puerto Rico), Mexico and Canada
Products sold	Easy-to-assemble furnishings and fittings, DIY tools and equipment, paint, flooring, garden furniture
Hispanic community in US	15 per cent of population: nation's largest ethnic minority
Numbers	More than 100 million by mid-century – nearly a quarter of the population
Home2u's recent campaign	Targeted Hispanics with emphasis on family, soccer (football) and salsa music
Problem with campaign	Stereotypical, didn't appeal to younger Hispanics (a massive majority – more than 90% – were turned off by it)
Reasons	Younger Hispanics have high aspirations Interested in new social media and pop culture Prefer info to be bilingual (more than half want store signage and assembly instructions in Spanish as well as English)
Plan	Relaunch campaign – edgy (teach this word), appealing, not patronising to young Hispanics
	(nearly three-quarters of young Hispanics think that the store staff patronise them, and less than a quarter would currently recommend the chain to friends, colleagues and family)

- Explain Task 1 and divide the class into groups of three. Point out particularly the instruction ... *brainstorm some [ideas] of your own.*
- Start the activity. Circulate, monitor and assist if necessary, but don't interrupt the groups if they are functioning acceptably.
- Note good points of language use, as well as half a dozen points that need further work, for example in relation to numbers, etc. and add these on one side of the board. (For example, note down any tendency of students to say *the most* rather than *most, the half* rather than *half*, etc.)
- Call the class to order and ask two or three of the groups to explain their conclusions, and the ideas of their own that they brainstormed.
- Praise good use of language, especially numbers language, that you heard in the activity. Then go over any points that need more work, getting individual students to say the right thing.

Stage 2: Task 2

- For the time being, work with the class as a whole. Tell students to read the celebrity profiles on their own. Circulate, monitor and assist if necessary, but don't interrupt students if they do not ask for help.
- Call the class to order and, books closed, get a student to summarise Eddie Velázquez's profile. Then do the same for the other three celebs (teach this abbreviation if students don't know it).
- Explain the task and get students to discuss the suitability of each celebrity in their groups of three.
- As ever, note good points of language use, as well as half a dozen points that need further work, and add these on one side of the board.
- Call the class to order and ask two or three of the groups to explain their choice.

Suggested answers

- **Eddie Velázquez** might be rejected on the basis that he is pushing 40, he is unknown in the US market, and he's the only male candidate. As a Latin rapper, he might also project the wrong kind of image for Home2u, but he's popular in Mexico and may appeal to 20- and 30-somethings.
- **Leona Pedraza** has already been approached by a sportswear brand. Leona should appeal to the up-and-coming market of students, single women and young mothers, as well as middle-aged women, because of her girl-next-door image, although Leona isn't as well known as the other candidates.
- **Elvira Olivas's** strong image might appeal to women wanting to do DIY, and she is also popular with the teen market and housewives. However, her contract may be expensive or problematic because she prefers to do advertising and promotional work in overseas markets.
- **Vanessa Flores** is probably the strongest candidate, but she's also a risky option, as her boyfriend problems might bring Home2u bad publicity and possibly reputational damage. Like Vanessa, her contract will probably be costly – a different offer of an endorsement deal fell through, as her fees were high.

- Praise good use of language that you heard in the activity. Then go over any points that need more work, getting individual students to say the right thing.

Stage 3: Listening CD1.35

- Work with the whole class again. Bring students' attention to the rubric. Play the recording and elicit the answer.

Suggested answers

Jodie, the Marketing Director, wanted Vanessa Flores for Home2u's TV commercial, but Emilio says she's gone on an international tour. Jodie then asks about Elvira Olivas, but he says she prefers to do endorsement deals overseas and he also criticises her for being a prima donna (explain this if necessary). He then rejects Eddie on the grounds that he's too old, 'pushing 40'. Emilio says they should go with Leona, but Jodie isn't convinced, as Leona might be too young and/ or have the wrong kind of image for the Hispanic market.

- Get students to discuss the information. (For example, you could ask younger students if they would consider a 40-year-old rapper as 'old'. They might also have things to say about the use of real Hispanic stars in product endorsement, e.g. Eva Longoria Parker for ice-cream.)

CD1.36

- Still working with the whole class, get students to look at the rubric. Play the recording and then elicit the answer.

Suggested answers

Leona doesn't sound very confident or experienced during the filming of the TV commercial. This doesn't bode well, and students might argue that Home2u needs to pick a different candidate. Others may give her the benefit of the doubt and blame her performance on a poor script.

- Again, get students to discuss the information. For example, in their own cultures, would a 24-year-old woman golfer have a profile among young people that could be exploited for endorsement purposes, even if she could say her lines correctly in an ad?

Stage 4: Task 3

- Explain the task, underlining the key points that students have to cover.
- Get students to work in the same groups of three as before, or get them to change groups.
- Get them to work on the task using pen and paper at first. When they are ready with some ideas, they could start working on some PowerPoint slides for their presentation, if facilities are available. (Otherwise, you could hand out transparencies and pens if an overhead projector is available.)
- Circulate, monitor and assist if necessary, but don't interrupt the groups if they are functioning acceptably. However, do make sure that they cover all the points in the task, rather than just some of them.
- Note good points of language use, as well as half a dozen points that need further work, and add these on one side of the board.
- When most groups have finished, call the class to order and praise good use of language that you heard in the activity. Then go over any points that need more work, getting individual students to say the right thing, especially points that will come up in their presentations.
- Then get some of the groups to give their presentations, which could be given by just one member of the group, or shared between all three.
- After each presentation, get the rest of the class to give their reactions. Get students to comment (encourage tact!) on the quality of the slides, for example in relation to the points in Writing (CB page 41), if you did that section of the unit with them.

One-to-one

Go through the activities, discussing the information as if you are both marketers. (Perhaps your student is one!)

Monitor the language that you both use. After the discussion, draw attention to some key language that your student used correctly and give praise. Also work on five or six points for correction, e.g. pronunciation, vocabulary, structural errors.

Of course, in one-to-one situations like this, student presentations can be worked on in great detail. For this presentation, it might be good to concentrate on PowerPoint slides as part of the 'Making an impact' theme introduced in the Writing section of Business Skills (even if you did not do this section with your student).

Record the presentation for intensive correction work.

DVD-ROM: Case study commentary

Stage 5: Writing

- Point out the format of press releases in the Writing file. Tell students that they can write a press release based on the outcome of the role play that they participated in, or they can write about a different decision. Get them to do this for homework. As ever, get them to e-mail it to you if possible and go through corrections in the next class.

➡ Writing file (Course Book page 148)

➡ Resource bank: Writing (page 207)

5 Employment trends

AT A GLANCE

	Classwork – Course Book	Further work
Lesson 1 *Each lesson is about 60–75 minutes. This time does not include administration and time spent going through homework in any lessons.*	**Listening and discussion: The future of work** Students listen to Ian Brinkley, an expert in employment trends, talking about the future of work. They then develop related language knowledge through exercises and discussion.	**Practice File** Word power (pages 28–29) **Resource bank: Listening** (page 193) **i-Glossary** (DVD-ROM)
Lesson 2	**Reading and language:** ***Giganomics: And what don't you do for a living?*** Students discuss the changing nature of work, read an article about portfolio working and do some related vocabulary exercises.	**Text bank** (pages 134–137) **Practice File** Text and grammar (pages 30–31)
Lesson 3	**Business skills: Resolving conflict** Students look at anger-related language and at ways of resolving conflict. They re-enact a conflictive conversation that they hear, and participate in a role play where conflict-resolution techniques and language are used. **Writing: avoiding conflict in e-mails** Students listen to a communications expert talking about possible misunderstandings in e-mails and ways of avoiding them. They then practise tactful e-mail language by improving some inappropriate e-mails.	**Resource bank: Speaking** (page 181) **Practice File** Skills and pronunciation (pages 32–33)
Lesson 4	**Case study: Delaney: call-centre absenteeism** Students read about the problems of absenteeism and low morale in a Dublin call centre, role-play an interview about absenteeism with a member of staff, prioritise the issues and discuss how to resolve the problems.	**Case study commentary** (DVD-ROM) **Resource bank: Writing** (page 208)

For a fast route through the unit, focusing mainly on speaking skills, just use the underlined sections.

For one-to-one situations, most parts of the unit lend themselves, with minimal adaptation, to use with individual students. Where this is not the case, alternative procedures are given.

BUSINESS BRIEF

Fifty years ago, experts were predicting an age of decreasing work hours and increasing freedom from work, but we now look back on what we think of as the relatively leisurely attitudes to work of the 1950s and 1960s – at least for **professionals** and **white-collar workers** – with a kind of nostalgia. Things seem to have gone in the opposite direction, with many employees being told no longer to expect a **job for life** and to be ready for the joys of **freelancing** and **portfolio** working – working for a number of clients – from their mid-40s onwards, after learning their **professional skills** in an organisation or series of organisations. (One problem for them is keeping their skills up to date after they have left the organisation that originally 'taught' them.) Some find this **stressful**, others **liberating**, happy to be **salary slaves** no longer, but **work–life balance** has become a hot topic for everyone, whether freelance or salaried employees.

Governments have understood the demands of the **information economy** and have been trying to prepare for it. In the UK, for example, there has been a great expansion in the number of university places, with three times as many **graduates** coming out of UK universities as only 20 years ago. Governments are looking increasingly to the industries of this **knowledge-based economy** for future **job growth**. And the knowledge-based economy leaves those without any particular skills, who can only offer manual work, feeling increasingly beleaguered.

However, those in **skilled manual work,** such as building or gardening or care for the elderly, may feel relieved that their jobs will not be **outsourced** to China or India (even if they face competition from **developing country workers** who move to the developed world to find work in areas such as these). The Internet means that after the move of much of the world's manufacturing to China, many **professional services** are now also moving to the **developing world**. English-speaking Indian graduates have now long benefited, of course, from the demand for call centres from businesses in the US and the UK. But India is now experiencing a second wave of service **'exports'**, this time for legal and accounting work for its graduates, educated in the Anglo-Saxon traditions of law and accountancy. These services, along with its strong home-grown IT industry, will bring even greater economic benefits to the country, as they offer higher **added value**.

However, there is still a place for the knowledge-driven **hi-tech manufacturing** in the older economies of the West. After the **economic downturn** of 2007–2009, Germany, in particular, has experienced enormous demand for its beautifully engineered products. Much of this demand is from Asia, where, thanks to the change in the world **balance of economic power**, an increasingly large and prosperous middle class has emerged, its members keen to buy such products as BMWs and Mercedes. The added value of German products is more than enough to counteract the effects of its **high salaries** and **social charges**. Economies with high salaries and charges that cannot offer competitively priced products or services will find themselves increasingly **squeezed**.

Employment trends and your students

Your in-work students will be able to talk about how their jobs and careers have changed as technology has developed and attitudes to work have changed. Pre-work students will be able to talk about the jobs of members of their family and the type of job they expect to be doing in the future. Both pre-work and in-work students will certainly have views on employment trends in their country/region and in the wider world.

Read on

Daniel H Pink: *A whole new mind: Why right-brainers will rule the future*, Marshall Cavendish, 2008. See also his website http://www.danpink.com

Barrie Hopson and Katie Ledger: *And what do you do? 10 steps to creating a portfolio career*, A & C Black, 2009

Ilan Oshrie et al.: *The handbook of global outsourcing and offshoring*, Palgrave Macmillan, 2009

Julia Hobsbawm: *The see-saw: 100 ideas for work–life balance: 100 recipes for work–life balance*, Atlantic, 2009

LESSON NOTES

Warmer

- Ask students where they see themselves in 10, 20 and 30 years' time in terms of their own work – freelance contractor, salaried employee, part-time worker, etc. They could do this in small groups and report back to the whole class. (This will provide insight into students' expectations – those of pre-work students will be particularly interesting to hear about. With in-work students over a certain age, be tactful in discussing this, of course.)

Overview

- Tell students that they are going to look at some key employment issues. Go through the overview panel at the beginning of the unit in the Course Book, pointing out the sections that your students will be looking at.

Quotation

- Ask students what they think of the quotation. Is it true that jobs-for-life no longer exist in their own countries? (You could ask them if civil servants and academics still benefit from this, and if the attraction of careers in these professions has increased or not over the past few years.)
- If interested, students can look at Homa Bahrami's Haas School of Business website page on http://www2.haas.berkeley.edu/Faculty/bahrami_homa.aspx (especially if they are interested in seeing the areas that an expert in the field of organisations and employment can get into).

Listening and discussion: The future of work

Students listen to Ian Brinkley, an expert in employment trends, talking about the future of work. They then develop related language knowledge through exercises and discussion.

A CD2.1–2.8

- Tell students that they are about to hear eight short extracts from people (1–8) talking about different work situations (a–h), and that they will have to decide which situation each person is talking about and the advantages of each for employers and employees.
- Play the recording, stopping at convenient points and eliciting the answers.

1 g **2** h **3** b **4** f **5** e **6** c **7** a **8** d

B

- Go through the questions and get students to work on them in pairs.
- Circulate, monitor and assist if necessary, but don't interrupt the pairs if they are functioning acceptably.
- Call the class to order and get different pairs to relate their 'findings', comparing and contrasting them. Don't be surprised if they have very different ideas and attitudes to yours, for example about self-employment, and what people think about work–life balance. Treat tactfully. Also, see the Business brief on page 42 for arguments for and against strict legislation on working hours.

C CD2.9

- Tell students that they are going to listen to an expert on the future of work: Ian Brinkley, of the Work Foundation, a UK body which describes itself as 'the leading independent authority on work and its future'. It aims to 'improve the quality of working life and the effectiveness of organisations by equipping leaders, policymakers and opinion-formers with evidence, advice, new thinking and networks.' Students can have a look, after the lesson, at http://www.theworkfoundation.com if interested.
- Tell students to take notes while listening, as they will have to write a summary afterwards. Tell them that the word count is very important and expressing the key points within this limit is very important. (Most students will want to write too much.)
- Play the recording twice, stopping at convenient points so students can take notes.
- Get students to write their notes individually, before getting them to read their summaries one at a time.
- You could photocopy this summary before the lesson and hand it out, or copy it onto a slide.

Suggested answer

His first point is that jobs have become more skilled in many countries. The second major trend is that new jobs are being created in the 'high-value' service industries, such as hi-tech, business, health, education and creative sectors. Thirdly, job growth is taking place in certain major cities and regions but not others. (53 words)

- Get students to say what they think of the ideas expressed by Ian Brinkley.

D

- Ensure students have the correct list of service industries from the recording.
- Do this as a quick-fire whole-class activity.

Suggested answers

high-tech: biochemist, software developer, technician, telecommunications engineer

business services: accountant, financial analyst, lawyer

education: lecturer

health: radiologist

cultural and creative: architect, games designer, journalist

- Ask both pre-work and in-work students (for the latter you could make a joke about a career change, but be tactful, especially with older participants) which of these careers they would find a) most attractive, and b) most likely to become (even) more important in the future.

E – F CD2.10

- Get students to focus on the task – they have to make a list of points about the impact of technology at work, not a complete summary this time.

Exercise E

He says three things: technology has led to quicker response times; it makes us work more quickly; and it improves communication.

- Continue from the previous discussion point to the ones in Exercise F. (With very large classes, you could get students to work on these points in pairs and report back.)
- Listen carefully to what students say, both pre-work and in-work, as this might provide some interesting pointers for the future. However, don't forget to work on language points that require it.

G CD2.11

- Give students time to read through the text. Then play the recording and elicit the answers.

LESSON NOTES

When starting out on a career, it's important to get the ~~most specialist~~ **widest** set of skills and experiences possible. Nowadays, most employers are not looking for specialist staff; they want people who can perform a wide variety of tasks within the company. Employers especially want people who have good ~~organisational~~ **communication** skills, who can ~~manage~~ **get on with** other people, and who can work ~~independently~~ **in a team**, as well as people with some ~~intercultural~~ **technical** competence.

H

- Get students to work on this exercise in pairs. Circulate, monitor and assist if necessary, but don't interrupt the pairs if they are functioning acceptably.
- With the whole class, elicit the answers, and above all, discuss why they are correct. Work on stress of longer words, e.g. *adapta<u>bil</u>ity*.
- After each paragraph, discuss the implications of the information in it – don't just treat this as a language exercise.

1 knowledge **2** indispensable **3** compelling
4 success **5** unpredictable **6** adaptability
7 continually **8** increasingly **9** responsibility
10 requirements

- Depending on time and interest, get students to discuss these questions, either as a whole class, or in pairs with pairs reporting back as usual. Insist on correct use of work-related language.

Resource bank: Listening (page 193)

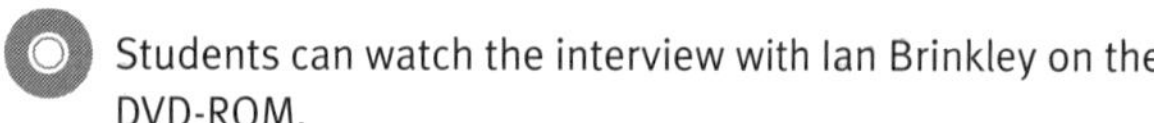

Students can watch the interview with Ian Brinkley on the DVD-ROM.

Reading and language: *Giganomics: And what don't you do for a living?*

Students discuss the changing nature of work, read an article about portfolio working and do some related vocabulary exercises.

A – D

- Discuss the questions in Exercise A with the whole class, perhaps referring to the attractions of a civil-service career (or referring back to this if you discussed in it in the Warmer).
- Get students to look at the photo and say what it suggests. At advanced level, students should know the word for what this shows: *juggling*. The man is juggling a series of part-time jobs to make a living. *Giganomics*, as the article will explain, is the activity of making a living from a number of 'gigs', i.e. part-time jobs, short-term projects, etc.
- Still with the whole class, and as a quick-fire whole-class activity, get students to suggest answers to the questions in Exercise C before they read the article. (Pre-work students, and students working in some industries (or as civil servants), may have difficulty with this. Help these students with some leading questions. (Publishing is the portfolio industry *par excellence*, with its writers only very rarely having been salaried employees, and now with its armies of out-of-house project managers, editors, designers, etc. But this model is spreading to many other industries, as students will see in the article.)
- Get students to read the article individually or in pairs. Circulate, monitor and assist if necessary, but don't interrupt students if they do not have particular questions.
- When most students have finished, elicit the answers to the questions in Exercise C. Discuss them in relation to students' own careers, or ones they hope to enter.

Exercise C

1 Jobs that portfolio workers might do, as mentioned in the article: career coach, writer, priest, magazine editor, non-executive director; also people who work in the creative industries such as advertising, graphic design and the media, as well as IT (line 103). Other possible fields and sectors: consulting, training and teaching.

2 *Suggested answers*

Benefits:
- By working for a variety of employers, no one has complete power over you to switch work on or off.
- It can be lucrative (for people like Suzy Walton).
- You keep up to date with different issues.
- It's a fantastic lifestyle.
- You have the freedom to pick and choose work, and to do it at a time that suits; you have control over what work you do.

Disadvantages:
- You have a busy diary.
- There is no job security.
- You don't have benefits like sick and holiday pay or a pension.
- The insecurity of not knowing where you'll be in six months can be more stressful.
- You have to keep up to date with different issues.
- There's a zero-tolerance attitude to being late or missing a commitment. You need to be excellent at time management.
- You feel you can't say no to anything.
- The people who employ you expect you to be on call whenever they want you.

E – F

- Get students to work on both the exercises in pairs. Circulate, monitor and assist if necessary, but don't interrupt if they are functioning acceptably.
- With the whole class, elicit the answers to both exercises, discussing *why* they are correct, and relating the information to students' own work experience (if any) where possible in order to get them to use some of the vocabulary about themselves or people they know. For example, *I'm not very good at juggling different projects – I prefer to work on one at a time.*

Exercise E

1 happening or done **only once**, not as part of a regular series
2 various kinds of **small** things
3 gives the impression that something is or will be **bad**
4 continue to learn about a subject so that you know all the **most recent** facts, etc.
5 used humorously to say something is **difficult** and **needs** a lot of effort
6 when two choices have **the same amount of** gains **and** losses so that there's little difference

Exercise F

1 a **2** b **3** a **4** a **5** a **6** b **7** a **8** b

G

- Depending on time and interest, get students to discuss this with the whole class or in pairs.
- If working in pairs and reporting back, get students to talk about the person they spoke to in relation to themselves, e.g. *Ana says she is pretty good at selling herself (though she says it herself!), but I'm not very good at this – it's something I have to work on.*
- Insist on correct use of work-related language.

- Get students to look at the Language reference section on page 132 of the Course Book and go through the information there before doing the exercise, either with the whole class or in pairs.

1 *-ing* form after a preposition
*... talk **about being** a career coach ...* (lines 2–3)
*... **by working** for a range of employers, no one has complete power over you ...* (lines 8–10)
*... **by setting** up as portfolio workers ...* (lines 19–20)
*... I am terrible **at selling** myself ...* (lines 44–45)
*... the insecurity **of not knowing** where I'll be in six months.* (lines 46–47)

2 infinitive after a modal verb
*... he **might talk** about being a career coach ...* (lines 2–3)
*Nick, 37, a graphic designer based in London, **can attest** to the stress ...* (lines 39–40)
*... you **can't say** no to anything ...* (lines 94–95)
*You **should** also **be** able to have a better work–life balance.* (lines 95–97)

3 *-ing* form as a noun
*And what don't you do for a **living**?* (headline)
*... there's a zero-tolerance attitude to **being** late or **missing** a commitment.* (lines 78–80)
*The creative industries such as **advertising** ...* (lines 100–101)
There's going to be much more multiple part-time working ... (lines 105–107)

4 *to* + infinitive after *It* + *is* + adjective
***It's hard to keep** up to speed ...* (line 75)

5 *to* + infinitive to express purpose
No examples in article

6 *-ing* form when we want to avoid repeating a subject + a relative + a vereb
Tina Brown paints a bleak picture of freelancers' lives [...],(freelancers that/who are) ***grafting** three times as hard for the same money ...* (lines 31–36)
*... with a background in central government, **including*** (that includes) *the Ministry of Defence, ...* (lines 53–55)

7 *to* + infinitive with certain verbs
*... **needs to be** excellent at time management.* (lines 83–84)
*... **be able to have** a better work–life balance.* (lines 96–97)
*... **expect** you **to be** on call ...* (line 98)

8 *to* + infinitive after certain expressions
*... in **a bid to survive**.* (line 16)
*... I'm **not** laid-back **enough to live** without ...* (lines 45–46)
*... there was **a price to pay** ...* (lines 49–50)
*... the **freedom to pick and choose** ...* (line 85)
*... you're **supposed to have** control ...* (line 92)

 Text bank (pages 134–137)

Business skills: Resolving conflict

Students look at anger-related language and at ways of resolving conflict. They re-enact a conflictive conversation that they hear, and participate in a role play where conflict-resolution techniques and language are used.

- The issue of conflict may be very culturally sensitive. Some cultures, for example Thais, don't like public displays of disagreement or conflict, which mean loss of face for those involved. Other cultures are more comfortable expressing themselves forcefully, e.g. Spanish and Americans, and yet others seem positively to thrive on it, e.g. the French.
- As a lead-in to this section, ask students about the last disagreement that they had with someone in the family (be very tactful), at work or with a stranger in the street. Ask them what the conflict was about and how they resolved it. Alternatively, you can give a simple example yourself, e.g. when someone jumped in front of you in a queue in a supermarket and what you did or said. Get students to look at the photo at the top of page 48. Ask students to imagine how the two speakers are feeling (work on advanced anger-related vocabulary, e.g. *She's upset, irate, losing her cool, going ballistic,* etc.) and what the conversation might be about. Get students in pairs to write a short dialogue for the photo. Circulate and help where necessary. Get one or two pairs of students to act out their dialogues for the whole class.
- Put students into pairs or small groups to discuss their views on the statements in Exercise A. There are no correct answers – this is a consciousness-raising exercise to make students aware of their own feelings about conflict and maybe think about their culture's attitude to conflict. Call the class to order and ask them about other types of workplace conflict that can arise, e.g. between departments, between boss and staff.

B

- Get students to look at the checklist. Deal with any questions, e.g. *sort something out*. Students work individually to answer the question 'Which do you most often use?'
- Put students into pairs to compare their answers and discuss the other two questions. Call the class to order and go through the last two questions with the whole class, asking students which conflict resolution techniques get the best results and other techniques that they have used or seen used.

C

- Get students to read the extract and deal with any questions. Tell them they have to memorise the essential information.
- Books closed, students then work in pairs to summarise what they've read.
- Ask the whole class if they think they are good listeners – most of us like to think we are. Ask them to give you examples of how they show other people they are listening such as: nodding, smiling, eye contact, asking more questions, etc. But don't forget cultures where listening in silence and waiting several seconds before talking oneself is often the norm, e.g. Finland and Japan.

D – E CD2.12

- Tell students that they are going to listen to a conversation between two work colleagues. Tell them to listen out for what the conversation is about and what techniques Carl uses to show he is listening to Yolanda. Play the recording once and get students to write their answers individually, then compare them in pairs. Ask what the conflict is about. (Carl's phone calls disturb Yolanda when she's working.)
- Play the recording again so that students can identify all the techniques Carl uses. Go through the answers with the whole class.

Exercise D

- Carl stops what he's doing and asks Yolanda to repeat what she's said: *Could you say that again?*
- He tries to show some understanding: *Got too much to do? I know the feeling.* But he has clearly missed the point.
- Then he paraphrases what's she's said – *So, what you're saying is ...* – but only to be funny, which annoys Yolanda.
- Later he does finally encourage her to continue, rather than interrupting or making fun of her or defending himself – *I'm sorry, I'm sorry. You were saying ...* and later *No, no, I'm listening. Please go on.*
- Next he shows he understands her point of view – *I appreciate how you feel ...* – before explaining the situation from his point of view.

Exercise E

a) 1, 5, 6, 9, 12
b) 3, 4, 10, 11, 13
c) 2, 7, 8, 14

- Get students to work in pairs. Refer them to the audio script on CB page 173. Deal with any remaining questions. Get students to read the dialogue aloud, paying attention to their intonation. Monitor students' performance and make a note of any problems students are having with the features of connected speech.
- Call the class together and drill any phrases students had difficulties reproducing at a natural speed and rhythm, e.g. *driving me up the wall, when I'm using the phone, most of the time,* etc.
- Students then swap roles and repeat the dialogue, trying to reproduce it at as natural a speed and rhythm as possible.
- Finally, call the class together and ask students how they would resolve the situation. Don't reject any ideas at this stage. One suggestion is that they work in different offices, although then Carl might just be disturbing other people. It could also help if Carl could learn to speak more quietly, but that seems unlikely.
- Ask students at the end to decide what they thought was the best solution mentioned. For further practice, students, in the same pairs, might like to finish the conversation between Carl and Yolanda.
- Circulate and help as necessary. Then call the class to order and ask one or two pairs to re-enact the resolution of the conflict between Carl and Yolanda that they enacted when in parallel pairs.

F

- Explain the task, read the text together with your students, or get one of them to read it, and divide students into two groups. Group A and Group B look at their corresponding information on pages 151 and 159 respectively – make sure that students turn to the correct page. Then put students into A+B pairs to carry out the role play.
- Circulate, monitor and assist if necessary, but don't interrupt the pairs if they are functioning acceptably. Make a note of students who carry out the task successfully, any target language used and five or six language points for correction, including pronunciation.
- When most pairs have finished, go through feedback with the whole class, praising appropriate language used for active listening, paraphrasing and checking understanding. Write up any points that need further work on the board and get students to say the right things, in context.
- Ask students if they were able to resolve the conflict, and if so, how.

➡ Resource bank: Speaking (page 181)

Writing: avoiding conflict in e-mails

Students listen to a communications expert talking about possible misunderstandings in e-mails and ways of avoiding them. They then practise tactful e-mail language by improving some inappropriate e-mails.

- As a lead-in to this section, ask students what kind of e-mails they generally write and receive, how many e-mails they deal with in the course of a day, if they ever react badly to the e-mails people write to them and what sort of problems they sometimes have. (They might mention the danger – and in the worst cases, threat to one's career – of firing off an angry e-mail when letting feelings cool down for a few hours or days might be a better option.)
- Get students to say what they think a course on e-mail netiquette might cover. As the point above suggests, it might cover not only 'polite' language, but situations where it would be better to wait before writing e-mails, situations where it would be better to phone, etc. (Point out the origin, if students haven't got it, of *netiquette*: 'Internet etiquette'.)

H CD2.13

- Tell students they are going to listen to intercultural expert Rob Giardina's views related to the above questions and specifically on the three questions mentioned here. Split the class into three groups.
- Tell each group to listen for the answers to just one of the questions and to take notes while they listen. Students compare their notes in their groups and add any extra information their colleagues heard which they didn't. Circulate and monitor, dealing with any questions.
- Play the recording again, this time pausing briefly after each question to allow students time to complete their notes. Again, each group compares their answers. Put the students into groups of three, with one person from each of the previous groups. Tell them to exchange the answers to the three questions.
- Go through the answers with the whole class. Discuss students' views on what they heard. Have they ever experienced misunderstandings of the type mentioned in the interview? In-work students who work with multinational teams might be able to talk abut the different communication styles of their different cultures. As always, treat tactfully, and avoid negative comments about particular cultures.

1 No visual information, e.g. smiles or nods, being able to say, 'I don't understand'.
Your context is different from their context. For example, you write a quick e-mail, and they see it as brusque and direct.
Some people don't express themselves well in writing.

2 When you read an e-mail, don't always believe your first impression – think about other possible interpretations.
When you write e-mails, think about how the other person could maybe misinterpret what you're writing and then make it clear that you don't mean that.
Take into account the other person's perspective and context and, if necessary, ask open, neutral questions.
E-mail can be particularly useful for multi-cultural teams because you can avoid the misunderstandings that can be caused by different communication styles and differences in things like body space or eye contact, etc.
You can't interrupt or be interrupted.

3 You could talk about the problem face to face or on the phone, but if you're angry or frustrated, e-mail can help you to control what you communicate. You can make your e-mails more rational and less emotional.

I

- Get students to do this in pairs in the way suggested in the Course Book, then bring the class to order and go through the answers with the whole class. However, if you're running out of time, do as a quick-fire whole-class activity.
- In both cases, be sure to discuss the issues arising, rather than just ploughing through the possible answers.

Suggested answers

1 (Using *must* in requests can sound too direct. It helps to explain the reason why you are making the request. Remember to use *please* and *thanks* / *thank you* when making requests.)
Hello everyone. I need to get an update from you on each of your projects ASAP. What I'm looking for is any progress you can report on the projects. I'm working on a departmental report and I want to be able to include this information. Many thanks!

2 (It's common in British English to soften an order or instruction by wording it as a request. It's polite to allow for the fact that some people may not be able to attend.)
Hi guys, Samira wants us to have a meeting on Tuesday morning at 10.00. This meeting is very important, so please make every effort to be there. And let me know ASAP if you can't make it. Thanks.

3 (Don't write in capital letters in e-mails – many people associate this with shouting. Extra punctuation, such as the question marks here, can also seem rude. The use of humour and the 'smiley' at the end mitigates the directness of the request a little, but it's debatable whether emoticons are appropriate in business e-mails – most people would say not, as they can be seen as pretty infantile. Showing empathy for the position of the person you are writing to is a way to avoid misunderstanding and potential conflict.)
Hi Carol. I realise you're up to your neck at the moment, but could you please send me those monthly figures ASAP? Thanks.

4 (It's important not to get too emotional in an e-mail, as it may be seen as flaming, even when that was not the intention. Always check that your e-mails sound polite and rational before clicking on SEND.)
Hi David, This is a little awkward. I'd really like to help, but I'm just too busy at the moment to deal with this request. Can it wait, or could you find someone else to take care of it?

5 (A short e-mail is not necessarily rude. However, it's never a good idea to swear or use symbols to represent swear words in an e-mail, as it makes the tone much more negative.)
Hi, guys. What's happening with that product presentation?

6 (A misunderstanding involves both parties, and it's more common for misunderstandings to occur in asynchronous communication like e-mail. The use of the adverb *simply* here seems to intensify the negative tone of the message. It's typical in British culture to apologise when such misunderstandings arise, but it isn't essential.)
(I'm sorry) There appears to be a misunderstanding here. What I'd like you to do is follow up with them and report back to me. Let me know if anything isn't clear. Thanks.

➡ Writing file (Course Book page 143)

CASE STUDY

Delaney: call-centre absenteeism

Students read about the problems of absenteeism and low morale in a Dublin call centre, role-play an interview about absenteeism with a member of staff, prioritise the issues and discuss how to resolve the problems.

Stage 1: Background and Report on absenteeism

- As a lead-in, ask students what *absenteeism* means (regular absence from work or school without a good reason), work on its stress: *absenteeism*, and ask students why they think staff at a call centre might be absent from work regularly.
- Don't spend too long on this discussion, as most of the issues come up later on in the case study. Get students to study the background information. Read it aloud, or ask students to read it aloud. Deal with any questions they may have. Write the headings from the left-hand column of the following table and elicit information from students to complete the right-hand column.

Company	Delaney
Based in	Dublin, Ireland
Client	Major car-hire company, which has outsourced its European booking operations to Delaney
Number of staff	260 full-time and part-time
Staff profile	Mostly young women in their mid- to late-20s. Many of them are fluent in English, Spanish, Italian, French or German.
Average employment tenure	three years
Problems associated with staff turnover	High costs of recruitment, selection and training Newer staff have lower productivity levels The competitiveness of the Irish call-centre industry

- Use the same approach to go through information from the report.

Instigator	Delaney's HR department
Subject	Absenteeism in the company
Length of study	12 months
Findings:	
Average no. days taken per year	seven
Reported causes	Headaches, migraine, colds, flu, back problems, stress
Consequences	Delays answering calls Extra work and stress on colleagues Cost of finding replacement staff Uncertainty in planning
Long-term consequences	Caller/client dissatisfaction
Solution	Find ways to reduce absenteeism and effective ways to deal with it when it does arise

Stage 2: Task 1 and Listening

- Divide students into two groups. Refer each group to a different role card: Group A turns to page 151, and Group B turns to page 159.
- Ask them to read their role cards and deal with any questions they have, after they have discussed their ideas as a group. It's a good idea in the first instance to allow time for peer teaching.
- Tell Group A to think about possible reasons why the agent is off sick so often and what you, as her manager, could say to her in the interview.
- Tell Group B to discuss and plan what the agent could say in this delicate interview with her manager. Giving students time to prepare for the role-play helps to increase the length of their utterances and the level of accuracy.

Possible reasons for absence

- Personal problems she doesn't want the company to know about
- Pretending to be ill to take a day off work when she feels like it
- Lack of motivation, low morale, low pay
- Pressure of workload, lack of control over workload
- Feeling bored, undervalued, or overqualified for the job

- Pair students up with someone from the other group to do the role play. Circulate and monitor the language that they use. Make a note of any target language used and five or six common errors for later correction.
- After the discussion, draw attention to some key language students used correctly and give praise. Also work on the points for correction, put these on the board and elicit the correct form, pronunciation, word, etc. from students.
- Ask students for feedback on how their discussions went, if they were able to avoid a conflict and resolve the problem, and if so how? Ask the students who played the agent if they felt their manager had been supportive or not.

CD2.14–2.19

- Get students to look at the rubric relating to the Consultant's findings. (The consultant was commissioned by the HR department, following the findings of its report on absenteeism.)
- Emphasise that students will have to summarise what they hear: get them to take notes.
- Play the recording once or twice and check students are indeed taking notes.
- Get one or more students to summarise what they heard.

- Agents and team leaders alike complain about the pressure of workload, the need to rush callers through bookings, and difficulties meeting the strict performance targets.
- It's not always possible to deal with customers in five minutes and customers can get angry when agents rush them.
- Agents feel suspicious about the purpose of call monitoring.
- Staff feel unsupported by management. Team leaders complain there is no flexibility and they aren't allowed to make decisions. Agents complain that they can't have a break after dealing with a difficult customer and that e-mails from team leaders are rude.

- With the whole class, get students to anticipate some of the solutions that the consultant might suggest, but don't pre-empt Task 2 too much.

Stage 3: Task 2

- Get students to read Task 2. Deal with any questions. Divide the students into groups of five or six. Tell them that each group will be the management team from Delaney during this task. Get them to allocate roles among themselves (e.g. the Operations Manager, the Human Resources Manager, the Chief Financial Officer, one or two Team Managers) – The Operations Manager is the senior member of staff that all the others report to. They could also have a representative from the consultants, APP. Get students to draw a 'name plate' that they can stand on the desk in front of them e.g. 'OPERATIONS MANAGER' so all students know the roles of the others.
- One of the managers, probably the Operations manager or HR manager, should lead the discussion and one student should be note-taker. When students are ready and clear about the task, get them to begin.
- Circulate and monitor, checking students are carrying out the task correctly. Make a note of any useful language being used and five or six common errors for correction, including pronunciation, for later feedback.
- When most groups have finished the task, bring the class to order. Praise the strong points that you heard and work on five or six points that need correction.
- Ask the note-taker from one or two groups to report back on how they prioritised the tasks and any solutions they came up with. There is no right answer to this question. Students may or may not reach a consensus.
- To round off the activity, highlight and summarise some of students' best ideas. As further practice, students could be asked to write up action minutes from their management meeting (see Writing file CB page 144).

One-to-one

Go through the information in the Course Book with your student. Explain any difficulties.

In Task 1, you and your student are a team manager and a call-centre agent.

Allow the student time to prepare their role. During the role play, monitor the language that your student is using, and language that you choose to use.

Note down any good examples of your student's language and points for error correction or improvement. Come back to these later. Praise any good examples of language used and go over any errors, including pronunciation.

Do Task 2 together, with each of you playing a different manager – decide which manager you are each playing at the start. Don't dominate the conversation in this task, but say enough to keep it going and allow your student to suggest ways to resolve these issues. You could record the discussion on audio or video, if the student agrees, and use it for intensive correction work afterwards.

 DVD-ROM: Case study commentary

Stage 4: Writing

- Get students to study the writing task and deal with any questions. Brainstorm the information that should go in the e-mail and put these points on the board. Alternatively, this could be made into a report-writing task.
- Get students to look at the model e-mail on page 143 of the Writing file in the Course Book again (or report writing on pages 146–147). Get students to write the final e-mail or report for homework, as this could probably be quite a long piece of work in either case. As ever, get them to e-mail it to you if possible and go through corrections in the next lesson.

Writing file (Course Book page 143)

Resource bank: Writing (page 208)

UNIT 6 Ethics

AT A GLANCE

	Classwork – Course Book	Further work
Lesson 1 *Each lesson is about 60–75 minutes. This time does not include administration and time spent going through homework in any lessons.*	**Listening and discussion: Trust me: corporate responsibility** Students listen to Philippa Foster Back, Director of the Institute of Ethics, talk about current thinking on business ethics; they work on language in this area and discuss their own opinions.	**Practice File** Word power (pages 34–35) **Resource bank: Listening** (page 194) **i-Glossary** (DVD-ROM)
Lesson 2	Reading and language: *The corporate conscience: Sherron Watkins, Enron whistleblower / Drug whistleblower collects $24m* Students compare and contrast two articles about corporate scandals. They also work on the modal perfect, to talk about what could have been done differently.	**Text bank** (pages 138–141) **Practice File** Text and grammar (pages 36–37)
Lesson 3	**Business skills: Ethical problem-solving** Students discuss two situations involving ethical problem-solving at work, listen to an 'agony aunt' giving her opinion about them, and work on expressions for giving advice. Writing: meetings and action points Students look at some tips for successful meetings, listen to a meeting about making staff redundant, then hold a meeting themselves and write the action minutes following it.	**Resource bank: Speaking** (page 182) **Practice File** Skills and pronunciation (pages 38–39)
Lesson 4	**Case study: Dilemmas at Daybreak** Students study a food company that is accused of putting too much sugar in its products and poor labelling. They role-play executive meetings to plan a new ethical approach and write a press release.	**Case study commentary** (DVD-ROM) **Resource bank: Writing** (page 209)

For a fast route through the unit, focusing mainly on speaking skills, just use the underlined sections.

For one-to-one situations, most parts of the unit lend themselves, with minimal adaptation, to use with individual students. Where this is not the case, alternative procedures are given.

BUSINESS BRIEF

Business ethics is a module taught at many business schools – MBA students discuss ethical issues to prepare them for the dilemmas they will face when they return to corporate life. **Corporate social responsibility**, or **CSR**, is the name increasingly used by companies to talk about their efforts to do 'the right thing' both locally and as **global citizens**.

A brand's value nowadays may not just be about profit and loss, but also **accountability** – for example, being able to demonstrate clearly a product's **sourcing**: where and how it was made. Companies produce **social audits** to talk about their performance in relation to all their **stakeholders** – not only suppliers, but all **employees**, **customers**, **suppliers**, **shareholders** and the countries where they operate as a whole. (In **stakeholder theory**, shareholders are just one of the many interested parties.)

These reports are designed to reassure everyone that companies are behaving **ethically** in everything from **working conditions** and **labour practices** to their **environmental impact**, not only of factories but also of warehouses and offices. Another aspect is the **effect** of companies' products in terms not only of the sourcing of the materials and parts put into them, but their **impact when in use** and the degree to which materials used to make them can be **recycled** when they are replaced. Companies talk increasingly about minimising their **carbon footprint** – the amount of carbon dioxide emitted by all their activities and products – as part of the effort to combat **global warming**.

This is all part of companies' efforts to underline their **sustainability** – the idea that their activities can continue indefinitely without causing harm – and **transparency** – the idea that they have nothing to hide. (Sceptics may describe efforts to hide or relativise the environmental impact of a company's activities as **greenwash**.)

Pressure from consumers is causing companies to be increasingly transparent about labour practices. Clothing companies are keen to demonstrate that their suppliers in developing countries do not use **sweatshop labour** or **child labour**. Multinationals argue that they have an interest in making working conditions at overseas suppliers a model for others to follow. They point out that conditions at their suppliers are often better than at local suppliers, who do not work with the outside world.

As in so many areas, the Internet is having an impact – people can see local conditions for themselves by looking at videos shot in local factories or industrial sites, sometimes clandestinely. **Consumer activists** unhappy about a company's behaviour may hack into its websites or cause them to crash in **denial of service (DOS) attacks**, where a company's website is overloaded with traffic. Activists who carry out these attacks are called, informally, **hacktivists**.

Business ethics and your students

In-work students will often be able to talk about the sustainability of their company's products or services, labour conditions, ethical manufacturing and purchasing, the effect of their company's products/services on society and the environment, the company's financial and non-financial reports and contribution, or lack of contribution, to CSR. (But be careful not to alienate students by 'egging them on' to criticise their companies' efforts or lack of them in this area, and in most organisations, even small ones, do not expect them to know all the details of operations that are a long way from their own responsibilities.)

Pre-work students may have experience of labour conditions and environmental impacts when working for companies on work placements or as part-time or temporary employees. Pre-work students may also be more aware than in-work students regarding issues such as (un)ethical fashion labels.

All students will have general world experience of buying (non-)ethical brands as consumers and may discuss the importance of corporate social responsibility when creating a positive or negative corporate image. They can also talk about whether companies should demonstrate greater responsibility and accountability to stakeholders such as employees, the local community and developing countries.

Read on

Stephen Asbury and Richard Ball: *Do the right thing: The practical, jargon-free guide to CSR,* IOSH Services, 2009

Andrew Crane and Dirk Matten: *Business ethics,* OUP, 2010

Matthew Gill: Accountants' truth: *Knowledge and ethics in the financial world,* OUP, 2011

Paul Griseri and Nina Seppala: *Business ethics and corporate social responsibility*, Cengage, 2010

Manfred Pohl and Nick Tolhurst: *Responsible business: How to manage a CSR strategy successfully,* Wiley, 2010

LESSON NOTES

Warmer

- Ask students to brainstorm a list of adjectives to describe attributes of an ethical business leader or manager. Write on the board: *An ethical business leader or manager should be ...* (*honest, trustworthy, open, fair, transparent*, etc.).
- Then ask students to brainstorm nouns related to ethics. Write on the board: *An ethical business should establish a corporate culture based on ...* (e.g. *honesty, trust, integrity, good conduct, values, openness, fair-mindedness, courage, transparency*, etc.) and write students' ideas up on the board.
- Alternatively, or in addition, ask students what they understand by the title of the unit, 'Ethics'.
- Point out that *ethics* is singular, even if many native speakers use a plural verb after it. The related adjective is *ethical*, not *ethic*. However, *ethic* can be used as a singular noun in expressions like *work ethic*.

Overview

- Tell students that they will be discussing business ethics and corporate social responsibility (CSR). Go through the overview panel at the beginning of the unit, pointing out the sections that students will be looking at.

Quotation

- Get students to look at the quotation and ask them what they think of it. (For those with a literary bent, you could point out that Shaw wrote the play *Pygmalion*, on which the musical *My Fair Lady* was based.)
- In addition, you could quote Groucho Marx: 'These are my principles. If you don't like them, I have others!'

Listening and discussion: Trust me: corporate responsibility

Students listen to Philippa Foster Back, Director of the Institute of Ethics, talk about current thinking on business ethics; they work on language in this area and discuss their own opinions.

A – B

- Go through the quotes with your students and explain any difficulties, e.g. meaning and pronunciation of *ingenious*. (You could point out that the first quote is from the 1987 film rather than the 2010 sequel, that had the secondary title *Money never sleeps*. Ask students if they have seen either of these films.)
- Get students to discuss the quotes in pairs or small groups. Circulate, monitor and assist if necessary, but don't interrupt the groups if they are functioning acceptably.
- Call the class to order and compare and contrast the opinions of different groups.
- Use the same procedure for Exercise B. If students are short of ideas, as homework you could ask them to do an Internet search on 'Bhopal', 'Enron', 'BP Gulf of Mexico', etc. to find out more about these particular scandals, and 'sweatshop labour/labor', 'pricing cartels', etc. to see what comes up in general, and come back with their findings in the next lesson. Don't forget to check their findings if you ask them to do this.

C CD2.20

- Tell students they are going to hear Philippa Foster Back, director of the Institute of Business Ethics, talking about corporate responsibility. (If students ask, you can tell them that *OBE* stands for 'Order of the British Empire', an honour given under the UK honours system, similar, for example, to the *Légion d'Honneur* in France. They can find out more about her organisation at www.ibe.org.uk.)
- Get students to read the three summaries individually. Explain any difficulties. Tell students that they have to identify the correct summary of what they are about to hear.
- Then play the recording, stopping at convenient points. Elicit the answer.

> Summary 2

- Discuss any issues arising and work on pronunciation of any words causing difficulty, e.g. *environmental*.

D CD2.21

- Get students to focus on the question. Play the second part of the recording and elicit the answer.

> 1 'Trust me' model: 100 years ago, when there were family-run companies, there was a great deal of trust around the way that companies were being run. Companies were more paternalistic, so there was an attitude of 'Don't worry, we'll look after you'.
> 2 In the 1980s/1990s, there were some corporate scandals that caused people to doubt the trust model. There was also more awareness of how companies were behaving, especially concerning environmental issues and in the oil and gas industries.
> 3 'Involve me': the attitude of 'Involve us in how you do your business. We would like to help you to do it better'. The 'involve me' model worked for some companies but not for others, and then it evolved to the 'show us' model: 'Show us you are doing business in the right way'.

- As ever, discuss the points with students rather than rushing through them.

E CD2.22

- Get students to read through the text and suggest what might go in the gaps.
- Then play the recording and see if their predictions are confirmed.

> **1** corporate responsibility **2** prove to
> **3** corporate responsibility reports
> **4** sustainability reports **5** stakeholders **6** obey me
> **7** not behaving **8** enforce the law / enforce laws

F

- With the whole class, get students to say which of the models in Exercise E is used a) by their organisation, or in the case of pre-work students, an organisation that they are interested in, and b) by most companies in the world today.

G – H

- Get students to work on these exercises in pairs or small groups. Circulate, monitor and assist if necessary, but don't interrupt the groups if they are functioning acceptably.
- Call the class to order and elicit the answers to Exercise G. Explain any difficulties and work on pronunciation and stress, for example of *paternalistic*.

> **Exercise G**
> **1** paternalistic **2** account; scandals
> **3** reports; irregularities **4** supply **5** labour
> **6** stakeholders **7** reputation **8** unethical

- Then get students, again in pairs or small groups, to comment on the statements using the system shown in Exercise H.
- Circulate, monitor and assist if necessary, but don't interrupt the groups if they are functioning acceptably.
- When most groups have finished, call the class to order and compare and contrast their findings – there are no right answers – the idea of the statements is to stimulate discussion.
- Work on any remaining difficulties, getting students to say the right forms.

Resource bank: Listening (page 194)

Students can watch the interview with Philippa Foster Back on the DVD-ROM.

i-Glossary

Reading and language: *The corporate conscience: Sherron Watkins, Enron whistleblower / Drug whistleblower collects $24m*

Students compare and contrast two articles about corporate scandals. They also work on the modal perfect, to talk about what could have been done differently.

A

- Do this as a quick-fire whole-class activity.

Definition c)

(Definition a) is a red herring. There isn't a specific word in English for this. Definition b) is an industrial spy, someone who commits industrial espionage.)

The term *whistleblower* derives from the practice of English policemen, who would blow their whistles when they noticed the commission of a crime. The whistle would alert other law enforcement officers and the general public of danger.

B

- Focus students' attention on the five questions and allocate the articles to Students A and B. (Don't let students choose, as this wastes time.)
- Get students to read their articles. Circulate, monitor and assist if necessary, but don't interrupt if students are reading without problems.
- When students have finished, call the class to order and elicit the answers.

1. Sherron Watkins worked for Enron, the world's biggest energy trader at the time.
   David Franklin worked for the pharmaceutical company Parke-Davis, later bought by Pfizer.
2. Sherron Watkins uncovered accounting fraud. She first exposed the fraud via an anonymous memo and later spoke to the founder and Chairman in person.
   David Franklin exposed illegal and fraudulent marketing of a drug. He took the company to court.
3. Sherron Watkins was an internal whistleblower.
   David Franklin was an external whistleblower who reported the wrongdoing outside the company.
4. Yes, David Franklin has become a millionaire.
5. There are no obvious traits that they have in common other than that they are both whistleblowers.

You could point out that today Sherron Watkins is now a lecturer in business ethics. You could show the following videos of interviews with her to your class, or get them to watch them outside the class and report back:

http://www.cbsnews.com/video/watch/?id=2116787n

http://news.yahoo.com/video/business-15749628/whistleblowers-a-different-breed-18390807

David Franklin has chosen to remain out of the public eye and has rarely given interviews, but students can read about him at http://en.wikipedia.org/wiki/David_Franklin_(scientist). (Give them the full web address as there are a number of people with this name on Wikipedia.)

C

- Depending on the level of the class, get students to look again at the same article, of if they are more advanced, get them to swap articles for this activity.
- Get students to do the exercise and circulate, monitor and assist if necessary, but don't interrupt the students if they have no particular questions.
- Call the class to order and elicit the answers for each article.

1 mired **2** stumbled across **3** work up the guts
4 taken the helm **5** dismissed **6** cooks the books
7 come clean **8** plead guilty **9** to settle **10** reported
11 hefty (speaker's) fees **12** reimbursement
13 filed a (whistleblower's) lawsuit **14** compliance

D – F

- With the whole class, get students to say what Sherron Watkins could have done, should have done, would have done, etc. and write correct forms of some of the students' utterances on the board, for example, *She should have (should've) seen the warning signs sooner, She could have (could've) gone outside the company,* etc.
- This is to focus students' attention on modal forms. Get students to look at the Language reference section in the Course Book, page 134, and talk them through the explanations and examples.
- Then get students to discuss the questions in Exercise F in parallel pairs. Circulate, monitor and assist if necessary, but don't interrupt the pairs if they are functioning acceptably. Note good points of language use, as well as half a dozen points that need further work, especially in relation to modal perfect forms, and add these on one side of the board.
- Call the class to order. Ask pairs for their answers to the questions, comparing and contrasting those of different pairs.
- Praise good use of modal perfects that you heard in the activity and get students to correct mistakes that you heard by asking them to repeat the correct forms.

Exercise E

- To hypothesise about and comment on the past: She could have gone outside the company;
  I would have gone to the company's auditors;
  I doubt that would have helped.
- To criticise past actions: Sherron Watkins should have done something sooner
- To express regret: She herself says she should have seen the warning signs.

Exercise F

Suggested answers

1. Because it means risking your job and career; because the situation might correct itself without you saying anything.

2 There is the risk that people may say the wrong things if payment is an incentive. It is better to guarantee the protection of genuine whistleblowers rather than offer to pay them.

3 It could be argued that whistleblowers like David Franklin forced the pharmaceutical company to pay money back to the government. Sherron Watkins believes her actions helped to convict people at Enron, and helped get important legislation passed, the 2002 Sarbanes Oxley Act, requiring CEOs and CFOs to certify that financial accounts are true.

 Text bank (pages 138–141)

Business skills: Ethical problem-solving

Students discuss two situations involving ethical problem-solving at work, listen to an 'agony aunt' giving her opinion about them, and work on expressions for giving advice.

A

- Teach the expressions *agony column* and *agony aunt* as a lead-in to this exercise. Then get students to read the dilemmas individually and check their understanding with some quick-fire questions. (You could ask them what the situation of getting jobs/promotion from relatives, as in the second situation, is called, though the word is not actually used there: *nepotism*.)
- Then get students to say how they would respond in each situation, comparing and contrasting their responses.
- Alternatively, if there is a good class atmosphere, you may want to describe a moral dilemma of your own that happened in the workplace and then ask students these questions:
  What kind of ethical problems have you faced at work?
  What happened?
  Do you think you took the right decision? Why? / Why not?
  If you were facing an ethical dilemma at work, who would you ask for advice? Why? / Why not?

B CD2.23–2.24

- Explain to students they are going to listen to two podcasts by the agony aunt about the situations in Exercise A. Play each recording once and ask students for their initial reactions, comparing the agony aunt's comments with their own.

C CD2.23–2.24

- Play the recordings a second time, pausing, if necessary, to give students time to mark their answers individually. Get early finishers to compare their answers in pairs.
- Then go through the extracts from the speakers with the whole class.

1 to do the right thing
2 neither here nor there
3 If it was up to me
4 you're in a tricky situation
5 Another thing you could do is
6 this is a clear-cut case
7 weigh up the pros
8 put your reputation at risk
9 On the other hand
10 is up to you
11 What I would say, though

- Get students to look at the expressions in the Useful language box and ask individual students to read them out with feeling. Work especially on the stressed *would* of *What I would say, though, is* ... and the stressed *really* of Are you *sure you really want to* ...?
- As a quick-fire whole-class activity, get students to say which are more diplomatic/neutral, and which more forceful/direct. (Point out that these latter expressions are not aggressive, just forceful/direct.)

Expressions that sound more diplomatic/neutral
Another thing you could do is ...
You might like to ...
What you finally decide is up to you.
Oh dear, that's a tricky/tough one.
You have to weigh up the pros and cons.
On the other hand, you might ...
On balance, I think you should ...

Expressions that sound more forceful/direct
The most important thing is to ...
If it were up to me, I'd ...
What I *would* say, though, is ...
I wouldn't do that if I were you.
Are you sure you *really* want to ...?

- Get students to think of typical ethical dilemmas at work (everyday ones, like use of the computer network to surf the Internet for private purposes) or, if they are pre-work, ethical dilemmas in relation to their educational institution, e.g. seeing that someone is cheating in exams.
- Divide the class into groups of three: Student A, Student B and an observer. Allocate roles and get students to do the activity in parallel groups. The observer's job is to note the relative forcefulness/directness of Student B.
- Circulate, monitor and assist if necessary, but don't interrupt the groups if they are functioning acceptably.
- When most groups have finished, call the class to order and get the observer from each group to comment on the relative forcefulness of the language they heard. Get the Student B from each group to say if that was what they intended, and ask the Student As to comment as well.

Resource bank: Speaking (page 182)

Writing: meetings and action points

Students look at some tips for successful meetings, listen to a meeting about making staff redundant, then hold a meeting themselves and write the action minutes following it.

- With the whole class, ask students to look at the tips for effective meetings and for writing up action points. Explain any difficulties. Point out that the tips use the mnemonic *PARTAKE*. (Practise the pronunciation of *mnemonic* – the initial *m* is silent.)

G CD2.25

- Tell students they are going to listen to a group of people having a problem-solving meeting, discussing procedures for employing staff. Tell them to focus on what the agenda was, and whether the meeting was managed effectively or not.
- Play the recording once. Ask students to compare their answers in pairs.

- Go through feedback with the whole class. Play the recording a second time, asking the students to note down all the things that go wrong in the meeting. Refer to the audio script on page 174 if necessary.

Suggested answers

The meeting was effective in that a couple of decisions were taken regarding communicating job losses to employees. However, it was quite a conflictive meeting.

There was some conflict from the Human Resources Manager, John, and the Sales Manager, Vincent, neither of whom wanted to communicate the bad news to employees. There was also some antagonism (teach this word) between John and Vincent, e.g. Vincent accused John of taking on unnecessary staff in production earlier that year.

Becky didn't handle the meeting too badly, considering it was fairly conflictive and she tried to keep them on track. But she could have used the 'round robin' technique earlier before things got out of hand. She also sounded very direct towards the end of the meeting, when she was briefing the other managers, although others might prefer this more directive approach.

H – I

- Make sure students are given plenty of time to absorb the information for the next tasks. Write the purpose of the meeting on the board so as to focus students' attention on it: a meeting at Maynard Electronics to discuss ways of monitoring employees and surveillance (practise pronunciation of this word) measures.
- Tell students that they will later have to write the action points for the role-played meeting, and get them to turn to the Writing file (CB page 144) to give them a flavour of what they will have to do.
- Ask students in work what kind of action points or minutes they generally receive or write. Ask pre-work students what they would expect to read in action points of a company meeting. Tell students they will have to write up a summary of the meeting that they are about to have.
- Get students to look at the agenda and get one student to expand on it in full sentences, e.g. *The firm wants to look at the possibility of installing security cameras, and if so, where.*
- Divide the class into groups of four and allocate the roles: make sure students turn to the correct pages. Get them each to write a job title nameplate for themselves and put it in front of them, e.g. 'HUMAN RESOURCES MANAGER'. Appoint a chair for each group, and tell students that they should each make enough notes to be able to write the action minutes afterwards.
- When they are ready, the role plays can begin. Circulate, monitor and assist if necessary, but don't interrupt the groups if they are functioning acceptably.
- Note good points of language use, as well as half a dozen points that need further work, and add these on one side of the board.
- When most groups have finished, call the class to order and ask different groups for a quick summary of what happened in each.
- Praise good use of meetings language that you heard in the activity, and work on half a dozen points that need improvement/correction, getting individual students to say the right thing.
- Students now write up action points as discussed in the meeting on managing effective meetings. Make it clear that they do not need to write detailed minutes.
- Circulate, monitor and help students whilst they write. Make a note of any useful expressions used on the board, together with five or six common errors. Early finishers can be referred to the board to see if they can correct the errors.
- After completing the task, students may compare their action minutes with another pair. Were all the main points mentioned? Is it clear who is responsible for each point? Are there deadlines or suggested dates for the actions? What could be improved?
- To help students be more aware of the impact their writing has on the reader, put each pair of students with another pair who had the same roles. They exchange and read each other's action points: students compare their summaries and ask their colleagues about any differences.
- If peer correction is appropriate in your setting, students could also be asked to proofread each others' writing task and point out any spelling mistakes or grammatical errors they spot. Be on hand to help with this, but leave most of the feedback and discussion to students.
- Go through feedback with the whole class, praising good examples of language used and pointing out five or six areas that need further work. Go through any common errors and the useful phrases on the board to round off the activity. This writing task could also be set for homework, with students e-mailing you their work. If they do this task as homework, don't forget to correct it / come back to it in a later lesson.

Suggested answer

Action points of meeting: Security and Workplace Surveillance

Date: 8 February

Venue: Head office, Room 4

Present: Ingvar Koning, Urszula Podalska, Ashkan Behdad and Siobhan McCarthy

Apologies: Pascal Beauvois, Ethan Rooney

		Action	By
1	**Installation of security cameras** Following the suggestion to install more security cameras throughout the building, we agreed that more cameras are essential in certain areas to prevent theft, e.g. in the warehouse and production area, but not in office areas. The IT dept will look into costs. It was also suggested that the company draws up a series of guidelines for Security and Workplace Surveillance.	UP/AB/ER	8 Mar
2	**Monitoring of e-mail and Internet usage** The majority of attendees agreed tighter measures are called for, and there is particular concern about the use (and abuse) of social media during office hours. The IT dept will review the current policy, together with the Production and HR depts, and send a report before the next meeting.	IK/UP/AB	15 Feb

	Action	By
3 Recruitment background checks Various ideas were discussed. The most contentious was that of investigating criminal records of new staff. Concerns were also raised regarding security of employees' records and privacy issues. The HR dept will look into these areas in more detail and consult an employment lawyer. To be discussed further at the next meeting.	IK/PB/SM	22 Feb
4 Communication to staff It was agreed that AB will take on the new role of Security Officer and would coordinate any subsequent actions concerning security and surveillance. A decision on AB's request for a full-time assistant is pending. It was stressed, however, *all* managers need to assume responsibility for their respective areas.	IK/AB/SM	22 Feb

Next meeting confirmed: 15 March, 9.00 a.m.
Venue: Maynard Electronics head office, Room 7
Aim of meeting: Guidelines for Security and Workplace Surveillance

Writing file (Course Book page 144)

CASE STUDY

Dilemmas at Daybreak

Students study a food company that is accused of putting too much sugar in its products and poor labelling. They role-play executive meetings to plan a new ethical approach and write a press release.

Stage 1: Background, Listening and Task 1

- Explain the background to the case study: a food company is accused of putting too much sugar in its products, and has to improve labelling, but is also forced to review its approach to its ethics as a whole.
- Get students to read the Background and elicit information from them to complete this table.

Company/ country	Daybreak, UK
Bad publicity due to	Mislabelling of products, including children's breakfast cereal, Ready-to-go
Whistleblower	An ex-employee, expert nutritionist
Allegation	Cereal is high in sugar, salt, carbohydrates
Effects	Company's website froze Customer service switchboard jammed by angry parents and nutritionists, who claimed cereal is 50% sugar
Labelling	Described as unclear because details for 30g given rather than for 100g Sodium and salt listed separately – misleading
Daybreak's actions so far	No apology Promise to review nutritional content Promise to improve labelling Recognition of need to review its ethics

CD2.26

- Tell students that they are about to hear a news broadcast about the crisis. Tell them they should be ready to take notes on key points.
- Play the recording, stopping the recording at convenient points to give students time to take notes.
- With the whole class, elicit answers from several students, going round the class, rather than just relying on one student.

Suggested answers

Key points:

- Some children's breakfast cereals are more than 50% sugar by weight.
- A study found children's cereals have more sugar, salt, carbohydrates and calories per gram than cereals not marketed to kids.
- A single serving of a cereal, including Ready-to-go by Daybreak, can have as much sugar as a doughnut.
- Eight cereal brands in the study were at least 40% sugar by weight.
- The food industry spends £145 million annually advertising cereals to children.
- An expert nutritionist said obesity is a problem and that children serve themselves over 50% more than the suggested serving.
- The study also found two cereal brands that only had one gram of sugar per serving.
- The consequences of this report are that at least two cereal brands are healthier than Daybreak's and it could result in damaging the company's reputation. Daybreak may need to issue a press statement and confirm or deny these findings.

- Tell students that in this role play, they will be discussing the issues as executives of Daybreak, but they won't have individual job titles.
- Underline the purpose of the meeting: executives discuss a) how they could have prevented the scandal, b) recommendations for the future, talking about the suitability of the ones shown here and adding some ideas of their own.
- Go quickly through the items on the agenda, explain any difficulties (e.g. *escalate*) and divide the class into groups of four or five.
- When groups are ready, start the role play. Circulate, monitor and assist if necessary, but don't interrupt the groups if they are functioning acceptably.
- Note good points of language use, as well as half a dozen points that need further work, and add these on one side of the board, especially in relation to the language of ethics, and to modal perfect forms.

- When most groups have finished, call the class to order and get students from one or two groups to say briefly what happened in their groups, and the conclusions that they came to.
- Praise good use of ethical and modal perfect language that you heard in the activity. Then go over any points that need more work, getting individual students to say the right thing.

Stage 2: Task 2

- Explain the task. The last meeting was more about the past, but the upcoming one is about the future – how to move on from the current crisis.
- Get students to absorb the information in the panel. Underline the need for students to make preparatory notes before the actual role play begins.
- Then allocate roles, ensuring that students turn to the correct page. This time, students have particular jobs and should show these on nameplates that they put in front of them, e.g. 'HEAD OF MARKETING AND SALES'. Appoint this person to lead the discussion and get him/her to draw up an agenda. (It doesn't matter if it's not exactly the one below, or if the points are in a different order, as long as it's coherent and relevant.)

Suggested agenda

1 How to improve food labelling
2 How to regain consumer confidence
3 Other suggestions for improving Daybreak's business ethics.
4 AOB

- Circulate, monitor and assist students with note preparation if necessary, but don't interrupt them if they are already doing this acceptably.
- When groups are ready, get them to begin. Circulate and monitor. As before, note good points of language use, as well as half a dozen points that need further work, and add these on one side of the board, especially in relation to the language of ethics, and to modal perfect forms.
- When most groups have finished, call the class to order and get students from one or two groups to say briefly what happened in their groups, and the conclusions that they came to, comparing and contrasting the outcomes in each group.
- Praise good use of ethical and modal perfect language that you heard in the activity. Then go over any points that need more work, getting individual students to say the right thing.

Stage 3: Listening  CD2.27

- As a final activity, get students to listen to another TV report, six months after the crisis.
- Get students to look at the instructions.
- Play the recording, stopping at convenient places.
- Then elicit the answers and discuss them with the whole class – as ever, don't just plough through them.
- Ask students what Daybreak could/should have done differently to avoid its current fate. Try to relate the issues to the students' own industry/ies, asking about parallel situations that they might be familiar with – what happened, what might have been done differently, etc.

Suggested answers

- **What action(s) did Daybreak take to improve their business ethics?**
  Daybreak standardised its food labels and claims that its children's cereals are healthier now. But experts found that sugar content had only been reduced by 10 per cent. Its sugar content is still higher than it should be.
- **Was it successful?**
  No, sales of Ready-to-go have dropped, despite them giving away cereal packs in supermarkets as part of a promotional campaign.
- **What else could they have done?**
  An expert/former employee says Daybreak should have reduced its levels of sugar, salt and carbohydrates in children's cereals, and increased the fibre content, too. Daybreak is trying to improve its image and is donating to a children's project in Mali, but it seems it's too little, too late.

One-to-one

Go through the information and activities in the Course Book with your student as above. Play the recording.

In Task 1, you and your student discuss the issues as two unidentified Daybreak executives.

Allow the student time to prepare their role. During the role play, monitor the language that your student is using, and language that you choose to use.

Note down any good examples of your student's language and points for error correction or improvement. Come back to these later. Praise any good examples of language used and go over any errors, including pronunciation.

Do Task 2 together, with each of you playing a different manager – decide which manager you are each playing at the start. Don't dominate the conversation in this task, but say enough to keep it going and allow your student to suggest ways to resolve these issues. You could record the discussion on audio or video, if the student agrees, and use it for intensive correction work afterwards.

Play the final recording and get your student to react to the outcome. Ask what Daybreak could/should have done differently to avoid its current fate.

Try to relate the issues to the student's own industry, asking about parallel situations that your student might be familiar with – what happened, what might have been done differently, etc.

DVD-ROM: Case study commentary

Stage 4: Writing

- Get students to study the writing task and deal with any questions. Underline the information that should go in the press release issued just after the meeting in Task 2 above.
- Get students to look at the model press release on page 148 of the Writing file again. Get students to write the press release for homework. As ever, get them to e-mail it to you if possible and go through corrections in the next lesson.

➡ Writing file (Course Book page 148)

➡ Resource bank: Writing (page 209)

Task

- Get students to look at the task description and instructions. Outline what they have to do and explain any difficulties.
- Point out that the discussion between Wright International executives will follow the agenda shown.
- Divide the class into groups of four or five and get students to start the meeting role play. Again, get someone to lead the discussion – tell them that they are the CEO of Wright. This time, you could name one of the members of each group as an observer who does not take part in the discussion, but who follows it and takes notes so as to be able to explain what happened in the meeting to the rest of the class when it is over.
- When the groups are ready, tell the CEOs to start the discussion role play. Circulate, monitor and assist if necessary, but don't interrupt the groups if they are functioning acceptably.
- Note good points of language use, as well as half a dozen points that need further work, and add these on one side of the board.
- When the groups have finished, call the class to order and ask the spokespersons for each group to say what happened in it. Encourage whole-class discussion to compare and contrast the results from each group.
- To round off, praise good use of language that you heard in the activity, and work on things that need improvement in the usual way.

UNIT B Revision

This unit revises and reinforces some of the key language points from Units 4–6 and from Working across cultures 2, and links with those units are clearly shown.

For more speaking practice, see the Resource bank section of this book, beginning on page 171. The exercises in this unit can be done in class, individually or collaboratively, or for homework.

4 Marketing

Vocabulary

- This exercise revisits some key marketing vocabulary on customer relationship management from Unit 4.

1 special offers **2** marketing tool **3** store
4 loyalty scheme **5** customised **6** personalise
7 reductions **8** privacy concerns **9** social networks
10 marketers **11** attract **12** online

Relative clauses

- Here, students get further work in relative clauses, from page 38. They can also look at the Language reference section on page 130 of the Course Book.

1. You can have a great, powerful brand in a company **whose** reputation has been damaged.
2. Conversely, you can have some companies **which/that** enjoy a great reputation, but don't own any world-class brands.
3. There are aspects of the company's reputation **which/that** will affect their brands.
4. As more consumers worry about obesity, leading fast-food brands have altered their menus to provide healthier choices, **which** has led to significant growth as a result.
5. The people **who/that** go out and buy the product ...
6. ... are not always the same ones **who/that** notice corporate reputations.

Skills

- Here, students revise key presentation expressions from page 40.

1 **1** b **2** g **3** a **4** f **5** c **6** e **7** d
2 **1** b **2** e and d **3** c **4** e **5** a, b and e **6** a and c **7** f and d

5 Employment trends

-ing form and infinitives

- Revision of the two forms discussed on page 47, and in the Language reference section, page 132.

Exercise 1

1 being; be; working **2** to find; being; not knowing
3 offer; to work; to give **4** having; keeping; juggling
5 working; having; to go **6** Recruiting; training/retaining; retaining/training **7** to reduce; to look at; to manage
8 change; working; to do

Exercise 2

1 (to) devise **2** meeting **3** to fix **4** ranging **5** working
6 listening **7** being **8** being **9** taking over
10 setting up **11** to think **12** including

Writing

- Another chance for students to practise polite e-mails, as on page 51 of the Course Book.

Suggested answer

To all staff

It has unfortunately come to my notice that one of the new in-house projectors has gone missing. Could the person who last used projector ref. no. PRO-5 please make sure it is returned as soon as possible?

As you know, these projectors should remain on site. That way we can all have access to such equipment whenever we need it. It is not for personal use. If you need to take a projector outside the office, e.g. for an external presentation, please remember to check with me first, or let one of the IT technicians know.

Thanks for your cooperation.

[Name]
Office manager

6 Ethics

Modal perfect

- Students get another opportunity to work on this area, presented on page 54 and in the Language reference section, page 134.

Suggested answers

The person leading the meeting should have sent the agenda in advance to all participants.

The participants should have arrived on time and they should have read all the relevant documents.

The meeting could have been scheduled at a more convenient time.

The chair should have asked for everybody's opinion.

The person leading the meeting should have finished on time.

The participants should have stuck to the agenda. etc.

Vocabulary

- Another look at ethical vocabulary.

1 renewable **2** standards **3** sustainable **4** conditions
5 reported **6** low-paid **7** Migrant **8** sources
9 awareness **10** take **11** respect **12** responsibilities

Skills

- Another opportunity to practise useful language for giving advice, presented on page 56.

1 What you finally decide is completely **up** to you.
2 Oh dear, that's a **tricky** one. Decisions, decisions ...
3 You have to weigh up the **pros** and cons.
4 I **wouldn't** do that right now if I were you. If it were up to me, I'd wait a bit.
5 On balance, I think you should say yes. On the other **hand**, you might want to say 'maybe'.
6 What I would say, **though/however**, is don't do anything unless you're absolutely sure.

Cultures 2: Ethical international business

- Another chance to look at the vocabulary related to this area.

1 criticised **2** food makers **3** fault **4** responsibility
5 obesity **6** Alarmed **7** put pressure **8** cut back
9 irresponsibly **10** processed

UNIT 7

Finance

AT A GLANCE

	Classwork – Course Book	Further work
Lesson 1 *Each lesson is about 60–75 minutes. This time does not include administration and time spent going through homework in any lessons.*	**Listening and discussion: Sustainable banking** Students listen to the Managing Director of a bank that operates on unusual lines and develop banking-related language in discussion and exercises.	**Practice File** Word power (pages 40–41) **Resource bank: Listening** (page 195) **i-Glossary** (DVD-ROM)
Lesson 2	**Reading and language:** ***Day of reckoning for innumerate bankers*** Students read about the banking debacle of 2007, discuss the reasons for it and work on finance vocabulary and multiword verbs.	**Text bank** (pages 142–145) **Practice File** Text and grammar (pages 42–43) **ML Grammar and Usage**
Lesson 3	**Business skills: Managing questions** Students look at the art of answering difficult questions in different contexts, listen to some situations where this is happening, and develop their own skills in this area.	**Resource bank: Speaking** (page 183) **Practice File** Skills and pronunciation (pages 44–45)
Lesson 4	**Case study: Dragons & Angels** Students, as angel investors, talk to entrepreneurs looking for funding, evaluate their projects and make a decision about the one to invest in.	**Case study commentary** (DVD-ROM) **Resource bank: Writing** (page 210)

For a fast route through the unit, focusing mainly on speaking skills, just use the underlined sections.

For one-to-one situations, most parts of the unit lend themselves, with minimal adaptation, to use with individual students. Where this is not the case, alternative procedures are given.

BUSINESS BRIEF

You have a brilliant but unusual business idea. You could put all your life savings into it, and ask friends and family to invest in it as well. But this may not be enough. Or your friends may, perhaps wisely, refuse to lend you money. You go to your local bank, but they don't understand your idea and suggest you look elsewhere.

You go to a **venture capitalist**. Venture capitalists are used to looking at new ideas, especially in hi-tech industries, and they see the potential in your brilliant idea. The venture capitalist also recommends it to some **business angels** (private investors looking for new **start-ups** to invest in). They provide you with **seed capital** to set up your business. Investors like this who share in the risk get a share of the business: they get **equity** in the business. (Lenders like banks do not get equity.)

You launch your business and it's a great success. But the amount of money it generates from sales is not enough to invest in further expansion: it's not **self-financing**. So you decide to raise more capital in an **initial public offering** or **IPO**: your company is **floated**, and you issue shares on a stock market for the first time, perhaps a market or a section of one that specialises in shares in hi-tech companies.

You wait anxiously for the day of the **issue** or **float**. Interest from investors is high, and all the shares are sold. Over the next few weeks, there is a stream of favourable news from your company about its sales,
new products and the brilliant new people it has managed to recruit. The shares increase steadily in value.

Now look at this process from the point of view of investors. The venture capitalists and business angels, for example, know that most new businesses will fail, but a few will do reasonably well and one or two will, with luck, hit the jackpot, paying back all the money they lost on unprofitable projects and much more. This exemplifies the classic trade-off between **risk and return**, the idea that the riskier an investment is, the more profit you require from it.

In your IPO, there may be investors who think that your company might be a future IBM or Microsoft, and they want to get in on the ground floor, holding onto the shares as they increase inexorably in value. They make large **capital gains** that can be **realised** when they sell the shares. Or they may anticipate selling quickly and making a quick profit.

Other investors may prefer to avoid the unpredictable world of **tech stocks** altogether and go for steady but unspectacular returns from established, well-known companies. These are the **blue chips** that form the basis of many conservative investment **portfolios**. One day, in a few years time, when your company is **mature** and growing at five or 10 per cent a year, rather than doubling in size every six months, your brilliant business idea may have become a blue-chip company itself.

Governments increasingly depend on investment from the private sector in public projects. These **public–private partnerships** are financed by a combination of commercial investment and public money from taxation and government borrowing.

Finance and your students

In-work and pre-work students will all have something to say about banking and banks. You could get them to talk about their experiences as bank customers, and about their opinion of the UK, US and Irish bankers who went on paying themselves **bonuses** after having been **bailed out** by the State. (If your students are bankers, be extremely tactful, of course!)

You could also get students to talk about whether banks in their countries are lending to companies and individuals. In the UK, for example, banks are often refusing to lend to even well-established businesses.
Ask students whether they think this is, in a way, understandable, following the enormous losses on bad loans that led to the banking crisis in the first place.

Read on

Michael Brett: *How to read the financial pages,* Random House, 2003

Ron Chernow: *The house of Morgan: an American banking dynasty and the rise of modern finance,* Grove Press, 2001

Longman Business English Dictionary, Pearson Education, 2007 edition

Michael Ramsden: *Teach yourself finance for non-financial managers,* Teach Yourself Books, 2010

Gillian Tett: *Fool's gold: How unrestrained greed corrupted a dream, shattered global markets and unleashed a catastrophe,* Abacus, 2010

LESSON NOTES

Warmer

- As suggested in the Business brief on page 62, ask students to talk about their experiences as bank customers, and about their opinion of bank bonuses following the events of the last few years. (Try to relate this to a recent development on this front, e.g. the latest figures on bank profits, bank lending, etc. This may require a bit of research before the class, e.g. on www.ft.com.)

Overview

- Tell students that they will be looking at finance in this unit.
- Go through the overview panel at the beginning of the unit, pointing out the sections that students will be looking at.

Quotation

- Get students to look at the quotation and ask them if they agree with it, or if they are less cynical than Ernest Haskins about the virtues of saving!

Listening and discussion: Sustainable banking

Students listen to the Managing Director of a bank that operates on unusual lines and develop banking-related language in discussion and exercises.

A

- Students work in pairs to discuss the question and the comments. Circulate, monitor and assist if necessary, but don't interrupt the pairs if they are functioning acceptably.
- Then get students' feedback as a whole class. (Don't correct relatively minor language mistakes at this point, so as to encourage students to get into the subject.)

1 A saver keeps money or other assets usually in a bank account, without any risk of making profit (apart from the interest) or loss (unless the bank fails).
Investors use their money to generate wealth in the future. Investors can gain much higher returns, but there is also a risk of some loss.

B CD2.30

- Prepare students for what they are about to hear, without giving too much away. Explain that Charles Middleton is the UK Managing Director (= Chief Executive) of Triodos, an ethical bank. Get a student to read the description of the bank in the margin for the whole class.
- Get students to predict what might go in the gaps in the text.
- Play the recording, stopping at convenient points.
- Elicit the answers and work on any difficulties, e.g. pronunciation of *expert<u>ise</u>* and the fact that it can be a countable or uncountable noun here.

Suggested answers
1 social **2** environmental **3** real economy
4 individuals **5** businesses **6** (actually) doing things
7 (an) expertise **8** triple bottom line

- Ask students if there are any banks like this in their own countries.

C CD2.31

- Get students to look through the text before they hear the recording, and predict what they think might be the mistakes, e.g. it seems unlikely that Triodos invests in nuclear power.
- Play the recording and elicit the answers.

Triodos invests in over 9,500 projects. They cover a ~~very limited~~ **vast/huge/enormous/wide** range of activities.
One such activity is ~~nuclear~~ **renewable** energy. The bank is lending to some of the major providers in the ~~EU~~ **UK**. It is also financing some of the big providers of social ~~networks~~ **housing**, such as Mencap. And it is involved in ~~training~~ **trading** activity, for instance with organisations like Café Direct, a major ~~wholesale~~ **fair-trade** provider of hot drinks. The bank provides these organisations with debt funding, so the return is just the interest on the loan.

D

- Adapt this exercise to your students. For example, if they are finance specialists, they will probably have some quite technical ideas for change. If they are pre-work or non-financial students, talk about bank charges, the difficulty of getting an overdraft or a loan, mistakes made by banks, etc.
- Get students to discuss these points in pairs or small groups. Circulate, monitor and assist if necessary, but don't interrupt the groups if they are functioning acceptably.
- With the whole class, elicit their ideas. As mentioned, adapt the discussion to the students' level and help with any vocabulary where necessary. (For example, they should know *overdraft* and *go overdrawn* at this level, but be prepared to help with terms like this.)
- Work further on banking-related language, getting individual students to say the right thing if they have made mistakes, for example using *credits* in the plural when they should say *loans*. (Point out simple but potentially useful words like *lending* and *borrowing*, which refer to the same thing, but seen from the point of view of each side of the transaction.)

E CD2.32

- Now play the recording and get students to see if any of their changes are mentioned by Charles Middleton.

Firstly, he'd like to see a focus on banking in the real economy, as opposed to creating products and services that are removed from the bank's business, because it's been proven that a bank can't manage that risk when it's not in direct contact with the business.
Secondly, he'd like to see some separation of the more investment-banking type of activities from commercial banking, because investment banking is a riskier business and customers are put at risk of banks failing.

F – G

- Do these as quick-fire whole-class activities, getting students to call out the answers and working on any difficulties, e.g. pronunciation and meaning of *ex<u>pos</u>ure*.

Exercise F
1 customer **2** loan **3** money **4** savings
5 deposit **6** down
You could also point out further word partnerships:
1 high-street / piggy / savings / central / the World
2 consumer / Third World / foreign / international
3 state / research / government / mortgage
4 unsecured / student / home / high-interest / low-interest
5 market / global / prosperous / world
6 insider / invisible / passing / external / foreign / international

LESSON NOTES

Exercise G

	a)	b)	c)
1	Investing	investors	investment
2	lend	lending	loan
3	deposited	deposit	deposits
4	exposed	expose	exposure

H

- Do this in pairs or with the whole class, being sure to deal with the two types of bank customer – retail clients and business clients. Insist on correct use of financial language.

Resource bank: Listening (page 195)

Students can watch the interview with Charles Middleton on the DVD-ROM.

i-Glossary

Reading: *Day of reckoning for innumerate bankers*

Students read about the banking debacle of 2007, discuss the reasons for it and work on finance vocabulary and multiword verbs.

A

- Ask students to look at the first exercise in pairs. Circulate, monitor and assist if necessary, but don't interrupt the pairs if they are functioning acceptably.
- Call the class to order and elicit students' ideas. If students come from different countries, compare and contrast the status/salaries of these jobs in different countries.

B

- Don't explain *innumerate* at this point if students don't know the word. Get students to scan the article in pairs or individually fairly quickly and choose the best headline.
- Circulate, monitor and assist if necessary, but don't interrupt students if they do not have any particular difficulties.
- Elicit the answer.

c) The collapse of the financial world because bankers couldn't count

- Explain and practise the stress and pronunciation now of *innumerate* if necessary. (Point out the parallel in meaning with *illiterate*.)

C – F

- Get students to read the statements in Exercise C.
- Then get students to read the article again in pairs or individually in more detail to find the answers.
- Circulate, monitor and assist if necessary, as before, but don't interrupt the students if they do not have any particular difficulties.
- With the whole class, elicit the answers to Exercise C, and discuss them with students (e.g. Were there similar problems in banks in their own countries?).

Exercise C

1 ✓ (All businesspeople know that you can carry on for a while if you make no profits, but that if you run out of cash, you are toast. Bankers, as providers of cash to others, understand this well. (lines 14–19))

2 ✓ (In general, banks have no measures of cashflow that work for banking. They do think about liquidity – can you borrow from other market participants, can you get money from the central bank? (lines 21–26))

3 ✗ (The article refers to banks spending money, but it does not name the government or consumers as such: ... and in the mid-noughties they [the banks] began to splash out. (lines 37–38); Not only has the industry – and by extension societies that depend on it – been spending money that is no longer there, it has been giving away money that it only imagined it had in the first place. (lines 73–78))

4 ✗ (From my own experience, in the mid-nineties, no more than four or five employees of Barclays' then investment bank were paid more than £1m, and no one got near £2m. (lines 54–59))

5 ✗ (How could they pay this imaginary wealth out in cash to their employees? Because they had no measure of cashflow to tell them they were idiots, and because everyone else was doing it. Paying out 50 per cent of revenues to staff had become the rule ... (lines 81–88))

6 ✓ (How did the shareholders let them get away with this? They were sitting on the gravy train too, enjoying the views from the observation car. How did the directors let it happen? Innumeracy and inability to understand accounts. How depressing the shame and folly of it all is, ... (lines 90–97))

- Get students to find the expressions in Exercise D in pairs or with the whole class and elicit the answers.

Exercise D

1 are toast (line 17) **2** folly (line 97)
3 dividends (line 42) **4** rampant (line 101)
5 liquidity (line 23) **6** colossal (line 71)
7 the City (line 52)
8 sitting on the gravy train (line 92) **9** fuss (line 8)
10 means curtains (line 27) **11** go bust (line 72)
12 shame (line 97)

- Then get students to give the meanings of the multiword verbs in Exercise E and get them to suggest other meanings for those that have them. (For item 6, *pay out,* tells students that there are also other occurrences of this multiword verb in the article, on lines 70 and 81.)

Exercise E

Suggested answers

1 continue doing
2 use all of something and not have any left
3 refuse an offer, request or invitation
4 spend a lot of money on something
5 suddenly start being successful
6 pay or give money (literal meaning)
7 give something without asking for any money, rather than selling it to them)
8 not be caught or punished when you have done something wrong; also, get away with murder
9 cause the collapse of

Other meanings:

- **turn somebody/something down**
  turn the switch on a machine such as an oven, radio, etc. to produce less heat, sound, etc., e.g. Could you turn it down?
- **take off; take something off**
  - when an aircraft rises into the air from the ground, e.g. The plane took off.
  - remove something, e.g. He took his jacket off.
  - have a holiday from work on a particular day, e.g. She took the day off.

- **give somebody/something away**
  - give something to someone because you do not want it or need it yourself
  - show where someone is or what they are doing or thinking when they are trying to keep this a secret;
  - tell someone something that you should keep a secret;
  - lose in a game or competition by doing something badly or making mistakes
- **get away with something**
  - receive only a small punishment for something
  - do something without experiencing any problems or difficulties, even though it isn't the best thing to do
- **get away**
  - leave a place, especially when this isn't easy
  - take a holiday from the place you normally live (get away from it all);
- **get away from**
  escape from someone who is chasing you or trying to catch you
- **bring somebody/something down**
  - reduce something to a lower level
  - fly a plane down to the ground
  - force a government or ruler to stop ruling a country
  - make someone fall over
- **bring down on/upon**
  make something bad happen to someone, especially yourself or people connected with you

F

- Get students to look at the Language reference section on page 135 of the Course Book, going through the points and writing up key sentences on the board.
- Then get them to identify the multiword verbs in Exercise E that don't take an object, and discuss the questions about word order.

Multiword verbs that are intransitive (don't take an object):

1 carry on (= continue doing something), e.g. *you can carry on for a while* (lines 14–15)

2 run out of, e.g. *Time is running out. She ran out of the room.* We say *run out **of*** before an object, e.g. *if you run out of cash, you are toast* (lines 16–17), *She has run out of ideas.*

4 splash out, e.g. *they began to splash out* (line 38) But we can say *splash out on something*, e.g. *We splashed out on an expensive meal.*

5 take off (= do well; leave), e.g. *things began to take off* (lines 60–61), *He just took off five minutes ago.* But we also say *take something off* (= remove), e.g. *He took off his glasses.*

8 get away (from) (= escape), e.g. *The bank robbers got away. We'd like to get away this weekend.* But we say *get away **with** something*, e.g. *How did the shareholders let them get away with this?* (lines 90–91)

We can change the order when the multiword verb is separable, i.e. when you can separate the object (or object pronoun) from the particle (the preposition or adverb), e.g. *How could they **pay** this imaginary wealth **out** in cash to their employees?* (lines 81–83)

We can't change the word order when the multiword verb is inseparable, e.g. *if you **run out** of cash, you are toast.* (lines 16–17) NOT *If you run cash out of…; societies that **depend on** it* (lines 74–75) NOT *societies that depend it on.*

A good dictionary like the *Longman Dictionary of Contemporary English* will show which multiword verbs, or which of their meanings, are intransitive or transitive, and which are separable or inseparable.

G

- To round off the section, get students to discuss the three questions in small groups. (Again, you will need to adapt this to the level of knowledge of your students.)
- Circulate, monitor and assist if necessary, but don't interrupt the groups if they are functioning acceptably.
- Call the class to order and discuss findings of the groups, insisting on correct use of financial vocabulary and getting students to say the right forms if there are any problems.

➜ Text bank (pages 142–145)

Business skills: Managing questions

Students look at the art of answering difficult questions in different contexts, listen to some situations where this is happening, and develop their own skills in this area.

A

- Books closed, ask the students this question orally, and get their answers as a quick-fire whole-class activity, adapting it to their own context(s). (Look at the suggested answers below if students run out of ideas – ask students leading questions to try and get them to suggest some of these situations.)

By your boss about something that has gone wrong; in a job interview; being interviewed by a journalist; meeting with your bank manager; in a police investigation; in a formal presentation; presenting an academic thesis to a panel of judges; giving a training session; in a meeting with a group of potential investors; etc.

B

- Go through items a–f and explain any difficulties. (An *audit* can refer to any detailed examination of an organisation, but here refers specifically to specialised outside accountants who check if a company's accounts are accurate or not.)
- Get students to work on the exercise in pairs. Circulate, monitor and assist if necessary, but don't interrupt the pairs if they are functioning acceptably.
- Call the class to order and elicit the answers. As ever, talk about the reasoning behind each answer, rather than just ploughing through them.

1 e **2** f **3** b **4** a **5** c **6** d

C CD2.33–2.36

- Tell students they are going to hear four speakers in four of the situations from Exercise B.
- Go through the possible answers a–g and explain any difficulties, e.g. the pronunciation of *rapport* (*t* not pronounced).
- Play the recording, stopping at convenient points, and elicit the answers.

LESSON NOTES

Speaker 1: b and c
Speaker 2: a and f (e.g. asking the questioner to identify him/herself)
Speaker 3: a, f (e.g. referring to the questioner by name) and g
Speaker 4: a, b, d and e

Other ways of dealing with Q&A:

- Say you've already answered the question and briefly sum up what you said, e.g. *As I said/mentioned before, ...*
- Comment on the kind of question to gain some thinking time, e.g. *That's a good/interesting question.*
- If the questioner is incomprehensible or inaudible, or you don't understand the question, ask them to repeat it.
- Avoid answering, e.g. say the last/next speaker will deal with that topic, or that it's not your area of expertise.
- Say the question is not relevant to your talk.
- Ask the questioner what he/she thinks, or put the question to the audience.
- Use humour as a distractor.

D

- Explain the task and get students to look at the tips in pairs. Circulate, monitor and assist if necessary, but don't interrupt the pairs if they are functioning acceptably.
- Call the class to order and get pairs to say what their conclusions were. Discuss and develop some of the ideas – for example, paraphrasing not only allows you check you've understood, but also allows other members of the audience to hear the question clearly. You could also say that hand gestures have to be used in moderation to avoid looking insincere.

E CD2.37

- Explain the task and explain what a *private equity firm* is (a financial organisation that invests in companies privately, i.e. the shares are not publicly traded on the stock market).
- Get students to write down, individually or in pairs, their questions.
- Play the recording, stopping at convenient points, and elicit the answers.
- Get individual students to say how their questions differed in form/wording from what they heard in the recording.

Suggested questions

What do you do exactly? / What do you do on a typical day?
How did you get into finance?
What aspect of your work do you enjoy the most/least?
How much do you earn? / Do you mind me asking how much you earn?
What are the secrets of your success?
What advice would you give ...? etc.

Questions actually asked by the interviewer:

1. Do you think you could describe what you do in 10 words?
2. How do you think your personal assistant would describe you?
3. Did you ever predict you would end up where you are today?
4. I'd like to know who has been your biggest influence.
5. Can you tell me what's the worst job you have ever done?
6. Would you mind telling me what's the worst thing you've ever had to do at work?
7. I was wondering if you had any guilty pleasures.
8. What would you say was your number-one rule?
9. Have you ever lied at work?
10. Have you ever praised someone and not meant it?
11. How important is money to you?
12. If you hadn't gone into finance, what would you have done?
13. I'd like to ask how you would like to be remembered.

The interviewer's questions might be different from the ones formulated by the students because she uses indirect or embedded questions (explain this) to sound less direct.

F CD2.37

- Get students to look at the expressions in the Useful language box, suggesting possible continuations based on situations covered in the previous exercises.
- Get individual students to read out complete expressions including continuations, with feeling and, above all, correct stress and intonation.
- Now play the recording again, getting students to tick the expressions that the financier actually uses.

She uses six of the expressions (in the order we hear them):

- **Do you think you could** describe your job in 10 words?
- **Would you mind telling me** what's the worst thing you've ever had to do at work?
- **I was wondering if** you had any guilty pleasures?
- **What would you say was** your number-one rule?
- If you hadn't been in business, **have you any idea** what would you have done?
- **I'd like to ask** how you would like to be remembered.

We often use indirect questions when we want to sound less direct, or more tentative and polite; also when asking personal or challenging questions, when rephrasing and insisting on the question, or when the questioner is playing for time.

G CD2.37

- Play the recording again, stopping after each item, this time getting students to complete the gaps.

1. evaluate investment proposals
2. ended up; had no idea; to go into; took off from
3. My grandfather; built himself up
4. Fire people; a necessary evil
5. taking it easy; feel guilty
6. to the full

- Elicit the answers and explain any difficulties, e.g. *necessary evil.*

H

- Explain the task and get students to do the activity in parallel pairs. Circulate, monitor and assist if necessary, but don't interrupt the pairs if they are functioning acceptably.
- Call the class to order and get some of the pairs to give public performances of their exchanges.
- Work on any difficulties, especially in relation to questions.

- This role play further develops students' question-and-answer skills.
- Explain the task, allocate the scenarios and the roles and get students to turn to the correct page.
- When students are ready, they can begin their scenario.
- Circulate, monitor and assist if necessary, but don't interrupt the pairs if they are functioning acceptably.
- Note good points of language use, as well as half a dozen points that need further work, especially relating to questions and answers, and add these on one side of the board.
- Get early finishers to study the points on the board.
- When most pairs have finished, call the class to order. Praise good use of question-and-answer language that you heard in the activity, and work on the points on the board, getting individual students to say the right thing.
- Get public performances of one or more of the scenarios, ensuring that students incorporate your corrections and improvements.

Resource bank: Speaking (page 183)

CASE STUDY

Dragons & Angels

Students, as angel investors, talk to entrepreneurs looking for funding, evaluate their projects and make a decision about the one to invest in.

Stage 1: Background, Task 1 and Listening

- Tell students that an investment organisation, often referred to as *angel investors* or *business angels*, is going to look at some business ideas in which to invest. Get students to read the Background and elicit information from them to complete this table.

Name of angel investors	Dragons & Angels (D&A)
Make-up and location	Syndicate, some members successful entrepreneurs, based in Edinburgh, Scotland
Advantage of syndicate in relation to individual investor	Larger, more frequent investments
Investment targets	Start-ups or established companies seeking to expand
Typical investment	£50k to £500k
Typical contact with entrepreneurs	Speed-funding events[1]: five minutes per entrepreneur
Rationale of one of senior partners	Spread risk away from stock market and property by investing in businesses that would otherwise have looked to bank loans for funding
Average rate of return	22% over four years[2]

[1] Point out similarity with speed-dating events if necessary.

[2] Point out that this is over four years, not the annual rate. This includes all projects invested in, including those that fail.

- Books closed, go round the class and get individual students to talk about D&A in their own words, based on the notes on the board.
- By this time, UK-based students (and those from the many countries where this programme format exists) might see the similarities with the TV programme *Dragons' Den*. If students know the programme, ask them what they think of it (and of the follow-up programmes where investors go out to see the progress of businesses that they have funded).
- Introduce Task 1 by telling students that they will be role-playing angel investors at a speed-funding event. Get students to look at the instructions, but not to look at the profiles of the three entrepreneurs for the moment.
- When students have absorbed the information, get one or two students to summarise it for the whole class. Work on any difficulties. (The vocabulary should be familiar at this level, but you might need to explain that *stake* refers to the percentage of the equity (= share capital) that each shareholder of the company has – by investing in a business, an angel investor becomes a shareholder, and a big issue for entrepreneurs is how much control they are willing to give to investors – the more the angel investor puts in, the bigger the say they will have in how the company is run, of course.)
- Say that you will be dividing the class into groups of three angel investors, all members of D&A. Each investor will 'specialise' in explaining to the other two members of the group about one of the three projects in which D&A might invest.
- Divide the class into groups of three and allocate each of the investment projects to one of the three students in each group, who then reads, summarises and comments on it to the other two members of the group in turn.
- Circulate, monitor and assist if necessary, but don't interrupt the groups if they are functioning acceptably.
- Call the class to order and work on any difficulties, e.g. pronunciation of *sceptical*. (Tell students to think of the AmE spelling *skeptical* to help them remember how to pronounce it.)

CD2.38–2.40

- Get students to listen to the recordings and make notes, stopping after each one to explain any difficulties.
- Get individual students to talk about the entrepreneurs in complete sentences of their own, based on the notes that they took.
- Get them to say which entrepreneur answered the questions best.
- Then, with the whole class, get students to suggest questions that they, as investors, could ask the entrepreneurs.

Suggested questions for investors to ask entrepreneurs

How are you going to use the equity capital/money?

How will this investment result in a profit for me?

Have you any idea what kind of returns we could expect if we invested in your business?

Your expected return on capital is very high at 40–45% over four years. How realistic do you think that is?

What's your business plan?

What's your exit strategy for investors?

Have you received equity/funding from other business angels?

Do you think you have the right expertise for this kind of business?

What did you use to do before you became an entrepreneur?

How motivated/passionate/committed are you?

Can you build and work with a team?

Where do you see the business in five years' time?

CASE STUDY

Stage 2: Task 2

- In this task, students move on to evaluating the projects they have seen. Go through the questions with them and explain any difficulties, for example that *quality* in point 4 is being used as an adjective – the expression means 'good-quality contacts'.
- Divide the class into the same threes as before and start the activity.
- Circulate, monitor and assist if necessary, but don't interrupt the groups if they are functioning acceptably.
- Note good points of language use, as well as half a dozen points that need further work, and add these on one side of the board.
- When most groups have finished, call the class to order and ask representatives of the groups to say which project they are going to back, and, briefly, why. (If there is time you could work on language for comparing and contrasting, e.g. *On one hand, on the other hand...* and concluding, e.g. *We looked in detail at all the projects, but finally we chose ...*) You could do this more formally, by getting individual students to come to the front of the class to make mini-presentations about who they chose and why.
- Praise good use of financial/investment language that you heard in the activities, and work on the points on the board, getting individual students to say the right thing..

One-to-one

Go through the information in the Course Book with your student. Explain any difficulties.

In Task 1, you present one of the entrepreneurs in your own words to give your student the idea, and your student can then present the other two.

Go through the Listening and Task 2 as above.

During the role plays, monitor the language that your student is using, and language that you choose to use.

Note down any good examples of your student's language and points for error correction or improvement. Come back to these later. Praise any good examples of language used and go over any errors, including pronunciation.

Don't dominate the conversation in the tasks, but say enough to keep it going and allow your student to suggest ways to resolve these issues. You could record the discussion on audio or video, if the student agrees, and use it for intensive correction work afterwards.

 DVD-ROM: Case study commentary

Stage 3: Writing

- Get students to study the Writing task and deal with any questions. Brainstorm the information that should go in the e-mail and put these points on the board. Alternatively, this could be made into a report-writing task.
- Get students to look at the model e-mail on page 145 of the Writing file again if necessary. Get students to write the final e-mail for homework. As ever, get them to e-mail it to you if possible and go through corrections in the next lesson.

Writing file (Course Book page 145)

Resource bank: Writing (page 210)

UNIT 8 Consultants

AT A GLANCE

	Classwork – Course Book	Further work
Lesson 1 *Each lesson is about 60–75 minutes. This time does not include administration and time spent going through homework in any lessons.*	**Listening and discussion: Operations consulting** Students discuss the benefits of taking on operations consultants, listen to an experienced consultant in this area and work on consultancy-related language.	**Practice File** Word power (pages 46–47) **Resource bank: Listening** (page 196) **i-Glossary** (DVD-ROM)
Lesson 2	**Reading and language:** ***Day in the life of a management consultant*** Students discuss what makes a good management consultant, read a consultant's blog and work on its language.	**Text bank** (pages 146–149) **Practice File** Text and grammar (pages 48–49) **ML Grammar and Usage**
Lesson 3	**Business skills: Negotiating** Students look at different negotiating styles, listen to recordings of negotiations, study the related language, then put it into practice in role plays. **Writing: summarising terms and conditions** Students work on the language in this area and apply it themselves in an e-mail.	**Resource bank: Speaking** (page 184) **Practice File** Skills and pronunciation (pages 50–51)
Lesson 4	**Case study: New market opportunities** A consulting firm is asked to study the mobile-phone market in South Africa for a new client. Students represent the two organisations and prepare for the negotiation internally following an initial feasibility study, working on their tactics and priorities. They then negotiate with the other company.	**Case study commentary** (DVD-ROM) **Resource bank: Writing** (page 211)

For a fast route through the unit, focusing mainly on speaking skills, just use the underlined sections.

For one-to-one situations, most parts of the unit lend themselves, with minimal adaptation, to use with individual students. Where this is not the case, alternative procedures are given.

BUSINESS BRIEF

A **consultant** is a **contractor** or outside supplier who provides **specialised services** or **skills** to a client for a **fee**. Some consultants work on their own, often drawing on **experience** and **knowledge** they have gained previously as salaried employees in companies. Others work for organisations large and small: one well-known firm, for example, is McKinsey, which describes itself as 'a management consulting firm advising leading companies on issues of strategy, organisation, technology and operations'. The **Big Four accountancy firms** (Deloitte, Ernst & Young, KPMG and PwC) also offer consulting services, and an issue for them has been the way that **auditing** (where they verify the accuracy and completeness of company accounts) has been sold alongside consultancy, which, some say, has inherent conflicts.

As experts in their fields, consultants can help with **analysing** and **solving problems, completing projects** and **specific tasks**. Consultants can bring an **independent eye** to bear on an organisation, offering an external, hopefully more **objective view** of its **strengths and weaknesses** than those working for it can possess – this objectivity is one of the advantages of the **arm's-length** relationship that outside consultants have with clients. They can also help a company not just to **formulate strategy** but also to **focus on results**, relating client's **objectives** to actual **outcomes**. Of course, this requires a longer-term relationship with clients than the traditional one of a short study period, submitting a report and sending in the invoice. The degree to which consultants' objectives are achieved is an important measure of success.

Consultants bring with them knowledge of **best practice** in their clients' industries, and can hopefully find ways of **transferring** it to other organisations, and also transfer the best practices of one industry to others. (One problem here is **confidentiality** – obviously, consultants must not reveal confidential information that they have gained from other clients.)

There are different types of consultants. At the highest level, **management consultants** advise on a company's overall **strategy** (see Unit 9) and propose ways to improve its **structure** to fit that strategy, in the long run bringing, hopefully, higher **profits**, or, in the preferred phrase, **enhanced shareholder value**.

Organisations depend increasingly on the sophistication of their **information technology (IT). Technology consultants** provide **implementation, support** and **training** services in this area. **Web consultants** provide assistance with **websites**, optimising **site design,** for example to maximise **usability** and thus sales on **e-commerce sites** (see Unit 10.) This is one of the latest areas of **IT consultancy** to develop – a large proportion of consultancy work relates to IT projects, and firms such as IBM, that used to make most of their money from hardware and software, now put consultancy services first in the way they present themselves to the world.

Consultants have to be able to handle the **human dimension** of the **client relationship** extremely well, as many managers will resent outsiders coming in to tell them how to run their business, a business that the managers may have been in all their working lives. There are issues of **ownership** and **'not-invented-here' syndrome**, where managers may be asked to put consultants' plans into action, plans where the managers may have had very little **input**. And, of course, potentially the most tense relationships are ones where consultants are brought in to **restructure** an organisation and make some or many of its employees redundant – here consultants' advice on **outplacement services** will be important, helping people find new jobs.

Consultants and your students

All students will hopefully have heard of some of the major consultancy firms mentioned above.

In-work students will be able to describe projects or tasks that have been or could be outsourced to consultants. Some students may also have had first-hand experience working alongside consultants. You could ask them, tactfully, to talk about their experiences of this.

Pre-work students will be able to talk about whether they could be interested in a career in consulting. (Many MBA graduates, some with only a few years behind them as relatively junior managers in organisations, go into prestigious consulting firms. If relevant and the opportunity arises, you could discuss, tactfully, the analytical skills that students bring from their MBA, hopefully making up for this lack of hands-on experience.)

Read on

Simon Burtonshaw-Gunn: *Essential tools for management consulting: Tools, models and approaches for clients and consultants*, Wiley, 2010

Mick Cope: *The seven Cs of consulting: The definitive guide to the consulting process*, Financial Times / Prentice Hall, 2010

Fiona Czerniawska and Paul May: *Management consulting in practice: award-winning international case studies*, Kogan Page, 2006

Calvert Markham: *The top consultant: Developing your skills for greater effectiveness*, Kogan Page, 2004

LESSON NOTES

Warmer

- Ask students to give a definition of a *consultant* – see the Business brief. (Tell them that *contractor* is increasingly used to refer to outsiders who work on projects for organisations. *Freelancer* refers more to journalists, writers, etc. and would not be used to talk about consultants.)
- Ask students to brainstorm problems at home, in their work or place of study where the services of a consultant (as opposed to someone already working there) could be useful, and why.
- Write students' ideas quickly on the board and discuss them briefly, but don't pre-empt the rest of the unit too much.

Overview

- Go through the overview panel at the beginning of the unit, pointing out the sections that students will be looking at.

Quotation

- Get students to look at the quotation and discuss it. Presumably Drucker had such vast knowledge of the workings of organisations in general that he was able to 'situate' the answers to his questions in this knowledge, so as to make sense of the answers. (Students can learn more about his long and illustrious career on http://en.wikipedia.org/wiki/Peter_Drucker.)
- If students are keen on quotations, you could give them another one: 'A consultant is someone who borrows your watch to tell you the time, and then keeps your watch.' (Robert Townsend, one-time CEO of Avis, the car-rental company)

Listening and discussion: Operations consulting

Students discuss the benefits of taking on operations consultants, listen to an experienced consultant in this area and work on consultancy-related language.

A

- Get students to discuss the questions in pairs or with the whole class.
- If the discussion is in pairs, circulate, monitor and assist if necessary, but don't interrupt the pairs if they are functioning acceptably. Then call the class to order and get representatives from each pair to talk about their 'findings', discussing them rather than just ploughing through them.

Suggested answers

1 The extract in Exercise B gives some examples of the services consultants provide: financial management, human resources services (e.g. headhunting, recruitment, training), IT implementation, change management, strategy development and improving operational efficiency.

2 Companies might hire management consultants for a variety of reasons:
- Companies don't have enough staff to do the work themselves.
- It can be a way to distance internal management from desired, but sensitive, changes (e.g. job layoffs, salary and benefit changes/reduction, major operational and strategic shifts).
- A company doesn't have the specialist know-how to deal with a specific problem or project (e.g. controlling costs, improving managerial performance, manage special projects).
- Consultants have developed knowledge of best practices across industries and functions, which helps them to identify effective solutions, e.g. by benchmarking (measuring an organisation's internal processes and adapting them to best practices).
- Companies often need a fresh perspective. Consultants can add a lot of value through their observations and insights.
- Training: a large part of what consultants do is educate client employees on necessary knowledge, skills and mindsets.

3 Implied criticisms:

1. Some consultants may use a lot of management buzzwords and clichés but may not have the specialist knowledge the company is looking for. The consultant may be inexperienced in the industry/sector.
2. Despite being costly, the consultant's fees are not usually based on the success of the project; there is little or no guarantee the consultancy will be successful, depending on the contract negotiated and which party is assuming most risk.
3. The report is often the most tangible deliverable, and the fee will not involve implementation unless it has been previously negotiated and included in the contract.
4. With so many consultancies in the market and increased competition, it is sometimes difficult to see how they differ from each other or what a consultancy's 'added value' may be. More prestigious consultancies may offer the same advice and services as cheaper, lesser-known ones.
5. Consultancies are given work based on the premise that there is a problem with the company or the company requires a specialist service or task that they are unable to do in-house. Consultants are unlikely to turn down a possible contract, or they may find a problem in the way a company works, even if one does not exist.

4

1. What can you tell us about managing change?
2. How much were you planning to charge? / What sort of fees were you expecting for this project?
3. Will you help us with the implementation of your recommendations?
4. Why should I hire you? What is the difference between you and (a rival firm)?
5. So, what do you think about how things are run around here?

- Go through the five utterances you'll never hear from consultants and see if they raise a smile, perhaps, in some cases, one of recognition!

B

- Explain the task, go through the vocabulary (some of which will already have cropped up), where necessary working on pronunciation and stress of longer words, e.g. *deliverable*, and explaining any difficulties.
- Get students to work on the exercise in pairs. Circulate, monitor and assist if necessary, but don't interrupt the pairs if they are functioning acceptably.
- Call the class to order and elicit and discuss the answers.

1 performance **2** specialised expertise
3 best practices **4** implementation **5** operational
6 techniques and methods **7** deliverable
8 tangible **9** scope **10** brief

LESSON NOTES

C CD2.41

- Tell students that they will be listening to an interview with Peter Sirman, Head of Operations Consulting at the PA Consulting Group.
- Get them to look through the text, anticipating the answers where possible; remind students that between two and four words are missing from each gap.
- Play the recording, stopping at convenient points, and get students to check if their hunches are confirmed. Discuss possible variations.
- After you have played the recording, go through any remaining difficulties.
- Discuss the ideas expressed, especially if they relate to students' own experiences.

1 order to cash **2** should be delivering **3** serving customers **4** service they value **5** level of quality **6** features of the product / product features / products and services **7** shape the way

D CD2.42

- Get students to look at the statements and explain *duplication* if necessary.
- Play the recording, elicit the answers and discuss them.

1 False: The technique mentioned is called Value Stream Mapping.
2 True
3 False: The technique looks at the period of time spent on each stage of the process, and the levels of quality.
4 True

E CD2.43

- Get students to look through the questions and anticipate the answers.
- Play the recording, stopping at convenient points, and getting students to give the answers as they come up. Again, discuss the answers rather than just plough through them.

1 Redesigning the work / Coming up with better ways of doing things
2 Stop doing things the customer doesn't value, or that are a waste of time and money and/or do things differently.
3 lead time(s) (These have to be reduced in order to improve efficiency.)
4 What the customer wants, e.g. shorter delivery times
5 The 'drivers' of improved performance, e.g. lead time; reducing (driving down) costs; improving (driving up) quality

F – **G** CD2.44

- Tell students that this time you will play the recording without stopping, so they will have to take notes on the answers to the questions.
- Play the recording and elicit the answers relating to Exercise F.
- Then play the recording again and get students to make notes on the answer to the question in Exercise G.
- Elicit the answers based on their notes after each recording, and discuss them with the whole class.

Exercise F

1 Taking out unnecessary steps, e.g. outsourcing some activities
2 Restructuring the company, e.g. by consolidating into a larger site
3 The management infrastructure, e.g. helping managers to understand and improve their performance

Exercise G

Through discussions with the client staff in workshops and meetings, in order to reach consensus around the changes they are recommending.

H

- Get students to discuss these questions in pairs. Circulate, monitor and assist if necessary, but don't interrupt the pairs if they are functioning acceptably. Pre-work students might need quite a lot of help with this. Don't spend too much time on it if they are stuck.

Suggested answers

1 Many people don't see the need to change; managers and staff don't want to lose their jobs; staff don't 'buy into' (point out this expression) the changes, especially if these are seen to be imposed from outside; there are budget constraints which make it impossible to make changes.
2 The company could overcome the resistance by communicating the need for change to staff; emphasising that the changes to the process will minimise delays and waste, maximise profitability, add value to the customer and thereby strengthen the business.
3 By involving the client in the project (e.g. through workshops, as Peter Sirman mentions in his interview); by handling sensitive information discretely (e.g. employee salaries); by offering tailor-made – not ready-made – solutions to the client; by delivering what was promised and expected; by following up on developments w ith the client after the project is completed.

Resource bank: Listening (page 196)

Students can watch the interview with Peter Sirman on the DVD-ROM.

i-Glossary

Reading and language: *Day in the life of a management consultant*

Students discuss what makes a good management consultant, read a consultant's blog and work on its language.

A

- Get two outgoing students to read the speech bubbles in the cartoon. (You could make the joke that laughter is not obligatory.)
- Do this as a whole class activity or in pairs. This time, it's the in-work students who have not done management studies courses (unless they assiduously read the *Harvard Business Review*) who might be at a disadvantage.
- Go through the answers and discuss them in relation to students' own level of knowledge.

1 c) James Dyson is not a business guru. He is an English industrial designer, best known for the Dyson vacuum cleaner.
   - C.K. Prahalad, born in India, is a business professor at the University of Michigan, and specialises in corporate strategy.

- Henry Mintzberg, Canadian professor and author, is an expert on business strategy.
- Tom Peters, US consultant and best-selling author on business management practices, is best known for *In Search of Excellence*.
- Rosabeth M. Kanter, author and professor in business at Harvard Business School, is an expert on management techniques, particularly change management.
  (Students can research these people on the Internet and report back in the next class if you think they will be interested in them.)

3 The question of why manhole covers are typically round, at least in the US and UK, was made famous by Microsoft when they began asking it as a job-interview question. Originally designed as a psychological assessment of how one approaches a question with more than one correct answer, the problem has produced a number of alternate explanations:
- A round manhole cover cannot fall through its circular opening, whereas a square manhole cover may fall in if it were inserted diagonally in the hole.
- Round tubes are the strongest and most efficient shape against the compression of the earth around them, and so it is natural that the cover of a round tube has a circular shape.
- Circular covers do not need to be rotated to align them when covering a circular manhole.
- Human beings have a roughly circular cross-section.
- A round manhole cover can be more easily moved by being rolled.
- Tradition.
- Supply. Most manhole covers are made by a few large companies. A different shape would have to be custom made.

B

- Ask students if they read blogs, and if so, which ones. (You could point out that blogs are a form of expression where, on a global level, there is probably more writing than reading going on!)
- Go through the questions with the whole class, then get students to work on the blog entry in pairs. Circulate, monitor and assist if necessary, but don't interrupt the pairs if they are functioning acceptably.
- When most pairs have finished, call the class to order to elicit and discuss the answers.

1 An operations turnaround project with a focus on personnel

2 It can be hard for companies to do a sensitive job like this, which involves major operational changes, e.g. job cuts, salary and benefit changes/reduction. Also, the company may not have the expertise internally to do this. Hiring consultants can be a way to reach the desired conclusions without company management being directly involved.

3 The consultant attends four formal meetings:
1) team meeting to prepare for the client meeting at 12 noon; 2) client (monthly progress) meeting at 2 p.m.; 3) post-meeting debrief at 3 p.m.; and 4) meeting between project team and three partners to discuss scope of the project at 4 p.m.
The lunch at 1.30 p.m. with the client team might also be considered an informal meeting in preparation for the meeting with the CEO.

4 The consultant appears to be quite young (*I briefly wonder if she'll ask me how old I am*), conscientious and enthusiastic (e.g. he prepares and revises the slides well, memorises key facts for the meeting, is keen to please the team manager, plans to work late on the new data for the next day, etc.).

5 The CEO seems happy at the end of the meeting and congratulates the partner on the team. On the other hand, it seems that the client has said the scope of the project is too narrow, i.e. the consultants are not doing enough.

6 It was a good day in that the Production team sent the slides, which saved the consultant a lot of work and time. He prepared a good presentation that impressed the CEO of the client company. The manager also seemed pleased with the team's work. The surprise news is that the team could have more work to do. A minor setback is the quarterly data appears to be a mess, so the consultant will have to work on it this evening. Another setback was the inconclusive teleconference call with the partners, who could not agree on what needed doing.

C – D

- Get the students to work on both the exercises in pairs. As before, circulate, monitor and assist if necessary, but don't interrupt the pairs if they are functioning acceptably.
- Call the class to order and elicit and discuss the answers to each exercise, working as much on the process of why they are correct as on the answers themselves.

Exercise C

1 wraps up **2** packs up **3** run [...] through
4 hammer out **5** go through **6** debrief
7 circle back **8** having a catch-up **9** a small nit
10 piled up **11** breathe a sigh of relief **12** left out

- Work on any difficulties, e.g. the pronunciation of *breathe*, ensuring that students distinguish it from *breath*.

Exercise D

Some examples:
(The) Hotel alarm wakes me.
(I) Breathe (a) sigh of relief.
(My) BlackBerry buzzes.
(The/My) Manager says ...
All (of my shirts) are wrinkled.
(There's) No extra sleep for me.
(It) Could have been much worse.
(The) Team meeting starts.
(The) meeting (is) over!

The words omitted are mainly articles (especially the), subject pronouns (e.g. it) and possessive adjectives (e.g. my). Notice there are no hard-and-fast rules, and these words are not always left out.

This style gives the blog entry a sense of immediacy and urgency. It also makes it sound more chatty and informal.

E

- Depending on time and interest, discuss in pairs or with the whole class.
- If the discussion is in pairs, circulate, monitor and assist if necessary, but don't interrupt the pairs if they are functioning acceptably. Then call the class to order and get representatives from each pair to talk about their 'findings', discussing them with the whole class.

➡ Text bank (pages 146–149)

LESSON NOTES

Business skills: Negotiating

Students look at different negotiating styles, listen to recordings of negotiations, study the related language, then put it into practice in role plays.

A – C

- Discuss the points in Exercise A, do the matching activity in Exercise B and the gap-fill in Exercise C in pairs or with the whole class. The principles in Exercise A could even be applied to parent–child negotiations, and you could get students with children to talk about these instead.
- If students work in pairs, circulate, monitor and assist if necessary, but don't interrupt the pairs if they are functioning acceptably. Then call the class to order and get representatives from each pair to talk about their 'findings' in Exercise A and to give the answers to Exercises B and C, discussing them with the whole class, as ever.

Exercise A

Students' own answers. But being flexible, being prepared to make concessions and achieving a win–win situation is probably the most widely acceptable style, certainly if you want to continue doing business with the other party in the future.

Exercise B

1 b, g **2** a, e **3** d, f **4** c, h

Other possible negotiating techniques:

- Play it cool, i.e. pretend you're not interested, e.g. when buying a property or bargaining in a market.
- Use a personal approach – think of the other party as a partner, not as an adversary.
- Call their bluff, pretending that you have a better offer elsewhere, although this can be very risky.
- Use your power, or threaten.
- Don't get personal or angry – stay objective.
- Negotiate as a team.

Exercise C

1 big concession **2** one by one
3 some sort of compensation
4 understands its full value **5** get a concession
6 willing to make concessions
7 'take-it-or-leave-it'; ill-will **8** walk away

D CD2.45, 2.46

- Tell students they are going to hear two negotiations. Get them to focus on the questions, then play the recording, stopping at convenient points and at the end of each negotiation to elicit and discuss the answers.

Suggested answers

Negotiation 1

1. They are effective negotiators because both parties are prepared to make concessions:
   Mr Khilawala agrees to deliver one week sooner and his client will probably pay him sooner (30-day credit terms), so it's a win–win situation.
2. Mr Khilawala, the supplier/seller, practises the silent technique. The buyer/customer (Irene) is the first to talk and does most of the talking. Irene also refers to a higher authority, John Himona, although it's not clear whether he's actually a real person, or she is calling his bluff – pretending to check with someone else first, probably to play for time.
3. They seem to know each other, although their relationship seems as little strained, as Mr Khilawala uses the silent technique.

Negotiation 2

1. Claude is 'effective' in that he negotiates a good price for the 30ml bottle. Kevin is also effective in that he agrees to take on a new product, but drops one that isn't selling well and negotiates a smaller size for the baby talc. They are both prepared to make concessions, but it isn't a win–win situation: Kevin is left feeling cheated, and we don't know if he will honour the oral agreement.
2. Claude, the supplier/seller, uses sales techniques, such as offering a special price because of their special relationship, which is a common salesploy: *Our usual price is €10 per 50ml. But for you, we're offering it at €9.50!* Claude also states the benefits for his client: *And economical, too. /That's a 5% saving, Kevin.* However, in the end Claude outwits Kevin and calls his bluff by pretending they're negotiating for a 50ml bottle of perfume/body spray and not for the 30ml bottle.
3. The buyer and the seller have a friendly relationship and adopt a personal approach. They seem to treat the other party as a partner, calling each other by first names and using humour, but there is also an element of oneupmanship. (Explain this word if necessary.)

E

- Play the recordings again, getting students to put up their hands when they hear the expressions. If necessary, get them to look at the scripts on pages 177–178 to check their answers.
- Then discuss the relative tentativeness or politeness of each expression.
- Work on any remaining difficulties.

Negotiation 1

Buyer (Irene)

I was wondering if you could deliver a bit sooner? (T)

Maybe we could talk a little about terms of payment at this point. (T)

I suppose I could look into it.

I'd have to check with my supervisor first.

He'd have to confirm the payment terms, you see.

I think that should be do-able. (T)

Leave it with me. I'll see what I can do.

Seller (Mr Khilawala)

We could deliver sooner, provided you paid in cash. (T)

What if we delivered one week earlier and you gave us ...? (T)

I'll wait to hear from you, then.

Negotiation 2

Buyer (Kevin)

Actually, it seems a couple of the products aren't doing that well. (T)

It might do better if it wasn't in a 500g container. (T)

So, we were wondering whether you'd be able to ... (T)

What would you say to a 10% discount? (T)

So, do we agree on €9 per bottle, then?

Consider it a deal.

Seller (Claude)

Our usual price is ... But for you, we're offering it at ...

That's a 5% saving.

It's always good doing business with you.

You'll put it all in writing, won't you?

- Explain the task. Tell students that you expect them to use some of the expressions they heard in the previous exercise in the role plays.
- Divide the class into pairs (at this point you could change the make-up of the pairs) and allocate the roles. Make sure students turn to the correct page. If time is short, allocate different role-play situations to different pairs, so they don't do all of them but just one or two.
- Circulate and assist with preparation of tactics if necessary, but don't interrupt the pairs if they are functioning acceptably. However, make sure that they are preparing tactics, and ask one or two students to whisper to you how they plan to approach each negotiation, and give extra guidance to the whole class if you think they need it.
- When pairs are ready, get them to start the activity. Circulate, monitor and assist if necessary, but don't interrupt the pairs if they are functioning acceptably. Note good points of language use, as well as half a dozen points that need further work, and add these on one side of the board.
- When most pairs have finished, call the class to order and ask some of the pairs about the outcomes of their negotiations and about whether they were able to put their tactical plans into action: if so, how; and if not, why not? (You could quote the German general Helmuth von Moltke the Elder (1800–1891): 'No battle plan ever survives the first contact with the enemy.')
- Praise good use of negotiations language that you heard in the activity, and work on the points on the board, getting individual students to say the right thing.

Resource bank: Speaking (page 184)

Writing: summarising terms and conditions

Students work on the language in this area and apply it themselves in an e-mail.

G

- Talk the students through the expressions in the Useful language box. (Don't get them to read the expressions aloud, as they are for use in writing.) Tell them that it's important to get these expressions exactly right. For example, writing *I send you a copy of our agreement* ... rather than *I'm sending* ... would create a very bad impression.
- Get students to group the expressions as in the instructions and work on any difficulties.

a) with someone you know quite well, because the expressions are semi-formal, e.g. When it comes to .../ Re delivery charges, I'd (just) like to point out ...; Could/ Can you confirm ..., please? Thanks.
These kinds of expressions are more common in business e-mails nowadays, where people generally try to adopt a friendly but professional manner and use contracted forms more often.

Formal expressions

These would be used in letters and some might sound odd or officious (explain this) in an e-mail:

Opening remarks

Following our conversation / Further to our meeting on (date), ...

Please find attached a copy of ... as discussed on (date) ...

Confirming

We would be happy to offer you ...

As previously discussed/agreed, our policy on ... is as follows: ...

Regarding payment and delivery, ...

Where delivery charges are concerned, we would need to point out (that) ...

When things go wrong

In the (unlikely) event of a ..., we would like to remind you that ...

In case of ..., please note that ...

Making a request

Could you please confirm ... in writing at your earliest convenience?

We would be very grateful if you could confirm ...

Closing remarks

Should you require further information, please do not hesitate to contact me.

We look forward to doing business with you (again).

- Get students to do this for homework. As ever, get them to e-mail it to you if possible and go through corrections in the next lesson, when you should also get Students A and B in each pair to compare what they wrote and their understanding of what they agreed.

Suggested answer

To:	Claudio Timi
From:	Denise Hall
Date:	10 April
Subject:	Sunshine Beauty Products agreement

Dear Claudio Timi*

I'm writing to confirm what we discussed in our meeting on 8 April. Sunshine Beauty Products is pleased to offer Daisy Supermarkets the following terms of agreement:

Specification of goods and price agreed

Sunshine Beauty Products will provide Daisy Supermarkets with our extensive sun range at the special prices listed below:

- Sunshine sun cream, Factors 10 and 25 @ €8.00 and €10.00 respectively (minimum orders of 1,000 units each)
- Sunshine Kids sun cream, Factor 50 @ €12.00 (min. 500 units)
- Sunshine face cream at €11.00 (min. 500 units)
- Sunshine after-sun lotion at €8.00 (min. 500 units)
- Sunshine haircare holiday pack at €6.00 per pack (min. 500 units)

Please note: should Daisy Supermarkets place orders of less than the minimum amount agreed, Sunshine Beauty Products will have to review these prices.

Delivery and payment

Payment will be on a sale-or-return basis for the first 500 units of each product. As we agreed, 40% of payment will be paid on delivery, with the remainder paid 60 days after delivery – with the approval of Daisy Supermarkets.

I would like to point out that the expected delivery date is the week of 5 May, subject to confirmation and product availability.

Limitation of liability, cancellation, refunds and warranty policy

I'm sending you a document with details regarding these – see the attached pdf.

If you have any queries, please let me know. Could you also please confirm your initial orders as agreed in our meeting by e-mail as soon as you can? Many thanks.

We're looking forward to receiving written confirmation of the above terms and your first orders.

Best wishes,

Name, position and company

* You could point out that some people dislike being addressed in this way, preferring *Dear Mr Timi*, or *Dear Claudio* if on first-name terms. *Dear Mr Claudio Timi* is certain to raise even more hackles, and would be considered unacceptable by most native speakers.

Writing file (Course Book page 145)

CASE STUDY

New market opportunities

A consulting firm is asked to study the mobile-phone market in South Africa for a new client. Students represent the two organisations and prepare the negotiation internally following an initial feasibility study, working on their tactics and priorities. They then negotiate with the other company.

Stage 1: Background, Task 1 and Listening

- Explain the subject of the case study (see above). Get students to read the background individually, or get a student to read it aloud. Explain any difficulties, e.g. the pronunciation and stress of *dossier* which can be done with a neutral schwa sound in the second syllable and the *r* pronounced or not according to taste, or in French fashion, i.e. *doss-ee-ay*.
- Elicit information from students to complete the table below, in the usual way.

Consultancy, country	Heitinga T-com Consulting (HTC), South Africa (SA)
Its speciality	Telecoms
Client and their background	Bajaj-tel, India: one of largest mobile operators there Low-cost pioneer
Client aspirations	Enter the SA mobile market by buying local SA networks
SA mobile market	Worth $24bn Competitive
Potential obstacles	Approval may not be given by regulators SANphone considered 'national champion'*
Outlook for SA economy	Improved infrastructure and productivity One of G3 developing markets (with India and Brazil) Pop. < 50m, but expected to grow fast

* Explain that this means that the authorities wish to see SANphone remain the largest company, and that regulators do not want to do anything that would threaten its dominant position, especially in relation to foreign firms.

- Get students to look at Task 1. Explain that they will discuss telecoms opportunities in SA. (Practise stress and pronunciation, and explain meaning, of *feasibility report*: a report on whether a project can be carried out or not, from a practical point of view, perhaps without considering its potential profitability, etc.)
- Explain that the role play takes place between members of HTC and Bajaj-tel in pairs, separately and in parallel, during a meeting where previously they have all been together.
- Divide the class into groups of four, each containing two pairs, one pair representing HTC and the other Bajaj-tel, and allocate the roles, checking that students turn to the correct page.
- When they have absorbed their information, the role play can begin in parallel pairs. Circulate, monitor and assist if necessary, but don't interrupt the groups if they are functioning acceptably. However, ensure that students are working effectively on preparing tactics.
- When students are ready, the meetings can resume. Note good points of language use, as well as half a dozen points that need further work, and add these on one side of the board.
- When most groups have finished, call the class to order. In this role play, don't ask pairs to report on their discussions, as this would weaken their positions when doing the next role play!
- However, praise good use of language that you heard in the activity, and work on the points on the board, getting individual students to say the right thing.

CD2.47

- Tell students that they will now hear a recording of a meeting between
  - Jeff Carstens, one of HTC's senior partners (but not its boss)
  - Annabel Kuper, junior consultant at HTC, who prepared the feasibility report referred to in the previous activity
  - Sunil Sukkawala, Chief of Finance at Bajaj-tel. (Point out that he is *not* the CEO of Bajaj-tel.)
- When students are ready, play the recording, stopping at convenient points, getting students to make notes on the opportunities and challenges that they foresee, as representatives of HTC in working with Bajaj-tel.
- With the whole class, get individual students to comment on it, using the notes that they made.

Suggested answers

Opportunities for Heitinga T-com Consulting and its new Indian client

- Mr Sukkawala from Baja-tel says they can sell a phone at 15 dollars and still make money.
- Bajaj-tel has already developed a successful low-cost model in India which could work in South Africa.
- Bajaj-tel annual growth rate has been over 50 per cent.
- Mr Sakkawala says they want to implement in new mobile network in South Africa soon – over the next 12 or 18 months.
- Bajaj-tel are sports sponsors – they could sponsor the World Athletics Championships in South Africa next year.
- Mr Carstens says his partner, Andrew Heitinga, might have some useful government contacts, although he could be bluffing.
- Andrew Heitinga is away. Mr Sakkawala suggests they meet up at the weekend, which suggests he's interested in doing business with the consultancy.

Challenges for Heitinga T-com Consulting and its new Indian client

- They only have 12 months to set up a new mobile network in South Africa – in time for the World Athletics Championships.
- It is unclear whether the consultancy has government contacts to aid the Indian mobile operator's venture. (The South African government turned down another foreign mobile operator last year, which doesn't bode well.)

- The team from Heitinga T-com haven't met the Bajaj-tel's CEO yet, although this could be a negotiating tactic.
- Bajaj-tel hasn't met the other partner at the consultancy, Andrew Heitinga.
- Although the junior consultant, Annabel, seems informed and very keen, Mr Carstens, the senior consultant, seems less enthusiastic about the project.

Stage 2: Task 2

- Get students to look at the agenda on page 81 for the meeting between HTC and Bajaj-tel and work on any difficulties, e.g. students may not be familiar with *deliverables*, things that have to be delivered.
- Explain that in this role play, Mr Bajaj himself has appeared and will be played by Student C, with the Chief of Finance now being played by Student D. (Students A and B keep the same roles as in Task 1.)
- Get students to work again in pairs with their 'colleagues' for five or so minutes to make sure that they are up to speed with the situation. Circulate, monitor and assist if necessary, but don't interrupt the pairs if they are functioning acceptably.
- When each group of two pairs is ready, they can start to the main HTC/Bajaj-tel negotiation, using points 2 to 6 on the agenda on page 81 as the basis for their discussions.
- Circulate, monitor and assist if necessary, but don't interrupt the groups if they are functioning acceptably. Note good points of language use, especially negotiations language, as well as half a dozen points that need further work, and add these on one side of the board.
- When most groups have finished, call the class to order and ask some of the groups to say quickly what the outcome of their negotiation was.
- Praise good use of language, especially negotiation language, that you heard in the activity, and work on the points on the board, getting individual students to say the right thing.
- To round off the case study, try to draw together some of its threads, getting students to extrapolate from this negotiating situation to negotiation in general. What have they learned in terms of a) negotiating techniques, and b) negotiating language.

One-to-one

Go through the information in the Course Book with your student. Explain any difficulties.

In Task 1, you can represent HTC or Bajaj-tel, and your student the other organisation, combining information from role cards for Students A and B, or C and D respectively.

Go through the listening as above.

Each of you should then make final adjustments to your strategies, and role-play Task 2, each of you being the head of the organisation that you represent.

During the role-plays, monitor the language that your student is using, and language that you choose to use.

Note down any good examples of your student's language and points for error correction or improvement. Come back to these later. Praise any good examples of language used and go over any errors, including pronunciation.

Don't dominate the conversation in the tasks, but say enough to keep it going and allow your student to suggest ways to resolve these issues. You could record the discussion on audio or video, if the student agrees, and use it for intensive correction work afterwards.

 DVD-ROM: Case study commentary

Stage 3: Writing

- Get students to study the writing task and deal with any questions. Get them to note down information from their role plays that should go in the e-mail while it is still fresh in their minds.
- Get students to look at the model e-mail on page 145 of the Writing file again if necessary and to write the final e-mail for homework. As ever, get them to e-mail it to you if possible and go through corrections in the next lesson.

➡ Writing file (Course Book page 145)

➡ Resource bank: Writing (page 211)

UNIT 9

Strategy

AT A GLANCE

	Classwork – Course Book	Further work
Lesson 1 *Each lesson is about 60–75 minutes. This time does not include administration and time spent going through homework in any lessons.*	**Listening and discussion: Strategy, goals and values** Students are encouraged to discuss the concepts of strategy, vision and mission and talk about the strategy process in (their) companies.	**Practice File** Word power (pages 52–53) **Resource bank: Listening** (page 197) **i-Glossary** (DVD-ROM)
Lesson 2	**Reading and language:** ***Living strategy and death of the five-year plan*** Students read an article about the usefulness or otherwise of strategic planning and work on related language.	**Text bank** (pages 150–153) **Practice File** Text and grammar (pages 54–55) **ML Grammar and Usage**
Lesson 3	**Business skills: Brainstorming and creativity** Students look at some ideas about brainstorming, work on related language and put it work in a brainstorming session about possible strategies for a retailer **Writing: mission statements** Students write a mission statement for their company or organisation.	**Resource bank: Speaking** (page 185) **Practice File** Skills and pronunciation (pages 56–57)
Lesson 4	**Case study: Stella International Airways: strategy for the skies** An airline needs to make strategic changes to secure its long-term future. Students work on possible strategies and suggest a marketing campaign to back it up.	**Case study commentary** (DVD-ROM) **Resource bank: Writing** (page 212)

For a fast route through the unit, focusing mainly on speaking skills, just use the underlined sections.

For one-to-one situations, most parts of the unit lend themselves, with minimal adaptation, to use with individual students. Where this is not the case, alternative procedures are given.

BUSINESS BRIEF

Strategy is not just 'having a **plan** to reach **objectives**' – it's about deciding what those objectives should be in the first place, and how **resources** will be **allocated** and **deployed** to reach them.

A **corporate mission statement** might set out a **bold vision** of how the company sees itself in 10 or 20 years, but unless they are **realisable**, these plans are just so much hot air. For a **vision statement** such as this to be achievable, senior management must decide how it is going to use the company's assets to achieve its goals – these assets could be **finance**, **physical equipment**, **managerial skill** and, increasingly, **knowledge**. If an organisation doesn't have these assets, it might be able to acquire them, but the debate then is about whether it has the wherewithal to acquire the right ones. In human-resource terms alone, it has to think carefully about recruitment (including graduate recruitment); management development; whether to recruit executives from outside the organisation, and if so, who; how its top management should be structured to provide the **best leadership**, and so on. A similarly long list could be made about the deployment and acquisition of a company's other types of assets. And despite all this, the objectives might become irrelevant and even harmful if something unexpected and **disruptive** comes along, like a **new technology**.

Another strategic issue is **commitment**. It's a commonplace to say that an organisation's strategy has to have the commitment of all its managers and employees. The commitment that really counts is that of its senior executives – hence the fact that **boardroom rows** are often about the **strategic direction** that the organisation should take. And because a strategy is something that requires total commitment of particular resources over a period of years, it cannot be easily changed – if it can be, it's not really a strategy at all. However, strategists do refer to an organisation's **strategic agility**, the flexibility to recognise when a strategy isn't working and to develop a new one.

A lot of strategic discussion is about the **industries** that a company should be in: should it stay in its current industry, or should it leave them? Should it try to enter new industries – if so, which ones? Which are the best for future **growth** and which are the most suitable, in relation to the company's existing **competencies**? If it decides to **enter an industry**, should it start from scratch, or should it **buy growth** by acquiring a company that is already successful or with the potential for success in that industry? The history of corporate strategy is littered with **failed acquisitions**, where the acquiring company has not been able to **integrate** the acquisition, perhaps because the **cultures** of the two companies are too different, or even because the culture and nature of the new industry is one that the acquiring company did not really understand. There was a fashion at one time for **conglomerates**, where the acquiring company made many purchases of companies, with the goal of applying its resources to improve their **performance** and **profitability**. But big heterogeneous **groups** like this are now out of fashion, an example of a failed **generic strategy**.

Despite their **strategic planning departments**, even very powerful companies make **strategic errors**. IBM's error was not to retain control over the PC, and Microsoft's was not to see the importance of the Internet. As John Kay has written, if IBM had been able to see the future, it would have tried to prevent it. Some established companies make valiant attempts to anticipate and influence the future, like BP with its 'Beyond Petroleum' aspirations, but then find that the ever-present concerns of today make that future vision seem irrelevant. It will be interesting to see how the new giants like Google and Facebook will deal with the future – they seem impregnable now, but what will the strategic mistakes or unexpected developments be that turn them into 'ordinary' companies? Who and what will emerge to confound their best-laid strategies?

Strategy and your students

In-work students will be able to discuss strategy and growth, vision and mission statements in the context of their own organisations and competitors. (You could encourage them to do research on their company's and competitors' declared strategies if they are not familiar with them, and report back.) Both in-work and pre-work students will have something to say about the strategies of the companies whose products and services they buy. What is the key to their success, and how might they maintain and develop it? They can also talk about the vision and purpose of the organisations where they study.

Read on

Robert M Grant: *Contemporary strategy analysis*, Wiley, 2010

Henry Mintzberg et al.: *Strategy safari: The complete guide through the wilds of strategic management*, FT / Prentice Hall, 2008

Michael Porter, *Competitive strategy: Techniques for analysing industries and competitors*, Free Press, 2004

Kevan Scholes et al.: *Exploring corporate strategy: Text and cases*, FT / Prentice Hall, 2009

LESSON NOTES

Warmer

- Ask students to brainstorm some very successful companies and write the names that students come up with on the board. Then ask students to discuss in pairs or small groups why they think these companies have been so successful, and what their differentiating factors are (what makes them better), compared to other companies in their industry. Students' answers will depend on the companies they choose, but they may come up with some of the following factors: innovation, new technologies, corporate values, leadership, pricing/marketing/growth/organisational strategies, etc. Go through feedback with the whole class.
- Alternatively, ask students what they understand by the title of the unit, 'Strategy' (a plan or series of plans for achieving an aim, especially success in business, or the best way for an organisation to develop in the future: *Longman Business English Dictionary*.) As always, with more complex topics such as this one, or with pre-work students, you may choose to give students the Business brief on page 000, getting them to look at it for homework before the first class on this unit and to talk about it then.

Overview

- Tell students that they will be looking at strategy and growth in this unit. Go through the overview panel at the beginning of the unit, pointing out the sections that students will be looking at.

Quotation

- Get students to look at the quotation and ask them what they think of it. (It would be hard to argue with it.) Ask them if they think companies are often guilty of being more concerned with strategy than with results.

Listening and discussion: Strategy, goals and values

Students are encouraged to discuss the concepts of strategy, vision and mission and talk about the strategy process in (their) companies.

A

- Students work in pairs to discuss the questions. Set a three-minute time limit for this. Then get students' feedback as a whole class. Help them with vocabulary on strategy.
- It's not necessary to spend too long on this, as it forms part of the listening section.
- Call the class to order and discuss the pairs' findings. As ever, get them to discuss their reasoning rather than just give their opinions.

Suggested answers

1 Ideally, everyone in the organisation should be committed to its strategy and imbued with it, but this may be a pious wish when it comes to the workers in the post room! Many companies make great efforts to communicate their strategy to all employees, others less. The mission statement is very important here, often addressed, as it is, as much to people within the organisation as to those outside it.

2 Students might contrast this with what Milton Friedman said, that the only social responsibility of a business is to make a profit (see Unit 6). However, many companies like to vaunt their contributions to society, through both their commercial activities and their charitable donations

3 Many successful businesses have prices that are not cheap: it's the perceived value of their products and services that is important, in relation to the price: low prices suit a 'high-volume' approach, but many companies differentiate themselves in ways that enable them to charge higher prices. However, whichever route is taken, profit is essential in most years if a public company is to survive the scrutiny of investors and the rigours of the stock market. Non-public companies, like Virgin for example, are less subject to this sort of scrutiny.

4 There are companies that change perceptions so much that they create new conditions by which they are judged, for example by selling a completely new product that consumers didn't think was possible, let alone one that they would desire. (Think of Apple's iPad.) Other companies (think perhaps of MacDonald's) are sometimes accused of changing behaviour for the worse.

B CD3.1

- Ask students if they know anything about Pearson. Tell them the name should be familiar, as they will have seen it in the Course Book, for example on the back cover, as the publisher of *Market Leader*. Pearson also owns many famous publishing brands such as Penguin, is big in educational testing and publishing, for example with Longman and Prentice Hall, and is the publisher of the *Financial Times*.
- Tell students that they will hear an interview with Marjorie Scardino, Pearson's CEO.
- Get them to look at the summary and resolve any difficulties. Explain the task and play the recording once or twice, stopping at convenient points. Make sure that students can distinguish the central consonant sound in *mission* from the one in *vision*.
- Get them to work on adding extra details in writing, individually or in pairs. (You could hand out pens and transparencies, getting students to present their texts for the whole class on an overhead projector, if you have one.)
- Call the class to order, elicit students' answers and compare and contrast them.

Suggested answer

Pearson has always been devoted to high-quality or digital / digitally-enabled content, so, for example, a child can study math(s) using interactive tools. Pearson starts with the premise that the company has to communicate what its goals and values are. Chief Executive Marjorie Scardino thinks the best organisations have a strong company culture. Whenever it's necessary, she personally writes to all staff in Pearson via the Internet / e-mail. Management also makes an effort to communicate in a transparent way, so that every one of the company's (35,000) employees understands.

(You could photocopy this text to give to students or put it on a transparency or PowerPoint slide. It would take too long to write it on the board.)

- Discuss any difficulties, e.g. her use of AmE *math* rather than BrE *maths* (Marjorie Scardino grew up in Texas), and *premise* (nothing to do with *premises*, of course.)

C CD3.2

- Get students to focus on the task here and play the recording, again stopping at convenient points so that students can take notes on which to base their summaries.
- Get students to work on their summaries, individually or in pairs. (Again you could hand out pens and transparencies,

getting students to present their texts for the whole class on the overhead projector, if you have one. As before, you could prepare the text below on a transparency or PowerPoint slide.)

Suggested answer

Pearson's goal is to help individuals make some progress in their lives through education. This goal enables people to do something larger than themselves and is part of a 'bigger-thinking' strategy. The Chief Executive says the exciting strategies are those that might influence people or schools. She adds that Pearson's strategy is about how you deliver education in a personalised way, that is accessible to everyone.
(66 words)

D

- Do this with the whole class. Perhaps students will raise the idea of mission statements (see the Business brief), or mention Marjorie Scardino's idea of sending e-mails to all employees at key moments.
- As supplementary questions, you could ask
  1. In order to grow, businesses sometimes either diversify or narrow down their business. Which strategy do you think proves to be more successful?
  2. How do companies establish what their goals are?

Suggested answers

1. The answer here is that it all depends. Students might mention Google, which seems to be expanding in all directions on the Internet, and has now developed a computer operating system to rival Windows and Apple's. An example of narrowing down is when IBM sold its PC manufacturing division to Lenovo in China, so as to concentrate more on IT services to corporations. (You might mention how sticking to a core business can be referred to as *sticking to your knitting*.)
2. See Business brief (page 79), and refer also to the importance of consultants with MBAs and managers with MBAs in setting strategy: there are fashions in strategy, as in many other things.

E

- With the whole class, go through the letter, getting one or two students to read different parts of it. Explain any difficulties, for example the meaning of *exposure* in this context.
- Then get students to work on their own version individually or in pairs, in 120 to 140 words. Tell them it should be in the first person, using *I* and *we*, as if they were CEO of Pearson.
- Circulate, monitor and assist if necessary, but don't interrupt students if not.
- Call the class to order and get students to read out their versions in a loud and confident voice, as if they were Pearson's CEO at a press conference where strategy is the subject. Compare, contrast and discuss them.

Suggested answer

Pearson's strategy is long-term investment in quality content, focusing primarily on digital and services businesses, through a policy of international expansion and growth. We are also committed to long-term investment through efficiency gains; by that I mean reducing costs.

I believe we have several reasons to be confident. Firstly, we're in a strong financial position, because we didn't take on a lot of cheap debt during the financial crisis. Secondly, we're a truly global company, not just an American or British one, which gives us access to markets all over the world. Thirdly, we have a strong advantage over our competitors, despite being in industries that are subject to frequent change. And finally, we offer our customers two essential services: namely, the need to understand a fast-moving digital world and the need to be educated.

F

- Get students to do this as a quick-fire whole-class activity, looking back at the letter in Exercise E.
- As ever, discuss with them *why* the correct answers are correct and the incorrect ones not.

1 businesses **2** expansion **3** position **4** diversity
5 markets **6** economies **7** position **8** world

G – H CD3.3–3.6

- Play the recordings, stopping after each one to get students to give their answers for Exercise G, and discuss each one, getting students to say if they agree with it. (You could mention that Toyota's recent travails with stuck accelerator pedals, etc., were great blows to its reputation for quality.)

Exercise G

1. Admires the chipmaker Intel for its innovation, e.g. smaller, faster, more powerful chips. Every year, their goal is to introduce new cutting-edge products. Intel calls it its 'tick-tock' strategy.
2. Admires the Spanish supermarket Mercadona, which offers fresh produce at competitive prices. Its business strategy is called ALP – Always Low Prices. The speaker is also impressed by the way they treat employees, e.g. staff are always friendly and helpful and there doesn't seem to be a high staff turnover.
3. Admires Toyota cars, because of their production system of producing 'perfect goods'. He adds they're the most reliable cars, especially for long distances. Other vehicles he's driven have broken down and have had to be towed.
4. Admires H&M, because they offer customers the latest fashions at affordable prices. The strategy involves regular quality controls, and manufacturing clothes with the least possible impact on the environment. They have a cost-conscious strategy of buying in large volume and limiting the number of middlemen. They also work with top designers.

- For Exercise H, go through points 1–8 first, working on any difficulties, for example *differentiate* (if necessary: you may have used this word in the Warmer above).
- Warn students beforehand that the points do not occur in the same order in the recordings as here, and one is not mentioned at all. Play the recordings again, getting students to hold up their hands when they hear the points mentioned.
- As ever, discuss the answers in class.

Exercise H
Suggested answers

1. not mentioned
2. Speaker 2/Mercadona (*there doesn't seem to be a high staff turnover*)
3. Speaker 1/Intel (*they just keep innovating*)
4. Speaker 1/Intel (*Every year, their goal is to introduce new cutting-edge products.*)

5 Speaker 2/Mercadona (*develop their own brand at competitive prices*)
Speaker 4/H&M (*H&M offers customers the latest fashions at affordable prices*)
6 Speaker 4/H&M (*we sometimes get top fashion designers to design exclusive collections*)
7 Speaker 3/Toyota (*Ohno believed in producing perfect goods and said, 'If a machine is not producing perfect goods, it is not working.'*)
8 Speaker 2/Mercadona (*They say they source directly without any go-betweens.*)

LESSON NOTES

I

- Depending on time and interest, get students to discuss this in pairs, or do it with the whole class.
- By now, students should be using strategic vocabulary well, so insist on this in the discussion.

Resource bank: Listening (page 197)

Students can watch the interview with Marjorie Scardino on the DVD-ROM.

i-Glossary

Reading and language: *Living strategy and death of the five-year plan*

Students read an article about the usefulness or otherwise of strategic planning and work on related language.

A

- Get students to look at and discuss the quotes in the margin and work on a statement in pairs. (Tell them that if they have irreconcilable differences, they can produce two different statements!)
- Circulate, monitor and assist if necessary, but don't interrupt the pairs if they are functioning acceptably.
- When pairs have finished, with the whole class get representatives from some of the pairs to read out their statements in a clear, loud voice.
- Compare, contrast and discuss them.

Suggested answers

Students may use the two quotes as a springboard for discussion of the pros and cons of long-term planning. Here are some of the issues they could mention, or you could introduce to stimulate discussion:

Advantages

- Strategic planning helps management to take a step back from the day-to-day business to think about the future of the organisation, rather than just working through the next issue or problem without consideration of the bigger picture.
- By setting objectives and priorities, a company can allocate resources appropriately and measure success and progress towards the goals.
- By establishing objectives and priorities, management and staff have a framework for decision-making about more day-to-day operational procedures.
- Having a sense of a bigger picture for the future can encourage staff and management support of the plan and active participation (buy-in).

Pitfalls

- In fast-moving, fast-changing industries, a long-term plan can soon become outdated and irrelevant.
- Long-term planning is inflexible and you can't predict the future.
- The planning process can take a lot of time and money, and the end result might be a long report that gathers dust on a shelf.
- Markets and the economic climate can be unpredictable and the plan can't cover all eventualities.
- Likewise, consumer preferences may be difficult to foresee and can change.
- Change of people in the senior management team might see the plan scrapped.

B

- Ask students to look at the four logos and say something about what they know about each of the companies. (If they don't know, tell them that P&G is Procter and Gamble, famous for its consumer goods.)
- Then get them to read the article quickly, individually or in pairs, to find information about the four companies.
- Call the class to order and get students to make brief statements summarising what they have learned about each company. Briefly discuss, but don't pre-empt the following activities too much.

- Google processes relevant data fast to get closer than anyone else to understanding how online advertising works.
- Amazon uses a network of valuable partners to support its Kindle e-book reader.
- Toyota reacted to social change and shifting customer preferences by introducing the hybrid Prius car.
- Procter & Gamble experiments effectively when it trials products.

C

- Get students to predict what might be in the gaps. Then get them to read the article again to find the answers and see if their predictions were confirmed. Discuss any issues.

1 growth **2** (economic) recession **3** recovery
4 adaptive advantage **5** relevant data/signals/changes
6 networks of partners / valuable partners
7 society/customer preferences **8** people/talent/resource
9 flexible/dynamic/adaptive

D

- Get students to look at the four questions individually or in pairs. Circulate, monitor and assist if necessary, but don't interrupt the students if they have no particular problems.
- With the whole class, elicit the answers.

Suggested answers

1 The primary audience would appear to be business leaders and senior executives who are involved in strategic planning in their companies.
2 There appear to be a number of purposes:
   a) to inform readers that old-style strategy planning is no longer viable and to explain why that is
   b) to persuade readers that a strategy for growth is always necessary
   c) to inform readers about the latest thinking in strategy planning and how some companies are applying a new style of strategy
   d) to motivate business leaders to take these ideas on board.
3 Yes, the writer quotes two expert sources throughout the article (see paragraphs 2, 4, 5 and 8, 9, 10) to add weight to his purpose.

4 He uses rhetorical questions – twice at the start of a paragraph (1 and 6) and twice at the end (3 and 8).
He contrasts points several times, especially in the opening and closing paragraphs (e.g. *Chief strategy offers will deny it ... But markets are predictable. If old-style strategy formulation is not exactly dead, then it is hardly in the best of health.*). A third technique is the use of adverbs for emphasis through the text (e.g. *hardly, simply, unsurprisingly, quickly, effectively*). He also uses examples from real companies to emphasise his points.

- The final point above is about rhetorical questions. Get students to look at the Language reference section on page 137 and walk them through the information there and discuss it.

E – F

- Again individually or in pairs, get students to work on the exercises.
- Elicit the answers and explain any difficulties, e.g. the meaning and pronunciation of *resilience*.

Exercise E
1 b **2** d **3** g **4** h **5** f **6** c **7** a **8** e
Exercise F
1 thriving **2** sharp **3** free-flowing **4** hardly
5 are alive to

G

- Get students to work on the task in pairs. If they don't have information available, it might be easier for students to work on this as homework and report back in the next class.
- Here are some links that may be useful for your students. However, tell them that they are free to talk about any companies that they are interested in.
  - Hyundai's advertising atrategy: Wait for the fire sales http://www.bnet.com/2403-13240_23-346169.html
  - PepsiCo's big steal: The middle man at a **$1** billion discount http://www.bnet.com/2403-13241_23-346150.html?tag=content;col1
  - How big lots is turning the real-estate bust into its own boom http://www.bnet.com/2403-13241_23-346386.html?tag=content;col1
  - ITT staffs up while the getting is good http://www.bnet.com/2403-13241_23-346170.html?tag=content;col1

➡ Text bank (pages 150–153)

Business skills: Brainstorming and creativity

Students look at some ideas about brainstorming, work on related language and put it to work in a brainstorming session about possible strategies for a retailer.

A

- As a lead-in to this section, ask students what they understand by the terms *brainstorming* (a way of developing new ideas and solving problems by having a meeting where everyone makes suggestions and these are discussed); and *creativity* (producing or using new and interesting ideas; also used in marketing, relating to producing advertisements, etc.). Then ask students the following questions:
  - In what situations do/would you need to brainstorm at work? Who with?
  - Do you enjoy brainstorming? Why? / Why not?
  - How could it be useful in business?
  - In what situations is it useful to be creative at work? Why?

There are no right or wrong answers for these questions, but students may think of brainstorming and creativity as marketing and advertising skills, when they are also useful in terms of product innovation and design, as well as being a useful management skill for problem-solving and strategy.

- Get students to look at the photo of Linus Pauling and ask if they know who he was (a US molecular biologist and multiple Nobel prize winner, 1901–1994). Students can find more about him on Wikipedia.
- Get students to discuss the questions in pairs or small groups.
- Go through initial reactions with the whole class.

Students' own answers. It has also been argued that people are more creative when they work on solutions alone and that group brainstorming sessions tend to take fewer risks and produce less radical ideas.

B – C CD3.7, 3.8

- Ask students to try to predict the brainstorming tips in Exercise B before they listen.
- Play the recording once without stopping. Get students to answer both exercises on brainstorming tips (B) and the principles of Koinonia (C).
- Students can check their answers in pairs. Replay the recording if necessary, referring them to the audio script on pages 178–179 if necessary.
- Go through the answers with the whole class and discuss them.
- Then play the second part of the recording and get students to take notes on the seven principles of Koinonia.
- Go through the answers with the whole class and discuss them.

Exercise B
1 problem or task **2** eight to 10 people
3 ideas **4** Encourage **5** discussing any one item
6 uncritical **7** contributions **8** Study and evaluate
Other suggested points and ideas: Stay focused on the task at hand; build on the ideas of others (leapfrogging).
Some people argue that remaining uncritical and suspending judgement during a brainstorming session just means you get lots of ideas that aren't very useful.
Exercise C
1 Establish dialogue.
2 Exchange ideas.
3 Don't argue.
4 Don't interrupt.
5 Listen carefully.
6 Clarify your thinking.
7 Be honest.
(Some students might say that the principles are contradictory. For example, it might be impossible to be honest about your opinion of someone's bad idea if you can't argue with it.)

- As a follow-up, ask students if they are familiar with any other brainstorming techniques or tips (e.g. writing down ideas on different coloured Post-its and putting them on a board).

- Refer students to the Useful language box on page 86. Ask them if they can think of any more expressions that they use for brainstorming or suggesting and reacting to ideas. Work on pronunciation, stress and intonation. Don't get students to repeat all the expressions, just one or two from each section that might be difficult in terms of pronunciation and intonation (e.g. *Would anyone like to get the ball rolling?*).
- Then get them in pairs, or with the whole class, to divide the expressions into the three categories.

a) Leading the session
So, who'd like to get the ball rolling?
Let's just get the ideas down at this stage.
Does anyone have any more ideas?
The rule is there are no bad ideas.
Try and suspend judgement until later.
Let's go around the table once and then open the discussion up.

b) Contributing and building on ideas
I've got one! What if we ...? / How about ...?
Yes, and here's what I'd add to your suggestion ...
I'm thinking (more) along the lines of ...
I'd like to expand on that ...
Here's another thought....

c) Responding to ideas
That's a great/wacky/cool/unusual idea!
I'm thinking (more) along the lines of ...
You've taken the words right out of my mouth.
I was just going to say that!
Yes, I like that.

E CD3.9

- Explain to students that they are later going to brainstorm some marketing strategies for a company in order to turn it around.
- Get students to read the information about the retailer, Ross & Franks. (Explain that this is a fictitious company, loosely based on the British retailer Marks & Spencer.) Deal with any vocabulary questions they have, e.g. *rejuvenate*.
- Make sure to give students preparation time to make notes, as this will improve the quality and length of their contributions in the upcoming brainstorming activity.
- Circulate, monitor and assist if necessary, but don't interrupt the students if they are working acceptably on the notes.
- Then play the recording and get students to take notes on it, to add to the information from the text.

F

- You can get students to do the activity as themselves, i.e. as strategic experts brought in to advise on R&F's strategy, in groups of any size up to five or six, or you could tell students that they will be working in groups of four, playing different Ross & Franks executives:
  Student A: Director of Marketing
  Student B: CEO
  Student C: Head of Corporate Communications
  Student D: A member of the marketing team
- Be clear in your own mind about which approach you have decided to use, and explain it to students. Divide students into pairs or small groups. Tell them that one person in each group will need to take notes during this task (probably Student D if they are doing it as role play).
- Circulate and monitor the class as students do the task. Make a note of useful language used and five or six language points for correction, including pronunciation. Write these errors on the board. Get early finishers to correct the errors on the board.
- When students have finished, call the class to order and elicit their ideas about the future strategy of the company. Compare and contrast ideas – there are no right or wrong answers for this task. Do not reject ideas during feedback, as the idea was to encourage students to be as creative as possible.
- Go through language feedback with the whole class, praising appropriate language for brainstorming.
- Work on the points you wrote on the board, getting individual students to say the right thing.

Suggested answers

1 Promotional marketing and advertising campaigns using celebrities, and best-selling products, etc.
2 Diversification into other market segments, e.g. new clothing ranges for different segments of the womenswear market – teens and younger women, professional working women, more mature women, and a high-quality range. And new lines of furnishing (mix-and-match style) and food (organic, healthy ready meals, international cuisine).
3 Innovation in clothing material, e.g. easy-iron linen and cotton clothes and machine-washable woollens
4 'Economy' range products to attract new customers and daily offers on the website.
5 Product development of best-selling products or brands.
6 Opening stores overseas and marketing the idea of 'British quality products'.

(The scenario portrayed in the Ross & Franks story is based on the position of the UK high-street retailer Marks & Spencer between 2004 and 2006. M&S had an 11% share of womenswear market at the time. The company was highly successful in its 'advertising-led' recovery strategy.)

Resource bank: Speaking (page 185)

Writing: mission statements

Students write a mission statement for their company or organisation.

- As a lead-in to this writing section, ask students what is meant by *mission statement* (see the Business brief, page 00).
- Ask in-work students if they are familiar with the mission statement of their company or organisation. If there is Internet access in the classroom, you may like to ask students to quickly find one on a company website – otherwise, or if there is not much time, get them to do this for homework and continue with this activity in the next class. Further samples of companies' mission statements are as follows:
  - Siemens
    It is our mission, within the scope of Siemens' core activities, to find the best way of combining and developing our know-how and expertise, so that we can profitably channel them into outstanding value for customers.
    https://www.swe.siemens.com/belux/portal/en/about/Pages/mission_statement.aspx
  - Southwest Airlines
    The mission of Southwest Airlines is dedication to the highest quality of Customer Service delivered with a sense of warmth, friendliness, individual pride, and Company Spirit.
    http://www.southwest.com/about_swa/mission.html

- Get students to do Exercise G, then go through the answers with the whole class, getting students to comment on the statements.

1 b **2** d **3** e **4** f **5** c **6** a

- Get students to look at the extract in Exercise H in pairs to identify the four criteria. Circulate, monitor and assist if necessary, but don't interrupt the pairs if they are functioning acceptably.
- When the pairs have finished, get them to suggest possible answers. Compare and contrast the different answers.

Suggested answer

An effective mission statement should:

- define the purpose of the organisation
- say what we want to be remembered for
- be short and sharply focused
- be clear and simple/easily understood.

Other tips not mentioned in the text but suggested by Peter Drucker:

- An effective mission statement should also:
- provide direction for doing the right things
- match the organisation's competence
- inspire commitment among members in the organisation.

I

- Again in pairs, get students to start writing mission statements for their own organisations of educational institutions.
- Circulate, monitor and assist if necessary, but don't interrupt the pairs if they are functioning acceptably.
- Tell them to do a final draft of their mission statements for homework. As usual, get them to e-mail their work to you, correct it before the next class and discuss it in the class.
- When discussing mission statements students have written in your feedback, get students to compare their mission statements with other pairs or groups, referring to the four criteria discussed previously in Exercise H (see answers above).
- If peer correction is appropriate in your setting, students could also be asked to proofread each others' writing tasks, bearing in mind the following points:
  - What expressions were used?
  - How could the mission statement be improved?
  - Are there any spelling mistakes or grammatical errors?
- Tell students accuracy is extremely important in this kind of writing, as the mission statement would normally appear in company literature and/or be diffused on the Internet and therefore read by many people. Be on hand to help with this, if necessary, but leave most of the feedback and discussion to students. If necessary, change the pairs around and repeat the process.
- Go through any common errors and the useful vocabulary and phrases on the board to round off the activity.
- Tell students you are going to read them a text and they should concentrate on understanding the general sense of it, and not focus on every word. Before you read, write the proper names on the board and tell students these names are mentioned in the text (i.e. Tony Cram, Ashridge, Austin Mini).
- Read out the text at normal speed. Students take notes while you read, then compare their notes in pairs. Read the text a second time, at normal speed again. Students then reconstruct the text in pairs. Explain to them that the important thing is that the content should be accurate and their writing should be grammatically correct, but they do not need to reproduce the text word for word.
- If peer correction is appropriate, students compare each other's texts. Go through feedback with the whole class, showing students the original text as an overhead slide or a photocopied handout.

CASE STUDY

Stella International Airways: strategy for the skies

An airline needs to make strategic changes to secure its long-term future. Students work on possible strategies and suggest a marketing campaign to back it up.

Stage 1: Background, Listening and Task 1

- Explain the subject of the case study (see above).
  Get students to read the background individually, or get a student to read it aloud. Explain any difficulties, e.g. *offset*, the use of *mirror* as a verb.
- Elicit information from students to complete the table below, in the usual way.

Company	Stella International Airways (SIA)
Base country	Holland
Nature of company	Long-haul and short-haul flights: one of Europe's leading airlines
Competitive environment	Structural shift in European airline industry toward LCCs (low-cost carriers) – loss of market share on short-haul routes Rise in oil prices – fall in SIA's shares
SIA's response so far	Fuel surcharge, but this has led to fall in passenger numbers and move to economy from first- and business-class.
CEO's response now	Devise a new strategy

- Get students to look at the pie charts – you will get students to prepare mini-presentations about them. First, give them the idea by starting one yourself, e.g. *The pie chart on the left gives a breakdown of Stella's costs for the last quarter. Its biggest cost is fuel and oil, representing a third of its overall costs* ... etc.
- Get students to give mini-presentations like this to each other in pairs, each student talking about one of the pie charts to their partner. Circulate, monitor and assist if necessary, but don't interrupt the pairs if they are functioning acceptably.
- When pairs have finished, get two students each to do a mini-presentation of each pie chart for the whole class. Depending on time available, you could work with the class further on graph and numbers language.
- Get students to look at the two short articles below the pie charts: *Stella passenger numbers down* and *Not a stellar quarter*. You could 'animate' these by getting students to convey the information in the articles as stand-up business news reporters, giving a report from Schiphol airport in Amsterdam. They will also do a vox-pop interview with the 'tired traveller' who wrote the e-mail 'budget versus business class'.
- Give students an idea of what you want by giving the start of one of the reports in suitably dramatic tones, e.g. *I'm at Schiphol Airport outside Amsterdam. It's here that Stella International Airways is based. Today, Stella has announced yet another set of disappointing figures: its first-class and business passenger numbers are down by five per cent* ..., etc.

- Then demonstrate the start of an interview with the writer of the e-mail: e.g.
  - Interviewer (you): Do you travel on scheduled airlines or low-cost?
  - Passenger (a student): I try to fly on scheduled airlines because ...
- Only do the first 30 seconds or so of the report and the interview respectively, just to give students the idea.
- Students then prepare their reports and interviews in pairs. Circulate, monitor and assist if necessary, but don't interrupt the pairs if they are functioning acceptably.
- When students are ready, get two of them to come to the front of the class, one of them to give the report 'to camera' – get him/her to hold an imaginary microphone in their hand. After this student gives their report, get them to turn to the other student, the passenger, and interview them, starting in a way similar to the one that you demonstrated.
- You could do this once more, getting students to integrate any corrections/improvements from the first run-through.

CD3.10–3.15

- Explain Task 1. Students are going to hear Stella managers and staff talking about the airline, and they have to use this information to complete the SWOT analysis in Task 1.
- Play the recordings of managers speaking, stopping at convenient points, getting students to take notes. (Tell them just to take notes at this stage – they will use the information to complete the SWOT table shortly.)
- Then do the same for the recordings of staff.
- After that, tell students to use their notes to complete the SWOT analysis in small groups.
- Circulate, monitor and assist if necessary, but don't interrupt the groups if they are functioning acceptably.
- When students have finished, get one or two students to give an account of the SWOT analysis they did in their respective groups.

Suggested answers

Strengths (internal)	Weaknesses (internal)
• safety record • experience and expertise • quality service • large number of flights and routes • key long-haul destinations, popular routes and airports • fleet size and quality • excellent reputation for service • mainline carrier is heavily focused on first-class and business-class markets and on the (long-haul) routes where that revenue is higher.	• losses over two consecutive years • high operating costs • falling passenger numbers on short haul • average fare per passenger down this year • first- and business-class passengers down this month • slower growth – mature market • can't win the low-fare battle with LCC • company might also need to invest in new aircraft for some of the long-haul flights

Opportunities (internal and external)	Threats (internal and external)
• reducing operating expenses, esp. staff costs • ancillary revenue stream – charges for food, baggage, online check-in, etc. • strategic alliance or merger with another airline • more perks for frequent flyers to encourage customer loyalty • weed out some of the poorer routes and switch aircraft to new opportunities, e.g. more slots on popular routes and new routes in Asian, such as China and India • reduce number of routes according to seasonal demand, e.g. cut slots in winter time • negotiate prices with aircraft manufacturers • change aircraft manufacturers • buy one model of aircraft to reduce maintenance costs • develop a lower-cost vehicle for UK–Europe operations, such as a subsidiary LCC • speculative buying of fuel (hedging)	• competition from LLCs (low-cost carriers) • unpredictable fuel prices • industrial action by unions • main aircraft partner is unwilling to play its part in cost reduction • business passengers will continue to trade down on short-haul routes • how long before LCCs leverage network potential and find a long-haul partner? • market share and cost base now will secure the airline's long-term future • high-speed train links being a threat for airline for some slots, e.g. London to Paris

- Then get students to work again in their groups on the new strategy for Stella, taking into account their SWOT analysis.
- Circulate, monitor and assist if necessary, but don't interrupt the groups if they are functioning acceptably.
- When most groups have finished, call the class to order and get a representative of each group to summarise briefly the discussion in their session, and the strategy that they have adopted.

Stage 2: Task 2

- Explain the task: students brainstorm a marketing campaign for Stella's future strategy. Get them to look at the information in Task 2. Explain that the purpose of the brainstorming session is to come up with a marketing campaign for their new strategy, so the initial brainstorming phase will be followed by a decision on the campaign.
- Divide them into groups of five or six and get them to start the task. (There is no need to appoint a chair at this stage, as brainstorming is normally done without one.)
- Circulate, monitor and assist if necessary, but don't interrupt the groups if they are functioning acceptably. Note good points of language use, as well as half a dozen points that need further work, especially in relation to strategic language, and add these on one side of the board.
- When most groups have finished the brainstorming phase, call the class to order and tell them that now they will have to make a final decision on the marketing. For each group, appoint a chair to lead the more formal discussion to take this decision. Explain this, and get groups to work on the decision.

- When most groups have finished, call the class to order and get a representative of each group to say what happened in their brainstorming session, and briefly present the campaign that they finally decided on.
- Praise good use of language that you heard in the activity, and work on the points on the board, getting individual students to say the right thing, especially in relation to marketing and strategic language

One-to-one

Go through the information in the Course Book with your student. Explain any difficulties.

Get your student to role-play the reporter after you have given a short demo of what you require. Then you can get your student to interview you, the tired traveller.

Go through the recordings as above, working with your student on the SWOT analysis.

Then move on to the brainstorming session in Task 2 with both of you contributing, but getting your student to make the decision on the marketing campaign, of course.

Note down any good examples of your student's language and points for error correction or improvement. Come back to these later. Praise any good examples of language used and go over any errors, including pronunciation. Don't dominate the conversation in the tasks, but say enough to keep them going. You could record any of the activities on audio or video, if the student agrees, and use them for intensive correction work afterwards.

 DVD-ROM: Case study commentary

Stage 3: Writing

- Get students to study the writing task and deal with any questions. Get them to note down information from their brainstorming sessions that should go in the summary while it is still fresh in their minds.
- Get students to look at the model report on pages 146–147 of the Writing file again if necessary. Though the format there is not really applicable to the one they will need here, you could use it to point out the similarities and differences. Get students to write the final summary for homework. As ever, get them to e-mail it to you if possible and go through corrections in the next lesson.

Writing file (Course Book, pages 146–147)

Resource bank: Writing (page 212)

WORKING ACROSS CULTURES **3**

Socialising

This unit looks at socialising, the pitfalls of small talk and how to avoid them.

A

- Introduce the subject by asking students where socialising skills might be needed in business contexts. (Talking to suppliers and customers before getting down to business, at trade fairs and conferences ...) Get students to continue the list based on their own contexts and experiences or, with pre-work students, ones in the future careers that they imagine for themselves.
- Get students to focus on the potential for misunderstanding in small-talk situations by asking students for any experiences in this area.
- With the whole class, go through the points here, discussing things that can go wrong, but don't spend too much time on them, as they are also dealt with in the next exercise.

B – C

- Explain the tasks, run quickly through the points in both exercises and get students to work on them in pairs.
- Circulate, monitor and assist if necessary, but don't interrupt the pairs if they are functioning acceptably.
- Call the class to order after each exercise and discuss pairs' findings with the whole class.

Exercise B
Suggested answers

1 Saying no, or turning down an offer or invitation from your host, is socially unacceptable in certain cultures, e.g. in Asian countries like China or Thailand.
2 Socialising with the boss is common in Anglo-American and some Northern European countries.
3 Using humour is considered to be a part of building working relationships, not just with colleagues but with those in authority, e.g. in Anglo-American cultures.
4 Discussing politics with people you know well is acceptable in certain countries, e.g. the US and UK. But discussion of religion (when not in the context of social customs), illness or death is best avoided, and these kinds of topics are considered 'conversation stoppers' in most cultures.
5 Many women may feel uncomfortable socialising on their own with a male business contact. In certain cultures, especially the Arab world, it would be very unlikely, certainly without a male family member present and dining out in a family restaurant.
6 Socialising is extremely important if you want to do business in some cultures, e.g. the Arab world and in many Mediterranean and Latin American countries. It is also an integral part of the concept of *guanxi* in China, or *kibun* in Korea. In American or European countries, it may be argued that socialising is more important in certain professions or sectors, e.g. in sales, marketing, human resources, public relations, etc.

In addition, socialising with workmates and going out with the team is considered to be an important aspect of team-building in many cultures, e.g. in the UK and particularly in Japan. In Asian countries, such as Japan or Thailand, it would be unacceptable to say no directly or refuse someone in a position of authority. You would have to turn down the invitation very diplomatically with a sincere apology.

Exercise C
Suggested answers

1 On behalf of (*name of company or managing director*), I'd like to welcome you all to (*name of company or place*). / It's my pleasure to welcome you all to (*name of company/event*). Thank you for coming here today. I hope you had a good journey. etc.
2 To a work colleague, you might compliment something they're wearing or their physical appearance, e.g. *I like your tie/shoes/suit/bag/new haircut. You're looking great!* Or compliment their work, e.g. *You're doing a great job. / You must have worked hard on that project.*
To an overseas visitor, you might compliment their country, city or food, etc., e.g. *I love your town/city. It's a fantastic place to live, isn't it?* Or compliment their work or effort on a project, e.g. *I hear that deal was a success.* Possibly compliment them on their clothes, possessions or physical appearance if you know them. It isn't usual in the UK to pay someone a compliment as a way of breaking the ice, but it is more common in the US. British people and some other cultures might get embarrassed and not know how to respond.
3 When turning people down, it is usual to include an apology, thank the person for the offer or invitation, give a good excuse or explanation for refusing, and possibly offer an alternative, e.g. *I'm really sorry, but the thing is, I have family visiting from abroad this week /it's my son's birthday, etc. I would love to come next time, though.*

D CD3.16–3.18

- Explain the task and play the recordings one at a time, asking what the situation is after each one, and discussing it.

Suggested answers

1 A British manager welcomes a group of international visitors/delegates to a UK company. He's friendly and shows concern for his guests, but his jokes might not be understood by all. Some cultures might consider this kind of speech far too informal and might think his sense of humour inappropriate.
2 The British host, Gary, invites Elvira and Nathan to dinner, but the American turns down the invitation because he wants to work on (*fine-tune*) his presentation for the next day. Gary is disappointed, as he expected Nathan to socialise with the rest of the team.
3 Gary and Elvira are making small talk after dinner. Elvira compliments the meal, but says British food has a bad reputation, which might offend her host. Gary then mentions the carnival in Brazil and says his friends were robbed (*mugged*) there. Negative talk about crime in her country could make Elvira feel uncomfortable. Gary later asks Elvira about her children, but she doesn't have any. She then excuses herself to go outside for a cigarette, which could be seen as an excuse to get away from him and might offend Gary.

E CD3.19–3.21

- Explain that this situation follows on from the previous exercise, and point out the task in this one.

- Play the recordings and get students to summarise them. Then get their answers to the questions, as well as their reactions and comments.

Suggested answers

1 Elvira wasn't happy with Gary's use of humour and colloquial language. She thinks he didn't realise how tired they were after their long journey. Ironically, Gary probably thought he was just being friendly and putting his guests at ease by using humour. He should have graded his language accordingly and he could have omitted some of the jokes in his speech to an international group.

2 Nathan realises he may have offended Gary by turning him down, but he says Gary should have understood he had to prepare for an important presentation the next day. You may think Nathan should have attended the meal in order to get to know the team, although he made a concession by saying he would come later for coffee.

3 Elvira wishes Gary hadn't mentioned the carnival in her country, as it's a stereotypical perception of Brazil. She also seems annoyed that international colleagues assume Brazilians party all the time, when she works hard. On the other hand, she has a negative perception of the UK with the rain, no-smoking policy and 'watery' coffee.

F

- You could get students to turn to the audio script on page 180 to help them do this task. Get them to read the conversation first.
- Then get students to 'improve' the conversation in parallel pairs. Circulate, monitor and assist if necessary, but don't interrupt the pairs if they are functioning acceptably.
- When the pairs have finished, call the class to order and get public performances from one or two of the pairs.

Suggested answers

- Compliment the food without mentioning its bad reputation.
- Talk about the carnival in a more positive light, and not mention the mugging episode.
- Talk about things to do and places to see in Brazil / the UK.
- Talk about the educational system in the UK compared to Brazil.
- Talk about the visitor's hotel, etc.

G – H

- Get students to work on these exercises in small groups, discussing the possible answers in Exercise G and doing the matching in Exercise H. Circulate, monitor and assist if necessary, but don't interrupt the groups if they are functioning acceptably.
- When most groups have finished, call the class to order and discuss the answers. (The ones below for Exercise G are just a guide – be sure to get students to suggest alternatives.)
- After students have given answers to Exercise H, get different pairs to read the utterances and the responses aloud, working on natural intonation.

Exercise G
Suggested answers

1 Acceptable way of paying someone a compliment. But it might not be socially acceptable in the Arab world, where a host might feel obliged to give you the item as a present!

2 When refusing an offer of food, a more polite refusal would be: *They look delicious, but I couldn't eat any more, thanks. /Actually, I'm on a diet, thanks.*

3 When talking about a person you both know, a more acceptable response would be: *You know Marcello! What a coincidence! How is he? /What's he doing these days?*

4 Acceptable way of refusing an offer of food. However, in some Asian cultures, e.g. China, Thailand, Korea, etc., it's best to avoid saying 'no', and in most cultures it's best to try any food you are offered.

5 When disagreeing with someone about politics, a more acceptable response would be: *Do you think so? I think she's a brilliant head of state.* But it might be better not to mention politics in some cultures.

6 When talking about family, a more socially acceptable question might be: *Do you have any children?*

7 This question may be acceptable when talking about religion in the context of social customs, although it is often best to avoid talking about religious beliefs.

8 Acceptable way of turning down an invitation

9 It wouldn't be socially acceptable in many cultures to make this kind of joke, or talk about funerals and death. This comment also might offend people from cultures which are quieter than others.

10 Acceptable way of making an arrangement. Although it's common practice to have breakfast meetings in the US, it's not socially acceptable in other cultures.

Exercise H

1 d **2** g **3** i **4** f **5** a **6** h **7** b **8** j **9** c **10** e

- Explain the task and get students to work on these exchanges in parallel pairs.
- When they have finished, call the class to order and get performances of the different exchanges from individual pairs. (As before, the answers below are just suggestions.)

Suggested answers

1 All of this organisation. It must have been a lot of work. (*as Elvira says to Gary in track 3.17*) / I hear that deal was a success. / You've got a great team. / You must have worked hard on that project.

2 That must have been awful for you. By the way, would you like something from the buffet? The food here is great, isn't it?
I'm sorry to hear that. It must have been difficult for you. You know, I hear you're a good friend of Said. I used to work with him in Malaga.
It makes you appreciate good health, doesn't it? Do you have much time to go to the gym or practise sport these days?

3 That's very kind of you. I'd love to come, but do you mind / is it all right if I invite a work colleague of mine, too? I know he'd like to talk to you about ...

Task

- Go through the task and get students to work in pairs on it. (You could change the make-up of the pairs at this point.)
- Allocate roles and make sure students are looking at the correct page. When students are ready, get them to begin. Circulate, monitor and assist if necessary, but don't interrupt the pairs if they are functioning acceptably.
- Note good points of language use, as well as half a dozen points that need further work, especially in relation to socialising, and add these on one side of the board.
- When most pairs have finished, call the class to order and get different pairs to re-enact different parts of the activity.
- Praise good use of socialising language that you heard in the activities, and work on the points on the board, getting individual students to say the right thing.
- You could round off the unit by asking some of your students, books closed, for the three most important things they have learned from it.

UNIT C Revision

For more speaking practice, see the Resource bank section of this book, beginning on page 171. The exercises in this unit can be done in class, individually or collaboratively, or for homework.

7 Finance

Vocabulary

- These exercises revisit some of the vocabulary from the unit.

1 **1** lends **2** financial **3** debt **4** interest **5** finance **6** making **7** return **8** savings **9** savers **10** transparency

2 **1** ethical **2** figure **3** fund **4** profits **5** economies **6** sustainable **7** Business angels **8** start-up **9** investment capital **10** venture capitalists

3 **1** get away with **2** give away **3** pay out **4** carry on **5** run out of **6** turn down **7** bring down **8** take out

Skills

- Students get an opportunity to work on the skills from pages 68–69 again.

1 Do you think you could describe your business idea in one sentence?

2 Would you mind telling me what the projected sales are for year one? / Would you mind tell me what your projected sales for year one are?

3 Who would you say was your target market?

4 What makes you think people are going to buy your products?

5 I was wondering whether you had ever done anything like this before.

6 I'd like to know what sort of return on investment we are looking at.

8 Consultants

Vocabulary

- This exercise gives students another chance to work on some of the vocabulary from the unit.

1 b **2** d **3** a **4** e **5** f **6** g **7** c

Ellipsis

- Students work on ellipsis, i.e. missing out words in texts, as in Exercise D on page 77.

Suggested answer

(Hi/Hello) Martin

(There's) no need to thank me for doing the slides. (Thank you / Thanks) for the corrections. (It's) great that you picked up on my (typos / typing errors)!

(I) was wondering if there's any chance of you cleaning up the employee performance data by (this) Friday? (I'm) really busy this week – (I'm (on a business trip)) in Vienna.

(I'm (really)) sorry. Richard's been asking (me) for it. (I'll) owe you (one / a favour) ...

(I'm) looking forward to catching up with you guys (on) Monday morning. (Do you have) any idea what time (it will be) and where (we're having the meeting)?

(I hope to) speak (to you) soon.

(Best wishes / BW)

Sylvia

The level of ellipsis depends on the working relationship between Sylvia and Martin, the power relationship and also how much time Sylvia had to write the e-mail. But it would be a good idea to reduce the amount of ellipsis if she's asking Martin for a favour, i.e. to clean up the employee performance data by Friday. That way the request would sound more polite, and Martin might be more inclined to do the work.

Skills

- Students work on the skills language from pages 78–79.

1 c **2** d **3** e **4** f **5** a **6** b

Writing

- Students work again on missing words, this time ones that can't be missed out!

I'm writing to confirm what *we/was*[1] discussed in our meeting. Thanks again for taking the time to see me at such short notice.

We're pleased *to*[2] offer you our Moroccan Mist body spray at €9.50 per 30ml. I've also made a note that you may be interested *in*[3] stocking the complete Spa Gift pack in Dionysius department stores in the future – subject to confirmation.

As discussed, our usual payment terms are 30 days from date of invoice. As *for*[4] delivery, I'd like to point *out*[5] that it is completely free on your first order. But we do charge for deliveries of fewer than 50 items on any subsequent orders.

Please find *attached*[6] a copy of our terms of agreement, including details of our sale or return policy. In the unlikely event that you, or your customers, are not fully satisfied with our products, please let me know *as*[7] soon as possible.

Finally, I'd be grateful if *you*[8] could confirm your first order in writing by Thursday in order to ensure prompt delivery next month. In case you need any more information *about/on/concerning/regarding*[9] our product range or promotional offers, please don't hesitate to contact *me/us*[10].

Looking forward *to*[11] doing business with you.

9 Strategy

Vocabulary

- Further work on strategic language.

1 strategic **2** growth **3** creating **4** compete **5** existing **6** thriving **7** endure **8** values **9** performance **10** corporate

Rhetorical questions

- Students work on this type of question and possible answers, as seen in the article on page 85.

1. How do they get away with it?
2. How long is a piece of string?
3. Is it just me?
4. So, what else is new?
5. What's the point?
6. Are you serious?

Skills

- Another chance to look at the brainstorming language from pages 94–95.

1 go; open **2** like; get; rolling **3** get; down
4 taken; right; mouth **5** there; bad ideas
6 judgement; later

Cultures 3: Socialising

- These two exercises rework some of the language for gaffe-free socialising.

Exercise 1

Suggested answers

1. That's a great/smart/gorgeous designer suit, Dominique. Where did you get it?
2. The roasted grasshoppers look wonderful, but I've just had lunch / eaten. Thanks.
3. What a coincidence! / That's amazing! You know my friend Jason!
4. Actually, I think you might be wrong there ...
5. Er, excuse me, I think I'll just go and help myself to the buffet / get something to drink / make a phone call.
6. That's really/very kind of you / Thanks, but I'm playing tennis this Sunday. Maybe some other time?

Exercise 2

1 b **2** a **3** a **4** b **5** a

UNIT 10 Online business

AT A GLANCE

	Classwork – Course Book	Further work
Lesson 1 *Each lesson is about 60–75 minutes. This time does not include administration and time spent going through homework in any lessons.*	**Listening and discussion: Developments in online business** Students discuss the development of the Internet and the future of e-commerce. They listen to an expert on e-commerce and work on related language.	**Practice File** Word power (pages 58–59) **Resource bank: Listening** (page 198) **i-Glossary** (DVD-ROM)
Lesson 2	Reading and language: *The new corporate firefighters* Students read an article about the problems of organisations maintaining their reputation on the Internet in an age of social networking. They also work on rhetorical devices such as metaphor and techniques for emphasising points.	**Text bank** (pages 154–157) **Practice File** Text and grammar (pages 60–61) **ML Grammar and Usage**
Lesson 3	**Business skills: Presentations: thinking on your feet** Students look at presentation situations that call for quick thinking on one's feet, listen to a speaker dealing with questions and then give a short presentation, themselves dealing with questions.	**Resource bank: Speaking** (page 186) **Practice File** Skills and pronunciation (pages 62–63)
Lesson 4	**Case study: The fashion screen** An online tailored-clothing retailer wants to improve its reputation. Students look at its business model, and comments that are being made about it online. They then try to come up with some improvements in both these areas.	**Case study commentary** (DVD-ROM) **Resource bank: Writing** (page 213)

For a fast route through the unit, focusing mainly on speaking skills, just use the underlined sections.

For one-to-one situations, most parts of the unit lend themselves, with minimal adaptation, to use with individual students. Where this is not the case, alternative procedures are given.

BUSINESS BRIEF

E-commerce has become established surprisingly quickly in many places. The early worries about having one's credit card details stolen, or the goods not arriving, seem to have dissipated. Five-and-a-half per cent of all retail purchases in Europe were made online in 2010, with much higher figures in some countries.

Some of the key issues for e-commerce are:

- The frustration of using **e-commerce sites.** The best, like Amazon's, are a pleasure to use, but 15 years after the start of **e-tailing**, many are still surprisingly inefficient, so purchases are not completed, with the resulting **virtual shopping trolleys** abandoned in the **virtual aisles** of many sites – an **e-tailer**'s nightmare! This is one of the problems for traditional retailers who have developed e-tailing operations, part of the more general question of how the two types of operation are going to relate to each other. However, rather than one eliminating the other, the two can be quite **integrated**, with the possibility of picking up products ordered online at a nearby store. This alleviates a key problem in e-commerce, which is:
- Physical delivery of goods. Parcel delivery companies have benefited enormously from e-commerce, where goods have to be **physically delivered** to homes. But they deliver at times of day when most people are out at work, especially the type of working people who tend to order things online. (However, clever e-tailers have managed to make money out of this by charging for goods to be delivered in a particular **time slot**.)
- The future of services. There has been especially fast progress in the sale of services such as travel and financial products, where the value of each transaction can be quite high, and goods do not have to be physically delivered. Airline tickets have now virtually (literally!) disappeared.
- **Business-to-business (B2B) e-commerce.** Some say that one of the biggest impacts of the Internet (and one unnoticed by consumers) is in business-to-business applications, where suppliers can competitively bid for orders. Competing companies, for example in the car industry, have set up networks where they can get suppliers to do this. One issue here is **anti-competition laws**: suppliers collaborating like this must avoid being perceived as illegally **fixing prices** in a **cartel**.

Of course, getting people to sites in the first place is key. Here, Google's **rankings** are all-important. **Webmetrics** allow e-commerce managers to know where the people who visit its site come from in terms of sites they have just **clicked on**, how many visits are **converted** into actual purchases of goods, how many abandon the process, etc. – all this information is now readily available. (Hack journalists are now paid to write screeds of material on the Internet about different subjects – really a type of **advertorial**, fodder for Google to list the e-tailer mentioned in the articles high in its rankings.)

Another factor is **social networking**, where companies are finding it increasingly difficult to keep control of their products' reputations. A brand can have **'friends'** on Facebook, and the brand's marketers would often prefer that presence to be maintained and enhanced mainly by the company (or its **web-hosting agency**), rather than by consumers, even friendly ones. And comments on blogs and Twitter are much less within a company's control. In an attempt to do this, companies are increasingly recruiting 20- and 30-something managers who understand how social media work. **Reputation management** has become a key issue.

Online business and your students

You can approach e-commerce by asking students how their organisation uses the Internet in general – don't forget to ask about business-to-business applications, too. If they don't buy things online as consumers, find out why not. (This should become less and less the case as time goes on – it's becoming difficult to use planes and even trains without using the Internet.)

The younger your pre-work students are, the more likely they are to think of the Internet as the normal way to do things in almost every area. If you are 10 years or more older than them, you probably have a lot to learn from them!

Read on

Dave Chaffey et al.: *Internet marketing: Strategy, implementation and practice*, Financial Times / Prentice Hall, 2008

Sarah Clelland: *Internet retailing: A practitioner's guide*, Kogan Page, 2011

Steve Johnston, Liam McGee: *50 ways to make Google love your website*, Random House, 2010

Ted Soskin: *Net profit: How to succeed in digital business*, Wiley, 2010

The latest stats on e-commerce in Europe can be found on: http://econsultancy.com/uk/blog.

LESSON NOTES

Warmer

- Get students to talk about their use of the Internet and attitudes towards it, without pre-empting the rest of the unit too much.
- In addition, you could get them to complete this table of common word partnerships related to e-commerce by writing it on the board and revealing the letters of the second word one by one until they get the answers. Then get students to talk about their attitudes to, and experiences (if any) of, these Internet activities.

online	banking dating gambling/gaming travel fundraising (for non-profit organisations)

Overview

- Go through the overview panel at the beginning of the unit, pointing out the sections that students will be looking at.

Quotation

- Get students to say what they think of the quotation. (If they want to know more about John Hagel, they can look at his website: http://www.johnhagel.com.)

Listening and discussion: Developments in online business

Students discuss the development of the Internet and the future of e-commerce. They listen to an expert on e-commerce and work on related language.

A

- Ask students how much they know about the history of the Internet and e-commerce before looking at the exercise. You could ask them when the Internet really 'took off' in their own countries, for example when people started using e-mail for the first time. (But with younger students, for whom the Internet has always been there, don't pursue this too much.)
- Do the exercise with the whole class and discuss any points arising from each year – don't just plough through it. For example, for 1998, you could ask your students when they started using Google – in that year or later? Do they use Twitter? What has happened to Napster?

1 Tim Berners-Lee **2** Amazon **3** eBay **4** Dell
5 Google **6** Napster **7** Amazon **8** Facebook
9 YouTube **10** Twitter

B

- Get students to look at this exercise in pairs and report back, comparing and contrasting their online business 'behaviour'.

C – F CD3.22–3.25

- Tell students that they are going to listen to David Bowen, a website consultant. (He also writes about the subject on ft.com.)
- Get students to focus on the question in Exercise C and anticipate the answers. (The previous exercise will have given them some ideas.)
- Play the recording and elicit the answers. Ask students if they are surprised by answers 2 and 3. If so, why?

Exercise C

He identifies three sorts of 'winners' in online business:

1. Companies that were set up specifically to do business online, e.g. booksellers, like Amazon, and eBay, the auction site
2. Small companies that have been able to sell outside their traditional markets
3. Companies – both large and small (e.g. your local plumber) – that can buy things around the world online more cheaply than in the past

- Get students to predict what might go in the gaps in Exercise D and then play the recording, stopping at convenient points.
- Elicit and discuss the answers.

Exercise D

1 complex **2** geographically dispersed
3 shareholders **4** journalists **5** signposting
6 usability **7** branding **8** homogeneous

- For Exercise E, get students to read through the text to see if they can already spot the six factual errors.
- Then play the recording and elicit and discuss the answers.

Exercise E

Through the use of social media, businesses can get their messages across in a different way from the method they use on the web (itself). They can have more engaging, two-way conversations with customers. Companies can also use social media for other purposes, such as using Facebook to contact young people looking for jobs.

On the other hand, social media present a big reputation risk. A story can spread very fast, so companies have to react much faster to counter the risk. One example is a story that was going around that Ford had tried to close down a very small dealership's website. Ford's Social Media Manager sent out messages on Twitter to find out Ford's side of the story and he was able to put that out on social media sites and successfully deal with the problem.

- Before playing the recording for Exercise F, get students to make three predictions themselves about the future of the Internet. It will be interesting to hear from younger students about the future of social networking in relation to e-commerce. Ask if they have themselves joined up as a 'friend' of a brand on its Facebook page, for example, and if they see this trend continuing.
- Play the recording and elicit and discuss the answers.

Exercise F

He mentions that customers will go and ask other customers about their experience with social media, and that's going to develop enormously.

He thinks we're going to get quite a lot more 3D, going into a virtual shop.

And also that we're going to get the convergence of television and computers.

G

- Get students to work on these predictions in pairs. Circulate, monitor and assist if necessary, but don't interrupt the pairs if they are functioning acceptably.
- Note good points of language use, as well as half a dozen

points that need further work, and add these on one side of the board.

- When most pairs have finished, call the class to order and elicit, compare and contrast the pairs' views.
- Praise good use of e-commerce-related language that you heard in the activity, and work on the points on the board, getting individual students to say the right thing.

Resource bank: Listening (page 198)

Students can watch the interview with David Bowen on the DVD-ROM.

i-Glossary

Reading and language: *The new corporate firefighters*

Students read an article about the problems of organisations maintaining their reputation on the Internet in an age of social networking. They also work on rhetorical devices such as metaphor and techniques for emphasising points.

A

- With the whole class, discuss the questions. You could point out that this is the first writing genre in history, where, on a global scale, there is probably more writing than reading! Also mention that, like diary writers, most bloggers give up their blogs after a few weeks or months – but encourage your students to give persuasive counter-examples of successful blogs. Another feature of blogging is that it is often done by journalists, so this sort is really journalism with another name.

B

- Go through the questions. Get students to read the article individually or in pairs. Circulate, monitor and assist if necessary, but don't interrupt if students are functioning acceptably.
- Elicit and discuss the answers.

1. There are six different job titles mentioned: Director of Social Media, Vice-President of Experiential Marketing, Digital Communications Manager, Director of New Media, Vice-President of Communities and Conversation, Director of Digital Care
2. In three different ways: a) the core team works on 'blog resolution'; b) others manage the company's Twitter accounts and Facebook pages; c) another group manages IdeaStorm, Dell's forum for customer feedback.
3. Dell has used customer feedback to help it develop new products, by incorporating consumer ideas into the design.
4. There are two mentioned in the article: a) by broadcasting discount alerts on Twitter, it may be possible to generate more sales; b) by solving a customer's problem by writing on a blog, it is more cost-effective than dealing with a customer by phone because other people can read the information online and find answers to their queries.
5. It's a fast and efficient way to get your message out to consumers, especially if there is a problem or crisis.

C

- Get students to read the article again specifically to find the answers to these questions.
- Elicit the answers and explain any difficulties, e.g. *make amends*.

1 engagement **2** (broad) shift **3** It's no longer **4** showed up **5** be attuned to **6** trawling **7** make amends **8** broadcasting **9** realised **10** put out [...] fires *(figurative)* **11** defuse **12** a brewing crisis

D

- Tell students that they are going to look at business metaphors. Get them to turn to the Language reference section on page 138 and take them through the material there.
- Then get them individually or in pairs to go back to the article and find metaphors in it.
- Explain any difficulties.

The principal metaphors used here are fire, war and natural phenomena: *corporate firefighters, to put out ...fires, erupt, defuse, a 'brewing' crisis.*

E – F

- Talk students through the three techniques in Exercise E and, with the whole class, get them to match the techniques and the examples.
- Then get them, in pairs, to find examples in the article.
- Elicit the answers and explain any difficulties.

Exercise E

1 b **2** c **3** a

Notes:

a) Full article available on http://psychology.suite101.com/article.cfm/a-social-paradox

b) Adapted from 'This is it. This is exactly what I look for in my summer popcorn flicks. Fun, fun, fun.' (http://www.joblo.com/reviews.php?mode=joblo_movies&id=1230).

c) Based on some of the media hype surrounding Apple's iPad on its launch.

Exercise F

1 Anaphora

They may not be press and they may not be customers ... (lines 25–27)

It's always worth talking directly with your customers. It's always worth listening to them ... (lines 63–66)

'If you solve someone's problem on the phone, nobody knows,' says Mr Sernovitz. 'If you solve that same problem in writing on a blog ...' (lines 86–90)

2 Hyperbole

Everybody's job is now social media. (lines 37–38)

multimillion-dollar savings (line 95)

3 Paradox

It's the wisdom of crowds. (line 67)

G

- Get students to discuss the questions in pairs. Give students help in relating the questions to their own organisations. For example, if they are pre-work students, get them to think about how social media could help their school in telling future students about what to expect, for example by reading current students' blogs.
- Circulate, monitor and assist if necessary, but don't interrupt the pairs if they are functioning acceptably.
- Call the class to order and elicit their opinions, comparing and contrasting them.

Text bank (pages 154–157)

Business skills: Presentations: thinking on your feet

Students look at presentation situations that call for quick thinking on one's feet, listen to a speaker dealing with questions and then give a short presentation, themselves dealing with questions.

A

- Ask students what they understand by the expression *thinking on your feet*. Ask them if they have ever had to do this in a presentation, for example when the equipment breaks down or someone asks an unexpected question. Get students to tell their stories about this. (Pre-work students will probably have little experience of this, so move swiftly on to the exercise.)
- Get students to discuss the situations in pairs and report back. If short of time, you could get different pairs to concentrate on different points. Circulate, monitor and assist if necessary, but don't interrupt the pairs if they are functioning acceptably.
- Call the class to order and compare and contrast their advice.

B CD3.26

- Explain the task, get students to focus on the questions and play the recording.
- With the whole class, elicit and discuss the answers rather than just plough through them.

Suggested answers

Strategies used:

Question 1: She says she's already talked about it. *Well, it's really what I was talking about at the start of my presentation.* She also says the next speaker will address the issue. *I don't want to go into too much detail at this stage, as Peter Adams will be dealing with ... in the next session.*

Question 2: She asks the questioner to repeat the question: *I'm really sorry, could you just repeat that question because I don't think everyone heard.* Again, she says the next speaker will address the issue: *Well, as I've already said, Peter will be dealing with those kinds of issues later ...* She also checks that the questioner is happy with her response: *I hope that answers your question.*

Question 3: She replies positively to the question at the start: *That's a really interesting question.*

Question 4: She rephrases the question at the start: *So, your question is what kind of language should we avoid?* She also tries to deal with the question in a humorous way: *Well, apart from the obvious, you know, offensive language, ...* Also, when she has finished answering, she refers the audience to the handout: *You'll find some guidelines on copywriting in the handout.*

Sophie finally indicates it's time to stop: *Is that all? OK, great, well, let's break for 15 minutes, then ...*

Other possible strategies:

- Simply admit you don't know, saying it's not your field/ department, etc.
- Refer the questioner to another expert or authority.
- Say you don't have the information on you, but will check it and, for example, send an e-mail to the questioner.
- Say you're running out of time but will be happy to discuss the question in more detail in the break, after your talk, etc.
- If you feel a member of the audience is being too aggressive or is undermining you, dismiss or ignore the question, or ask *Anyone else?*, or bring the Q&A to a close.

C CD3.26

- Explain the task. Get students to anticipate what might be in the gaps and play the recording again, getting them to check if they were right or not.

1 I was just wondering what you thought
2 I'd like to know
3 I'd be interested to know more
4 I mean to say, could you tell us
5 Yes, but I was wondering whether

We use these kinds of indirect questions to play for time, to sound more polite or tentative, or to soften a challenging question because the questioners are aware they're putting the presenter on the spot. See also Unit 7 (Managing questions).

D

- Go through the expressions in the Useful language box and work on natural intonation, getting students to read the different expressions with feeling.
- Then ask the question and elicit the answers.

Suggested answers

Playing for time – when you don't know the answer, thinking of what to say, and when the question is difficult

I'm glad you asked me that question.
I'm sorry, could you speak up, please?
Sorry, could you speak up a bit?
Do you mind using the microphone so that everyone can hear?

Repeating ideas – when you're asked about something you've already talked about

As I mentioned/said before/previously, ...
As I explained earlier / at the start of my talk.
In fact, this goes back to what I was saying earlier, ...
Actually, this is precisely what [name of speaker] meant when he/she said ...

Delaying an answer – when the questioner interrupts you; when you're planning on talking about the point later in your talk; when you need more time to think about the answer; when you're running out of time

That's an interesting point, but perhaps we could discuss it later?
If you don't mind, I'll be happy to answer that question at the end of my talk.
If you'd like to find me after the presentation, I can answer that in detail.
I'd be happy to discuss that with you in more detail in the break.

Saying you don't know – when you're asked about something that's not in your field, or an irrelevant question, or when you simply don't know!

To be honest, that's not really my area of expertise.
I'm afraid I can't say off the top of my head.
I'm not really an expert on that, but I could refer you to my colleague, or [name of expert].
I think you'll find the next speaker will be dealing with that (issue/question).
I'm afraid it's not my field exactly, but I believe [name of colleague or expert] has a theory about that.
I imagine the answer is ..., but don't quote me on that.

E

- With the whole class, get students to suggest how to express these ideas in acceptable ways. (Underline that they should never actually say these things! You could ask what might happen in students' own cultures if presenters did say these things.)

Suggested answers

1 That's an interesting / a very specific question ...
I'm afraid I don't have that information at hand, but ...
2 As I've already said, ...
Well, it's really what I was talking about at the start of my talk.
Well, it goes back to my main point about ...
3 Could I come back to you about that later?
I'm sorry, but we're running out of time now.
4 I'm sorry, do you mind speaking up / using the mike / repeating the question, please?
So, if I've understood you correctly, you're asking whether ...?
5 I'm sorry, but that's not really the aim of my talk today.
I'm sorry, but that's not really my field / area of research.
6 I don't want to go into too much detail at this stage, but what I might say is ...
Actually, [*name of expert*] has a theory about this.
I hope that answers your question.
7 I'm afraid that's all we've got time for. Thank you.
I'm afraid we've run out of time, but I'd be more than happy to discuss that with you during the break.
8 That's a very interesting point. I'd be happy to discuss this with you further after my talk.
That's quite a specific question. If you'd like to find me after the presentation, I'd be happy to discuss that with you in more detail.

F – G

- Get students to discuss the points in Exercise F in pairs and report back. Don't spend too long on this: tell students that the main idea is to put these points into action later in their own presentations.
- Allocate the tasks in Exercise G and get students to turn to the correct pages. Get students to start preparing their presentations in pairs as outlined in the task description. Circulate, monitor and assist if necessary, but don't interrupt the pairs if they are functioning acceptably.
- Get pairs to give their presentations to each other. This could be done in parallel pairs first (circulate and monitor language being used, especially in relation to 'thinking on your feet'-type reactions to questions.) Then get public performances from each pair for the whole class.
- In large groups, you may like to ask half of the students to give their presentations in one class, and the other half in another class so that students do not have to listen to each other for more than 45 minutes. Students who are listening should prepare challenging questions for the presenters. You may also like to put students in groups of four at the end, so that one pair can give feedback to another pair.
- With some of the stronger students, you may give out information to one of the other students, asking them to 'hijack' the presentation or throw the speaker, e.g. interrupt three times during the talk, start talking on a mobile phone or get it to ring, walk out and walk back in again, explain there has been a power failure and ask the speaker to continue without using slides, or point out an imaginary error on the slide.
- Alternatively, if short of time, students could improvise two of the situations from Exercise A.

➡ Resource bank: Speaking (page 186)

CASE STUDY

The fashion screen

An online tailored-clothing retailer wants to improve its reputation. Students look at its business model and at comments that are being made about it online. They then try to come up with some improvements in both these areas.

Stage 1: Background and Task 1

- Explain the subject of the case study (see above). Get students to read the background individually, or get a student to read it aloud.
- Elicit information from students to complete the table below in the usual way.

Company/founder	Meerza Tailoring Fashions (MTF)/ Zayna Meerza (ZM)
Based in	Paris
Reputation/award	ZM one of leading figures in tailoring – Best Female Entrepreneur in France
Clientele	Leading executives – men and women
Typical price for suit	€750
Business model	From 'bricks-and-mortar' outlet to online. Clients' measurements saved for future ref/updating
Other outlets	London, Frankfurt, Brussels, where suits are also made and from where they are delivered
New service	Shirts sold online – customers just enter measurements
Threats	Cut-price fashion sites Competitors are using viral marketing including blogging and social networking

- Books closed, get one or two students to rephrase the above information in their own words.
- Books open again, get students to look at the blog entries on page 103. Explain any difficulties and ask students if they have ever contributed to blogs like these for products, travel, etc., bought online or signed an online petition.
- Then get students to look at Task 1 and discuss the points in small groups. Circulate, monitor and assist if necessary, but don't interrupt the groups if they are functioning acceptably.
- Call the class to order and get groups to say what their findings were.

Suggested answers

There are several complaints about Meerza Tailoring Fashions, their garments and their website:

1 Lidia complains the pics (photos) on the site should be high resolution, as they are difficult to see.
2 The entry posted by an 'unhappy customer' complains that her suit was a copy of one worn by a singer and wasn't original.
3 The navigation on the website may need improving, as Stevie says the self-measuring guide isn't easy to follow; also, his tailored shirt was a bad fit, so he sent it back and he's still waiting for a refund.

4 Aaron complains that the company claims the shirts are made in Paris, but his was made in Frankfurt.
5 The two entries posted by Bombay Chique-chick suggest that Zayna is *not* opposed to sweatshop labour, and therefore condones it.
6 Meerza Tailoring Fashions has only posted one entry to advertise its shirts, and its lack of presence on the blog is noted e.g. *Meerza Tailoring Fashions and your ill-fitting shirts – are you out there?*

The most urgent issue is that Meerza Tailoring Fashions should improve its online communication with customers by replying more quickly to the entries on such blogs and dealing with both complaints and rumours more effectively.

Secondly, the company seems to be making false advertising claims about where its clothes are made (item 4 above), and this should be clarified immediately.

Thirdly, they could improve the online experience for customers by making their website more user-friendly, and providing clearer instructions for taking measurements, with easy-to-follow instructions and clearer, high-resolution photos.

Stage 2: Listening and Task 2

CD3.27

Get students to look at the questions. Then play the recording, elicit the answers and, above all, ask students how well they thought ZM dealt with the questions.

Suggested answers

Zayna comes across fairly well in the first part of the interview when she describes her business success, but then falters when she's asked about digital/social media, although it sounds as if she's considering taking on a social media manager.

The interviewer also asks her about the (false) advertising claim that the garments are made in Paris when they are actually made elsewhere. Zayna replies by saying it's a false accusation and that it depends on customer location, but the interviewer doesn't give Zayna the chance to explain further.

Zayna is then asked whether the company is experiencing financial difficulty. Zayna replies, *Those are just rumours. Meerza Tailoring Fashions is going from strength to strength.* It is not clear whether the company is actually experiencing financial difficulty, or whether these are only rumours.

The business owner is finally challenged about not signing the *don't-shop-sweatshop* campaign. Zayna says she's thinking about it, but the presenter puts words into her mouth, concluding, *Zayna Meerza is going to sign the petition.*

- Get students to look at Task 2 and explain the task and the structure of the role play: students will role-play technology consultants and company directors.
- Divide the class into groups of four: two consultants and two company directors in each group. (In smaller classes, you could have groups of two: one consultant and one company director.)
- Get students to turn to the correct page and give them time to absorb their information. Circulate, monitor and assist if necessary, but don't interrupt the groups if they are functioning acceptably.
- If students playing the directors are stuck, you could give them the following suggestions:
  - how to stay ahead of the competition, e.g. spot fashion trends and be innovative in online content;
  - how to improve the online experience, e.g. help customers when taking their own measurements; maybe offer computer-generated image assessment which could recommend certain styles and colours for customers according to their age, height, hair/eye colour, etc.;
  - how to manage the face-to-face measuring sessions and help customers when taking their own measurements, e.g. employ more staff as measurers/fitters across Europe?
  - how to manage your brand reputation, e.g. incidents of 'flaming' (*a sudden burst of anger that is usually short-lived*); employ a social media manager or a social media team?
  - how to retain control of website content, e.g. social media manager should check with you first in the event of an incident of 'flaming';
  - outline where you want to be in two years' time, e.g. are you a quality tailor first, and an online business second? Or should you just concentrate on the online business?
- When groups are ready, tell them to begin the role play. Circulate and note good points of language use, as well as half a dozen points that need further work especially in relation to e-commerce, and add these on one side of the board.
- When most groups have finished, call the class to order and praise good use of e-commerce language that you heard in the activity, and work on the points on the board, getting individual students to say the right thing.
- Ask representatives of some groups to say what happened in them. Try to draw some of the threads together from the various role plays, comparing and contrasting the discussions of each group.

One-to-one

Go through the information in Task 1 in the Course Book with your student and discuss it. Explain any difficulties.

Then do Task 2 with you as a consultant and your student as a company director. If there is time and interest, do the task again, or part(s) of it, reversing the roles.

Note down any good examples of your student's language and points for error correction or improvement. Come back to these later. Praise any good examples of language used and go over any errors, including pronunciation.

Don't dominate the conversation in the tasks, but say enough to keep your student going. You could record any of the activities on audio or video, if the student agrees, and use them for intensive correction work afterwards.

DVD-ROM: Case study commentary

Stage 3: Writing

- Get students to study the writing task and deal with any questions. Get them to note down information from their brainstorming sessions that should go in the summary while it is still fresh in their minds.
- Get students to look at the summarising e-mail on page 145 of the Writing file again if necessary (although the format there is not really applicable to the one they will need here, you can still use it to point out the similarities and differences). Get students to write the final summary for homework. As ever, get them to e-mail it to you if possible and go through corrections in the next lesson.

Writing file (Course Book page 145)

Resource bank: Writing (page 213)

UNIT 11 New business

AT A GLANCE

	Classwork – Course Book	Further work
Lesson 1 *Each lesson is about 60–75 minutes. This time does not include administration and time spent going through homework in any lessons.*	**Listening and discussion: Advice for start-ups** Students discuss their entrepreneurial potential, listen to an expert on start-ups, and work on related language.	**Practice File** Word power (pages 64–65) **Resource bank: Listening** (page 199) **i-Glossary** (DVD-ROM)
Lesson 2	**Reading and language:** ***Go the distance with a one-trick pony / Work longer, work older*** Students read about the difficulty of starting a new company with a single product, work on entrepreneurial language, and put it to work in discussing entrepreneurship.	**Text bank** (pages 158–161) **Practice File** Text and grammar (pages 66–67) **ML Grammar and Usage**
Lesson 3	**Business skills: Chasing payment** Students look at one of the key problems of small businesses. They listen to a phone call between a supplier and a customer about a payment, look at tips on reducing late payments, do a role play and write a follow-up e-mail.	**Resource bank: Speaking** (page 187) **Practice File** Skills and pronunciation (pages 68–69)
Lesson 4	**Case study: Healthy growth for OTC Tech** A start-up making diagnostic test kits is looking for ways to grow its business. Students, as directors of the company, suggest ways to do this, and then role-play a negotiation between the company and a potential retailer.	**Case study commentary** (DVD-ROM) **Resource bank: Writing** (page 214)

For a fast route through the unit, focusing mainly on speaking skills, just use the underlined sections.

For one-to-one situations, most parts of the unit lend themselves, with minimal adaptation, to use with individual students. Where this is not the case, alternative procedures are given.

BUSINESS BRIEF

The success of *Dragons' Den*, a TV format seen around the world where **budding entrepreneurs** submit their sometimes no-hope ideas to a bunch of ruthless investors, is testimony to the interest that many people have in becoming their own boss. More than half of start-ups are out of business after a year, and nearly all after five years. **Drive** and **determination** may not be enough, but this does not discourage people from trying, especially where there is a **can-do culture** that encourages entrepreneurs, which, even within Europe, is a very variable factor. (More dream of being civil servants than entrepreneurs.) **Acceptance of failure** is the other side of this coin, and the US is famous for being very tolerant in this regard, where other cultures confer **stigma** on it.

The ease with which you can start your own business is a concern of many governments, who rightly see this as part of the process of encouraging change in public attitudes to entrepreneurship. There are interesting lists on the Internet of the level of **red tape** in different countries: how many days it takes, typically, to start a business; how many forms there are to fill in and different authorities to inform. Many governments have streamlined the process to the point where it can all be done **online** (and perhaps with a good **accountant**) at a **one-stop shop** (or website) – this is a measure of their **business-friendliness**. Countries compete in league tables as the **'best to do business in'**, but it's rarely specified whether this refers to multinationals or one-person start-ups. Some countries are great for one but not the other.

A new business needs to offer an **innovation** – a new product or service – or to be able to do something that already exists better or more cheaply than before. An inventor might **tout their idea** round established companies, but they risk having their idea **stolen**, even if they have **patented** it, as large organisations have vast resources for **litigation**, unlike most entrepreneurs.

Investment can come from **backers** of various kinds. In the current climate, a large enough **bank loan** is not always available, so entrepreneurs might go to **business angels** or **venture capitalists**, both experienced in putting money into business ideas, knowing that many will lose money but that some could make a lot. These backers will bring **expertise** that an independent entrepreneur will not have – in evaluating **business plans**, and then in **market research, marketing, operations** and in **sustaining innovation** so as to go beyond the **initial**, usually **single, product**.

Some people are **serial entrepreneurs**, starting up a series of businesses, perhaps funded by the previous ones. But once the businesses reach a certain size, they may prefer to take their profit by selling and move on to the next one. It's true that once businesses reach a certain size and **mature**, they need a different type of **business acumen**, one which mercurial entrepreneurs may not possess. For example, perhaps they are unwilling or unable to work further on **team building** and **recruitment**, and deal with all the hassles of human resources management. This is just one of the management areas that a start-up specialist might prefer to leave to someone else. Beyond that might come the rigours of an **initial public offer (IPO), floating the company on the stock market** so as to be able to tap new **sources of capital**. (Some entrepreneurs, like Richard Branson, go through all this but then decide to **take their companies private** again, so as to have, in their view, more control of events.)

New business and your students

Students might know about the businesses of family members. Your in-work students could talk about the businesses that people in their industry typically start up if they leave their employers (for example, consultancies). Ask them to talk about businesses like this that they have heard about, perhaps ones they themselves might have had in the past before joining their current organisation. However, be tactful about past business failures! (See above.)

In this age of 20-something billionaires, your pre-work students might already have business plans, perhaps Internet-based. Ask your students to talk about them, but don't be surprised if the real entrepreneurs don't want to say too much about them.

Read on

Rachel Bridge: *How to make a million before lunch*, Virgin Books, 2010

Alexander Osterwalder, Yves Pigneur: *Business model generation: A handbook for visionaries, game changers, and challengers*, Wiley, 2010

Philip A Wickham: *Strategic entrepreneurship*, Financial Times / Prentice Hall, 2006

Sara Williams: *The Financial Times guide to business start-up*, FT / Prentice Hall, 2010

LESSON NOTES

Warmer

- Ask students if any of them would one day like to start a business. If so, what businesses would they start? If not, why not? Discuss this briefly, but don't pre-empt the rest of this unit too much.

Overview

- Go through the overview panel at the beginning of the unit, pointing out the sections that students will be looking at.

Quotation

- Get students to say what they think of the quotation. (It would be difficult to argue with it. You could point out how, when they open, the shops of many first-time-shopkeepers seem to reflect the personal tastes and interests of their owners, rather than being based on any business plan or rationale. These shops tend not to last very long.)

Listening and discussion: Advice for start-ups

Students discuss their entrepreneurial potential, listen to an expert on start-ups and work on related language.

A

- Explain the task and get students to do it in pairs. Circulate, monitor and assist if necessary, but don't interrupt if pairs are functioning acceptably.
- When they have finished, get them to check their score by looking at page 154. (The scoring system is reproduced below for convenience.)
- Then, with the whole class, get students to say what their scores were and the conclusions that they draw from this. Compare and contrast students' answers, but be tactful with the non-entrepreneurial!

Count up the number of questions that you answered 'yes' to.

0–3 Although you might like the idea of setting up your own business, it's not really for you. You are much better off working for someone else and wouldn't be able to handle the risk or uncertainty. Who wants to work 24/7 anyway?

4–6 You probably have lots of initiative and good ideas, but remember you need to be fully committed before getting a business venture off the ground. You may need to work more on your entrepreneurial business skills or getting hold of some risk capital.

7–9 You are a serial entrepreneur in the making. Make sure you find a good mentor or a suitable business partner, and work on your sales pitch. If you haven't started your own company yet, what are you waiting for? Go for it!

B – C

- Get students to continue to work in pairs on the matching task in Exercise B.
- When pairs have finished, get students to give the answers, and, above all, use them as a basis for discussion about skills that students already have, or would like to develop.

Exercise B

1 e **2** c **3** d **4** a **5** b

Other key business skills (suggested answers)

- Business planning
- Assessing the strengths and weaknesses of your business and planning accordingly
- Marketing skills
- Setting up and overseeing sales and marketing operations, analysing markets, identifying selling points for your product and following these through to market
- CRM (customer relationship management: see Unit 4)
- Managing your relationship with customers and keeping them happy; managing customer data and adapting your products, services and delivery accordingly

- Get students, still in their pairs, to work on Exercise C, and then discuss their answers with the whole class. (Again, the information from the Course Book is reproduced below for convenience.)

The entrepreneurial quality check

1. **Self-confidence**
   A self-belief and passion about your product or service – your enthusiasm should win people over to your ideas.
2. **Self-determination**
   A belief that the outcome of events is down to your own actions, rather than external factors or other people's actions
3. **Being a self-starter**
   The ability to be resourceful and take the initiative; also to be able to work independently and develop your ideas
4. **Judgement**
   The ability to be open-minded when listening to other people's advice, while bearing in mind your objectives for the business
5. **Commitment**
   The willingness to make personal sacrifices through long hours and loss of leisure time
6. **Perseverance**
   The ability to continue despite setbacks, financial insecurity and risk

- Work on any difficulties, e.g. the stress of *perseverance*.

D – F CD3.28–3.30

- Students listen to Mike Southon, an expert in starting new businesses. (He writes a regular column for the FT. His site is at www.mikesouthon.com.)
- Get students to look at the question in Exercise D. Then play the recording and get a student to give the answer.

Exercise D

Mike says there are basically two types of start-ups. One solves a problem or brings new services to a local area. This is usually a services business, a physical business, for example a plumbing firm or accounting company. The other type of start-up is an Internet business, selling information or products from a website.

- Go through the points in Exercise E and work on any difficulties. (For point 4, you could teach the expression *when the going gets tough, the tough get going*.)
- Play the recording and elicit the answers.

Exercise E

Classic mistakes that Mike mentions are:

2 Spending too much time developing your products/ services

3 Not having a good team

6 Not finding customers

- Then focus attention on the three questions in Exercise F and play the recording.
- Elicit the answers.

Exercise F

1 A mentor is somebody who can give you good advice and is probably somebody you know, maybe a family friend and who's got some business experience and contacts. He recommends getting a good mentor firstly, to test your idea and give you advice on how to improve your product or service, or how to get customers and secondly, to make contacts for you and open doors for you.

2 An elevator pitch* is being able to sell your idea to a potential customer or investor (in one or two minutes). A good pitch should include the five Ps:
- Pain: Where is the pain or problem that you solve?
- Premise: What does your business actually do?
- People: What makes your people better than somebody else's people?
- Proof: You have to have some proof (that you have a good business idea), and the best proof is some happy customers that you can direct potential customers to.
- Purpose: What is the purpose of your business?

3 The first purpose of a business is to make money; the second purpose is why you are doing this business and not something else, e.g. Are you making the world a better place? Are you having fun?

* If students ask, point out that *elevator* is AmE, but *elevator pitch* is used everywhere. No BrE speaker would say *lift pitch*!

- As ever, discuss the answers with your students. What do they think, for example, of the idea that having fun is a key part of starting a new business?

G

- Depending on time and interest, discuss these points in pairs or with the whole class. (Refer back, where appropriate, to the ideas that students came up with in the Warmer.)
- When most pairs have finished, call the class to order and compare and contrast pairs' findings (if you did the activity in pairs).
- Note that there are no 'right answers' for many of the points in question 3. It would often depend on the type of business. However, it's hard to envisage situations where knowing about potential customers and the competition would be disadvantageous.

Resource bank: Listening (page 199)

Students can watch the interview with Mike Southon on the DVD-ROM.

i-Glossary

Reading and language: *Go the distance with a one-trick pony / Work longer, work older*

Students read about the difficulty of starting a new company with a single product, work on entrepreneurial language, and put it to work in discussing entrepreneurship.

A

- With the whole class, discuss the questions. If students (and you yourself!) are not sure of the answer to the second question, tell them they will find it in the article they are going to read. Maintain the suspense by not giving it away now.

B

- Get students to read through the questions and anticipate some of the answers before reading the article, for example if they already know what a *one-trick pony* is.
- Then get them to read the article individually or in pairs. Circulate, monitor and assist if necessary, but don't interrupt the individuals or pairs if they are functioning acceptably.
- Call the class to order and elicit the answers.

1 *A one-trick pony* (informal) is a person or thing considered as being limited to only one single talent, capability or quality. In the article, it means a business with a single product for sale.

2 The most challenging task for start-ups is finding a buyer/customer; for more established businesses, it's getting paid.

3 Mandy Haberman's Anywayup Cup's is unique because it's a child's cup that you can hold anyway up but it won't spill. It's been very successful, as it is sold worldwide, generating annual sales of about £40m, and is now what's known as a mature product.

4 By accident by attending a trade fair: Haberman meant to attend a show called The Nursery Fair, but booked one called Nursery World that was aimed at childcare providers and nursery managers. She owes part of her success to luck because her initial error actually put her into contact with customers who were eager to buy her product in large volumes.

5 Her selling tip is to try and find something that will grab someone's attention. (It is very hard to get a meeting with buyers at large retailers – and even harder to achieve a deal.)

- Explain any difficulties and discuss the answers. For example, have students had experiences where making a mistake was a good thing in the long run?

C – E

- Get students to continue working on the exercises individually or in pairs, explaining any difficulties, and stopping after each exercise to elicit the answers and discuss them.
- Work on any other expressions that students might have trouble with. For example, *a complete cock-up* (line 35): something that has been totally spoiled by someone's stupid mistake (informal); *netting* her up to about £1m a year (line 49): earning a particular amount of money as a profit after tax (informal).

Exercise C

1 b **2** a **3** a **4** b **5** a **6** a

Exercise D

Suggested answer

The lessons to be learnt from Mandy Haberman's experience of starting a business are that you need an innovative product, but also a certain amount of luck; also a great deal of determination and an unusual idea that will grab the attention of buyers.

Exercise E

Suggested answer

Olderpreneurs are older people who are starting a business. A recent study says that one in six Britons aged 46–65 hopes to embark on a new business venture rather than retire.

F

- Get students to look at the Language reference section on cleft sentences on page 139 of the Course Book and talk them through the information there.
- Then get them to do this exercise in pairs. Circulate, monitor and assist if necessary, but don't interrupt the pairs if they are functioning acceptably.

- Call the class to order and elicit the answers, referring students back to page 139 if necessary.

1 'It wasn't that he wasn't interested. It was just that he didn't talk a number that was acceptable.'
2 'What I find interesting – and what could change the face of business – is that they may prefer to do that working for themselves.'
3 It was then that she realised she had to find something that would grab someone's attention.
4 What Mandy did next was to go to see the buyer of a larger retailer.
5 It is the motto 'If at first you don't succeed, try, try again' that has a particular resonance for many entrepreneurs.
6 It was Billy Wilder, the Hollywood director, who said, 'Trust your own instinct. Your mistakes might as well be your own, instead of someone else's.'

The sentences are cleft sentences, where the information which could be given in one clause is divided into two parts, each with its own verb. Writers use this device to be more emphatic, e.g.

It wasn't that he wasn't interested. It was just that he didn't talk a number that was acceptable. (It cleft sentences with two verbs.)

(He was interested. But he didn't talk a number that was acceptable.)

What Mandy did next was go to see a buyer of a larger retailer. (*wh-* cleft sentence)

(Mandy next went to see a buyer of a larger retailer.)

What I find interesting [...] is that they may prefer to do that working for themselves. (*wh-* cleft sentence where *what* means 'the thing that')

(I find it interesting that they may prefer to do that working for themselves.)

G

- Depending on remaining time and interest, discuss the questions with the whole class or get students to discuss them in pairs and report back. (Don't push students aged 20 too hard when you ask them what they will be doing at 65!)

Text bank (pages 158–161)

Business skills: Chasing payment

Students look at one of the key problems of small businesses. They listen to a phone call between a supplier and a customer about a payment, look at tips on reducing late payments, work on a role play and write a follow-up e-mail.

A CD3.31

- Ask in-work students in companies if late payment and suppliers' invoices containing mistakes is a problem in their organisation, as far as they know. Then play the recording and elicit the answer.

Dunbarry Jewellers appears to have made a mistake in an invoice and billed Carswell Department Stores for 300 instead of 260 items.

B

- Get students to look through and complete the tips in pairs. Circulate, monitor and assist if necessary, but don't interrupt the pairs if they are functioning acceptably.
- Call the class to order, elicit the answers and discuss them, in relation to students' own contexts. (For example, they might not agree with the advice on use of first names, even in some European cultures. Also, the advice might not work – if someone doesn't want to pay, they won't pay.)

1 (first) name **2** relationship **3** numbers
4 paperwork/documents/documentation **5** show/indicate
6 person/speaker/caller/customer/client **7** understood
8 details/information **9** action **10** deadline

Other possible tips:

- Stay calm, polite and professional.
- Confirm what has been agreed in a follow-up e-mail.
- Offer some form of compensation if appropriate.

C CD3.31

- Play the recording again and get students to suggest ways for Val and Max to improve their approaches.

Suggested answers

Max doesn't have all the paperwork in front of him and seems disorganised, so he should prepare better.

Val shows she is listening closely by restating and checking the details, which is good, but she doesn't apologise or empathise with Max's problem, nor does she confirm Max's phone number, so she should work on these aspects.

D

- With the whole class, read the tips and get students to comment on and add to them. (Work also on the expressions in this area, e.g. *run credit checks*, *chase payment* and *withhold payment*.)
- Ask about charging interest on late payments. Is this possible in students' countries?

Suggested answers

Run credit checks on all new non-cash customers.

Offer discounts to customers who pay their bills rapidly.

Chase payment promptly (or you will be behind others creditors in the queue).

Find out if the customer is having cashflow problems and offer to let them pay in instalments if necessary.

Ask customers to make deposit payments at the time orders are taken.

Issue invoices promptly and follow up immediately if payments are slow in coming.

Track accounts to identify and avoid slow-paying customers.

Adopt a policy of cash on delivery (c.o.d.) as an alternative to refusing to do business with slow-paying customers.

Charge interest on the overdue amount (not possible in all countries).

Threaten the late payer with legal action (worst-case scenario).

E – **F** CD3.32

- Explain the task in Exercise E, play the recording and elicit and discuss the answers.
- Then get students to look through the expressions in the Useful language box, practising natural intonation. Explain any difficulties.
- Then play the recording again and get them to tick the expressions that they hear.
- Explain any remaining difficulties.

Exercise E

Max agrees to settle the invoice for 28 May this week. He also agrees to pay the other invoice within 15 days. Val will contact Max again on 30 July if she hasn't received both payments.

Exercise F

Chasing payment

I'm phoning about the outstanding payments on ...

I/We (also) sent you an e-mail reminder on ...

As you know, our credit terms are 30 days.

Payment is now (well/way) overdue on ...

Reaching agreement

Would that be acceptable?

I think we can work with that.

Confirming follow-up action

Can/Could you tell me when that will be?

I'll get back to you when/if/at/on ...

Being firm but polite

I'm sorry, (but) we'd like/expect/want ...

(Given the situation), we'll have to consider ...

Other useful expressions

I'll authorise payment as soon as possible. (*Chasing payment*)

Look, I'm sure we can sort this out ... I can make an exception and ... (*Reaching agreement*)

We would prefer payment of the other outstanding invoice within ... (*Chasing payment/Being firm but polite*)

G

- Students role-play a phone call about late payments. Explain the task, divide the class into 'new' pairs if possible and allocate the roles. Get students to turn to their respective pages and give them time to absorb the information.
- When ready, tell them to sit back to back and start their phone conversations. Circulate, monitor and assist if necessary, but don't interrupt the pairs if they are functioning acceptably.
- Note good points of language use in relation to the topic of this section, as well as half a dozen points that need further work, and add these on one side of the board.
- Call the class to order. Praise good use of language that you heard in the activity, and work on the points on the board, getting individual students to say the right thing.
- Get one or two of the pairs to give public performances of their conversations, ensuring that they integrate your suggestions for language improvement.

Resource bank: Speaking (page 187)

H

- Students could start this writing task in class and finish it for homework. Tell them they should look at the e-mail models on page 143. As ever, get them to e-mail their work to you and give feedback in the next lesson.

Suggested answer

Dear Mr Bryson

I am writing to inform you that, despite earlier requests for payment, invoices no. BJ1728 for €2,915, dated 13 June, and BJ1735 for €2,670, dated 22 June, remain unpaid. Please find attached copies of the invoices for your information. As you know, our agreed payment terms are 30 days from date of invoice.

In view of our good commercial relationship in the past, we would like to resolve this matter amicably. We ask that you settle this account within five working days. In the event that you have already paid these invoices, please ignore this reminder.

If there is a problem with our goods which has caused you to withhold payment, please contact me immediately at the telephone number below, so that we can resolve the issue.

Should you fail to pay this invoice by the stated date, then we may have no alternative but to review your account with us, which means that we will no longer be able to supply your company with our jewellery.*

Best regards,

* If students ask, tell them that this is the BrE form of AmE *jewelry*.

Writing file (Course Book page 143)

CASE STUDY

Healthy growth for OTC Tech

A start-up making diagnostic test kits is looking for ways to grow its business. Students, as directors of the company, suggest ways to do this, then role-play a negotiation between the company and a potential retailer.

Stage 1: Background, Listening and Task 1

- Explain the subject of the case study (see above). Tell students to look at the device on page 111 to give them a concrete idea of what OTC Tech wants to make.
- Get students to read the background individually, or get a student to read it aloud.
- Elicit information from students to complete the table below, in the usual way.

Company	OTC Tech
Founders	Anders Larsen (engineer), Ulla Hofmann (research chemist in pharma*)
Based in	Copenhagen, Denmark
Rationale	Avoid the three-week rigmarole when doing blood tests and waiting for results
Products	Easy-to-use home diagnostic kits, incl. ones for cholesterol, diabetes and allergy testing

* Point out this spoken and written abbreviation for the adjective *pharmaceutical* and the noun *pharmaceuticals*.

- Books closed, get one or two students to rephrase the above information in their own words.
- Books open again, get students to look at the question under the background information and elicit possible answers.

- Regulatory approval needed in different countries before products can be sold
- Unwillingness of people to test themselves, wanting to rely on the medical profession (Ask students if they would use these products themselves.)
- Ease or otherwise of using tests
- False positives and negatives (showing you have a problem when you don't, and vice versa)
- Lawsuits from doctors and patients if the above happens
- Competition, actual and potential

Students may suggest more.

CD3.33

- Get students to look through the three questions. Explain the task, play the recording, stopping where necessary to give time to students to make notes, and elicit and discuss the answers.

1 Not very effectively. Most people in target EU markets have never heard of the products, and the instructions for use were too long and complicated.
2 Suggested improvements: make the instructions for use simpler and more user-friendly; provide support on the website; carry out some publicity, e.g. a launch event to create greater impact and promote for the products; find ways to get customers to want to buy more, or take customers from competitors, or attract new customers, or preferably all three; try to get pharmacies and shops to display the products more prominently, such as on the counter.
3 No, they need to hire someone with suitable marketing expertise.

- Get students to look at Task 1. Quickly run through points 1–8 in the report and explain any difficulties.
- Divide the class into groups of four directors (the directors' functions are not and don't need to be specified, but appoint someone in each group to take notes), and start the discussion.
- Underline the instruction about pros and cons of the suggestions, and whether they are high or low risk.
- Circulate, monitor and assist if necessary, but don't interrupt the groups if they are functioning acceptably.
- Note good points of language use, as well as half a dozen points that need further work, and add these on one side of the board.
- When most groups have finished, get the note-takers from several groups to say what they decided for each option. Compare and contrast ideas from different groups.
- Praise good use of language that you heard in the activity, and work on the points on the board, getting individual students to say the right thing.

Suggested answers

Risk level of the options and some points to consider

1 low risk: Experts say it's best to keep sight of a company's core competency and make sure all expansion radiates from it. If a company strays far from what it does very well, it can be very risky.
2 low risk: Although in future the product range may have no significant gaps, and a new strategy will be needed. Another risk is if competitors start a price war.
3 higher risk: See option 1. It is outside their field of expertise and could be expensive and more risky, especially the investment required in high-tech monitors.
4 higher risk: High spending levels are essential in this sector, but this brings higher risk. On the other hand, collaboration with a university or hospital research facilities will increase the company's prestige, expertise and network of contacts.
5 low risk: Expanding sales channels is a good option. A basic website can be developed into a fully functional e-commerce, marketing and customer-support site. It can both help grow sales in the EU and help OTC Tech expand into overseas markets.
6 higher risk: Running a business overseas will mean appointing a reliable manager to oversee the set up and running of the operation. The laws, regulations, bureaucracy, sales processes and ways of doing business could all be very different.
7 higher risk: Similar issues to option 6; also quality control is an important consideration.
8 higher risk: Finding a suitable partner and trying to work together can be stressful.

Stage 2: Listening and Task 2

CD3.34

- Get students to listen to the recording and take notes.
- Elicit a summary of the radio report from different students, based on their notes.
- Explain any difficulties and underline the importance of getting approval from the all-powerful FDA in the US to be able to sell products there.
- Explain the task, divide the class into pairs and get them to look at the correct pages. Give students time to absorb the information.
- When ready, get students to start the task. Circulate, monitor and assist if necessary, but don't interrupt the pairs if they are functioning acceptably.
- Note good points of language use, as well as half a dozen points that need further work, and add these on one side of the board.
- When most groups have finished, get some of the pairs to say what they happened in their negotiations. Compare and contrast outcomes from different groups.
- Praise good use of language that you heard in the activity, and work on the points on the board, getting individual students to say the right thing.

One-to-one

Go through the information in the Course Book with your student. Explain any difficulties.

Get your student to role-play one of the directors in Task 1, with you playing another.

Task 2 can be done with you as Student A and your student as B. If there is time and interest, you could reverse the roles and do the task (or parts of it) a second time.

Note down any good examples of your student's language and points for error correction or improvement. Come back to these later. Praise any good examples of language used and go over any errors, including pronunciation.

Don't dominate the conversation in the tasks, but say enough to keep them going. You could record any of the activities on audio or video, if the student agrees, and use them for intensive correction work afterwards.

DVD-ROM: Case study commentary

Stage 3: Writing

- Get students to study the writing task and deal with any questions. Get them to note down information from their brainstorming sessions that should go in the summary while it is still fresh in their minds.
- Get students to look at the model on page 145 of the Writing file again if necessary (though the format of e-mails like this should be very familiar by now). Get students to write the e-mail for homework. As ever, get them to e-mail it to you if possible and go through corrections in the next lesson.

➡ Writing file (Course book page 145)

➡ Resource bank: Writing (page 214)

AT A GLANCE

UNIT 12 Project management

AT A GLANCE

	Classwork – Course Book	Further work
Lesson 1 *Each lesson is about 60–75 minutes. This time does not include administration and time spent going through homework in any lessons.*	**Listening and discussion: Issues in project management** Students discuss project management, listen to managers talking about the qualities required for it, and listen to an expert talking about what makes for a successful project.	**Practice File** Word power (pages 70–71) **Resource bank: Listening** (page 200) **i-Glossary** (DVD-ROM)
Lesson 2	**Reading and language:** ***Fine-tune your project schedule*** Students discuss statements about delegation, read an article about project management, work on related language and give a short presentation.	**Text bank** (pages 162–165) **Practice File** Text and grammar (pages 72–73) **ML Grammar and Usage**
Lesson 3	**Business skills: Teleconferencing** Students look at tips for teleconferencing, listen to some teleconference extracts, study the language for teleconferencing, and put it to work in role plays.	**Resource bank: Speaking** (page 188) **Practice File** Skills and pronunciation (pages 74–75)
Lesson 4	**Case study: Creating a world-class port** An international consortium is developing a major port in India, but the project has hit troubled waters. Students role-play participants in the project and suggest solutions to the impasse.	**Case study commentary** (DVD-ROM) **Resource bank: Writing** (page 215)

For a fast route through the unit, focusing mainly on speaking skills, just use the underlined sections.

For one-to-one situations, most parts of the unit lend themselves, with minimal adaptation, to use with individual students. Where this is not the case, alternative procedures are given.

BUSINESS BRIEF

In 1961, John F. Kennedy promised to put a man on the moon 'before this decade is out' and that is what happened – there was no **slippage**. Less well known is the fact that the project had a budget of $7 billion, but that the final cost was $25.4 billion (in 1970 dollars) – it was 260 per cent **over budget**. Think also of massive civil-engineering projects, such as the one to build the tunnel under the English Channel, often way **over budget** and **behind schedule**. However, the **final achievement** makes it all seem worth it. **Underestimation** of the time and money required for projects seems to be a necessary part of them getting accepted in the first place.

Being a project manager requires a special form of leadership and the ability to **juggle priorities** and **multi-task** – to be good at **parallel processing**. **Constituting a project team** requires skill in itself, finding people with **complementary skills**; but team members will often be unknown to the leader before the project starts and sent by the head of the department where they work, rather than chosen by the project manager. When people come from different departments in an organisation, there may well be a **political dimension**, and when they come from different companies, for example working on **joint ventures**, there will inevitably be conflict and misunderstandings due to their different **company cultures**. These will be multiplied further when the companies are from different **linguistic or cultural backgrounds**. Inevitably, different parties will have different **agendas** and **priorities**. The project manager needs to establish a **realistic schedule** and **budget**, but these will often be imposed from elsewhere.

There are four main project stages: **initiation**, **definition**, **implementation** and **completion**. When designing a **project lifecycle** process, it's important to set out the project **objectives** clearly. Various **graphic tools** and systems exist to help with project planning, such as **flow charts** and **Gantt charts**. The latter is a diagram showing **phases** and **sub-phases** of the project, indicating which of these are **sequential** (can only be done when the previous one is complete) and which are **overlapping** or able to be done **in parallel**. This chart was developed by Henry Laurence Gantt (1861–1919), an American mechanical engineer. It was 19th-century engineers who first established project management as a discipline. Even if, now, projects can be in many different areas, the tools and techniques of project management are the same. IT and the Internet mean that **project management tools** have moved on a long way from the Gantt chart. **Web-enabled project management** allows people to work on a project at any time – organisations can have **virtual project teams** with people located all over the world, using the specialities of people in different countries, for example designers in London and IT developers in Bangalore.

Project managers talk about **delivering** particular results. There will probably be **deliverables** for each phase – particular results that demonstrate **progress**, and if it can be shown that they are happening as scheduled, these will be seen as **milestones** that help people to remain **on board** and **committed to the project**. If this does not happen, and the project falls behind schedule, there may be **loss of morale**, and it may be necessary to bring in a new team leader to provide the impulse to bring the project **back on track**. There are firms and consultancies that advertise and promote their ability to come in like this and **turn round** failing projects, a business speciality in itself.

Project management and your students

A lot of business at managerial level is about the management of projects, and your in-work students should have experience of it as participants or managers. Draw on their experience as much as possible when doing this unit.

Pre-work students will be able to talk about project work they have done with others at their educational institution and the practical and psychological factors involved. This could be interesting if they are doing business studies, as this revolves more around projects than many other areas of teaching. They may also be able to talk about 'projects' with friends and family, such as holidays.

Read on

Delegating work, Harvard Business School Press, 2008

Stephen Barker, Rob Cole: *Brilliant project management: What the best project managers know, do and say,* Prentice Hall, 2009

Sebastian Nokes: *The definitive guide to project management,* Financial Times / Prentice Hall, 2007

Stanley Portney: *Project management for dummies*, Hungry Minds Inc., 2010

http://www.pmforum.org is a not-for-profit resource that gives information on international project management affairs.

LESSON NOTES

Warmer

- Prepare some or all of the sentence stems (in bold) below on a PowerPoint slide or an overhead transparency, or dictate them to students. Deal with any questions. Then ask students how they could complete the sentences. Do this as a quick-fire activity.
- Read out the second half of the quotes and ask students to match them with the correct stems. Write the answers on the board one at a time and/or get students to complete the sentence stems they have written down.
  A two-year project will take three years, *a three-year project will never finish.*
  Any project can be estimated accurately *once it's been completed.*
  If it wasn't for the 'last minute', *nothing would get done.*
  The more ridiculous the deadline, *the more money will be wasted trying to meet it.*
  The sooner you get behind schedule, *the more time you have to make it up.*
  What is not on paper *has not been said.*
  When all's said and done, *a lot more is said than done.*
  Everyone asks for a strong project manager *– when they get one, they don't want her.*
  (from http://en.wikiquote.org/wiki/ Project_management)
- Ask students for their reactions to the quotes. Do they think there is an element of truth in any of these or not? What has been their own experience of working to deadlines? What tasks do they tend to leave until the last minute?

Overview

- Go through the overview panel at the beginning of the unit, pointing out the sections that students will be looking at.

Quotation

- Get students to say what they think of the quotation, and ask them to recount their experiences in this area. Do they think it is a realistic or cynical view of project management?

Listening and discussion: Issues in project management

Students discuss project management, listen to managers talking about the qualities required for it, and listen to an expert talking about what makes for a successful project.

A

- Discuss these two questions with the whole class. With pre-work students, adapt the activity: they could talk about project work they have done with others at their educational institution, or 'projects' with friends and family, such as holidays.

Keeping the project to schedule; budgeting and making sure the project doesn't go over budget; delegating tasks; planning tasks that may be happening at the same time or overlapping; knowing how to create and use a Gantt chart*; communicating project aims to a variety of people; etc.

* See Business brief above. Students can look at the entries for him and his chart on Wikipedia if they are interested.

B CD3.35

- Get students to look at the instruction and to anticipate what words might go in the gaps. If necessary, remind students that each gap needs between one and four words.
- Then play the recording, stopping at convenient points, elicit the answers, and, as ever and above all, discuss them in the light of students' own experiences.

Suggested answers

1 roles (in the team) **2** acting like a boss / giving orders
3 decision-making process **4** delegate **5** multi-tasking
6 big/whole picture **7** directing/motivating
8 goals/aims (of the project)

C

- Explain the task, work on any of the items in the box that require this (e.g. BrE pronunciation of *scheduling* is 'sheduling' and AmE 'skeduling'; the fact that *criteria* is the plural form of *criterion*), and get students to work on it in pairs. Circulate, monitor and assist if necessary, but don't interrupt the pairs if they are functioning acceptably.
- When most pairs have finished, call the class to order and elicit and discuss the answers.

1 Aim of the project **2** Outputs **3** Quality criteria
5 Management structure **7** Tolerances
8 Dependencies **9** Risks **10** Scheduling

D – **E** CD3.36, 3.37

- Introduce Tom Taylor and get students to focus on the three questions in Exercise D.
- Play each part of the recording, stopping at convenient points, and elicit the answers to both exercises and discuss them.

Exercise D

Suggested answers

1. Tom Taylor says a successful project is one that is on time, on budget and to performance, but is often something else. (Other people also use the terms *to scope* or *to quality*.)
2. A wedding and a power station
3. A wedding: to be on time, on budget, to performance: they get married – but it is not enough. The stakeholders/ interested parties might have other criteria, e.g. *We'd like a nice day, we'd like some nice photographs or a video, or we'd like everyone who should come to arrive.*
   A power station: to be on time, on budget, to performance, but also other criteria are important, such as, *We'd like it to be safe, we'd like it to have minimum environmental impact* and *We'd like it to last for 50 years.*

Exercise E

Tom Taylor mentions the following issues:

c) *tight budgets*
i) *value for money requirements*
e) *needing things to be delivered on time, maybe not just at the end of the project but at stages during the project*)
j) *The best use of technology, technology appropriate to the project*
f) *sustainability, the environment and green issues*
h) *dealing with people ... you can't project-manage from behind a computer*

F

- Get students to work on this in pairs. Circulate, monitor and assist if necessary, but don't interrupt the pairs if they are functioning acceptably.
- Note good points of language use, especially in relation to project management, as well as half a dozen points that need further work, and add these on one side of the board.

- When most pairs have finished, call the class to order and praise good use of language that you heard in the activity, and work on the points on the board, getting individual students to say the right thing. Elicit and discuss the answers.

Resource bank: Listening (page 200)

Students can watch the interview with Tom Taylor on the DVD-ROM.

i-Glossary

Reading and language: *Fine-tune your project schedule*

Students discuss statements about delegation, read an article about project management, work on related language and give a short presentation.

A

- As an introduction to this area, ask students for examples of workload 'nightmares' they have had. Pre-work students might talk about finishing essays at 4 a.m. In-work students might talk about intolerable pressures that they have been under at work.
- Move on to the subject of delegation. Work on the associated language: You *delegate* work to people in a process of *delegation*, but the people you delegate to are not, in this context, *delegates* – you can only refer to them as *the people I've delegated [this task, etc.] to*.
- Ask students whether delegation is always a good thing, and ask if they have expressions in their own language(s) that are equivalent to *If you want something done, do it yourself.*

B

- Get students to discuss these points in pairs. Circulate, monitor and assist if necessary, but don't interrupt the pairs if they are functioning acceptably.
- Call the class to order and elicit and discuss the answers, but don't pre-empt the discussion you will have after they have read the article.

C

- Get students to read the article, individually or in pairs, to see what it says about the points in Exercise B.
- Again, circulate, monitor and assist if necessary, but don't interrupt the students if they are functioning acceptably.

Suggested answers

1 One ~~minor~~ **major/important** aspect of project planning is knowing which tasks are dependent on one other.
Identify the task dependencies. Some tasks cannot start until prior tasks are finished. Obviously, you can't install a roof over a house with no walls. (lines 58–62)

2 ~~Project managers~~ **Clients** often set their expectations too high and ~~clients~~ **project managers** complain timelines are unrealistic.
One of the most common problems that project managers weep about is 'unrealistic timelines', a common consequence of clients having set their expectations too high. (lines 5–9)

3 Periods of non-productivity or inactivity are ~~unacceptable at any time during a project~~ **a normal phenomenon in project schedules.**
Managers tend to remove it from the schedule to impress their bosses or clients. ... accept the fact that slack times are a normal phenomenon in project schedules. (lines 79–87)

4 ~~All team members should work however many hours it might take~~ **Key team members should work longer hours** on crucial tasks.
Also, make sure you are not over-assigning critical tasks to your best team member. It is mindless to assume that your best resource can work 16 hours a day for three weeks. (lines 110–115)

5 One way of speeding up a project is getting more than one person to work on a critical task at the same time.
You can put two people to work in parallel and have the task completed in half the time. (lines 105–107)

6 By focusing on key tasks, a project manager can ensure the project is delivered on time or is finished ahead of schedule.
... focus your attention on the critical path. When the critical path is shortened, the project is finished early. When the critical path is maintained, the project is finished on time. When the critical path is extended, the project is delayed. (lines 30–37)

7 The project manager's aim should be to complete the project as soon as possible without compromising ~~the original schedule~~ **its scope and the quality.**
... the project manager's objective is to create the shortest schedule possible without sacrificing its scope and quality. (lines 24–27)

D – F

- Get students to work on these exercises individually or in pairs.
- Call the class to order and elicit and discuss the answers when they have finished each exercise.

Exercise D

1 fine-tuning* **2** scope **3** For one **4** Chances are
5 mindless **6** clouds **7** shout foul **8** slack **9** weep
10 over-assigning **11** idly

Exercise E

a) Words like *weep* and *idly* are more formal and literary.

b) *For one* (also *For starters* in the text), *Chances are* and *shout foul* are more informal or colloquial expressions that are usually spoken.

c) The other items are 'neutral' and can be used in any context. *Resource* is also more formal than *person* – both are used in the text.

The writer probably uses this mix of formal and informal vocabulary and grammatical forms because although it is an instructive article, he wants the information to be accessible to the reader and he is sometimes being humorous or ironic. The article is also written for reading on a website rather than for a formal academic paper or report.

Exercise F

1 Gives definitions
The basic foundation of managing a project is creating an efficient and realistic project schedule. (lines 17–19)
Slack time, as the name implies, is the time when ... (lines 76–77)
The role of a manager is to identify and minimise them. (lines 87–89)

2 Illustrates points with examples
For starters, accept the fact that slack times are a normal phenomenon ... (lines 85–87)
For one, do not crash tasks that are strictly interdependent on one another, such as applying a second coat of paint. (lines 97–100)

3 Uses imperative forms

Make a list of tasks first. (line 53)

Do not put them directly into the Gantt chart ... (lines 53–55)

Don't try to schedule putting on the roof and building walls in parallel. (lines 66–68)

Identify your critical path(s). (line 69)

... accept the fact that slack times are a normal phenomenon ... (lines 85–87)

... do not crash tasks that are strictly interdependent on one another ... (lines 97–99)

... make sure you assess the risks. Also, make sure you are not over-assigning critical tasks to your best team member. (lines 110–113)

4 Exaggerates for dramatic or humorous effect

Does the project manager shout foul and blame other people? (lines 13–14)

Obviously, you can't install a roof over a house with no walls. (lines 60–62)

Don't try to schedule putting on the roof and building walls in parallel. (lines 66–68)

5 Repeats certain grammatical forms

When the critical path is shortened, the project is finished early. When the critical path is maintained, the project is finished on time. When the critical path is extended, the project is delayed. (lines 32–37) (conditional sentences with *when* and passive forms)

You can put two people to work in parallel and have the task completed in half the time. Or you can assign a more productive resource who can finish the work earlier. (lines 105–109) (modal verb *can*)

* Point out that this is used for cars, machines, etc. When referring to musical instruments, the expression is just *tuning*.

G

- Get students to prepare their presentation in pairs. For this task, PowerPoint is probably not necessary. Tell students that presentations should be snappy and, if they like, funny. (But don't forget strictures on the non-transference of humour between cultures – if you have a multicultural class, this might be an interesting test case!)
- These should be short, fun presentations – students can experiment with using humour and irony. Here are a few alternative topics to those in the Course Book:
  How (not) to get on with the project manager
  How (not) to create a Gantt chart
  How (not) to install new software
  How (not) to change a computer network
  How (not) to build a house
  How to paint your house/flat
  How to play jazz / tune a violin, etc.
  How to change a car tyre
  How to organise a great party
- Circulate, monitor and assist if necessary, but don't interrupt the pairs if they are functioning acceptably.
- When pairs are ready, get one of them to give the presentation, or they can share it between them.
- As these may be the last presentations they give in the course, you could give them a break from language correction – spontaneity is key here.
- Do no more than two or three presentations, keeping the others for later classes.

➡ Text bank (pages 162–165)

Business skills: Teleconferencing

Students look at tips for teleconferencing, listen to some teleconference extracts, study the language for teleconferencing and put it to work in role plays.

- Introduce the idea of teleconferencing if it is unfamiliar: managers in different locations who participate in virtual meetings by phone. (Compare this with videoconferencing, where they also see each other.)
- Ask in-work students if they have experience of this and what they think of it, e.g. the frustration of not being able to see the other participants, the difficulty of finding a time that is suitable for people in different time zones, etc. (You could mention the annoyance of Europeans who have to stay late at work to be able to talk to people on the west coast of the US, for example.)
- With the whole class, ask students to look at the questions and discuss them. If they have no experience of teleconferencing, this will be difficult for them – in this case, talk them through the answers and move swiftly on to the next exercise.

Suggested answers

- It's even more important to be on time for a teleconference than in a face-to-face meeting.
- It's more essential that there is no background noise.
- Participants usually have to identify themselves before speaking.
- You have to address people by name when speaking to them or asking them a question because there are no visual cues. If you just ask a question or make a remark without indicating who you are speaking to, it's very difficult for other participants to know who is being addressed.
- It's important not to call from a mobile phone or on a speakerphone, because the sound quality can be bad due to static, echoes and background noise.
- Leading teleconferences is more difficult than leading a face-to-face meeting. The host needs to control the conversation more and summarise/check more often what's being said.
- It is also harder for the host to make sure everyone understands and is contributing to the discussion because of the lack of visual information.

Others features of a teleconference

- A teleconference is usually shorter and more productive, because it reduces casual conversation and allows the host to keep the meeting on track.
- It enables quick decision-making; problems can be handled quickly (with staff and clients anywhere in the world).
- Because members can't see each other, they tend not to interrupt as much as in face-to-face meetings, this also helps keep the meeting on track.

When might a teleconference not be ideal for a meeting?

There are two key situations that teleconferencing is not ideal for: negotiating and rapport-building. (A face-to-face meeting is a tried-and-tested way to create a lasting relationship between business and client, company and employee. Body language is a huge part of sensing someone's intentions, and this isn't possible via the telephone. In negotiations, such as the exchange of money or property, the physical presence of people is often required. These types of meetings are sometimes delicate and require many exchanges between participants, which is not easily done through teleconference, and also not useful in creating an atmosphere of trust.)

- As a follow-up, if students have experience of tele- and videoconferencing, they could talk about whether video conferences are any better than teleconferencing. You could also ask what sort of advanced planning is necessary for a teleconference.

Suggested answers

- Make a list of all attendees and check to see if their availability on the date and time planned.
- Contact all participants and give them the date and time of the teleconference. Be sure to specify which time zone you are referring to.
- If you are going to provide handouts and supplementary material to participants, send it early enough so that it arrives before the teleconference, and participants have time to read it and generally prepare for the meeting.
- Include a written agenda of the teleconference, and the list of participants.
- Remind participants of the telephone number and access code the day prior to the meeting, as they frequently mislay it and can't find it when needed.

B CD3.38–3.41

- Explain the task and get students to look at the questions. Then play the recordings, stopping at the end of each extract to elicit the answers.

Extract 1

1 Two of the people are late, then one of them gets cut off or leaves the telecon unexpectedly.

2 People arriving late can happen in both types of meetings, but is arguably more annoying and disruptive in teleconferences, e.g. listening to 'musak' for minutes on end.

3 Technical problems, such as getting cut off, are unique to telecons and video conferences.

Extract 2

1 Two of the people have not received the agenda in advance.

2/3 People not receiving an agenda in advance can be typical of both types of meetings, but it's even more important in teleconferences to make sure that people, who may be globally dispersed, get sent documents beforehand.

Extract 3

1 An issue that is not on the agenda is brought up for discussion, and one participant checks her e-mail half-way through the telecon.

2 People side-tracking the discussion is common in both types of meetings, and the leader has a key role to play here.

3 People checking their e-mail can be a common problem during teleconferences, because as they can't be seen, they decide to use the opportunity to 'multi-task' and do other work (e.g. check e-mail) rather than focus on the meeting.

Extract 4

1 Martha doesn't identify herself when she asks Pierre a question. A mobile phone also rings during the telecon.

2 Interruptions and background noise, such as people arriving late and mobile phones ringing, is common in both types of meetings, but arguably more disruptive to teleconferences where people have to make more of an effort to tune in to what is being said.

3 Not identifying yourself when speaking is important etiquette unique to telecons, because you can't always be sure people will recognise your voice, especially with a big group or when people don't know each other well.

C

- Do this exercise with the whole class, especially if they have no experience of teleconferencing.
- Go through the items first – point out the spelling and meaning of *roll call*, noting that this not spelled 'role call' – it just means checking who is present, like at primary school or in the army, but hopefully done in a more business-oriented way!
- Then elicit the answers and work on any difficulties.

1 take a roll call – g
2 the agenda – a
3 basic rules – f
4 an eye on – b
5 keep track of – d
6 get feedback – c
7 go over what was discussed – e

D – F CD3.42

- Get students to focus on the question in Exercise D, then play the recording, elicit the answer and discuss it.
- After that, get students to look at the language box and guess what's in the gaps, based on what they've just heard.
- Then play the recording again, and get them to focus on the expressions in order to complete the gaps in Exercise E, stopping at convenient points.
- Work on any remaining difficulties and move on to Exercise F – which expressions are most useful?

Exercise D

Suggested answers

Rachel generally does a good job. She follows the etiquette by starting with a roll call, and introducing the main objectives and agenda. She also states some ground rules, e.g. *We only have 45 minutes*. She also introduces Daniel, who is new to the group. She deals with attempts to side-track the meeting well.

The report should have been sent to everyone in well in advance of the meeting to give participants time to read it. Some students might feel that she is too brusque and doesn't allow any time for necessary small talk and relationship-building. She also says they only have 45 minutes, which puts pressure on the participants to stay focused. She deals with the turn-taking issue well, as members will often overlap in teleconferences. Everyone is good at identifying themselves when they want to speak.

Exercise E

1 roll call **2** This is **3** speaking **4** joined us **5** the items **6** a start **7** question **8** go ahead **9** after you **10** going to

Exercise F

Suggested answer

Most useful for the host of a teleconference are the expressions for moving things along, turn-taking and clarifying action points at the end of the meeting.

G

- Depending on time and interest, students can do one or both meetings, or some students could do one task and others the other.
- Ensure students know which task they are doing and allocate the roles, checking that they turn to the correct page. Check that all the Student As know that they are the host.

- With a one-to-one class or a group of two, you can ignore the separate role cards A–D, and just look at the meeting information.
- If there are more than four students per group, students can double up on the roles. You might also like to assign observers to note down any useful language used.
- Give time for students to absorb their information. Circulate, monitor and assist if necessary, but don't interrupt the groups if they are functioning acceptably.
- Tell each group to sit round a table with their backs to it, to simulate a teleconference. With a one-to-one student or a small group it may be possible to work in two separate rooms and simulate the call on phones or mobile phones, with a hands-free option. When groups are ready, the role play can begin.
- Note good points of language use in relation to teleconferencing, as well as half a dozen points that need further work, and add these on one side of the board.
- When most groups have finished, call the class to order and ask students what happened in their groups.
- Praise good use of teleconferencing language that you heard in the activity, and work on the points on the board, getting individual students to say the right thing.
- If you have time, get one of the groups to give a public performance of their teleconference, integrating the language improvements and corrections.

Resource bank: Speaking (page 188)

CASE STUDY

Creating a world-class port

An international consortium is developing a major port in India, but the project has hit troubled waters. Students role-play participants in the project and suggest solutions to the impasse.

Stage 1: Background, Report, Listening and Task 1

- Explain the subject of the case study (see above).
- Divide the class into two halves. Get one half to read, individually, the background article *A bottleneck on the road to growth* and the other half to read, also individually, the panel on Blake Ports Management.
- Prepare these two tables on the board with the headings in their left-hand columns. Then elicit information from students in each half of the class to complete them.

Country	India
Obstacles to economic development	Poor infrastructure, including ports and roads
Major projects	Delhi–Mumbai industrial corridor High-speed rail links Improved cargo-handling at ports
Resources	Trying to attract: – more private investment – management expertise in infrastructure development

Project	Raghavan port, Gujarat, western India
Development consortium	Blake–Martins: – Blake Ports Management, Australia – Martins, civil engineering firm, Denmark
Schedule and location	three phases over four years 600 acres reclaimed land
Financial structure	Gujarati Ports Authority (GPA) – *15%* Gujarati State Government – *15%* Blake–Martins – *70%* (*30*-year tenure)

- Books closed, get two students to rephrase the above information in their own words, preferably students from the half that did not originally read the relevant information.
- Then, with the whole class, get students to anticipate the delays the project might encounter.

Suggested answers

- Cost overruns and budget overruns, due to:
- *force majeure* (teach this expression), e.g. bad weather
- cultural misunderstandings
- changes in specifications after project has started
- change of government

- Get students to look at the questions under 'Report findings' at the top of page 119.
- Then get them to read the report on delays to the first phase of the project, individually or in pairs.
- Elicit the answers to the questions.

Suggested answers

Issues under the project manager's control and how the PM could solve the problems:

Change of scope: to some extent, this is under the PM's control in that it can be negotiated with the developer. The PM could negotiate more a realistic opening date with the developer and suggest a staged opening.

Road conditions: This is more difficult for the PM to control, as it's part of the government infrastructure. However, the project developers are in partnership with the port authorities and state government on the port project, so it does have some contacts and influence there. One option might be to help fund and construct the rail and road links, which would be two more major projects for the consortium.

Procurement: This seems to be under the PM's control. One option would be to find additional storage space for the steel. Another option would be to negotiate a fixed price for the steel, although the delivery dates changes.

Water and power supplies: This is something the PM should have allowed for in the planning stage of the project. Fresh water could be brought in via tankers. The site might need its own generators as a back-up source of energy if the electricity grid is unreliable.

Weather: The PM has no control over weather conditions, but, again, some allowances should have been made in the planning stage for local weather conditions. The PM will need to make modifications to the schedule if there are extreme weather conditions, as in this case.

CD3.43–45

- Re-introduce the idea of teleconferencing that students saw in the Business skills section (if you did it) – managers in different locations who participate in virtual meetings by phone.
- Ask students to look at the panel of times in Sydney, Delhi and Copenhagen and ask them to anticipate the problems for teleconferences.
- Then get students to focus on the 'Feedback from the team' panel. (If necessary, explain that *multi-disciplinary* refers to different specialities, rather than different forms of punishment!)
- Tell students to take notes while you play the recordings, stopping at convenient points.
- Get students to summarise what they heard from each specialist.

The project developer

- Not everyone knows how to use the software/Internet-based application correctly. Some team members use e-mail, telephone, paper-based systems and their own IT systems instead.
- It's causing problems with communication and tracking and work is duplicated or missed.
- The developer calls for a 'good-enough' approach so that the work is done on time.

The civil engineer

- The design layout had to change to accommodate the increased traffic.
- The client wants the redesign and construction to be completed within the original timeframe.
- Not enough time allocated for quality design and revisions to the plans.
- Engineering staff unhappy about schedule changes.
- Postponing vacation was not an option for them.
- Client blamed engineers because the revised plans were delayed.
- There's no sense of working towards a common goal.
- More telecon meetings needed to improve communication.

The lead contractor

- Teleconferences aren't easy because of the time differences. Can only communicate for half a day.
- Teleconferences are set at the Australian team's convenience.
- He doesn't like speaking at telecom meetings. He feels he's confronting the client by discussing schedule slippage or other potential risks and problems. It's creating misunderstandings.
- Feedback from the client is always so negative.

- Get students to look at Task 1. Run through the points 1-4 quickly.
- Divide the class into pairs and get them to discuss the points, as project manager and project sponsor – allocate these roles. Circulate, monitor and assist if necessary, but don't interrupt the pairs if they are functioning acceptably.
- When most pairs have finished, call the class to order and ask some of the pairs for the conclusions that they reached.

Stage 2: Task 2

- Explain the task and get students to work on it in groups of three or four. (The Student D role can be omitted if necessary.)
- Allocate the roles and get students to turn to the correct page. Point out that Student A is going to host or chair the teleconference. Give them time to absorb their information.
- When students are ready, the role play can begin. Circulate, monitor and assist if necessary, but don't interrupt the groups if they are functioning acceptably.
- Note good points of language use, as well as half a dozen points that need further work, and add these on one side of the board.
- When most groups have finished, call the class to order and praise good use of language that you heard in the activity, and work on the points on the board, getting individual students to say the right thing.
- Then get representatives of different groups to say what happened in their group, comparing and contrasting the outcomes.

One-to-one

Go through the information in the Course Book with your student. Explain any difficulties.

Get your student to role-play one of the managers in Task 1, with you playing another.

Task 2 can be done with your student hosting the teleconference as Student A and you taking one of the other roles. If time and interest, you could reverse the roles and do the task (or parts of it) a second time.

Note down any good examples of your student's language and points for error correction or improvement. Come back to these later. Praise any good examples of language used and go over any errors, including pronunciation.

Don't dominate the conversation in the tasks, but say enough to keep them going. You could record any of the activities on audio or video, if the student agrees, and use them for intensive correction work afterwards.

 DVD-ROM: Case study commentary

Stage 3: Writing

- Get students to study the writing task and deal with any questions. Get them to note down information from their brainstorming sessions that should go in the summary while it is still fresh in their minds.
- Get students to look at the format of reports on pages 146–147 of the Writing file again if necessary. Get students to write the report for homework. As ever, get them to e-mail it to you if possible and go through corrections in the next lesson.

Writing file (Course Book pages 146–147)

Resource bank: Writing (page 215)

Managing an international team

This unit looks at the intercultural issues that can arise in international teams and suggests ways of dealing with them.

A – B CD3.46

- Introduce the subject of the section (see above). Get students to read the text in Exercise A in pairs and predict what the problems might be. (They might anticipate some of the problems below before they hear the recording.)
- Then move on to Exercise B. Play the recording, stopping at convenient points, to allow them to take notes under the three headings, then elicit and discuss the answers.

Exercise A

Students' own answers. They may pick up on the potential for cross-cultural conflict or think of other reasons why the project failed, such as budget constraints. The idea is to get students thinking about possible problems before listening to what actually happened in Exercise B.

Exercise B

Suggested answers

The German and Japanese teams clearly had different ways of thinking and doing things which caused them to misinterpret the behaviour and attitudes of the other team. For instance:

Participation in meetings

The German and Japanese obviously had different attitudes to participating in meetings and decision-making processes. The Japanese expected decisions to be made in a series of informal pre-meeting meetings and then ratified in formal meetings.

Communication styles

Their communication styles were very different, with the Germans being more direct about giving opinions, interrupting each other and disagreeing. The Japanese interpreted this as being rude and inconsiderate. Saving face, by not openly contradicting or disagreeing with someone, is an important priority for the Japanese. At the same time, the German team probably found the Japanese indirectness and tolerance of longer silences frustrating.

Attitudes to time

The Japanese felt the Germans were lazy because they went home from work on time. This shows the two teams had different attitudes to time and the length of the working day.

C CD3.47

- Get students to say what they would have done to avoid the failure of the project. Then play the recording and get students to compare their answers with the ones they heard. Explain any difficulties.

Suggested answer

To avoid the failure of the team, an attempt should have been made from the start to get the new team to discuss their differences (and similarities, e.g. both the Japanese and Germans generally expect punctuality and clear, detailed agendas). The team had no chance to explore their similarities and differences and to establish the best way to work together (e.g. establish SOPs for meetings, decision-making, problem-solving processes).

D

- With the whole class, get students to look at the words in the box and get them to give different possible related forms, before they do the exercise, e.g. *behaviour, behavioural; decision, decisive*; etc.
- Then get them to work on the exercise in pairs. Circulate, monitor and assist if necessary, but don't interrupt the pairs if they are functioning acceptably.
- When most pairs have finished, call the class to order and elicit the answers.
- After getting the correct item for each tip, discuss the tip before moving on to the next one. Don't just plough through them.

1 behaviour **2** patience **3** decision
4 punctuality **5** sharing **6** loss **7** effectively

E CD3.48

- Before doing this activity, ask students if they know anything about Carlos Ghosn (pronounced 'gone' in French) and his multicultural background: he is Franco-Lebanese, grew up in Brazil, speaks six languages fluently and was the first non-Japanese to manage a Japanese car company, Nissan. The recording is about the partnership between Nissan and Renault under Ghosn's leadership. Get your students to have a look at his entry on Wikipedia after the class.
- As ever, get students to look through the questions before you play the recording. Also point out the stress in *al<u>li</u>ance*.
- Play the recording, stopping at convenient points – you could get students to give the answers after the relevant part of the recording rather than all at the end.
- Elicit and discuss students' reactions. You could ask if having English as the official (and neutral) language of communication, rather than getting the Japanese to learn French, and the French Japanese, might have been a key factor.

1 To help team members learn about the cross-cultural differences and similarities of their new colleagues and give them useful insights into how they can best work together.

2 Renault invested massively in cross-cultural training, teambuilding and consultancy for managers at all levels, so that staff had a good understanding of the cultural norms and expectations of their partners and respected their cultural identity. This helped to build trust and create a harmonious partnership.

3 English is now the official language of meetings and communication, there is an exchange of people between companies, and a culture of equality between partners. The alliance is also sensitive to cultural practices, for instance vacations such as the Fourteenth of July in France and Golden Week in Japan.

F – G

- Get students to look quickly through the points, then discuss them in pairs or small groups. (If you have a multicultural class, put students of different nationalities in each group so they can compare and contrast their attitudes. In a monocultural class, get students to discuss their own culture. If students come from the same culture but from more than one organisation, you might be surprised at the differences of opinion on the differences between organisations even within one national culture.)
- Circulate, monitor and assist if necessary, but don't interrupt the groups if they are functioning acceptably.
- Note good points of language use in relation to intercultural issues, as well as half a dozen points that need further work, and add these on one side of the board.
- When most groups have finished, call the class to order. Praise good use of language that you heard in the activity, and work on the points on the board, getting individual students to say the right thing.
- Then get students to give their findings, incorporating any language improvements that you have made, e.g. correct pronunciation of *dignity*.
- After that, get students, individually or in pairs, to rewrite the statements in relation to what is normal in a particular culture, perhaps not their own, but based on what they have discovered in the discussion above. If pairs have irreconcilable differences on the statements, tell students to put both opinions using suitable contrasting language, e.g. *In France, my experience is that older executives are addressed respectfully, using 'Monsieur' and 'Madame', but my colleague says that he has heard subordinates address bosses using their first names in some French companies. Perhaps it depends on the organisation and the industry – some are probably more conservative than others.*
- Get your students to finish this for homework and submit it to you by e-mail in the usual way for feedback in the next class.

H

- Depending on time and interest, discuss this with the whole class, or, especially if your students have experience of this area, ask them to do it in writing (ask them, for example, for three specific difficulties), submitting the work along with the statements from Exercise G above.

Suggested answers

Possible challenges

- It's more difficult to build trust in a virtual team than in a face-to-face team.
- Team members might feel more isolated; help, psychological support, encouragement and acknowledgment of efforts are often neglected.
- People can be overloaded with unnecessary or overlong e-mails.
- Decision-making and problem-solving via teleconference and videoconference may be harder than in face-to-face meetings.

What the team leader could do

- Hold a kick-off face-to-face meeting in order to allow the team to get to know each other, explore cultural differences and similarities and establish a code of practice (e.g. response time to e-mails).
- Ensure that the team has a shared vision and is working towards a common goal, and that everyone knows what the goal is.
- Get small groups from different cultures to work together on small tasks initially in order to get used to working together, build trust and encourage them to learn from each other.
- Remember to provide support and encouragement through e-mails.
- Know how to summarise relevant information for the group without inundating (explain this if necessary, perhaps giving the alternative 'overloading') people with e-mails.

Task

- With the whole class, go quickly through the task and explain any difficulties.
- Tell students they will be working on the task in pairs on points 1 and 2 – this would be a good time to change the make-up of the pairs in relation to earlier activities.
- When students are ready, go quickly through the different steps and tell them to work on point 1 only, getting them to compare answers with one of the pairs next to them when they have finished their list for point 1.
- Back in their pairs, get students to brainstorm the SOPs for the new team, as in point 2.
- Then put pairs together to form groups of four or six to work on point 3 – brainstorming the getting-to-know-you activities.
- Then get each group to prepare mini-presentations about their ideas for SOPs and kick-off activities that they will give to the whole class.
- During the different stages of the task, circulate, monitor and assist if necessary, but don't interrupt the pairs if they are functioning acceptably.
- Note good points of language use in relation to intercultural issues, as well as half a dozen points that need further work, and add these on one side of the board.
- Before students give their mini-presentations, work on this language. Praise good use of the language that you heard in the activity, and work on the points on the board, getting individual students to say the right thing.
- Then get representatives of each group to give a mini-presentation of SOPs and kick-off activities that they have come up with.
- Compare and contrast the suggestions of each group.

D Revision

This unit revises and reinforces some of the key points from Units 10–12 and from Working across Cultures 4, and links with those units are clearly shown. For more speaking practice, see the Resource bank section of this book beginning on page 171. The exercises in this unit can be done in class, individually or collaboratively, or for homework, except for Exercise 2 in Cultures 4, which involves students giving a presentation.

10 Online business

Vocabulary

- This exercise revisits the vocabulary of Unit 10.

1 dotcom **2** e-commerce **3** sites **4** Web **5** personalised **6** advertising revenues **7** search engine **8** digital media **9** online **10** social networking

Rhetorical devices

- Students look at rhetorical questions.

1 fuel **2** erupt **3** defuse **4** flood **5** put out; fire **6** brewing **7** grass-roots

Skills

- Students work further on presentation skills.

1 at hand **2** raised; point **3** into; stage **4** coming to **5** enough **6** pointed out **7** area **8** afraid; one

11 New business

Vocabulary

- Further work is provided here on the vocabulary from Unit 11.

Exercise 1

1 c **2** a **3** b **4** e **5** d

Exercise 2

1 bounce back from setbacks **2** draw on expert help **3** handle uncertainty **4** pitch an idea **5** set up a business

Cleft sentences

- Students extend their work on cleft sentences from page 107.

1 we need is
2 the one/person who
3 (why) the start-up failed was
4 an entrepreneur should identify is
5 I learned was (that)
6 is what she loves
7 was / when/while he was

Skills

- Students spot the errors relating to the e-mail on page 109.

We are writing to **advise/remind/inform**[1] you that, despite our previous requests, payment remains **outstanding/ overdue**[2] on invoice no. AU10-0093911 for €358. Our records also indicate that payment is now **due/overdue**[3] on invoice no. AU10-0096745 for €260. Please find **attached**[4] copies of both invoices for your information.

We would like to **remind**[5] you that our agreed payment terms are 60 days from date of invoice. Therefore, we would be grateful if you could give this **matter/issue**[6] your urgent attention and **settle**[7] your account within the next five working days. Unless payment is received by this date, we may have to consider **withdrawing/reviewing**[8] your credit terms.

If there is a problem with our goods which is causing you to **withhold/delay**[9] payment, please contact us immediately in order to **resolve**[10] this issue.

In the **event**[11] that you have already paid these invoices, please accept our apologies and **disregard/ignore**[12] this message.

Writing

- Students write an e-mail about invoices.

Suggested answer

Dear Ms Antipova

My name is Natasha Reynolds. I have recently taken over from Claire Boyle and will be in charge of accounts payable.

I am pleased to inform you that we have paid invoice AU10-0093911 for €358 today by bank transfer. My sincere apologies for the delay. Unfortunately, there was a backlog of work here at the office because we recently upgraded the computer system.

As for invoice no. AU10-0096745 for €260, our records show that we have not yet received these goods and therefore I can not authorise payment. Could you let me know when we can expect delivery? Could you also cancel this invoice and reissue a new one when the goods are delivered.

If you have any queries about these payments or any other matters regarding our account with you, do not hesitate to contact me by e-mail or phone.

Best regards

12 Project management

Vocabulary

- Students get further practice in the vocabulary from Unit 12.

Exercise 1

1 d **2** f **3** a **4** e **5** c **6** b

Exercise 2

1 delegate **2** fine-tuning **3** reports **4** schedule **5** crashing **6** multi-tasking **7** assign **8** assess

Skills

- Students develop their knowledge of the language used in teleconferencing.

1 here **2** roll call **3** speaking **4** This **5** joining **6** make **7** moving on **8** item **9** agenda **10** again **11** comment on **12** go ahead **13** hear from **14** add to **15** go over

Cultures 4: Managing an international team

- Students work on the language of international teams and give a presentation about the subject.

Exercise 1

1 perceptions **2** communication style **3** less direct **4** working relationship **5** group-oriented **6** highly valued; deadlines **7** hierarchical; respectful **8** decision-making

Exercise 2

Get students to prepare these and give them in the usual way.

Text bank

TEACHER'S NOTES

Introduction

The Text bank contains articles relating to the units in the Course Book. These articles extend and develop the themes in those units. You can choose the articles that are of most interest to your students. They can be done in class or as homework. You have permission to make photocopies of these articles for your students.

Before you read

Before each article, there is an exercise to use as a warmer that helps students to focus on the vocabulary of the article and prepares them for it. This can be done in pairs or small groups, with each group then reporting its answers to the whole class.

Reading

If using the articles in class, it is a good idea to treat different sections in different ways, for example reading the first paragraph with the whole class, then getting students to work in pairs on the following paragraphs. If you're short of time, get different pairs to read different sections of the article simultaneously. You can circulate, monitor and give help where necessary. Students then report back to the whole group with a succinct summary and/or their answers to the questions for that section. A full answer key follows the articles.

Discussion

In the Over to you sections following the exercises, there are discussion points. These can be dealt with by the whole class, or the class can be divided, with different groups discussing different points. During discussion, circulate, monitor and give help where necessary. Students then report back to the whole class. Praise good language production and work on areas for improvement in the usual way.

Writing

The discussion points can also form the basis for short pieces of written work. Students will find this easier if they have already discussed the points in class, but you can ask students to read the article and write about the discussion points as homework.

JOB APPLICANTS' FIRST IMPRESSIONS

Before you read

What was your first impression of the organisation that you work for or the educational institution that you study at?

Reading

Read this article from the *Financial Times* by John Willman and do the exercises that follow.

FT

LEVEL OF DIFFICULTY ● ○ ○

Businesses urged to keep interview standards high

John Willman

1 A third of job applicants come away from their interview with a bad impression of the business, having faced questions unrelated to the job, poor interview preparation, sexism and bad personal hygiene, a survey has found. In some cases, applicants complained of racist questions and interviewers who were drunk.

2 Kevin Moran, a 29-year-old IT worker who went for a job in the City, said he had been surprised to find it was held in a bar. "I had to shout over the noise, and one of the interviewers kept going to the bar when I was still speaking, butting in rudely and talking about things that were completely unrelated," Mr Moran said.

3 The survey of more than 2,000 people, by Ipsos Mori for T-Mobile, found that applicants judged a potential employer on their impressions of the working environment and the people employed. They expected intelligent questions related to the job, and a clear career-progression plan. However, 40 per cent of those who judged their interview experience as bad said the questions asked were nothing to do with the job, while a third said the interviewer was unprepared. More than 31 per cent of those finding the encounter disappointing had never heard from the company again.

4 Among the complaints about interviewers' behaviour by those who rated their encounter a bad experience were lateness (18 per cent), sexism (16 per cent) and bad personal hygiene (7.5 per cent). Another complaint was that the interviewer ate during the process (5.2 per cent), while 11 of the 662 disappointed applicants said the interviewer was drunk. Almost 30 per cent complained they had not been offered any refreshments, while 10 per cent said the building was dirty. As a result, almost half those who had experienced a bad interview turned down the job when it was offered.

5 "Interviewees are always under pressure to create a good first impression, but it seems that businesses need to feel a bit of that pressure as well," said Mark Martin, Human Resources Director at T-Mobile UK. "Candidates are beginning to place a company's culture and values at the top of their agenda, so businesses need to think about how these are expressed in an interview situation – or their reputation and brand could be on the line."

1 Read through the whole article. Match each of these headings (a–e) to a paragraph (1–5).

a) Businesses should think more about the first impressions that they create
b) Job candidates' bad first impressions of potential employers
c) One candidate's bad experiences
d) Particular complaints about job interviews
e) What people expect at interviews, and what many actually get

2 Relate what these interviewees said with the complaints in paragraphs 1 and 2.

a) 'The guy looked as though he hadn't shaved for a week.'
b) 'He started slurring his words.'
c) 'She didn't really know anything about the job.'
d) 'They asked me, an experienced female executive, if I'd be willing to make tea for the boss!'
e) 'I was talking about my previous job in IT, and suddenly he asked me which football team I support.'
f) 'It was crowded, and I couldn't hear a word he was saying.'
g) 'They didn't let me finish my sentences when I was speaking.'

3 Decide whether these statements about paragraphs 3 and 4 are true or false.

The survey ...

a) was carried out by Gallup.
b) covered more than 2,000 people.
c) found that interviewees were only interested in their first job in the organisation, not their later career there.
d) found that 40 per cent of those surveyed said that the questions at the job interview had nothing to do with the job.
e) found that about 33 per cent of those surveyed thought that the job interviewer had not prepared properly for the interview.
f) found that nearly a third of those who had had a bad experience did not hear anything again from the company.

4 Complete this table with words from paragraphs 3 and 4, and related words.

verb	noun
survey	.........[1]
.........[2]	applicant, ...[3]
employ	employment, ...[4], ...[5]
expect	.........[6]
interview	.........[7], ...[8], ...[9]
.........[10]	encounter

5 Match the nouns in Exercise 4 to these definitions.

a) an informal meeting, often between two or just a few people
b) an organisation that gives people jobs
c) someone who asks for a job
d) an occasion when someone is asked questions to see if they are suitable for a job
e) the person who is asked the questions
f) the person who asks the questions
g) someone who works for an organisation
h) the act of asking for a job
i) the process of asking people about their opinions and publishing the results
j) what you think will happen (in a particular organisation)

6 Choose the best alternative (a, b or c) to complete these statements to reflect how the expressions in *italic* are used in paragraphs 4 and 5.

1 If you are *disappointed*, you feel unhappy because something you ...
   a) expected did not happen.
   b) expected did happen.
   c) did not expect happened.
2 If you *turn* an offer *down*, you ...
   a) accept it.
   b) think about it.
   c) refuse it.
3 If you feel *under pressure* to do something, you feel ...
   a) pleased to do it.
   b) obliged to do it.
   c) worried about doing it.
4 A company's *values* are ...
   a) its profits in the previous year.
   b) its physical assets.
   c) the ideas, ways of behaving, etc. that it thinks are important.
5 If something is *at the top of your agenda*, it is the thing ...
   a) that you think is most important.
   b) that is the most urgent.
   c) in your diary that you have to do next.
6 A company's *reputation* is people's ...
   a) good opinion of it.
   b) opinion of it, whether good or bad.
   c) bad opinion of it.
7 If something such as your reputation is *on the line*, it is ...
   a) unchangeable.
   b) at risk.
   c) unpardonable.

Over to you 1

If you were told that a job interview was going to be in a bar or café, would you go to it? Why? / Why not?

Over to you 2

Make a list of five key pieces of advice each for a) interviewers, and b) interviewees in your country.

TEXT BANK

COSMETIC SURGERY

Before you read

Would you consider having cosmetic surgery? Why? / Why not?

Reading

Read the article from the *Financial Times* by Matthew Garrahan and Emma Jacobs and do the exercises that follow.

FT

LEVEL OF DIFFICULTY ●●○

Men facing up to nips and needles

Matthew Garrahan and Emma Jacobs

1 Peter Burling believes that when it comes to business, first impressions are everything. "Anyone who says looks are not important is a liar," says the 33-year-old account manager, who works for a British marketing agency. "You need to look good – fresh and bright rather than tired and stressed out." So, three years ago, gripped by fears that the ageing process was taking effect, he went to Transform, a UK cosmetic surgery group, to have Botox injected into his forehead, brow and crow's feet. He was so pleased with the results that he has a top-up every six months. "I perform better if I feel confident, so it may have increased the number of contracts we have won," he says.

2 While some may see such treatments as frivolous luxuries, the people offering them say that increasing numbers of men are turning to non-invasive cosmetic treatments and even to plastic surgery for pragmatic career reasons. "There are definitely more business guys coming in, and they have very focused demands," says Cap Lesesne, one of Manhattan's leading cosmetic surgeons. "They are worried about their job futures and their professional longevity." Typical male patients might be in their mid-forties, he adds. "They're fairly successful and they're looking to work into their sixties." Dr Lesesne says the number of male patients coming through his doors has risen threefold in the past decade: "Sometimes they will come in because their wife is having something done. But usually a male friend will have told them about it."

3 The cosmetic-surgery sector has grown over the past decade. In the US, the American Society of Plastic Surgeons recorded almost 12 million procedures last year, with total spending on cosmetic surgery rising 9 per cent to $12.4bn.

4 Michael McGuire, President-elect of the ASPS, says: "People might say: 'You look tired.' What that implies is you're not as vigorous or energetic, or not as competitive as you might be." Dr McGuire says he recently operated on a Nebraska steelworker who wanted to improve his appearance, while Dr Lesesne says more male patients from overseas are consulting him. "I see a lot of guys from England. They arrive on the 7 p.m. British Airways flight, I see them that night and tell them to walk 20 blocks to get the circulation going. I see them the next day and they are on the flight home on Sunday."

TEXT BANK

1 Look through the whole article to find the name of ...

a) a cosmetic surgeon in New York.

b) a client for cosmetic surgery who works in marketing.

c) a UK company that offers cosmetic surgery.

d) a professional association for cosmetic surgeons in the US.

e) an office-holder in this organisation who has not yet officially started the job.

2 Find appropriate forms of expressions in paragraph 1 to replace these expressions in *italic*, keeping the same meaning. The number in brackets shows the number of words in each expression.

a) Anyone who says that they don't pay attention to how others dress is *wrong*. (2)

b) If you're *afraid* that you're looking older, you should do something about it. (3)

c) It's not good to look *exhausted and tense* when you go to meet clients. (4)

d) *Lines around the eyes* make people look tired and old. (2)

e) *Looking older and older* is not inevitable. (3)

f) When *you consider* job interviews, how you dress is very important. (3)

g) You *produce superior results* if you look your best. (2)

3 Complete these statements using expressions from paragraph 2.

a) Cosmetic procedures that do not involve cutting the skin are ....

b) If something increases by 300 per cent, it increases ....

c) Practical reasons for doing something are described as ....

d) Requests that are explicit are ....

e) Things that you do or have that are not serious or not necessary are ....

f) The length of time that someone can continue working is their ....

4 Complete the answers to these questions about paragraph 2 using appropriate forms of the expressions in Exercise 3.

a) Are men vague about what sort of cosmetic treatment they want?

No, they have very ...

b) Are they just thinking about the present?

No, they are thinking about ...

c) Do men undergo cosmetic treatments just for the fun of it?

No, they don't see this as a ...

d) Do they have non-practical reasons for undergoing these treatments?

No, their reasons are ...

e) Does Dr Lesesne only do plastic surgery?

No, he offers ...

f) Has the number of men treated by Dr Lesesne doubled in the last 10 years?

No, it has ...

5 In paragraphs 3 and 4, find ...

a) a noun that can be stressed either on the first or second syllable.

b) a verb with a related noun form that has a different stress pattern.

c) a verb where the spelling changes in the third person singular, as well as adding an *s*.

d) an adjective spelled the same in British and American English, whose related noun form is spelled differently in each of these.

e) an informal noun here referring to men, but that can be used to informally address a group of both men and women.

f) a noun that can relate to newspapers, but in the sense it is used here refers to health.

Over to you 1

Has your attitude to a) non-invasive, and b) invasive cosmetic treatments changed now that you have read the article? In what ways?

Over to you 2

What attitudes do people in your country have towards cosmetic treatments and surgery? Have these changed over the last few years? If so, in what ways?

TRAINING CIVIL SERVANTS

Before you read

How are senior civil servants recruited and trained in your country?

Reading

Read this article from the *Financial Times* by Michael Bleby and do the exercises that follow.

FT

LEVEL OF DIFFICULTY ●●○

Ivory Coast turns to HEC business school

Michael Bleby

1 The image of bureaucracy in the developing world conjures up pictures of red tape and demotivated, uncaring officials. But Charles Koffi Diby, Economy and Finance Minister for Ivory Coast, is working to overturn that image. "We aim to strengthen ethics, put in place a customer-oriented administration and put the human being back into the heart of the administrative system," he says. "We would like to have a public administration as competitive as the private sector."

2 In pursuit of this, Mr Diby has introduced a corporate training programme for the 8,400 public servants in his Ministry of Economy and Finance. The tailored course, run by HEC School of Management, Paris, is part of a wider programme of change that Mr Diby is promoting within his department. He hopes the HEC course will enable managers to bring about much-needed reforms.

3 Roger Dault, an affiliate professor at HEC who designed and runs the programme, explains where the weaknesses lie. "These people need to strengthen their managerial competencies in different areas, like how to set up a strategy, how to implement it within the fabric of the ministry as an organisation and how to align everybody behind this strategy."

4 The programme had its genesis in 2007, when Mr Diby, who has written a book on public-sector management in Africa, met staff from HEC. "He told us: 'I want to have real managers ... people able to run an efficient administration,'" says Professor Dault. "He said: 'Our citizens have needs and demands. We have to understand these needs and demands and try to answer in the best possible way. I want an administration taking care of its citizens and taking care of companies.'" Professor Dault says Mr Diby realised that taking care of industry and investors would be another factor of differentiation for Ivory Coast.

5 The programme consists of two courses for executive and middle managers and a shorter version for lower-level staff. The 10-day programme for executives, run over 10 months, studies strategy and implementation, leadership, people management, ethics, customer needs and change management.

6 Participants also take part in a group project. HEC conducts 10 workshops for groups of 20 executives at a time, meaning up to 200 are trained in a year. A similar course trains middle managers in similar numbers, with more emphasis on operations. At the third level, rank-and-file staff take part in one-day "mega-workshops" comprising 20 tables of 10 people. By conducting discussions on customer needs, followed by ethics, they encourage officials to respond to the changes being introduced by their managers.

1 Choose the correct alternative (a, b or c) to replace the expressions in *italic* from paragraphs 1 and 2, keeping the closest meaning.

1 The *image* of bureaucracy in the developing world ...
a) picture b) reputation c) icon

2 ... *conjures up* pictures of red tape and ...
a) evokes b) invokes c) provokes

3 ... *demotivated*, uncaring officials.
a) unmotivated b) disabused c) disinterested

4 But Charles Koffi Diby, Economy and Finance Minister for Ivory Coast, is working to *overturn* that image.
a) dismantle b) abolish c) change

5 'We aim to *strengthen* ethics, ...'
a) power b) reinforce c) robust

6 *In pursuit of this*, Mr Diby has introduced a corporate training programme ...
a) To finalise this
b) To action this
c) To achieve this

7 The *tailored* course, run by HEC School of Management, Paris, is part of a wider programme of change that Mr Diby is promoting within his department.
a) specially cut
b) specially designed
c) specially conceived

2 Decide whether these statements about paragraph 3 are true or false.

Roger Dault ...

a) wrote the programme for Ivory Coast civil servants.
b) thinks that managerial skills of civil servants in Ivory Coast need to be improved.
c) thinks that strategy should be decided by business school professors.
d) believes that putting strategy into action should be part of the course.
e) thinks that strategy can be applied without involving low-ranking officials.

3 Find the five groups of people/organisations mentioned in paragraph 4. Which groups are referred to by more than one expression?

4 Match these areas mentioned in paragraph 5 (1–6) to a related idea (a–f).

1 strategy formulation
2 strategy implementation
3 leadership/people management
4 ethics
5 customer needs
6 change management

a) Asking citizens what they want
b) Behaving in a moral way
c) Inspiring civil servants to work to the best of their ability
d) Persuading people to do things in new ways
e) Sitting down to discuss goals over the next 10 or 20 years
f) Thinking about how the grand plan can be put into practice

5 In paragraph 6, find ...

a) a verb (used twice here) that can also be used to talk about leading musicians.
b) a prefix that means 'very big'.
c) a noun that can also refer to medical procedures.
d) an adjectival expression used to refer to the ordinary members of an organisation.
e) a noun that can also refer to a place where things are made on a small scale.
f) a verb used to talk about reacting to events.
g) a verb (used in its *-ing* form here) meaning 'contain'.

Over to you 1

Look again at the areas in Exercise 4. To what extent can training designed for private-sector managers and employees be applied to the public sector? Think about specific examples where they would be a) the same, b) similar, or c) different.

Over to you 2

Imagine that you are Head of Training for your organisation, or one you would like to work for. Give the outlines of an ideal management course that you would like to run for its managers, using professors from a top management school.

DISTANCE LEARNING

Before you read

Could you imagine following, or have you followed, a course of study mainly or entirely online? Why? / Why not?

Reading

Read this article from the *Financial Times* by Charlotte Clarke and do the exercises that follow.

FT

LEVEL OF DIFFICULTY ● ● ○

Online MBAs: Flexibility and reach draw ever greater numbers

Charlotte Clarke

1 The data submitted to this year's *Financial Times* online MBA listing show two main trends compared with last year's: a rise in enrolment figures and a wider range of specialist programmes. Does this mean that online MBAs are set to become a dominant feature of business-school education? Marcel Cohen, Director of the MBA by Distance Learning at Imperial College Business School in London, strongly believes so. "Distance learning is the training for tomorrow's business world," he says, emphasising that it will eventually take centre stage.

2 He gives two main reasons for this: first, online learning recognises that people study at a different pace. Second, it teaches teams to collaborate virtually, in the same way global organisations have to. The list shows that the majority of schools set a generous five-year time limit for completing the degree. This gives students the freedom to follow a self-managed schedule, fitting their study hours around work, family and travel. Matt Smith, a graduate of the Athabasca online MBA, has been able to make room for a wedding, the birth of four children, three job promotions and two international relocations while studying for his MBA. "For my family, life is always changing, so I needed a flexible programme that would fit our lifestyle," he says.

3 Virtual collaboration with other MBA students is included in 66 of the 73 programmes listed. This usually involves video lectures, podcasting and videoconferencing. This is essential training, according to Mr Cohen, who argues that schools that are not willing to embrace these methods of teaching are living in "yesterday's world", held back by a desire to preserve the past.

4 He envisages a future where classroom teaching will be something only older generations will remember. Murat Tarimcilar, Associate Dean for Graduate Programmes at George Washington University in Washington DC, however, does not believe that the online MBA will ever replace the full-time version. "They offer completely different experiences," he says. Yet he does feel that the online degree will increasingly be on a par with its full-time counterpart. "The stigma that it is inferior is still there, but less and less every day," he says. Instead, the online MBA is "seductive" in its ability to reach thousands. This has also taken networking – a long-established feature of schools – to a new level, with message boards and social networking sites in constant use. People now recognise that virtual interaction can create close relationships, despite the lack of face-to-face communication.

1 Look through the whole article. Who are these people?

a) Murat Tarimcilar

b) Matt Smith

c) Marcel Cohen

2 Correct the expressions in *italic* in these statements with appropriate forms of expressions from paragraph 1. The correct forms contain the same number of words as the incorrect ones.

a) If something replaces the thing that was most important until then, it *occupies middle scene*.

b) If you bring attention to something when speaking, you *italicise* it.

c) If you *enlist* on a course, you become a participant on it.

d) If you really think that something is the case, you *powerfully consider* it.

e) If you *submerge* data, information, etc., you make it available.

f) The most important changes in something are its *principal themes*.

g) The most important characteristic of something is its *domineering aspect*.

3 Which of these things are *not* referred to in paragraph 2?

With an MBA course by distance learning, you can ...

a) study at the speed that suits you.

b) take up to five years to complete it, at some business schools.

c) link the subjects that you study specifically with the issues that you deal with at work.

d) study in the same way that people work together in international organisations.

e) study while you are sitting in your office.

f) get married and have children.

g) go and work abroad.

4 Complete the answers to these questions with appropriate forms of expressions from paragraphs 3 and 4.

a) Do students always meet face to face, at least some of the time?

No, they work together in a process of ....

b) Is this form of studying something that they can do without?

No, it's ....

c) Is it acceptable for business schools to use this form of collaboration in a half-hearted way?

No, they have to .... it.

d) If they resist, is it because they think that face-to-face methods are more effective?

No, they just want to ....

e) Does Marcel Cohen think that face-to-face teaching will continue?

No, he thinks that a future where people only have memories of this is something we can now ....

f) Does Murat Tarimcilar think that online MBAs will be worth less than traditional ones?

No, he thinks that they will be .... with them.

5 Decide whether these statements about expressions from paragraph 4 are true or false.

a) A *dean* is a senior person on a university's staff, and also a senior person in some religions.

b) A *counterpart* to something is its equivalent, and in talking about people, *counterpart* is used to talk about one of your colleagues in the same department or organisation.

c) A *stigma* is something that people are ashamed of.

d) *Seductive* means 'attractive' and relates to *seduction*.

e) *Long-established* could be replaced by the expression *long-existing* without changing the meaning.

f) *Constant* relates to the noun *constance*.

g) *Lack* could be replaced by *absence* without changing the meaning.

Over to you 1

If you have followed a distance-learning course, do the points in the article about the benefits of virtual collaboration relate to your own experience? Why? / Why not?
If you haven't followed one, do you think that virtual collaboration can be as good as face-to-face interaction? Why? / Why not?

Over to you 2

Will distance education with virtual collaboration eventually take over as the main form of learning? Why? / Why not?

TEXT BANK

ALTERNATIVE ENERGY

Before you read

Name as many sources of renewable energy as you can think of.

Reading

Read this article from the *Financial Times* by Hal Weitzman and do the exercises that follow.

FT

LEVEL OF DIFFICULTY ● ● ○

TEXT BANK

Wind of change sparks US renewables revival

Hal Weitzman

1 The history of the US is replete with images of extravagant fossil-fuel consumption: smoke billowing from gleaming trains; long, sleek, gas-guzzling cars; gigantic refineries endlessly pumping out plumes of dirty air. But the reputation is somewhat misleading. For much of the country's history, renewable energy played a far more central role than it does today.

2 By the early 1900s, hydroelectric power supplied more than 40 per cent of US electricity needs, and by the 1940s, hydropower provided about 75 per cent of all the electricity consumed in western and Pacific north-western states. Fossil-fuel consumption, however, rapidly eclipsed hydro, and in recent years environmental criticisms of the damage dams can have on aquatic ecosystems led to the decommissioning of some plants.

3 Nowadays, hydroelectric generation supplies only a small fraction of the US's electricity. However, its history goes to show that the country was not always the great global polluter it is today. And as the US moves to reduce its dependence on carbon fuels, alternative energy sources are back in vogue.

4 In fact, renewable energy already plays a relatively significant role in US electricity production. Discounting hydroelectricity, the US is the world's biggest consumer of renewable energy for electricity – consuming twice as much as Germany and three times as much as Japan.

5 Renewable energy, including hydro, accounted for more than 7 per cent of the US's total energy consumption in 2008, according to the US Department of Energy. Although that is still dwarfed by energy from petroleum, natural gas and coal, alternative energy sources are slowly but surely taking a bigger share of the country's energy use: in 2004, renewable energy's share of total US energy consumption stood at 6 per cent; and renewable energy consumption grew by 7 per cent between 2007 and 2008, despite a 2-per-cent decline in total US energy consumption.

6 At 7 per cent of the total, alternative energy sources are rivalling nuclear power's 9-per-cent contribution to the US's energy make-up. Although hydroelectricity remains by far the largest source of renewable electricity in the US, the real star of the renewable energy scene in recent years has been wind power. The sector has grown strongly in recent years. Wind power now provides 1.3 per cent of US total electricity generation, up from 0.4 per cent in 2004. Last year, the US overtook Germany as the world's biggest producer of power from wind.

1 Find adjectives in paragraphs 1 and 2 that mean the following.

a) excessive
b) using a lot of petrol
c) very large
d) not giving a true idea about something
e) able to be used again
f) relating to power produced by water
g) relating to nature, natural resources, etc.
h) relating to water

2 Decide whether these statements about paragraphs 1 and 2 are true or false.

In thinking about the US, ...

a) people imagine that fossil fuels have always been the main source of energy.
b) renewable energy has never played a big part.
c) hydroelectricity provided nearly half of energy in about 1910.
d) hydroelectricity provided three-quarters of energy in the US in the 1940s.
e) hydroelectric plants were closed because they were no longer economical.
f) fuels like oil and coal overtook hydroelectric energy.

3 Choose the alternative (a, b or c) that can replace the expression in *italic* from paragraphs 4 and 5.

1 In fact, renewable energy already plays a relatively *significant* role in US electricity production.

a) main b) principle c) important

2 *Discounting* hydroelectricity, the US is the world's biggest consumer of renewable energy for electricity – consuming twice as much as Germany and three times as much as Japan.

a) Reducing b) Apart from c) Selling

3 Renewable energy, including hydro, *accounted for* more than 7 per cent of the US's total energy consumption in 2008, according to the US Department of Energy.

a) represented b) audited c) balanced

4 Although that is still *dwarfed by* energy from petroleum, natural gas and coal, alternative energy sources are slowly but surely taking a bigger share of the country's energy use: ...

a) very little in relation to
b) a lot in relation to
c) average in relation to

5 ... in 2004, renewable energy's share of total US energy consumption *stood at* 6 per cent; ...

a) fell b) was c) rose

6 ... and renewable energy consumption grew by 7 per cent between 2007 and 2008, *despite* a 2-per-cent ...

a) although b) however c) in spite of

7 ... *decline* in total US energy consumption.

a) levelling off b) drop c) plummet

4 Look through the whole article and find what these percentages relate to.

a) 6 per cent
b) 7 per cent
c) 2 per cent
d) 9 per cent
e) 1.3 per cent
f) 0.4 per cent

5 Use expressions from paragraph 6 to answer these questions about energy in the US, using the number of words shown.

a) Is hydroelectricity still important as a source of renewable energy?

Yes, in relation to this kind of energy, it's still ... (*5 words*)

b) Is alternative energy almost as important as nuclear energy in the US?

Yes, alternative energy ... (*4 words*)

c) Has wind power in the US become more important than in Germany?

Yes, the US ... (*3 words*)

d) Has alternative energy developed fast over the last few years?

Yes, it ... (*3 words*)

e) Does wind power provide more that 1 per cent of electricity in the US?

Yes, it provided 1.3 per cent of total ... (*2 words*)

f) Are alternative energy and nuclear energy about as important as each other?

Yes, they each make a similar ... (*1 word*)

Over to you 1

Did the information in the article about alternative energy in the US surprise you? If so, in what ways?

Over to you 2

Do some research on the Internet into the contributions made in your country by the different forms of energy mentioned in the article.

TEXT BANK

PEAK OIL

Before you read

In which year do you think the world's oil reserves will run out?

Reading

Read the article from the *Financial Times* by Jeremy Leggett and do the exercises that follow.

FT

LEVEL OF DIFFICULTY ●●●

You have had the credit crisis – next it will be oil

Jeremy Leggett

1 As it now admits, BP "did not have the tools" to contain a deepwater oil leak in the Gulf of Mexico. Its failure with that risk must now raise questions about its approach to other risks. Top of the list must be the threat that global oil production will fall sooner than generally forecast, ambushing oil-dependent economies with a rapidly opening gap between supply and demand. The approach of the point at which global oil supplies reach an apex, "peak oil" as it is often known, worries growing numbers of people. But, until now, BP has poured scorn on the worriers, encouraging the oil industry's effort to reassure society about peak oil. The disaster in the Gulf of Mexico casts doubt on the viability of the deepwater production on which industry forecasts depend.

2 Every year, BP publishes a report that is effectively a risk assessment on peak oil arriving prematurely. Its Annual Statistical Review of World Energy routinely states that there are about 40 years of proved oil reserves, that advances in technology will enable much more to be found and produced, that rising oil prices can finance the necessary exploration and infrastructure, and that global oil supply can go on rising for decades. Every year, peak-oil worriers say they doubt the Opec oil producers' reserve statistics that are echoed in BP's review, that technology can only slow depletion not reverse it, that rising oil prices do not help when it takes so many years to extract new oil from increasingly exotic locations and that global supply is heading for an imminent fall.

3 BP's disaster has mired a regional economy, collapsed the company's value and dragged down the FTSE 100. Yet failure with the peak-oil risk assessment would render such wreckage insignificant. Leaders of the companies in the UK's Industry Taskforce on Peak Oil and Energy Security (ITPOES) – Arup, SSE, Solarcentury, Stagecoach and Virgin – argue that premature peak oil would be quite as bad as the credit crunch. In the foreword to ITPOES's report published in February, it urged the UK government to "act now ... don't let the oil crunch catch us out in the way the credit crunch did".

4 The credit crunch nearly gave us the second Great Depression. As for the oil crunch, the ITPOES companies fear an irrecoverable fall in global oil supply by 2015 at the latest and that if oil producers then husband resources, a global energy crisis could abruptly morph into energy famine for some oil-consuming nations.

1 Match each of these summaries (a–d) to one of the paragraphs (1–4).

a) An oil crunch will mean a global energy crisis.
b) BP's annual review of oil reserves is unrealistic.
c) BP failed to foresee the Gulf of Mexico disaster and, now, peak oil.
d) The forthcoming oil crisis will be as bad as the credit crunch.

2 Find expressions in paragraphs 1 and 2 that mean the following.

a) an unwanted escape (of oil)
b) the amount of something that is available
c) the amount of something that is required
d) the ability of something to be done, from the practical and financial point of view
e) the point when world oil production will be at its highest
f) the systems, equipment, etc. needed to do or produce something
g) the process of something becoming used up

3 Decide whether these statements about paragraphs 1 and 2 are true or false.

According to the writer, BP ...

a) did not have the right equipment to deal with the Gulf of Mexico leak.
b) is not able to judge risks effectively.
c) denies that oil production will ever fall.
d) says that people who worry about an early decline in oil production are wrong.
e) thinks that oil reserves will last another 50 years.
f) thinks that global oil production will remain steady over that time.
g) is of the opinion that new techniques for oil exploration will emerge.
h) agrees with people who say that oil may reach its maximum levels of production in the next few years.

4 Use these expressions (a–g) to replace the expressions in *italic* (1–7) in paragraph 3 (reproduced below), keeping the same meaning.

a) unexpectedly early
b) greatly reduced
c) make
d) surprise us
e) damaged
f) evaluation
g) destruction

BP's disaster has *mired*[1] a regional economy, *collapsed*[2] the company's value and dragged down the FTSE 100. Yet failure with the peak-oil risk *assessment*[3] would *render*[4] such *wreckage*[5] insignificant. Leaders of the companies in the UK's Industry Taskforce on Peak Oil and Energy Security (ITPOES) – Arup, SSE, Solarcentury, Stagecoach and Virgin – argue that *premature*[6] peak oil would be quite as bad as the credit crunch. In the foreword to ITPOES's report published in February, it urged the UK government to "act now ... don't let the oil crunch *catch us out*[7] in the way the credit crunch did".

5 Choose the alternative (a, b or c) that has the closest meaning to each of these sentences from paragraph 4.

1 The credit crunch nearly gave us the second Great Depression.
   a) The credit crunch should have led to the second Great Depression.
   b) The credit crunch would have led to the second Great Depression.
   c) The credit crunch could have led to the second Great Depression.

2 ... the ITPOES companies fear an irrecoverable fall in global oil supply by 2015 ...
   a) The ITPOES companies fear that global oil production will fall by 2015, never to rise again.
   b) The ITPOES companies are afraid that global oil production will go down by 2015, but may rise again.
   c) The ITPOES companies are certain that world oil production will go down by 2015.

3 ... if oil producers then husband resources, ...
   a) If oil producers then increase their supplies ...
   b) If oil producers then ration their supplies ...
   c) If oil producers then keep their supplies at the same level ...

4 ... a global energy crisis could abruptly morph into energy famine for some oil-consuming nations.
   a) A global energy crisis might suddenly change into an energy surplus for some of the countries that consume oil.
   b) A global energy crisis may rapidly evolve into severe energy shortage for some of the countries that consume oil.
   c) A global energy crisis would certainly change into severe supply shortages for some of the countries that consume oil.

Over to you 1

Has the answer that you gave in *Before you read* changed now that you have read the article? Why? / Why not?

Over to you 2

List all the effects that an oil shortage might have on the economy.

TEXT BANK

TARGETED MARKETING

Before you read

With the growth of the Internet, how long do you think newspapers will last as an advertising medium in your country?

Reading

Read this article from the *Financial Times* by Matthew Garrahan and do the exercises that follow.

FT

LEVEL OF DIFFICULTY ●●○

Marketing to minorities

Matthew Garrahan

1 Marketing was fairly straightforward when newspapers and television were the only media that brands much cared about. The Internet offers plenty of challenges for advertisers, but has also made it easier for companies to target specific ethnic and demographic groups. For UrbanAdserve, a New York digital-marketing agency, tailored online campaigns, e-mail newsletters and social media websites are the means by which brands can reach influential Latino, African-American and Asian consumers.

2 The company focuses on "urban trendsetters" – predominantly affluent black and English-speaking Latino consumers in the top 10 US metropolitan markets – running advertisers' banners everywhere from nightclub and dating websites to career and parenting sites. Staffed and owned by five women, the agency has built a network of 300 digital-publishing partners: websites aimed at Latino men, for example, or online TV shows targeted at African-American women.

3 When a client such as Ford or Procter & Gamble wants to reach one of these groups, UrbanAdserve distributes the campaign to the desired audience, says Sheila Marmon, co-founder. "The US multicultural market has $2.2 trillion in buying power," she adds, pointing to research from the World Bank and University of Georgia's Selig Center. "It's the largest domestic market, but it hasn't been tapped into to the highest potential."

4 The multicultural market is sophisticated, says Ms Marmon, a former investment banker. "There is a misperception that people of colour are not on the Web, but we show our clients that they are." Internet penetration among university-educated black and Latino people is as high as it is among whites, at about 90 per cent, while a Pew Center report shows that more blacks and Latinos use the Web via a handheld device than whites (48 per cent and 47 per cent respectively, compared with 28 per cent).

5 UrbanAdserve recently secured a digital campaign with Chanel, the first time the fashion brand has targeted the multicultural market online. The agency is distributing the campaign for Chanel's new men's fragrance alongside a series of profiles it has compiled of black and Hispanic rising stars, including Julian Castro, the mayor of San Antonio, and Laz Alonzo, an actor who appeared in Avatar.

6 Demographic trends are on the side of companies targeting the multicultural market. In California, the biggest media market in the US, Latinos are forecast to become the largest racial or ethnic group by 2020 and will constitute a majority by 2050, according to the Public Policy Institute of California.

1 Look through the whole article and find ...

a) a New York digital-marketing agency.
b) its co-founder.
c) three of its clients.
d) three consumer groups and a sub-group within one of these.
e) three ways in which they can be reached.
f) two Hispanic celebrities.
g) four bodies that do research into population and marketing trends.
h) four types of websites.

2 Find adjectives in paragraphs 1 and 2 that mean the following in the context of the article.

a) relating to the Internet
b) relating to computers and/or the Internet
c) relating to a particular race
d) relating to a particular part of the population
e) prosperous
f) living in cities
g) designed for a particular audience
h) easy and simple

3 Match the expressions (1–7) from paragraphs 2, 3 and 4 to their definitions (a–g).

1 desired audience
2 domestic market
3 Internet penetration
4 Latino consumers
5 multicultural market
6 metropolitan markets
7 urban trendsetters

a) consumers in the US
b) consumers who live in cities and start using particular products before other consumers do
c) people living in very large cities
d) people making up different ethnic groups
e) people of Central and South American origin
f) the degree to which people use the Internet
g) the people that advertisers want to reach

4 Decide whether these statements about expressions in *italic* from paragraphs 5 and 6 are true or false.

a) If you *secure* something, you lose it.
b) If an agency *distributes* an advertising campaign, the campaign is only run on TV and in newspapers.
c) If something happens *alongside* something else, it happens together with it.
d) A *demographic trend* is a fall in population.
e) If something is *forecast*, it is predicted.
f) If a particular group *constitutes a majority*, it is the biggest compared to others.

5 Choose the best alternative headline (a, b or c) for the article.

a) Urban trendsetters are the ones to watch
b) Internet marketers ignore ethnic groups at their peril
c) Ford and Procter & Gamble's Internet marketing campaigns

Over to you 1

How do advertisers reach particular demographic groups in your country?

Over to you 2

Design a website marketing campaign for a product that you know, targeted to reach a particular demographic group.

LUXURY BRANDS AND SOCIAL MEDIA

Before you read

Do you use social media like Facebook? Why? / Why not?

Reading

Read the article from the *Financial Times* by David Gelles and do the exercises that follow.

FT

LEVEL OF DIFFICULTY ● ● ●

Tarnish the brand or build an aspirational following?

David Gelles

1 It takes some gumption to walk into a Gucci store. One must be self-possessed, confident enough to meet the gaze of the shopkeepers, and presumably wealthy enough to afford a $4,000 handbag. No such confidence is needed on the Web. Anyone can visit a company's website, no matter how rarefied the brand. But if the Web has cracked the door open, social media has invited everyone into a brand's virtual boutique.

2 Through Facebook fan pages, Twitter accounts and private social networks, luxury brands are managing online communities of tens of thousands of fans. Many of them are eager to engage, yet only a small portion may be actual customers. "It is most definitely a tenuous relationship," remarks Samir Balwani, an Internet marketing strategist. "Luxury means inaccessibility, uniqueness. And social media means the opposite. Everyone can talk about it, everyone can pass it round."

3 The calculation for brands, then, is whether increased awareness on the Web can generate additional sales without tarnishing the brand. "It's about finding the balance where you don't lose your brand allure, but still are able to reach the core consumers," says Mr Balwani. To this end, the Facebook pages of Gucci, Chanel and Coach are no haphazard jumble. They are sleek, image-rich and meticulously curated. Despite Facebook's egalitarian ethos, there is little crowd-sourced content from fans on Facebook brand pages. Instead, the messaging, themes and promotions are entirely in sync with the brand's latest seasonal campaign.

4 "Facebook is the 800-pound gorilla in the room," says Reggie Bradford, Chief Executive of Vitrue, a social media management company. "Time spent is dominant. That's where people are connecting to the Internet. That has to be the centre point of your social media strategy. The result is classic word-of-mouth marketing – 78 per cent of consumers buy products based upon a recommendation from a peer or friend," says Mr Bradford. "Luxury brands should be thinking about 'how can we create a dialogue and get consumers connecting with our brand'."

5 When Gucci, for example, has 737,000 fans on Facebook, it is all but impossible to kick them out of the virtual boutique. And even if not every tweet and Facebook post is driving immediate sales, "it's worth it," says Mr Balwani. "You not only reach your consumers, but aspirational consumers. Getting the consumer early on is really where the win is in the long term."

1 Decide whether these statements using expressions in *italic* from paragraphs 1 and 2 are true or false.

If ...

a) you have the *gumption* to do something, you have the courage and determination to do it.

b) you are *self-possessed*, you have good self-control.

c) you can *meet* someone's *gaze*, you are unable to look them in the eye.

d) a brand is *rarefied*, it is luxurious and exclusive.

e) you are *eager to engage*, you are keen to communicate.

f) you have a *tenuous relationship* with someone, you are very close to them.

g) something has *uniqueness*, there are many examples of it.

2 What is the basic contradiction between luxury brands and social networking? Where in paragraph 2 is this mentioned?

3 Choose the best alternative (a, b or c) to replace each expression in *italic* from paragraph 3.

1 The calculation for brands, then, is whether increased awareness on the Web can generate additional sales without *tarnishing* the brand.

a) enhancing b) protecting c) damaging

2 'It's about finding the balance where you don't lose your brand *allure*, ... '

a) attractiveness b) share c) name

3 ' ... but still are able to reach the *core* consumers,' says Mr Balwani.

a) least important

b) most important

c) most influential

4 To this end, the Facebook pages of Gucci, Chanel and Coach are *no haphazard jumble*.

a) extremely well organised

b) extremely interesting

c) extremely helpful

5 They are sleek, image-rich and *meticulously curated*.

a) carelessly managed

b) very carefully managed

c) very beautiful

6 Despite Facebook's *egalitarian ethos*, ...

a) democratic nature

b) undemocratic nature

c) unplanned nature

7 ... there is little *crowd-sourced content* from fans on Facebook brand pages.

a) material written by advertisers

b) material written by the brand owners

c) material written by social website users

8 ... the messaging, themes and promotions are entirely *in sync with* the brand's latest seasonal campaign.

a) in harmony with

b) in conflict with

c) in timing with

4 Correct these statements with appropriate forms of expressions from paragraphs 4 and 5.

a) A very good example of something is a classical example of it.

b) If you start communication with someone, you fabricate a dialogue with them.

c) People who are not actual customers for a product, but who would like to be, are inspirational.

d) People with a similar age, background, etc. to you are your piers.

e) Something that brings sales drifts them.

f) The most important aspect of something is the one that is domineering.

g) The most important part of something is its hub point.

h) When people buy things because of personal recommendation, this is mouth-to-ear marketing.

i) You can refer to something very big, that you can't ignore, as the 400-kilo ape at the door.

5 Choose the best summary (a, b or c) for the whole article.

Luxury brands should ...

a) not allow access to their websites by people who never buy their products.

b) carefully manage their sites and links with social media, even if sales are not immediate.

c) allow anyone who wants to contribute to their sites to do so.

Over to you 1

Would you become a 'friend' of a brand on Facebook? Why? / Why not?

Over to you 2

Research on the Internet the social media strategy of a well-known brand and produce a short report about it.

THE FUTURE OF WORK 1

Before you read

Which will be the boom industries of the future?

Reading

Read this article from the *Financial Times* by Luke Johnson and do the exercises that follow.

LEVEL OF DIFFICULTY ●●○

Time to work on the jobs of the future

Luke Johnson

1 What the hell are the jobs that everyone is going to be doing in the future? That is the question that no one seems able to answer. Not many of those in power even appear to be thinking seriously about it. Yet it is perhaps the most important single issue facing the West: what are the industries and professions that represent our salvation, and how do we prepare our citizens for them?

2 Paying jobs do not just crop up through chance or political dreaming. New jobs in the private sector that add value generally only arise when there is optimism and new capital formation, in locations that are competitive in terms of costs and skills.

3 Three main structural trends are apparent in the world of work in the West. First, jobs are being shipped offshore to lower-cost economies such as China and India. Second, perhaps more significantly, technological advances mean many sectors such as manufacturing, mining and agriculture are much more efficient than they used to be, so less labour is required for a greater output. And third, employing people in countries such as Britain has become much more expensive: not simply because of wage inflation but other obligations such as increased holiday, entitlements such as maternity and paternity leave, higher payroll taxes and so on.

4 The three sectors that I hear about most are healthcare, education and green energy. But who is doing the research, who is placing the crucial bets? Poor venture capital returns mean the asset classes are attracting much less money and talent. This is likely to mean less innovation and commercialisation of new ideas.

5 There is superficial talk of "green" jobs and clean energy. Perhaps inventions will emerge to replace fossil fuels and create new industries. But the short-term burden of carbon-limiting legislation will increase costs and lead to more job losses, as companies shift yet more production to cheaper places. Service and support professions such as healthcare and education will no doubt require more people – if we can afford to pay them. Yet even in growth sectors such as pharmaceuticals and software, our competitive advantages are being swiftly eroded.

6 Think-tanks, civil servants, trade associations and business schools should be combining their intellectual resources to tell us where investors, entrepreneurs and the state should be directing their energies so as to boost job prospects. Because a nation without enough real jobs is a miserable place.

1 Look through the whole article to find the order in which these ideas occur. Two of the ideas do not occur.

a) What remains of the coal industry will decline even further.
b) Some industries are more productive than before.
c) No one in government seems to be thinking about how jobs are to be created in the future.
d) New industries may emerge based on new fuels.
e) Jobs are not created by accident.
f) Healthcare is often cited as an industry of the future.
g) Four types of organisation should pool resources to develop thinking in this area.
h) Companies need tax concessions to encourage them to create jobs.
i) Drug manufacturing is an area where the West is less efficient in relation to other countries than it was before.

2 Find expressions in paragraphs 1 and 2 that could be replaced by these expressions without changing the meaning.

a) in government
b) arguably
c) are the things that will save us
d) occur
e) positive sentiment about the future
f) creation
g) places

3 Decide whether these statements related to expressions used in paragraph 3 are true or false.

a) You can refer to big changes in the economy as *structuralist*.
b) If jobs are *shipped offshore*, they are done on ships going to developing countries.
c) If *less labour is required for greater output*, there is a fall in productivity.
d) *Wage inflation* is when workers' pay rises.
e) *Obligations* could be replaced by *entitlements*, and *entitlements* by *obligations* with no change of meaning.
f) *Payroll taxes* are a form of personal income tax.

4 Match the two parts of these expressions from paragraphs 4, 5 and 6.

1 asset	a) jobs
2 clean	b) advantages
3 fossil	c) fuels
4 competitive	d) resources
5 crucial	e) classes
6 green	f) energy
7 intellectual	g) bets

5 Match each of the expressions in Exercise 4 to one of these examples.

a) Coal and oil
b) Different activities in which venture capitalists can invest
c) The ideas produced by think tanks, etc.
d) Jobs making wind turbines
e) The activities of the future that investors decide to back
f) The ability to do or make something more efficiently than others
g) Tidal power

6 Complete this table with words from paragraphs 4, 5 and 6, and related words.

noun	verb
boost	1
.........2	burden
commercialisation	3
.........4	erode
innovation	5
legislation	6
shift	7

Over to you 1

Identify a competitive advantage that your country has. Will this advantage increase or decrease over the next 30 years? Give your reasons.

Over to you 2

Do some research on the Internet to see what the government of a country that you are interested in is doing to encourage development of industries of the future. (You could look at the websites of government departments, think tanks, universities, etc.)

TEXT BANK

THE FUTURE OF WORK 2

Before you read

What will be the biggest trend in the workplace over the next 30 years?

Reading

Read the article from the *Financial Times* by Lynda Gratton and do the exercises that follow.

FT

LEVEL OF DIFFICULTY ● ● ●

TEXT BANK

Winds of change head for the workplace

Lynda Gratton

I am halfway through a four-year research project involving academics and executives from across the world to try to figure out which direction we are heading in, and how it will affect the nature of work. Based on our study, here are some clues to the big challenges.

1 Most corporations have hung on to command and control structures, with reliance on strategic direction from the top. But what happens when, within 10 years, more than nine billion people will be actively connecting to each other and engaging in purposeful creation online? It could shift the balance of power from within companies to the microentrepreneurial-rich ecosystems that will increasingly dominate their value chains.

2 The baby-boomers' generation has pretty much been in control of the corporate agenda for the past 20 years. But what will happen when generation Y, a group now in their mid-20s, takes control? They want work–life balance and they tend to be cooperative and empathetic. This could create a shift from valuing careers that propel you to the top to valuing careers that enable a more balanced and creative life.

3 Developed economies have had a near monopoly on research and development spending and the high-value innovations that flow from this. So what happens when the frugal innovations from emerging markets begin to look a lot more exciting, when even old-timers move their labs to Bangalore and when more of the Indian and Chinese diasporas move home? Expect disarray in the classic Western talent pipelines and a dash for Asian talent.

4 The carbon footprints of US and European employees and consumers have dwarfed the rest of the world's for decades. What happens when Chinese and Indian employees and consumers (and by 2020 there will be three billion of them) get the same taste for fossil fuels and consumption? Suddenly, it looks like a challenge that will require a level of global cooperation never before witnessed.

5 Employees have tended to have some trust in their companies, their governments and their communities. The deal was that they worked hard to make money to buy stuff that made them happy. Plus, they spent about 20 hours a week of their leisure time watching television. But what happens when institutional trust ebbs, when it seems that the wealthy are no happier, and we now replace a couple of hours of television with connecting creatively with billions of other people online? Perhaps it is these billions of potential grassroots activists and workers that will make a real difference.

1 Match each of these headings (a–e) to one of the paragraphs (1–5).

a) Carbon emissions in industrialising economies
b) Work–life balance
c) Connecting with others
d) New management methods
e) R&D talent

2 In paragraph 1, find ...

a) an adjective whose opposite ends in *-less*.
b) a noun with a similar form with the same meaning that ends in *-ivity.*
c) a two-word expression relating to all the steps involved in making money.
d) a three-word expression referring to new types of work environment.
e) a verb used also to talk about changing gear in a car.
f) a three-word expression also used to refer to relationships between countries.
g) a four-word expression relating to traditional forms of management.

3 Decide whether these statements about expressions in paragraph 2 are true or false.

a) The *baby-boomers' generation* includes people born between about 1925 and 1940.
b) *Generation Y* includes people born between the mid-1970s and the early 2000s.
c) If you *tend* to behave in a particular way, you always behave that way.
d) If you are *cooperative*, you work well with others.
e) If you are *empathetic,* you don't understand how other people are feeling.
f) If something *propels* you in a particular direction, it prevents you from getting there.

4 Choose the correct alternative (a, b or c) to replace the expressions in *italic* from paragraph 3, keeping the same meaning.

1 Developed economies have *had a near monopoly on* research and development spending ...
a) controlled all
b) controlled most
c) controlled some

2 ... and the high-value innovations that *flow* from this.
a) result b) cause c) come out

3 So what happens when the *frugal* innovations from emerging markets begin to look a lot more exciting, ...
a) resource-hungry
b) resourceful
c) economical

4 ... when even old-timers move their labs to Bangalore and when more of the Indian and Chinese *diasporas* move home?
a) ex-patriots b) expatiators c) expatriates

5 Expect *disarray* in the classic Western talent pipelines ...
a) disorganisation
b) utter chaos
c) total breakdown

6 ... and a *dash* for Asian talent.
a) demand b) exodus c) rush

5 Look at paragraphs 4 and 5 and answer these questions.

a) Will it be possible for Chinese and Indian consumers to use oil and coal, and consume goods in the same ways as their Western counterparts?
b) What will be required to deal with the call on resources in relation to the trend mentioned in (a) above?
c) Did employees have total trust in companies, governments and communities in the past?
d) Has this trust increased?
e) What has been people's main leisure activity?
f) What will this be replaced by?
g) What will this bring about?

Over to you 1

Do you agree with the writer's ideas about these five future trends? Why? / Why not?

Over to you 2

Think about your own work–life balance and leisure activities. How would you like to see them develop in the future?

TEXT BANK

ETHICAL SUPPLIERS

Before you read

List some of the issues that must be considered in deciding if goods are being produced ethically.

Reading

Read this article from the *Financial Times* by Paul Tyrrell and do the exercises that follow.

FT

LEVEL OF DIFFICULTY ● ● ○

Buyers unravel the ethics behind the label

Paul Tyrrell

1 If you ever buy an item of clothing from Tesco, the UK supermarket chain, you can be sure it will not contain any cotton from Uzbekistan. The company decided to boycott Uzbek cotton following reports of forced and state-sanctioned child labour. "It was an enormously complex task," says Alan Wragg, the company's Clothing Technical Director. "Even the production of a simple garment such as a T-shirt requires materials to pass through four to seven pairs of hands, so the number of possible permutations in the supply chain was huge."

2 Traceability has become an especially pressing issue for the clothing industry in recent years, as stories of worker exploitation have emerged from the developing world. However, some supply-chain experts believe all retailers and their suppliers should be preparing for the sorts of challenge faced by Mr Wragg. We are approaching a tipping point, they say, beyond which everyone will want to know the provenance of their products.

3 At Tesco, Mr Wragg knew that in order to monitor his supply chain, he first needed to see it more clearly. "We learned quickly that our supply chain was very complicated and diverse," he says. "We knew that Uzbek cotton was taken mainly to Bangladesh, Turkey and China, but most producers of yarn don't use a single source, they blend cotton from a variety of countries." The quality of raw cotton can vary depending on local factors such as weather conditions, he explains, so blending prevents inconsistencies in the finished yarn.

4 The solution was provided by Historic Futures. This UK company has developed an online application called String, which enables users to see at a glance what has happened to a particular product at every stage in its supply chain. String can capture data about any event resulting in an output – for example, when raw materials are purchased from a third party, when production processes are performed on those materials and so on – including documentary evidence uploaded to the site. If anyone fails to provide such evidence, this is clearly visible to those further along the supply chain.

5 "We're not in the business of guaranteeing the data, we're in the business of automating the audit process," says Tim Wilson, Managing Director. "If you wanted to falsify your data, then you'd have to get everyone below you in the chain to falsify their data too. It's a tiny problem compared with the patchy recording of data, which is already commonplace where no such system exists. We want String to be the Facebook of supply chains."

1 Look through the whole article to find the name(s) of ...

a) a UK supermarket chain
b) its Clothing Technical Director
c) a country that produces cotton
d) three countries that this cotton is taken to
e) a company that provides information on supply chains
f) an Internet application that it has developed
g) the company's Managing Director

2 Complete the answers to these questions about paragraphs 1 and 2.

a) Do Tesco's clothes contain Uzbek cotton?
No, Tesco has ....
b) Does the Uzbek government allow children to work in cotton production?
Yes, child ....
c) Is it easy to trace where cotton comes from?
No, it's an ....
d) How many firms does the cotton for T-shirts go through before it reaches Tesco?
Between ....
e) Are there many different routes for T-shirts through the supply chain?
Yes, the number of ....
f) Is the supply chain an ethical concern for suppliers and customers?
Yes, ... is an ....
g) Are workers always treated fairly in the developing world?
No, ... is an issue.
h) Will the origin of supplies become more and more important?
Yes, interest in the issue is reaching a ....

3 Choose the correct alternative (a, b or c) to complete these statements about expressions from paragraphs 3 and 4.

1 Something that is *complicated* is ...
a) compound. b) complex. c) competent.
2 Things that are *diverse* are ...
a) different from each other.
b) the same as each other.
c) contradictory to each other.
3 Things that are *blended* are ...
a) separated from each other.
b) mixed together.
c) sorted out.
4 *Inconsistencies* are ...
a) deformations.
b) similarities.
c) irregularities.
5 If you see something *at a glance*, you see it ...
a) clearly. b) immediately. c) in focus.
6 A computer application that *captures* data ...
a) incorporates it. b) catches it. c) arrests it.
7 If a process is *performed* on a material, it is ...
a) carried off. b) carried away. c) carried out.
8 Evidence is a way of providing ...
a) proves of something.
b) probes of something.
c) proof of something.

4 Find one verb and three *-ing* forms in paragraph 5 used in relation to *data*. Complete this table with them and related forms. (Be careful with spelling.)

verb	*-ing* form	noun
guarantee	1	2
..........3	4	5
..........6	7	8
..........9	recording	10

5 Choose the correct alternative (a, b or c) to complete this sentence.

When Tim Wilson says 'We want String to be the Facebook of supply chains,' he means that he ...

a) wants it to provide photographs of users, updates about their private lives, give information on the status of their 'friends', etc.
b) is realistic in thinking that it will be as popular and profitable as Facebook.
c) thinks it can provide information about materials and products in the supply chain in the same way that Facebook provides information about people.

6 Look at the headline again and explain the use of *unravel* in the context of the article.

Over to you 1

Would you boycott goods produced in a way you considered unethical? Why? / Why not?

Over to you 2

Research on the Internet a website that allows you to trace the provenance of products, and prepare a short report on it. (Hint: Do an Internet search on *traceability*.)

TEXT BANK

UNIT 6 Ethics

THE TEACHABILITY OF ETHICS

Before you read

Can ethics be taught, or should businesspeople intuitively know the right thing to do in different situations?

Reading

Read the article from the *Financial Times* by Mary Gentile and do the exercises that follow.

FT

LEVEL OF DIFFICULTY ● ● ●

Ethics teaching asks the wrong questions

Mary Gentile

1 A few years ago, I suffered a crisis of faith. After working in the field of business ethics at Harvard Business School, I began to wonder if it was even ethical to try to teach the subject. Classes were typically based on thorny ethical dilemmas: the ones we termed "right versus right" discussions, although they often amounted to more of a search for the lesser evil. Students who argued for "ethical" positions would often appear to be less sophisticated; the way to demonstrate you were worldly wise was to argue that the competitive marketplace did not allow for self-serving morality, or even more cleverly, that it was wrong to behave in such a selfish way, putting one's own conscience over the good of the enterprise and shareholders.

2 But then I realized that the MBA graduates pictured in handcuffs were typically those who had been engaged in more clear-cut offences; rather than right-versus-right scenarios, their offences were not only unethical but illegal. And I wondered if our focus on distinguishing right from wrong was actually creating a kind of "school for scandal."

3 Were we asking the wrong questions? Shouldn't we invite students to think about how to do what was ethical and legal, rather than whether it was possible (or profitable) to do so? And what if we asked students to develop action plans and "scripts" for what they would say and do when they encountered the very predictable pressures to behave unethically? We could then tell them to practice these scripts with each other—not as adversarial role play but as peer coaching exercises. Students would prove their sophistication with the most feasible arguments and methods to do the seemingly impossible, that is, behave in accordance with their highest values in the workplace.

4 Just think what might have happened at BP in the Gulf of Mexico if individuals there not only knew what the right thing to do was (we know there was more than one engineer who tried to speak up about safety violations), but also knew how to do so effectively.

5 This idea is not rocket science. It amounts to educators asking students, and business leaders asking employees to bring their insights, their critical thinking, and innovative ideas to the task of getting the right thing done. We know that the heroes of business history comprise individuals who made "do-able" what previously seemed impossible. Let's invite students to apply that same passion and entrepreneurial spirit to building a values-driven economy.

1 Which alternative (a, b or c) *cannot* be used to replace the expression in *italic* from paragraph 1, keeping a similar meaning?

1 A few years ago, I *suffered* a crisis of faith.
a) experienced b) underwent c) submitted

2 After working in the *field* of business ethics at Harvard Business School, ...
a) area b) pasture c) discipline

3 ... I began to *wonder* if it was even ethical to try to teach the subject.
a) question b) ask myself c) interrogate myself

4 Classes were typically based on *thorny* ethical dilemmas: ...
a) complex b) sharp c) difficult

5 ... although they often *amounted* to more of a search for the lesser evil.
a) ended up as being
b) came down to
c) went in for

6 Students who argued for 'ethical' positions would often appear to be less *sophisticated*; ...
a) luxurious in their thinking
b) refined in their thinking
c) clever in their thinking

7 ... the way to demonstrate you *were worldly wise* ...
a) had no dreams
b) had no illusions
c) were quite cynical

8 ... was to argue that the competitive marketplace did not allow for *self-serving morality*, ...
a) morality that gives you an advantage
b) self-service morality
c) morality that benefits you

9 ... or even more cleverly, that it was wrong to behave in such a selfish way, putting one's own conscience *over* the good of the enterprise and shareholders.
a) beneath b) above c) before

2 Decide whether these statements about expressions in paragraph 2 are true or false.

a) If someone is in *handcuffs*, it is usually because they have been arrested.
b) A *clear-cut offence* is a crime that involves a grey area between right and wrong.
c) A *right-versus-right scenario* is one where both arguments could be equally valid.
d) If you have a *focus* on something, you consider it is equally important in relation to a number of other things.
e) If you *distinguish* x from y, you think they are the same.
f) A *school for scandal* is an expression for a place where people learn how to commit crimes, engage in wrongdoing, etc.

3 In paragraph 3, find ...

a) a noun referring to a plan for how to behave, what to say, etc. in a particular situation.
b) a noun that can refer to a member of the British House of Lords, but that here is used adjectivally to refer to people similar to others, in the same situation, etc.
c) a noun that refers to complexity, whose adjectival form is used in paragraph 1.
d) a three-word expression to say that something is done in a way that is compatible with something else.
e) a verb normally spelled with an *s* in British English.
f) a verb that could be replaced by *met*.
g) a way of making a suggestion using a modal verb.
h) a way of making a suggestion using a word beginning *wh-*.
i) an *-ing* form that can also refer to sports training.
j) an adjective to say that something is do-able.

4 What do these words and expressions in *italic* from paragraphs 4 and 5 refer to?

a) Just think what might have happened at BP in the Gulf of Mexico if *individuals* there ...
b) ... not only knew what the right thing to do was (we know there was more than one engineer who tried to speak up about safety violations), but also knew how to *do so* effectively.
c) *This idea* is not rocket science.
d) *It* amounts to educators asking students, and business leaders asking employees to bring their insights, their critical thinking, and innovative ideas to the task of getting the right thing done.
e) *We* know that the heroes of business history comprise individuals who made 'do-able' what previously seemed impossible.
f) Let's invite students to apply *that same passion and entrepreneurial spirit* to building a values-driven economy.

5 Choose the best summary (a, b or c) for the whole article.

Ethics teaching in business schools ...
a) is a waste of time and should be abandoned, as it just encourages people to think about the fastest way to make a profit.
b) should be reformed so as to concentrate not only on what to think about particular situations, but how to put that thinking into action.
c) produces perverse results and results in MBAs in handcuffs, with their pictures on television and in the newspapers.

Over to you 1

Do you agree with the ideas in the article? Why? / Why not?

Over to you 2

Think about a recent corporate scandal. Outline a 'script' for executives that might have prevented it.

TEXT BANK

FINANCIAL RESULTS

Before you read

List 10 expressions that you might find in an article about a company's financial results.

Reading

Read this article from the *Financial Times* by Rose Jacobs and do the exercises that follow.

FT

LEVEL OF DIFFICULTY ● ● ○

Al-Fayed goes out in style as Harrods leaps 40 per cent

Rose Jacobs

1 Mohamed Al-Fayed's swansong financial results at Harrods revealed that the department store saw strong growth in profits in the final year under its colourful owner. Mr Al-Fayed and his top directors – who resigned in May following the sale of the group to Qatar's sovereign wealth fund – pointed to a customer loyalty scheme and refurbishments of the group's Knightsbridge store as a few of the forces behind a 12-per-cent rise in sales and 40-per-cent surge in profit.

2 The £78m ($123m) in pre-tax profits reported for the year to January 31 are two-and-a-half times the £30m Harrods earned in 1985, when Mr Al-Fayed outbid rival businessman Tiny Rowland for the group, prompting a political furore. When Qatar Holding, a direct invesment vehicle for the Gulf state, bought Harrods in May for £1.5bn, Ahmad Al-Sayed, the fund's Chief Executive, said the move was part of a strategy of adding "prestigious, top-performing businesses" to its portfolio at low points in the economic cycle.

3 Last year's results show Qatar took on a group in the midst of a significant investment programme: Harrods put £35.6m into refurbishment of its Knightsbridge store, including the addition of two restaurants, and the opening of a shop and boutique in Heathrow's Terminal 4. The former management team promised "a similar level of capital investment in 2010".

4 That sort of capital expenditure may increase under the Qataris: Mr Al-Sayed this spring launched a three-month strategic review of the business, which included consideration of a makeover of the store. The review also focused on possible overseas expansion, development of an online offering and extending the sale of Harrods-branded souvenirs for the mass market.

5 Mr Al-Sayed has not spoken about the conclusions drawn from the review, but the company is developing its fashion portal, aiming to create a serious rival to online market leader Net-a-Porter. Meanwhile, while managers have said they would like to open a Harrods venue in Shanghai – a move that would capitalise on growing demand for luxury goods from Chinese shoppers – no plans have been announced. In 2009, £515.5m of the company's £519.8m revenue was derived from Harrods' UK operations, with Japan as the next biggest contributor, at £2.5m.

1 Look through the whole article to match the figures (1–9) to the things that they refer to in Harrods' accounts (a–i).

1 £2.5m
2 £30m
3 £35.6m
4 £515.5m
5 £519.8m
6 £78m
7 £1.5bn
8 12 per cent
9 40 per cent

a) increase in sales over the previous year
b) increase in profit over the previous year
c) price paid by Qatar Holding to buy the company
d) revenue worldwide
e) profits before tax
f) revenue in Japan
g) money put into improving the store
h) profit made in 1985
i) revenue in the UK

2 Decide whether these statements about expressions in paragraphs 1 and 2 are true or false.

a) If something is your *swansong*, it's the last time that you do it.
b) If you describe someone as *colourful*, you mean that they are boring.
c) If x is described as *a force behind* y, x is the cause of y.
d) A *surge* is a large increase.
e) If you *outbid* someone when buying something, you offer more for it.
f) A *furore* is a mild disagreement.
g) Something *prestigious* is of high quality and is famous.
h) A *portfolio* is a collection of different investments.
i) The *economic cycle* is a means of transport.

3 Complete this table with words from paragraphs 3 and 4, and related words.

noun	verb
investment	1
..........2	refurbish
expenditure	3
makeover	4
expansion	5
..........6 / 7	offer
..........8	extend

4 Find nouns in Exercise 3 to match each of these definitions.

a) something that is available for sale
b) when you improve the look of something (two expressions)
c) when you make something bigger
d) when you offer new products using the prestige, etc. of your existing products
e) when you put money into something for profit
f) when you spend money on something

5 Choose the best alternative (a, b or c) to replace each of the expressions in *italic* from paragraph 5, keeping the closest meaning.

1 Mr Al-Sayed has not spoken about the *conclusions drawn* from the review, ...
a) endings of b) results of c) effects of

2 ... but the company is developing its fashion *portal*, aiming to create a serious rival to online market leader Net-a-Porter.
a) website b) service provider c) doorway

3 Meanwhile, while managers have said they would like to open a Harrods *venue* in Shanghai ...
a) meeting place b) concert hall c) store

4 ... – a move that would *capitalise on* growing demand for luxury goods from Chinese shoppers – no plans have been announced.
a) invest in b) amortise c) exploit

5 In 2009, £515.5m of the company's £519.8m revenue *was derived from* Harrods' UK operations, ...
a) resulted in b) drew out from c) came from

6 ... with Japan as the *next biggest contributor*, at £2.5m.
a) second highest source of profits
b) second most important source of revenue
c) second greatest profit centre.

Over to you 1

Go back to *Before you read*, and the list of financial expressions that you made. How many of them actually occurred in the article?

Over to you 2

Think of another retailer that you are interested in. Research its financial results for the latest year and compare them with those for Harrods.

FINANCIAL MATHEMATICS

Before you read

How important is mathematics in the area of business that you work in or would like to join? Explain your ideas.

Reading

Read the article from the *Financial Times* by Gillian Tett and do the exercises that follow.

FT

LEVEL OF DIFFICULTY ● ● ●

What happens to markets when numbers don't add up

Gillian Tett

1 A few years ago, Tim Johnson, a British academic at Heriot Watt University, was appointed to act as an official public "champion" for financial mathematics. It initially seemed an easy job. After all, before 2007, politicians were not very interested in things such as probability theory. So Dr Johnson mostly used his huge grant to conduct his research in peace.

2 No longer. In the years since the financial crisis exploded, financial mathematics has come in the line of fire, with "quants" – analysts with qualifications in advanced mathematics – and their models blamed for fuelling the banking woes. Hence Dr Johnson now has his work cut out, as he tries to defend the world of maths. Or as he told a conference this week: "There is a sense of bewilderment amongst mathematicians about the view that mathematics was responsible for the crisis."

3 Is this sense of indignation fair? Up to a point, yes. During the past couple of decades, the world of finance has certainly borrowed heavily from disciplines such as maths and science, and some of this plagiarism has produced disastrous results. Just look at all those crazy investment decisions inspired by ultra-complex – and flawed – models to assess risk.

4 But if you peer closely at all this plagiarism, it is dogged by a bitter irony. In public, banks like to boast of their ability to buy the "brightest and best"; in practice, though, the specific ideas that banks have been importing from disciplines such as maths or economics in recent years have not always been "cutting edge". On the contrary, many of the imports that have been widely used – or abused – were distinctly out of date.

5 For example, when finance has borrowed ideas from physics, it has been an old-fashioned Newtonian branch of physics, not the Theory of Relativity. And insofar as bankers have used maths in the past two decades, they – like 18th-century scientists – have typically treated maths as a "mere" tool.

6 Most academic mathematicians, however, prefer to view their discipline as a form of intellectual inquiry. Many also feel uncomfortable about assuming that maths offers crude "absolutes". So, just as the Theory of Relativity has forced scientists to recognise that space and time can expand or shrink in a relativist manner, so too men such as Dr Johnson tend to think that calculations of "probability" can shift according to context. Money and statistics, in other words, are not crude, fixed entities (as bankers have tended to assume); instead, Dr Johnson's vision of "maths" sounds more akin to the financial version of quantum mechanics.

1 What or who from paragraphs 1 and 2 do the words in *italic* refer to?

a) Until the crash of 2007, *he* led a relatively quiet life.
b) *It* was a job that seemed easy.
c) *They* were not interested in the mathematical theories behind finance.
d) *It* is being increasingly criticised.
e) *It* is where Tim Johnson spoke this week.
f) Mathematicians feel *this* because they have been accused of responsibility for the crash.

2 Look at paragraphs 3 and 4 and find ...

a) a noun referring to a feeling connected to another feeling in paragraph 2.
b) a noun, used twice, meaning 'subjects'.
c) an expression meaning 'to a certain extent'.
d) a noun referring to the copying of ideas.
e) an expression referring to very difficult mathematical ideas that were mistaken.
f) a verb meaning 'to look closely'.
g) a form ending in *-ed* used to refer to something that has been subject to problems.
h) a noun for the feeling that something odd has happened, the opposite of what was expected.
i) an expression referring to the most intelligent people.
j) an expression referring to the most up-to-date ideas.

3 Choose the best summary (a, b or c) of the main point of paragraphs 3 and 4.

Financial mathematicians ...

a) are entirely to blame for the financial crash of 2007 because of the flawed and risky models they used at the banks.
b) are entirely blameless, as they were not responsible for the out-of-date ideas that were being used by the banks.
c) contributed to the crisis, but the ideas used by the banks were not as advanced as the theories developed by these people would have suggested.

4 Find 'linking' expressions from paragraphs 5 and 6 used to ...

a) give an illustration (two words).
b) say that something is true up to a point but not completely (two words – can also be spelled as four words).
c) contrast two ideas (one word).
d) add an idea (one word).
e) introduce a consequence of an argument (one word).
f) add an idea similar to the one just stated (two words).
g) re-express an idea that has already been stated (three words).
h) say that one idea is true, rather than another just stated (one word).

5 Choose the best summary (a, b or c) for the article as a whole.

a) Financial mathematicians played a role in the crash, but ironically banks were not using their most advanced ideas and might not have failed if they had been using them.
b) Bankers do not understand financial mathematics and misunderstood the models that they were using, intimidated by the brilliance of their 'brightest and best' financial recruits.
c) Financial mathematics as practised in universities has nothing to do with the maths used by financial institutions.

Over to you 1

How is working in the finance industry viewed in your country? What are the best qualifications to have if you want to work in it?

Over to you 2

Think about your own area of business, or one that you would like to work in. Is there a close link between it and universities? For example, is university research relevant to the business area? Why? / Why not?

HEADHUNTERS

Before you read

Headhunting is when executives are approached by consultants who try to persuade them to take another job. Some people think this is unethical. What do you think?

Reading

Read this interview with Nigel Parslow from the *Financial Times* and do the exercises that follow.

FT

LEVEL OF DIFFICULTY ●●○

Candidates in some sectors need a little coercing

Interview with Nigel Parslow, UK Managing Director, Executive Search, Harvey Nash plc

...............?[1]

The appeal lies in the development of long-term relationships with clients, where they embrace you in their strategic thinking and confidence, combined with the accolades received from candidates in securing great appointments for them. As in all walks of life, it is great to be remembered, respected and seen as contributing to clients' objectives and candidates' lives.

...............?[2]

The best are those candidates who get a role through me and progress rapidly in the client organisation over several years. Two examples: a UK marketing manager progressed to Sales and Marketing Director and then on to running one of the client's global businesses; and a manufacturing director of a German-owned food services organisation progressed over nine years to become the UK Managing Director and ultimately to managing its EMEA-region organisation, with more than 4,000 employees.

...............?[3]

Modern social and business media offer an excellent means of communication to wide groups of prospective candidates, and to an extent it has commoditised aspects of finding candidates. The best search is achieved through applying the principles of management consultancy within the search industry. This can only be done by dialogue and exchange.

...............?[4]

It's all in the preparation. The researcher or the search consultant should have researched the target thoroughly, assessing expertise and how the vacancy would be viewed by this candidate. There is no point in targeting a candidate for a role which takes their career backwards or doesn't play to their expertise.

...............?[5]

The search industry has evolved at a different pace in different countries. In the US, it is mature, and candidates work hard to be on the radar of search consultants and are very responsive to calls. Other geographies are less so. Even in the UK, there are some functions and sectors that need more coercing in accepting a call, such as engineering and parts of the industrial sector.

...............?[6]

The industry is based on trust and there are no "tricks". Successful recruitment is based on working closely with the candidate and the client to ensure that the courtship is managed in a timely fashion with absolute openness and integrity.

TEXT BANK

1 Read through the whole interview and match each of these questions (a–f) to the paragraph (1–6) that answers it.

a) Are executives in some sectors more receptive to calls than others?
b) How do you approach the big phone call when headhunting someone?
c) How do you persuade reluctant movers to take a post?
d) How do you see your job?
e) What is the most effective mode of communication?
f) What was your best placement?

2 Look at the headline of the article. Which two questions (a–f) in Exercise 1 does it most closely relate to?

3 Find expressions in paragraph 1 that mean the following.

a) attraction
b) dealings with people
c) different professions, etc.
d) goals
e) jobs
f) obtaining
g) praise
h) warmly accept

4 Decide whether these statements about paragraphs 2 and 3 are true or false, or the information is not given.

a) The best placements are the ones where the candidate goes on to be promoted quickly by the recruiting organisation.
b) The first example of a satisfying placement was of a British executive.
c) The second example of this relates to a German executive.
d) The manager in the second example ended up in the US.
e) Headhunting is still a sophisticated activity that only highly trained people can do.
f) Nigel Parslow uses the same ideas as other management consultants.
g) He tries to impose his ideas on his clients.

5 Complete these statements using grammatically appropriate forms of expressions from paragraphs 4 and 5.

If ...

a) you make an a.......... of a particular situation, you evaluate it.
b) you have a particular v.......... of something, this is your opinion of it.
c) you are an e.......... in a particular area, you have very good knowledge of it.
d) you do a t.......... job, you do it in a complete way.
e) you r.......... to a consultant's offer, you are willing to discuss it.
f) you c.......... someone to do something, you force them to do it.
g) something doesn't p.......... to something else, it doesn't correspond to it.
h) a market sector is m.........., a lot of people know about it, participate in it, etc.

6 In paragraphs 5 and 6, find ...

a) a four-word expression originally referring to aircraft or shipping, used here to talk about awareness of someone.
b) a three-word name (including *the*) for the activity of headhunters.
c) a noun used in the plural, whose singular form is the name of a subject taught in schools.
d) a noun that can refer to a physical area, used here to talk about a particular business activity.
e) a plural noun referring to situations where someone is cheated or fooled.
f) a noun that usually refers to the period before a couple are married.
g) a noun referring to honesty.
h) a noun referring to not hiding things.

Over to you 1

Go back to the answer you gave in *Before you read*. Would it be the same now that you have read the interview? Why? / Why not?

Over to you 2

'Modern social and business media offer an excellent means of communication to wide groups of prospective candidates, and to an extent it has commoditised aspects of finding candidates.' Nigel is here referring to sites like Facebook and LinkedIn. What other effects have sites like these had on the world of work, in your view?

TEXT BANK

CONSULTANCY IN A RECESSION

Before you read

When should organisations call in consultants?

Reading

Read this article from the *Financial Times* by Dave Ulrich and do the exercises that follow.

FT

LEVEL OF DIFFICULTY ●●●

Tips for when the tide turns

Dave Ulrich

1 If a rising tide lifts all boats, a falling tide exposes all flaws. In an upturn, companies may grow without outside advice, yet they have money for consulting services. In a downturn, companies have less money for consulting expertise, but need it more. And while demand for consultants falls, their supply increases as many former employees in other sectors naively view consulting as their career redemption.

2 These paradoxes reveal the realities and opportunities of consulting in current market conditions. First, consultants must offer unique value. While low-cost, generic products often prevail in a thrifty economy, consultants who offer generic ideas and insights will be exposed. Branded consulting, where the consultants have a deserved reputation for innovative ideas and pragmatic solutions, will continue to add value as clients scrutinise the value of such services.

3 Consultants who offer tangible results that clients could not otherwise find will continue to grow. In our work on organisational transformation, leadership brand, human resources and talent, we have found that, more than ever, clients need innovative solutions that may not be found in their own history. They need to access and apply ideas and actions from the experiences of others. Consultants transfer knowledge that leads to client productivity.

4 Second, to paraphrase Darwin, only the best survive. It has become trite to say that a crisis is a terrible thing to waste. The good news is that this economic downturn has exposed charlatans, fads and what we call "consulting foo-foo". Quick-fix consulting solutions are like fad diets, with bold promises and few sustainable results. Consultants who have creative ideas, thoughtful theories and research roots are likely to be more fit to serve and survive.

5 Third, successful consultants need to adapt and learn. Consulting firms must offer tailored, targeted and measurable solutions to client problems, both expressed and unexpressed. Tailored projects mean that off-the-shelf solutions are replaced by joint learning. Clients should prepare to adapt, not adopt, solutions found in other settings.

6 Creative consultants engage by listening and diagnosing more than recommending and solving. Targeted projects mean that clients should find consultants who scope and bound their interventions with outcomes and timelines. Clients should lease-to-own consultant knowledge rather than rent it.

7 Measurable projects come from consultants who see the value of their work for the clients' investors (economic value), customers (customer share value) and employees (emotional value). Innovative consultants share the risk and gain of successful projects. When consultants adapt their offerings by tailoring, targeting and measuring them, clients come to trust that consultants have their interests in mind.

1 In what order does this information occur in the article?

Consultants ...

a) must offer something unique.

b) need to produce tangible results.

c) need to adapt.

d) need to be innovative.

e) need to listen.

f) will only survive if they are creative.

g) work in an activity with many contradictions.

2 What are the contradictions outlined in paragraph 1?

3 Choose the best alternative (a, b or c) to replace each expression in *italic* from paragraph 2, keeping the most similar meaning.

1 These paradoxes *reveal* the realities and opportunities of consulting in current market conditions.

a) hide b) conceal c) show

2 While low-cost, generic products often *prevail* in a thrifty economy, ...

a) precede b) succeed c) recede

3 ... consultants who offer *generic* ideas and insights ...

a) standard b) genial c) specialised

4 ... will be *exposed*.

a) found up b) found out c) found in

5 Branded consulting, where the consultants have a *deserved* reputation ...

a) merited b) deserted c) important

6 ... for innovative ideas and *pragmatic* solutions, ...

a) theoretical b) practical c) positive

7 ... will continue to add value as clients *scrutinise* the value of such services.

a) severely criticise

b) casually look at

c) carefully examine

4 Complete this table with words from paragraphs 3 and 4, and related expressions.

verb	noun
survive	.........[1]
.........[2]	transformation
access	.........[3]
apply	.........[4]
.........[5]	experience
.........[6]	transfer
paraphrase	.........[7]

5 In paragraph 4, find ...

a) a noun referring to origins.

b) a plural noun meaning 'fashions', also used adjectivally in its singular form to mean 'fashionable'.

c) a plural noun referring to people who pretend to have knowledge and qualifications, but do not.

d) a two-word expression meaning 'rubbish' (used by the writer but probably not found in dictionaries).

e) an adjective meaning 'banal'.

f) an adjective to describe intelligent ideas.

g) an adjective to describe something that can be maintained.

6 Complete this table with contrasting ideas from paragraphs 5 and 6.

expressed problems	unexpressed problems[1]
tailored projects	.........[2]
.........[3]	adopt solutions
.........[4]	recommending and solving
lease-to-own knowledge	.........[5]

7 Choose the best alternative (a, b or c) to summarise the main point of paragraph 7.

a) Clients value tailored and targeted consultancy with measurable outcomes that are positive for three different groups.

b) Clients want consultants to bear all the risk in projects, especially during recessions.

c) Consultants should think first of all about the outcome for their clients' customers.

Over to you 1

What is the status/role of consultants in your country? What reputation do they have?

Over to you 2

Think of a company or school that you know (perhaps your own). If you could hire consultants to suggest improvements in a particular area, what would that area be? Explain your reasons.

THE GOVERNMENT'S ROLE IN INDUSTRIAL STRATEGY

Before you read

What should a government do to formulate strategy for the industries of the future?

Reading

Read this article from the *Financial Times* by John Kay and do the exercises that follow.

FT

LEVEL OF DIFFICULTY ●●○

The job of Business Minister is to put the future first

John Kay

1 If you were a government department pondering the future of the computer industry in the 1970s, you would naturally have turned to IBM for thoughtful experts and presentations. You would not have consulted Bill Gates or Steve Jobs, who were barely out of school, or Michael Dell, who was barely in it. But IBM did not know the future of the industry. If it had known, it would have tried to prevent it. The interests of the industry and of consumers were not only different from those of the dominant business: they were diametrically opposed.

2 If, a decade later, you had wondered what government could do to promote Britain's civil aviation industry, you would have asked British Airways – and perhaps its main rival, British Caledonian. The government tried to promote competition through liberal policies that particularly favoured Caledonian. All irrelevant, of course – Caledonian would disappear, and the people who controlled the future were Michael O'Leary of Ryanair and Stelios Haji-Ioannou of easyJet. But as Business Minister, you would have had no reason to give them the time of day.

3 Confusion between the interests of an industry and the interests of existing companies pervaded last year's Digital Britain policy document and the legislation that followed. An admirable desire to promote Britain's creative industries is translated into a wish list for corporate lobbyists, hired by large companies and trade associations. Who else could they be hired by?

4 So the proper interpretation of a business minister's task is the promotion of markets. Their job is not to reward grandees with knighthoods and favours but to encourage a new generation of people such as Gates, Dell and Jobs, Stelios and O'Leary, none of whom they are likely to meet unless they stay in their job for 20 years. Promoting innovation means making it easy for new entrants to develop new products and business processes, not subsidising existing research and development.

5 The interests of businesspeople do not necessarily coincide with the interests of a dynamic market economy. These include executive remuneration, obsession with mergers and acquisitions, and the toxic combination of quarterly investment performance and quarterly corporate reporting. A business minister should focus on issues such as these that enable business to improve how it serves the public. They should not act as a super lobbyist, collating the suggestions of the chief executives and public relations consultants constantly banging on their door.

1 Look at paragraphs 1 and 2. Which verb structure is used in the first, second and fourth sentences of paragraph 1, and the first and fourth sentences of paragraph 2?

2 Decide whether these statements about words and expressions used in paragraphs 1 and 2 are true or false.

If ...

a) you *ponder* something, you think about it briefly and superficially.
b) someone is *barely out of school*, they have been out of school for a long time.
c) a business is *dominant* in an industry, it is the most powerful firm.
d) something is *diametrically opposed* to something else, it is completely different from it.
e) something is *irrelevant*, it is meaningful and important.
f) you don't *give someone the time of day*, you don't consider them important.

3 This table contains words from paragraph 3, and related words. Correct them where necessary.

verb	noun
confound	confusion
pervade	pervasion
legify	legislation
lobby	lobbier (person lobbying)
hire	hiree (person hired, esp. AmE)
associalise	association

4 Answer these questions about paragraph 4.

a) What is the main responsibility of a minister for business?
b) Are they ever likely to meet the people who emerge as the founders of the next successful businesses? Why? / Why not?
c) Should a business minister promote R&D?

5 Find words and expressions in paragraph 5 that mean the following.

a) when two things happen together with negative results
b) occasions when one company buys another
c) occasions when companies join
d) when companies announce their financial results
e) when you think about certain things to the total exclusion of others
f) senior managers' pay

6 Choose the best ending (a, b or c) for this sentence summarising the article as a whole.

In setting its industrial strategy, a government should ...

a) try to choose future winners and losers.
b) encourage innovation and facilitate new entrants.
c) honour leaders of successful companies while encouraging new ones.

Over to you 1

Do some research on the Internet about one of the company founders in the article and write a short report about him.

Over to you 2

Think about a company that has emerged in the last 20 years that you are interested in (for example, Amazon, Google or Facebook). Why was it successful, and not its competitors?

STRATEGIC LOCATIONS

Before you read

Think about the headquarters and other sites of a company that you are interested in. Why are they located where they are?

Reading

Read the article from the *Financial Times* by Paul Tyrrell and do the exercises that follow.

LEVEL OF DIFFICULTY ● ● ○

The added value of a group

Paul Tyrrell

1 Babel Media is a company that could, in theory, be based anywhere. It provides the video-games industry with outsourced services such as localisation and quality assurance. Most of its 1,000 staff need only computers and reliable Internet connections to do their jobs. Yet they are concentrated in just a handful of places worldwide to take advantage of specific local conditions.

2 The company was founded in 1999 in Brighton, on the south coast of England, partly because the city has one of the highest concentrations of young foreign workers and students in the UK. Its latest production office was opened in Montreal, Canada – again, a source of young, multilingual talent but also, critically, home to one of the world's fastest-growing "business clusters" for video-games production.

3 The concept of the business cluster has become an increasingly important part of regional development and corporate strategies since 1990, when Michael Porter of Harvard Business School published *The Competitive Advantage of Nations*. In the book and subsequent research, Professor Porter found that as more companies of the same type cluster together in the same place, so they derive more benefits from their "collocation".

4 Companies have long recognised that siting themselves near to rivals could make life easier for customers, cut supply-chain costs, and – most important – make it easier to recruit specialists. However, Professor Porter identified other benefits, such as increased productivity, innovation and start-up activity. In his latest paper on the subject, written with Mercedes Delgado and Scott Stern, he finds that strong clusters produce "higher growth in new business formation and start-up employment" and "contribute to start-up firm survival".

5 For Babel Media, the benefits of being part of the Montreal cluster are numerous, says Steve Kingswell, the company's Chief Financial Officer. "It provides an enhanced labour pool, so recruiting is easier," he says. "The colleges and universities here are encouraged to offer courses in the creative media and technology, and research in the universities gets tailored to our industry. Also, the companies in the cluster can lobby together for changes in the locality."

6 The decision to open an office in Montreal, however, was largely influenced by generous incentives from the Quebec government. Software producers in Montreal can, for example, claim tax relief on up to 30 per cent of the salaries of their production staff, or up to 37.5 per cent if their work is published in French.

1 Look through the whole article to find the name(s) of ...

a) a video-games company.
b) a town on the south coast of England where this company is based.
c) an executive at the Canadian branch of the company.
d) the Canadian city where the company has an office.
e) the province where this city is situated.
f) a business-school professor.
g) two colleagues of his.

2 Find words and expressions in paragraphs 1 and 2 that mean the following.

a) translating video games and other software into other languages, adapting it to different markets, etc.
b) a few
c) testing products to check that they work correctly
d) present in large numbers in a small area
e) speaking many languages
f) places where many businesses of the same type are present
g) the way that things are in a particular place
h) not breaking down

3 Which of these ideas are *not* mentioned in paragraphs 3 or 4?

Clusters ...

a) have been the subject of work by Michael Porter.
b) benefit the firms that make them up, thanks to their being near each other.
c) benefit customers.
d) reduce costs.
e) make it easier to recruit people.
f) allow like-minded people to socialise together.
g) increase productivity.
h) encourage new businesses to form.
i) can provide support to companies in difficulty.
j) make it more likely that new businesses will survive.

4 Look at paragraphs 5 and 6. You are interviewing Steve Kingswell. Use the prompts given to ask questions containing the overall number of words indicated, corresponding to the answers that he gives. The first one has been done for you.

a) What / do (*4 words*) What do you do?
I'm Chief Financial Officer at Babel Media in Montreal.

b) Montreal cluster / bigger choice / potential recruit (*12 words*)
Yes, it provides us with an enhanced labour pool to recruit from.

c) universities here / offer course / creative / media technology (*11 words*)
Yes, colleges and universities here are encouraged to offer courses in the creative media and technology.

d) research / universities / suit / needs / industry (*9 words*)
Yes, research in the universities gets tailored to our industry.

e) presence / industry cluster / persuade / open / office here (*14 words*)
No, it was largely influenced by generous incentives from the Quebec government.

f) tax breaks / government / offer (*7 words*)
Software producers in Montreal can claim tax relief on up to 30 per cent of the salaries of their production staff, or more if their work is published in French.

5 Choose the best summary (a, b or c) for the article as a whole.

a) Tax breaks can help clusters to develop, and Quebec is encouraging a video-games cluster to develop there, like the one in Brighton, England.
b) Michael Porter's research shows the importance of clusters, and Brighton and Montreal are examples of these in relation to the video-games industry.
c) Clusters of video-games makers will no doubt crop up in other places, given the right tax incentives.

Over to you 1

Think about your own industry, or one you would like to join. Do the firms that make up the industry tend to cluster in particular places? If so, where, and what strategic advantages do they gain from being there? If not, why not?

Over to you 2

'Software producers in Montreal can, for example, claim tax relief on up to 30 per cent of the salaries of their production staff, or up to 37.5 per cent if their work is published in French.' Imagine you are a taxpayer in Quebec. Would you approve of this use of government money? Why? / Why not?

TEXT BANK

UNIT 10 Online business

MULTICHANNEL RETAILING

Before you read

Do you prefer shopping in shops to shopping online? Give your reasons.

Reading

Read this article from the *Financial Times* by Jonathan Birchall and do the exercises that follow.

FT

LEVEL OF DIFFICULTY ● ● ○

Digital-savvy shoppers drive change

Jonathan Birchall

1 Best Buy, the largest US electronics retailer, is testing a system that sends messages about special offers to customers' mobile phones when they enter its stores. Kohl's, the mid-price department store, is rolling out in-store touch-screen kiosks that will allow customers to order online items that are not available in the store. JC Penney, its rival, is moving towards the launch of a mobile e-commerce platform, and has just upgraded its website search system. Wal-Mart, the international retail group, is creating a global e-commerce platform.

2 Customer demand may still be sluggish, but US retailers have been continuing to spend money on technology aimed at their customers. "Retailers have maintained as spending priorities anything that may enhance the customer relationship or experience," says Nikki Baird of Retail Systems Research, a consultancy that specialises in retailers' information systems. "Everything else has struggled."

3 The current spending on customer-facing technology is supported by the need, in a slow-growth economy, to deliver increased sales by luring shoppers away from rivals, says Ms Baird. But it also reflects a significant shift in the traditional world of retail technology. Shoppers equipped with smartphones can now use tools from the online world in-store. They can check prices at rival stores and look for independent product reviews. They can use their phones to receive digital offers, and increasingly to access payment systems and complete transactions. But dealing with the digitally equipped "multichannel" shopper is presenting challenges for the industry that go well beyond what the customer sees in the store.

4 For retailers, the challenges of creating a single customer experience both online and in stores can encompass basic considerations such as ensuring the prices or offers are the same whether the customer is buying in a shop or via the Internet.

5 In one of the most radical responses to the challenge, Moosejaw, a small outdoor-equipment retail chain based in Michigan, has done away with a separate computer system for its point-of-sale devices. Instead, the in-store machines connect to the same IBM Websphere Commerce database as its e-commerce site, which is also used by its call-centre sales staff. The system also operates a loyalty reward scheme – the customer's purchase history is accessible in all channels. "All the channels are updated in real time and can each offer the exact same features," says Gary Wohlfeill, Moosejaw's Creative Director. With just seven stores, Moosejaw's multichannel transformation was relatively straightforward.

1 Look through the whole article to find the name(s) of ...

a) five US retailers.
b) the Creative Director of one of them.
c) software used to manage retail sales.
d) the computer company that developed it.
e) a retail consultancy.
f) a consultant who works there.

2 Look at the first four retailers in your answer to a) in Exercise 1, and their innovations in relation to retailing technology. Match each of these utterances by customers (a–d) to the retailer that they are talking about.

a) 'They didn't have it, so I ordered it online while I was in the store.'
b) 'Just as I walked in, my mobile rang, and I saw I could get 30 per cent off laptop computers that day.'
c) 'It's great – I can order anything online and have it delivered anywhere in the world.'
d) 'I can actually order stuff on my mobile.'

3 Decide whether these statements about expressions from paragraphs 2 and 3 are true or false.

a) If demand is *sluggish*, it is high.
b) If you *maintain* spending on something, you continue to spend money on it.
c) If sales of something *struggle*, they do badly.
d) *Customer-facing technology* is used only in companies' back-office operations.
e) If a retailer *lures* customers *away* from rivals, the customers continue to go shopping at competitors' stores.
f) A *significant shift* is a slight change.
g) A *multichannel* shopper is one who only goes shopping in stores.

4 Find expressions with these meanings in paragraphs 4 and 5.

a) the process that customers go through, whether they are buying in-store or online (*three words*)
b) extreme solutions (*two words*)
c) referring to a retailer, its size and the goods that it sells (*six words, including the article*)
d) equipment used in-store (*two expressions, one of four words and one of three words*)
e) people who sell over the phone (*four words*)
f) a programme for regular customers (*three words*)
g) relating to all the things that someone has bought in the past (*three words*)
h) recent changes in all the ways the retailer sells things (*two words*)

5 Choose the best alternative (a, b or c) to complete this description of the customer experience after Moosejaw's transformation.

Moosejaw's customers can ...

a) see on the website all the goods they have bought from Moosejaw, through whatever channel.
b) phone the call centre, but the staff there can only tell them what they bought in the past over the phone.
c) only see what they have bought in one of the seven stores when they visit the store in question.

Over to you 1

Would you be attracted as a customer to retail chains like Moosejaw with a multichannel approach? Why? / Why not?

Over to you 2

Will in-store selling decline in relation to Internet selling over the next 10 years? Justify your opinion.

THE NEXT BIG THING

Before you read

Make some predictions about how the Internet will evolve over the next 10 years.

Reading

Read this article from the *Financial Times* by Richard Waters and do the exercises that follow.

FT

LEVEL OF DIFFICULTY ● ● ●

Valley that thrives on hope of next big online fad

Richard Waters

1 A decade ago, it looked like the first generation of dotcoms had staked out all the online territory worth owning, with companies such as eBay and Amazon owning e-commerce and Yahoo the gatekeeper to online content. But eBay failed to adapt quickly enough as its customers decided they wanted different – and more secure – ways of shopping, while Yahoo responded late to the rise of both search and social networks.

2 The shift to a new computing architecture greatly amplifies the risks of faulty execution. Hand-held devices that draw on services from giant central datacentres – known by the term "cloud computing" – create new, disruptive possibilities. Take music. Apple's iTunes store may have represented the first successful legal approach to digital music, but new technology is creating alternatives. Pandora in the US and Spotify in Europe are proving that many listeners, clutching the latest generation of smartphones, are happy to listen to tunes being streamed from databases in the cloud.

3 The Internet leaders clearly see the risk and are working frantically not to miss a trick. Google has taken to hoovering up small Internet start-ups in its search for talent and fresh ideas. Apple bought a streaming music company, although it has yet to launch a service. There's no guarantee, though, that they can identify all the challenges.

4 The second reason to expect further disruption is that the behaviour of online users evolves in unexpected ways. Not so long ago, the idea that people would get hooked on broadcasting 140-character messages, or trusting an encyclopaedia that can be rewritten by anyone, would have sounded outlandish. Much current experimentation on the Web is focused in two areas – helping users find useful information in ways that don't involve a standard search box, and devising location-based services that tap into the potential of mobile handsets. Large areas of online content, communication and e-commerce could be at stake.

5 At first glance, the forms this experimentation take can seem odd. Quora, a company founded by ex-Facebookers, is generating considerable buzz in the Valley. Ask any question on the service, and leave it to Quora's other users – many of them anonymous – to provide the answer. Information is grouped in subject areas, giving it a flavour of Wikipedia, or around people you are interested in following, like Twitter. Whether valuable information can be filtered from the torrent of noise in a service like Quora is unclear. But out of experimentation like this, the next big online fad – and company – could be born.

1 Match each of these summaries (a–e) to one of the paragraphs (1–5).

a) The evolution of user behaviour is unpredictable.
b) Some established Internet companies have been slow to react to changes in what people want.
c) Quora may be one example of the way things will go.
d) New technology makes it even harder to predict future developments.
e) Google and Apple are buying up small Internet start-ups in order to keep up with technical developments.

2 Find the expression in paragraphs 1 and 2 that each of the words in *italic* relates to.

a) It seemed as if *they* had claimed all the possible 'positions' on the Internet.
b) When you wanted to find something on the Internet, *this* was the place to go to.
c) When you want to buy something, *they* were the places to go to.
d) *They* changed their behaviour in the areas of both search and e-commerce.
e) *This* means that it's easier to make mistakes in implementing strategy.
f) *They* allow users to access services directly on central servers, rather than downloading them.
g) *It* means that future development of the Internet may involve radical, unforeseeable changes in the way it is used.
h) *These* are two examples of music-streaming services.

3 Choosing the correct alternative (a, b or c) to complete each of these statements about expressions in paragraphs 3 and 4.

If ...

1 you work *frantically* to do something, you work
   a) extremely hard.
   b) extremely slowly.
   c) in a disorganised way.
2 you don't want to *miss a trick*, you don't want to miss
   a) an opportunity to play cards.
   b) the opportunity to cheat someone .
   c) any new ideas, developments, opportunities, etc.
3 one company *hoovers up* others, it
   a) destroys them.
   b) sells them.
   c) buys them.
4 you have *yet to do* something, you
   a) have done it.
   b) haven't done it.
   c) shouldn't do it.
5 you expect *disruption*, you expect things to
   a) go on as before.
   b) change enormously.
   c) end completely

4 In paragraph 4, find ...

a) an expression meaning 'more' or 'another'.
b) a verb that means 'develops'.
c) an expression to say that someone becomes addicted to something.
d) an adjective meaning 'very strange'.
e) a noun referring to a process of trial and error.
f) an *-ing* form relating to inventing things.
g) a multiword verb that means to exploit the usefulness of something.
h) a noun referring to the possibilities of something.
i) a two-word expression referring to something that may be 'won' by different competitors.

5 Complete the answers to these questions using appropriate forms of expressions from paragraph 5.

a) Does Quora look like a logical development for the Internet?
   No, it looks ....
b) Is Quora creating a lot of interest?
   Yes, it is ....
c) Is it possible to know the names of all its users?
   No, many of ....
d) Is it similar to Wikipedia?
   Yes, the way the subjects are grouped .... of Wikipedia.
e) What is one of the potential problems with it?
   It's not yet clear if .... from the noise.
f) What might come out of experimentation like this?
   The next big Internet company might ....

6 Look at the headline again and answer these questions.

a) Which valley is being referred to?
b) What is a *fad*?

Over to you 1

Imagine you are walking around an unfamiliar city on holiday with a handheld device connected to the Internet. Would you use local services that automatically came up on the device? What sort of services would be most useful?

Over to you 2

Think about your own industry, or one you would like to work in. What 'disruptions' do you predict in it, perhaps ones linked to developments on the Internet?

TEXT BANK

UNIT **11** New business

THE CAPITAL OF START-UPS

Before you read

Who would you go to for money if you had an idea for a new business?

Reading

Read this article from the *Financial Times* by Jonathan Moules and Tim Bradshaw and do the exercises that follow.

FT

LEVEL OF DIFFICULTY ● ● ○

Fledgling ventures flock to London for seed funding

Jonathan Moules and Tim Bradshaw

1 London has been crowned Europe's capital for start-ups by some of the global technology industry's leading players at a gathering to nurture some of the most promising upcoming entrepreneurial talent. Angel investors, venture capitalists and entrepreneurs from San Francisco, New York, Berlin, Vienna, Paris, Tel Aviv and Johannesburg descended on the campus of University College London in Bloomsbury for Seedcamp, a week-long incubator event and competition aimed at giving promising early-stage ventures a leg-up.

2 New York-born Hussein Kanji, a Seedcamp mentor who moved to the UK from Silicon Valley five years ago, said the past 48 months had seen a marked maturing in London's "ecosystem" for nurturing new companies. Start-up activity has been growing across Europe in recent years, he noted, but the UK capital is where these companies come to network and get investment. "London has turned into pretty much the definitive hub," he said. "You have pretty much all the major European venture-capital firms here and a considerable number of people who want to live here."

3 For the first time, some of this year's finalists received approaches from investors even before the event began, reflecting the reputation that Seedcamp has attained in the start-up community. Some finalists say they wanted to enter the competition as much for the marketing opportunities and access to other investors as for the prize itself.

4 Among the winners of this year's Seedcamp event were Geoff Watts and Julia Fowler, who met racing cars in their native Perth, Australia, before moving to London to set up EDITD, a fashion-industry data provider that describes itself as a Bloomberg for clothing brands. The positive attitude of all involved in Seedcamp provides a wealth of networking opportunities, Watts said, noting that he and Fowler have been invited to Vienna Fashion Week this Wednesday by fellow Seedcamp winner Garmz, another fashion industry start-up, based in the Austrian capital. "People are just so willing to introduce you, and it often turns out that their friend's friend's cousin is a potential customer of yours," Watts said.

5 London's emergence as an entrepreneurial cluster has been helped by the rise of start-up activity across Europe, particularly in the technology sector. Since 2004, seven of the 25 technology companies that went public or were acquired for at least $1bn were based in Europe, including Internet telephony service Skype and satellite navigation service TomTom.

1 Look through the whole article and find ...

a) an event for start-up companies.
b) where it was held.
c) three people who attended it, two of them prize winners.
d) two companies involved in the fashion industry.
e) a fashion event in Austria.
f) two well-known technology companies.

2 Match the two parts of these expressions from paragraph 1.

1 angel	a) capitalists
2 early-stage	b) event
3 entrepreneurial	c) industry
4 incubator	d) investors
5 leading	e) players
6 technology	f) ventures
7 venture	g) talent

3 Match each of the expressions in Exercise 2 with one of these meanings.

a) people with the knowledge and skills to start new companies
b) organisations and people that specialise in investing in start-ups
c) very new companies
d) wealthy individuals who put money into start-ups
e) important people and companies in a particular industry
f) a meeting like Seedcamp designed to help new companies
g) tech companies considered as a group

4 In paragraphs 2 and 3, find ...

a) an adjective meaning 'large'.
b) an *-ing* form referring to the way that something becomes more developed.
c) an *-ing* form referring to help given to new companies.
d) a verb meaning 'reach'.
e) a verb used to talk about making contact with people who may be useful to know.
f) a plural noun used in this context to refer to interest shown by investors in start-ups.
g) a noun used to talk about the centre for something, where people meet to exchange ideas, etc.
h) a noun from biology used here to talk about all the people and organisations involved with start-ups.
i) a noun for someone who helps people by giving them advice.

5 Decide whether these statements about paragraph 4 are true or false.

a) Geoff Watts's and Julia Fowler's business idea involved racing cars
b) They met in Australia.
c) Their start-up is a fashion house.
d) They are going back to Australia in the next few days.
e) They have been invited to Vienna by an investor.
f) Julia said that getting to meet useful people is easy in the world of start-ups.

6 Look at these expressions in *italic* replacing expressions in paragraph 5. Which of them can be used without changing the meaning of the article?

London's **a)** *emergency* as an entrepreneurial cluster has been helped by the **b)** *increase in* start-up activity across Europe, **c)** *especially* in the technology **d)** *segment*. Since 2004, seven of the 25 technology companies that **e)** *were listed on the stock exchange for the first time* or were **f)** *taken over* for at least $1bn were based in Europe, **g)** *comprising* Internet telephone service Skype and satellite navigation service TomTom.

Over to you 1

Is networking important in your industry, or one you would like to work in? What are the main events where networking is possible?

Over to you 2

Would you be willing to move to a) another city, b) another country, or c) another continent to develop your career? Why? / Why not?

TEXT BANK

THE PROTECTION OF NEW BUSINESS IDEAS

Before you read

Should people who steal intellectual property go to prison, like ordinary criminals? Why? / Why not?

Reading

Read the article from the *Financial Times* by Hugo Greenhalgh and do the exercises that follow.

FT

LEVEL OF DIFFICULTY ● ● ●

Theft of intellectual property "should be a crime"

Hugo Greenhalgh

1 Trevor Baylis is angry. The inventor of the clockwork radio believes inventors and entrepreneurs are having their intellectual property (IP) stolen, while the government and the courts fail to offer adequate protection. "The theft of intellectual property should become a white-collar crime," Baylis says. "If I stole from you, then I would probably go to jail. But if I were to steal your intellectual property, which potentially could be worth billions of pounds, it would only be a civil case – and, even then, most of us can't afford to pay £350 an hour for a lawyer."

2 Even with a patent, copyright or trademark (around a business name or brand) in place, IP theft is still extremely common. Gill Grassie, Head of IP and technology at Maclay Murray & Spens, a Scottish firm of solicitors, points out that recent studies have shown the impact of counterfeiters on all industry sectors in the UK is as much as £11bn a year. Adam Morallee, a partner in the IP Group at Mishcon de Reya, a commercial law firm based in London, says his firm recovered more than £100m in damages in the last five years alone for its clients who have had their IP rights infringed.

3 In 2006, Japan and the US established the Anti-Counterfeiting Trade Agreement (ACTA) to fight the growing tide of counterfeiting and piracy. Preliminary talks started that year, and it is hoped some sort of global agreement – now that the two founders have been joined by 35 other nations – can be reached later this year. Yet part of the problem faced by entrepreneurs and inventors is the sheer cost of registering a patent in the first place. "The patent process is slow, expensive and time-consuming," says Stephen Streater, Chief Executive of Forbidden Technologies and the founder of Eidos, a video-games company.

4 A simple way to protect an idea is to make sure potential colleagues or financial backers agree to sign a non-disclosure agreement. "You've got to make sure you have one, so that you have protection," says Clive Halperin at GSC Solicitors. "Once the idea is out there, you've lost your chance."

5 Indeed, when John Barrington-Carver, now Director at PRAM, a Leeds-based public-relations and marketing consultancy, worked with Baylis on the invention of the clockwork radio, he says his job was to keep it out of the media in general to prevent large south-east Asian electronics companies from taking the idea and throwing money at developing a successful production prototype before Baylis could protect the patent.

1 Imagine that each paragraph is the answer to a question. Match the questions (a–e) to the paragraphs (1–5).

a) Are there ways of protecting an idea apart from applying for a patent, copyright or trademark?

b) Does registering a patent, copyright or trademark guarantee protection for a product or idea?

c) What did Trevor Baylis do to protect his idea for a clockwork radio?

d) What has been done to prevent counterfeiting, and what's the main problem faced by entrepreneurs and inventors?

e) Why is Trevor Baylis angry?

2 Complete this table using information in paragraphs 1 and 2. If information is not given, write *NG*.

	property theft	intellectual property theft
criminal or civil case?		
punishment		
cost of lawyers		
cost to UK industry		
frequency of occurrence		

3 Complete these statements with appropriate forms of expressions from paragraphs 1, 2 and 3, and related expressions.

a) Applying for a patent is referred to as the p.......... ....

b) If you succeed in applying for a patent, you r.......... it.

c) The crime of using an idea for a product that someone has patented or copyrighted is patent or copyright i...........

d) Copying a product or using a brand name without permission is c.......... or p.........., and a person who does this is a c.......... or p...........

e) When people steal money through fraud, etc., this is w..........-.......... ....

f) Damages obtained from those who have infringed patents or copyright is r.......... from them.

g) An agreement about IP protection that is valid all round the world is a g.......... agreement.

4 Look at paragraphs 4 and 5. What does each of these words in *italic* refer to?

a) Apply for *this* if you want to stop people copying your invention.

b) *He* made sure that information about *it* was not published. (two expressions)

c) If *it* becomes known, there's nothing you can do about *it*. (two expressions)

d) *They* signed *one*, so they can't talk to other people about it. (two expressions)

e) *They* would have exploited the idea if they had known about it.

f) They would have developed *one* very quickly.

5 Choose the best summary (a, b or c) for the whole article.

a) Trevor Baylis wants those who infringe patents to go to prison in order to reduce the amount of money lost to the UK economy because of this every year.

b) Even if patent infringement was a crime, the best protection against having ideas stolen is to ensure that they are not published before a patent is obtained.

c) If your patent is infringed, you can always obtain damages from the counterfeiters or pirates who did it.

Over to you 1

Go back to your answer in *Before you read*. Would it be the same now that you have read the article? Why? / Why not?

Over to you 2

How long should patent protection for an invention like the clockwork radio last? Explain your reasoning.

TEXT BANK

BRINGING IN A PROJECT MANAGER

Before you read

You have been asked to identify a project in your organisation that could not be carried out using internal resources, and to bring in a temporary project manager with specialist skills to work on it. Which project would you most like to see happen?

Reading

Read this article from the *Financial Times* by Charles Batchelor and do the exercises that follow.

LEVEL OF DIFFICULTY ● ● ○

Interim managers work fast – there are bound to be mistakes

Charles Batchelor

1 In the early days, interim project management was often seen as a temporary berth for out-of-work executives looking for a job to tide them over until something permanent came along. But as the industry has become more professional, clients have become more demanding, and a definition of what makes a good interim project manager has emerged. The attributes required involve a combination of experience, personality and an attitude to the job that demands flexibility, curiosity and a willingness to accept the uncertainty of a series of relatively short-term contracts and no guarantee of future work.

2 Some of these qualities are required of permanent managers, who are also having to deal with a jobs market that has become less secure, but others require a very different approach. "One of the key things is experience of multiple environments," says Nick Robeson, Chief Executive of Alium Partners, an interim management provider. The individual who has worked in one organisation for a very long time might struggle to get up to speed quickly. "You do have to have the ability to make decisions quickly," he explains. "Interim managers are not necessarily 'details people' but they have to be able to prioritise. They need to focus on the important things that need to be delivered. Some mistakes are likely, but that is the price of operating at high speed."

3 The Interim Management Association (IMA) says: "Most functions and business leadership roles and project management tasks translate well into interim management assignments. You need to be an expert in your field with a background of progressive achievement, demonstrating clear success, budgetary and people responsibility. You are unlikely to have worked for the same company for the majority of your career."

4 Interim managers often get called into turnaround situations that require tough decisions on job and budget cuts. But contrary to the idea that the interim manager is a tough nut with a heart of stone, people skills are essential for the job. The interim has to be "capable of quickly establishing a rapport and building trust", according to the IMA. He or she will have "strong interpersonal skills, operating independently or as a team member". Yet, at the same time, the interim manager has to be aware that they are not part of the regular workforce and not get sucked into office politics – what Mr Robeson calls "the day-to-day blancmange of conversations around the water-cooler".

1 Choose the correct alternative (a, b or c) to replace each expression in *italic* from paragraph 1, keeping the same meaning.

1 In the early days, interim project management was often seen as a temporary *berth* for out-of-work executives ...
a) positioning b) position c) positing

2 ... looking for a job to *tide them over* ...
a) help them through a difficult period
b) increase their income
c) boost their morale

3 ... until something permanent *came along*.
a) turned down b) turned in c) turned up

4 But as the industry has become more professional, clients have *become more demanding*, ...
a) increased their attention
b) increased their expectations
c) increased their needs

5 ... and a definition of what makes a good interim project manager has *emerged*.
a) become known
b) become clear
c) become visible

6 The *attributes* required ...
a) character b) characters c) characteristics

7 ... involve a combination of experience, personality and an attitude to the job that demands *flexibility*, ...
a) ability to change so as to work in different ways
b) ability to work at different times of day
c) ability to bend in different directions

8 ... *curiosity* and a willingness to accept the uncertainty of a series of relatively short-term contracts and no guarantee of future work.
a) intrusiveness in different situations, etc.
b) nosiness about different situations, etc.
c) interest in new situations, etc.

2 Find words and expressions in paragraph 2 that mean the following.

a) understand what is required, and start delivering it fast
b) the potential disadvantages of working fast
c) put things into order of importance
d) inside knowledge of how different organisations function
e) decide things fast
f) concentrate on high-priority tasks

3 Decide whether these statements about expressions from paragraph 3 are true or false.

a) *Role* is used as a noun here, but you can also use it as a verb, as in the expression *to role someone with a particular task*.
b) *Task* is used here as a noun, and you can also use it as a verb, as in the expression *to task someone with a particular project*.
c) *Interim* is an adjective that means the same as 'temporary'. There is also an expression *in the interim* that means 'the period of time between two events'.
d) *Assignment* is an informal word meaning 'task'. It can also take the form *assignation*, which means the same thing.
e) If you *demonstrate* a particular achievement, you can show and prove it. The corresponding noun is *demonstration*.
f) *Unlikely* is an adverb, and it could be replaced here by *improbably*.
g) *Majority* is a noun, used here to mean 'most'.

4 Put these ideas from paragraph 4 into the order in which they occur.

Interim managers ...
a) should not get involved in employee gossip.
b) should not be cold and remote.
c) need to be good with people.
d) need to be good at working together with others.
e) need to be good at working on their own.
f) need to be able to deal with negative situations that need to be improved quickly
g) need to be able to build relationships.
h) need to be able to create a feeling of trust.

5 What is *blancmange*? Why is it mentioned at the end of the article?

Over to you 1

Look again at the qualities mentioned in the final paragraph of the article. Would you make a good project manager? Why? / Why not?

Over to you 2

What is the most difficult problem for an outside manager coming into an organisation to manage a project there?

TEXT BANK

PROJECT MANAGEMENT IN THE ARTS

Before you read

Imagine you are responsible for putting on a theatrical production.
Draw up a plan for all the stages in the project.

Reading

Read the article from the *Financial Times* by Rebecca Knight and do the exercises that follow.

FT

LEVEL OF DIFFICULTY ● ● ○

Handling arts projects

Rebecca Knight

1 What are the biggest human-resources headaches at the Paris Opera Ballet? How does the Director of the Berlin Philharmonic increase public appeal? How should the Tate Modern diversify its revenue stream? These are some of the questions that students at Cambridge University's Judge Business School will take up this year as part of the school's new course on cultural and arts management. The programme, which includes various specialised courses on the subject and culminates with a two-week final project on an arts-management theme, aims to give aspiring leaders of large cultural institutions a deeper understanding of the arts sector's most pressing issues.

2 "Many of the concerns emerging in the cultural and arts sector are the same as in other sectors: globalisation, commercialisation, brand development and the exploitation of intellectual property," says Jeremy Newton, the designated "coach" for the course. "But at the same time, running the Bank of New York is very different from running the New York City Ballet. We are going to tease out what it takes to run arts projects or cultural projects on the ground." The Judge MBA specialised programme, which is open to between 10 and 30 students, includes new courses in areas such as art valuation and film finance that incorporate real-world case studies from the UK and elsewhere.

3 There is an acknowledgement from the cultural institutions themselves about the need for leaders with solid management skills, according to Stefano Baia Curioni, the Director of Bocconi University's Master's in economics and management in arts, culture, media and entertainment programme. As the arts industry expands and changes, there is increasing recognition that business know-how is a necessary ingredient in figuring out new ways of assessing the value of cultural projects, or determining new methods of increasing public appeal.

4 "Arts and cultural institutions are very complex, and this complexity is often underestimated," he says. "In the last 15 to 20 years, the state provision that sustained these institutions has been dramatically reduced, and cultural production is in a huge transition. This transition has to be supported by people who understand culture, but also understand project management, and sustainability."

5 The year-long programme includes many specialised courses such as finance for the arts, the history of entertainment and live-entertainment business planning. There is also a field project at the Piccolo Teatro where students put into practice project management and marketing tools they have learned. In addition, the programme makes available internships in institutions including London's Globe Theatre, the New York Chamber Orchestra and Rome's Opera Theatre.

1 Look through the whole article to find the name(s) of ...

a) eight cultural institutions.
b) two academic institutions.
c) one financial institution.

2 Match these expressions from paragraph 1 (1–8) to their meanings (a–h).

1 human resources
2 public appeal
3 revenue stream
4 arts management
5 specialised courses
6 final project
7 cultural institutions
8 arts sector

a) the last piece of work that students do on a course
b) money coming into an organisation
c) what attracts people to something
d) places like art galleries, museums, opera houses, etc.
e) running and administering places like those in d)
f) the places above in d), when considered as a part of the whole economy
g) programmes of study in particular areas, rather than general ones
h) another expression for 'personnel'

3 Use appropriate forms of longer phrases from paragraph 2, containing the expressions in Exercise 2, to complete the utterances below. Not all the expressions from Exercise 2 are used.

a) 'I can't find a decent project manager anywhere! This is one of my ....-.......... ....'
b) 'How can we make ourselves more attractive to the public? How can we .... our ....?'
c) 'How can we find new ways of bringing in money? How can we .... our ....?'
d) 'We don't have the expertise to organise an exhibition like this. We need someone with a qualification in ....'
e) 'While I was at Judge Business School, I followed .... on arts management. And at the end of the course, I did a ....-.......... .... on running publicly owned theatres.'
f) 'Running museums, art galleries and opera houses in the capital is not easy – people who work in these .... need handling very tactfully!'

4 Decide whether these statements about paragraphs 2 and 3 are true or false.

Arts management involves ...

a) completely different skills to those needed in business.
b) totally different issues compared to business.
c) particular issues that Jeremy Newton will look at on his course.
d) finding finance for particular projects.
e) finding leaders with a purely artistic background.
f) finding people who know how to evaluate cultural projects.
g) finding people who will run projects and institutions that appeal only to the elite.

5 In paragraphs 3 and 4, find ...

a) an adjective meaning 'complicated'.
b) a noun related to the above adjective.
c) a past simple verb to say that something can be continued.
d) a noun related to the above verb.
e) a noun referring to funding.
f) a noun referring to a part of something, used mainly in cooking.
g) a noun referring to a change.
h) a noun meaning 'recognition'.
i) a noun meaning 'expertise'.

6 In paragraph 5, find expressions that these things are examples of.

a) work experience at a theatre where students have to write a dissertation at the end
b) unpaid or low-paid jobs to give work experience in theatre
c) planning all the stages of a theatre production, and then supervising it
d) an arts cinema's website and brochures
e) a university course on arts management that lasts 12 months
f) a course on how to organise and manage rock concerts so that they make a profit
g) a course on how to fund opera houses

Over to you 1

What are the main cultural institutions in your country? How are they managed?

Over to you 2

Would arts/cultural management attract you as a career? If so, which areas would you be most interested in? If not, why not?

TEXT BANK KEY

Unit 1

Job applicants' first impressions

1 1 b 2 c 3 e 4 d 5 a

2 a) bad personal hygiene b) interviewer was drunk
c) poor interview preparation d) sexism
e) question unrelated to the job
f) interview held in a bar g) butting in

3 a) false (It was carried out by Ipsos Mori.)
b) true
c) false (They expected a clear career-progression plan.)
d) false (Forty per cent of those *who had had a bad interview experience* said that the questions at the job interview had nothing to do with the job.)
e) true
f) true

4 1 survey 2 apply 3 application
4/5 employer/employee 6 expectation
7/8/9 interview/interviewer/interviewee
10 encounter

5 a) encounter b) employer c) applicant
d) interview e) interviewee f) interviewer
g) employee h) application i) survey
j) expectation

6 1 a 2 c 3 b 4 c 5 a 6 b 7 b

Cosmetic surgery

1 a) Dr Cap Lesesne b) Peter Burling c) Transform
d) American Society of Plastic Surgeons (ASPS)
e) Dr Michael McGuire

2 a) a liar b) gripped by fears c) tired and stressed out
d) Crow's feet e) The ageing process f) it comes to
g) perform better

3 a) non-invasive b) threefold c) pragmatic
d) focused e) frivolous luxuries
f) professional longevity

4 a) focused demands. b) their professional longevity. c) frivolous luxury. d) pragmatic.
e) non-invasive treatments. f) increased threefold.

5 a) decade b) record c) imply – implies
d) vigorous – vigour (BrE), vigor (AmE) e) guys
f) circulation

Unit 2

Training civil servants

1 1 b 2 a 3 a 4 c 5 b 6 c 7 b

2 a) true
b) true
c) false (Civil servants should be able to set up a strategy.)
d) true
e) false (Everybody must be aligned behind the strategy.)

3 1 staff from HEC 2 (real) managers/administration
3 citizens 4 companies/industry 5 investors

4 1 e 2 f 3 c 4 b 5 a 6 d

5 a) conduct b) mega c) operations
d) rank-and-file e) workshop f) respond
g) comprise

Distance learning

1 a) Associate Dean for Graduate Programmes at George Washington University in Washington DC
b) a graduate of the Athabasca online MBA
c) Director of the MBA by Distance Learning at Imperial College Business School in London

2 a) takes centre stage b) emphasise c) enrol
d) strongly believe e) submit f) main trends
g) dominant feature

3 c, e

4 a) virtual collaboration b) essential c) embrace
d) preserve the past e) envisage f) on a par

5 a) true
b) false (A *counterpart* to something is its equivalent, but in talking about people, *counterpart* is used to talk about someone who does the same job as you in another department or organisation.)
c) true
d) true
e) false (It could be replaced by *long-standing*.)
f) false (It relates to the noun *constancy*.)
g) true

Unit 3

Alternative energy

1 a) extravagant b) gas-guzzling c) gigantic
d) misleading e) renewable f) hydroelectric
g) environmental h) aquatic

2 a) true
b) false (For a long period, hydroelectric power was much more important than today.)
c) true
d) false (The figure relates to the western and Pacific north-western states only.)
e) false (Some were closed because they were environmentally damaging.)
f) true

3 1 c 2 b 3 a 4 a 5 b 6 c 7 b

4 a) Renewable energy's share of total US energy consumption in 2004
b) Renewable energy consumption growth, 2007–2008 / Alternative energy sources' contribution to the US's energy make-up
c) Decline in total US energy consumption, 2007–2008
d) Contribution of nuclear energy to US's energy make-up
e) Contribution of wind power to US energy consumption today
f) Contribution of wind power to US energy consumption in 2004

5 a) by far the largest source.
b) is rivalling nuclear power.
c) has overtaken Germany.
d) has grown strongly.
e) electricity generation.
f) contribution.

Peak oil

1 1 c 2 b 3 d 4 a

2 a) leak b) supply c) demand d) viability
e) peak oil f) infrastructure g) depletion

3 a) true
b) true
c) false (BP says production will fall at some point.)

TEXT BANK – Key

d) true
e) false (BP thinks that oil reserves will last another 40 years.)
f) false (BP thinks production will increase.)
g) true
h) false (BP 'pours scorn' on them.)

4 1e 2b 3f 4c 5g 6a 7d

5 1c 2a 3b 4b

Unit 4

Targeted marketing

1 a) UrbanAdserve
b) Sheila Marmon
c) Ford, Procter & Gamble, Chanel
d) Latino, African-American and Asian consumers; African-American women
e) tailored online campaigns, e-mail newsletters, social media websites
f) Julian Castro (the mayor of San Antonio) and Laz Alonzo (an actor)
g) World Bank, University of Georgia's Selig Center, Pew Center, Public Policy Institute of California
h) nightclub, dating, career, parenting

2 a) online b) digital c) ethnic d) demographic
e) affluent f) urban/metropolitan g) tailored
h) straightforward

3 1g 2a 3f 4e 5d 6c 7b

4 a) false (You obtain it.)
b) false (It could be on the Internet.)
c) true
d) false (It could be a change in population of any kind.)
e) true
f) true

5 b

Luxury brands and social media

1 a) true
b) true
c) false (You are able to look them in the eye.)
d) true
e) true
f) false (You are not close to them.)
g) false (There is only one example of it.)

2 Social media has opened up luxury brands to thousands of people. 'Luxury means inaccessibility, uniqueness. And social media means the opposite.'

3 1c 2a 3b 4a 5b 6a 7c 8a

4 a) A very good example of something is a *classic* example of it.
b) If you start communication with someone, you *create* a dialogue with them.
c) People who are not actual customers for a product, but who would like to be, are *aspirational*.
d) People with a similar age, background, etc. to you are your *peers*.
e) Something that brings sales *drives* them.
f) The most important aspect of something is the one that is *dominant*.
g) The most important part of something is its *centre point*.
h) When people buy things because of personal recommendation, this is *word-of-mouth* marketing.
i) You can refer to something very big, that you can't ignore, as *the 800-pound gorilla in the room*.

5 b

Unit 5

The future of work 1

1 1c 2e 3b 4f 5d 6i 7g
(a and h do not occur.)

2 a) in power b) perhaps c) represent our salvation
d) crop up e) optimism f) formation g) locations

3 a) false (The form of the adjective in this context is always *structural*.)
b) false (The jobs are done by people in other countries, usually developing ones.)
c) false (There is a rise in productivity.)
d) true
e) true
f) false (They are for things like social security cover, healthcare and so on.)

4 1e 2f 3c 4b 5g 6a 7d
NB *Green* also collocates with *energy* in the article, but *clean* does not collocate with *jobs*.

5 1b 2g 3a 4f 5e 6d 7c

6 1 boost 2 burden 3 commercialise/commercialize
4 erosion 5 innovate 6 legislate 7 shift

The future of work 2

1 1d 2b 3e 4a 5c

2 a) purposeful b) creation c) value chain
d) microentrepreneurial-rich ecosystems
e) shift f) balance of power
g) command and control structures

3 a) false (It includes people born between about 1945 and 1960.)
b) true
c) false (You normally or often behave that way.)
d) true
e) false (You do understand how other people are feeling.)
f) false (It helps you to go there.)

4 1b 2a 3c 4c 5a 6c

5 a) No, this will be a big challenge.
b) A high level of global cooperation
c) Yes, they tended to.
d) No, it has ebbed.
e) Watching TV
f) Connecting with others on the Internet
g) A big change in the way people think about companies and in the way they use their leisure time

Unit 6

Ethical suppliers

1 a) Tesco b) Alan Wragg c) Uzbekistan
d) Bangladesh, Turkey and China
e) Historic Futures f) String g) Tim Wilson

2 a) boycotted Uzbek cotton
b) labour is state-sanctioned
c) enormously complex task
d) four and seven
e) possible permutations is huge
f) traceability; especially pressing issue
g) exploitation
h) tipping point

3 1b 2a 3b 4c 5b 6a 7c 8c

4 1 guaranteeing 2 guarantee 3 automate
4 automating 5 automation/automaton
6 falsify 7 falsifying 8 falsification 9 record
10 record

5 c

6 *Unravel* is used to talk about a thread that comes apart into its separate parts, so this is appropriate to cotton, and the supply chain for cotton T-shirts is the subject of the article. *Unravel* is also used to talk about solving a mystery or problem, so it is also appropriate in this sense.

The teachability of ethics

1 1 c 2 b 3 c 4 b 5 c 6 a 7 a 8 b 9 a

2 a) true
b) false (It involves a clear case of right and wrong.)
c) true
d) false (You give it more importance than the other things and concentrate on it.)
e) false (You find differences between them.)
f) true

3 a) script b) peer c) sophistication
d) in accordance with e) practice
f) encountered g) Shouldn't we ... h) What if ...
i) coaching j) feasible

4 a) Engineers and others working there
b) Do the right thing
c) The idea of putting ethical thinking into action
d) The idea of putting ethical thinking into action
e) The writer, readers of this article, people interested in ethics teaching generally
f) Doing what seemed previously impossible

5 b

Unit 7

Financial results

1 1 f 2 h 3 g 4 i 5 d 6 e 7 c 8 a 9 b

2 a) true
b) false (They are interesting, create controversy, etc.)
c) true
d) true
e) true
f) false (It's a violent disagreement.)
g) true
h) true
i) false (It's the natural change in economic growth and recession over a period.)

3 1 invest 2 refurbishment 3 spend 4 make over
5 expand 6/7 offer/offering 8 extension

4 a) offer b) refurbishment/makeover
c) expansion d) extension e) investment
f) expenditure

5 1 b 2 a 3 c 4 c 5 c 6 b

Financial mathematics

1 a) Dr Tim Johnson
b) official public 'champion' for financial mathematics
c) politicians
d) financial mathematics
e) a conference
f) (a sense of) bewilderment

2 a) indignation b) disciplines c) Up to a point
d) plagiarism e) ultra-complex – and flawed – models
f) peer g) dogged h) irony i) brightest and best
j) cutting edge

3 c

4 a) For example b) insofar as c) however
d) also e) So f) so too g) in other words
h) instead

5 a

Unit 8

Headhunters

1 1 d 2 f 3 e 4 b 5 a 6 c

2 a and c

3 a) appeal b) relationships c) walks of life
d) objectives e) appointments f) securing
g) accolades h) embrace

4 a) true
b) true
c) not given
d) false (He/She ended up running the Europe–Middle East–Africa (EMEA) area.)
e) false (It has to an extent become widely available commercially.)
f) true
g) false (He believes in dialogue and exchange.)

5 a) assessment b) view c) expert d) thorough
e) respond f) coerce g) play h) mature

6 a) be on the radar b) the search industry
c) geographies d) sector e) tricks f) courtship
g) integrity h) openness

Consultancy in a recession

1 g, a, b, d, f, c, e

2 In a period of growth, companies can afford consulting services, but they can grow without advice from consultants. In a downturn, they need these services more, but are less able to afford them. During downturns, demand for consultants falls, but there are more of them, because people who have lost their jobs start to offer consulting services.

3 1 c 2 b 3 a 4 b 5 a 6 b 7 c

4 1 survival 2 transform 3 access 4 application
5 experience 6 transfer 7 paraphrase

5 a) roots b) fads c) charlatans d) foo-foo
e) trite f) thoughtful g) sustainable

6 2 off-the-shelf solutions 3 adapt solutions
4 listening and diagnosing 5 rent knowledge

7 a

Unit 9

The government's role in industrial strategy

1 third conditional ('impossible' conditional)

2 a) false (You think about it deeply and for a long time.)
b) false (They have only just come out of school.)
c) true
d) true
e) false (It is of no importance because it is not related to what is being considered or discussed.)
f) true

3

verb	noun
confuse	confusion
pervade	**pervasiveness**
legislate	legislation
lobby	**lobbyist** (person lobbying)
hire	**hire** (person hired)
associate	association

4 a) To promote markets, rather than reward leaders of existing businesses
b) No, because leaders of new businesses will take 20 years to emerge, by which time the minister will probably no longer be in the job.

   c) They shouldn't subsidise existing research and development, but encourage new entrants to develop new processes and products.

5 a) toxic combination b) acquisitions c) mergers d) corporate reporting e) obsession f) executive remuneration

6 b

Strategic locations

1 a) Babel Media b) Brighton c) Steve Kingswell d) Montreal e) Quebec f) (Professor) Michael Porter g) Mercedes Delgado and Scott Stern

2 a) localisation b) a handful c) quality assurance d) concentrated e) multilingual f) business clusters g) local conditions h) reliable

3 f, i

4 *Suggested answers*
   b) Does the Montreal cluster give you a bigger choice of potential recruits?
   c) Do universities here offer courses in the creative media and technology?
   d) Does research in universities suit the needs of industry?
   e) Did the presence of the industry cluster persuade you to open an office here?
   f) What tax breaks does/do the government offer?

5 b

Unit 10

Multichannel retailing

1 a) Best Buy, Kohl's, JC Penney, Wal-Mart, Moosejaw
   b) Gary Wohlfeill
   c) Websphere Commerce
   d) IBM
   e) Retail Systems Research
   f) Nikki Baird

2 a) Kohl's b) Best Buy c) Wal-Mart d) JC Penney

3 a) false (It is low.)
   b) true
   c) true
   d) false (It is used by customers.)
   e) false (They are attracted away from competitors.)
   f) false (It's a big change.)
   g) false (They access products in stores, online, on mobile devices, etc.)

4 a) single customer experience
   b) radical responses
   c) a small outdoor-equipment retail chain
   d) point-of-sale devices, in-store machines
   e) call-centre sales staff
   f) loyalty reward scheme
   g) customer's purchase history
   h) multichannel transformation

5 a

The next big thing

1 1 b 2 d 3 e 4 a 5 c

2 a) The first generation of dotcoms
   b) Yahoo
   c) eBay and Amazon
   d) Internet users/customers
   e) The shift to a new computing architecture
   f) Hand-held devices
   g) Cloud computing
   h) Pandora and Spotify

3 1 a 2 c 3 c 4 b 5 b

4 a) further b) evolves c) get hooked on d) outlandish e) experimentation f) devising g) tap into h) potential i) at stake

5 a) odd
   b) generating considerable buzz
   c) them are anonymous.
   d) gives it a flavour
   e) valuable information can be filtered
   f) be born

6 a) Silicon Valley b) a short-lived fashion

Unit 11

The capital of start-ups

1 a) Seedcamp
   b) University College London, Bloomsbury
   c) Hussein Kanji, Geoff Watts, Julia Fowler
   d) EDITD, Garmz
   e) Vienna Fashion Week
   f) Skype, TomTom

2 1 d 2 f 3 g 4 b 5 e 6 c 7 a

3 a) entrepreneurial talent b) venture capitalists c) early-stage ventures d) angel investors e) leading players f) incubator event g) technology industry

4 a) considerable b) maturing c) nurturing d) attain e) network f) approaches g) hub h) ecosystem i) mentor

5 a) false (It relates to the fashion industry.)
   b) true
   c) false (It provides information about the fashion industry.)
   d) false (They are going to Austria soon.)
   e) false (They have been invited by another start-up.)
   f) false (Geoff said this.)

6 b, c, e and f can be used without changing the meaning.
   a) An *emergency* is a dangerous situation that must be dealt with immediately.
   d) A *segment* is a particular group of customers in a market.
   g) *Comprising* would mean that Skype and TomTom were the only companies to go public in this period.

The protection of new business ideas

1 1 e 2 b 3 d 4 a 5 c

2

	property theft	**intellectual property theft**
criminal or civil case?	criminal case	civil case
punishment	jail	damages
cost of lawyers	NG	£350 an hour
cost to UK industry	NG	£11bn a year
frequency of occurrence	NG	extremely common

3 a) patent process
   b) register
   c) infringement
   d) counterfeiting; piracy; counterfeiter; pirate
   e) white-collar crime
   f) recovered
   g) global

TEXT BANK – Key

4 a) a patent
   b) John Barrington-Carver; the idea for the clockwork radio
   c) an idea for a product; the fact that it has become known
   d) potential colleagues / financial backers; a non-disclosure agreement
   e) large south-east Asian electronics companies
   f) a production prototype

5 b

Unit 12

Bringing in a project manager

1 1 b 2 a 3 c 4 b 5 b 6 c 7 a 8 c

2 a) get up to speed quickly
   b) the price of operating at high speed
   c) prioritise
   d) experience of multiple environments
   e) make decisions quickly
   f) focus on the important things (that need to be delivered)

3 a) false (*Role* is used as a noun here, but you cannot also use it as a verb.)
   b) true
   c) true
   d) false (*Assignment* is a fairly formal word meaning 'task'. The meaning of *assignation* is not the same: it's a slightly humorous expression for a meeting, perhaps secret, between two people in a romantic relationship.)
   e) true
   f) false (*Unlikely* is an adjective and could not be replaced here by *improbably.*)
   g) true

4 f, b, g, h, c, e, d, a

5 Blancmange is a cold, sweet dessert made from cornflour that is quite slippery and messy to eat. Here, it's used to talk about the 'messy' conversations that happen around the water-cooler in different organisations – the place where people often meet to gossip.

Project management in the arts

1 a) Paris Opera Ballet, Berlin Philharmonic, Tate Modern, New York City Ballet, Piccolo Teatro, Globe Theatre (London), New York Chamber Orchestra, Opera Theatre (Rome).
   b) Cambridge University's Judge Business School, Bocconi University
   c) Bank of New York

2 1 h 2 c 3 b 4 e 5 g 6 a 7 d 8 f

3 a) biggest human-resources headaches
   b) increase; public appeal
   c) diversify; revenue stream
   d) cultural and arts management
   e) various specialised courses; two-week final project
   f) large cultural institutions

4 a) false ('... running the Bank of New York is very different from running the New York City ballet', but not totally different.)
   b) false ('Many of the concerns emerging in the cultural and arts sector are the same as in other sectors')
   c) true
   d) true
   e) false ('There is an acknowledgement from the cultural institutions themselves about the need for leaders with solid management skills, ...')
   f) true
   g) false ('... business know-how is a necessary ingredient in ... determining new methods of increasing public appeal.')

5 **a)** complex **b)** complexity **c)** sustained **d)** sustainability **e)** provision **f)** ingredient **g)** transition **h)** acknowledgement **i)** know-how

6 a) a field project
   b) internships
   c) project management
   d) marketing tools
   e) year-long programme
   f) live-entertainment business planning
   g) finance for the arts

Resource bank

TEACHER'S NOTES

Introduction

These Resource bank activities are designed to extend and develop the activities in the main Course Book. The Resource bank contains exercises and activities relating to:

- **Speaking:** Each Speaking unit begins with a language exercise that takes up and takes further the language points from the Course Book unit, and then applies this language in one or more activities. The Speaking units are best done in the classroom, of course. You have permission to photocopy the Resource bank pages in this book. In some units, you will give each student a copy of the whole page. In others, there are role cards, which need to be cut out and given to participants with particular roles. These activities are indicated in the unit-specific notes below.
- **Listening:** Students listen again to the interviews from the Listening sections in the main Course Book, and do further activities on comprehension and language development. These activities can be done in the classroom, but they have been designed in a way that makes it easy for students to do them on their own as homework. Make photocopies for the students of the pages relating to the units you would like them to do. Follow up in the next lesson by getting students to talk about any difficulties that they had. You could play the recording again in the classroom to help resolve problems if necessary.
- **Writing:** A model answer is given for the writing task at the end of each Case study in the Course Book. There are then two or three extra writing activities. These can all be done as homework. Again, make photocopies for the students of the pages relating to the units you would like them to do. After correcting the writing exercises in the classroom, go over key points that have been causing problems.

Speaking

What to give the learners

The **language exercises** at the beginning of each Speaking unit in the Resource bank can be used to revise language from the main Course Book unit, especially if you did the Business skills section in another lesson. In any case, point out the connection with the Course Book material to students. These language exercises are designed to prepare students for the role plays/discussions that follow and in many cases can be done in a few minutes as a way of focusing students on the activity that follows.

When you go round the class helping students with exercises, work on the **process** of deducing the answers by looking at grammatical and sense clues. Do this again when you round up the correct answers with the whole class: don't just mechanically give the right answer and move on.

A typical two-person **role-play** might last five or 10 minutes, followed by three to five minutes of praise and correction. An animated group discussion might last longer; in this case, drop one of your other planned activities and do it another time, rather than trying to cram it in before the end of the lesson. If you then have five or 10 minutes left over, you can always go over some language points from the lesson again, or, better still, get students to say what they were. One way of doing this is to ask them what they've written in their notebooks during the lesson.

Revising and revisiting

Feel free to do an activity more than once. After one run-through, praise strong points, then work on three or four things that need correcting or improving. Then you can get students to change roles and do the activity again, or the parts of the activity where these points come up. Obviously, there will come a time when interest wanes, but the usual tendency in language teaching is not to revisit things enough, rather than the reverse.

Fluency and accuracy

Concentrate on different things in different activities. In some role plays and discussions, you may want to focus on fluency, with students interacting as spontaneously as possible. In others, you will want to concentrate on accuracy, with students working on getting specific forms correct. Rather than expect students to get everything correct, you could pick out, say, three or four forms that you want them to get right, and focus on these.

Clear instructions

Be sure to give complete instructions before getting students to start. In role plays, be very clear about who has which role, and give students time to absorb the information they need. Sometimes there are role cards that you hand out. The activities where this happens are indicated in the notes.

Parallel and public performances (PPP)

In pairwork or small-group situations, get all pairs to do the activity at the same time. Go round the class and listen. When students have finished, praise strong points and deal with three or four problems that you heard, especially problems that more than one group has been having. Then get individual pairs to give public performances so that the whole class can listen. The performers should pay particular attention to the problem areas.

One to one

The pairwork activities can be done one to one, with you taking one of the roles. The activity can be done a second time, reversing the role and getting the student to integrate your suggestions for improvement.

Unit 1 First impressions

Networking

A

- Relate this exercise to the expressions in the Useful language box on page 11 of the Course Book, practising pronunciation and intonation. Then get students to close their Course Books.
- Get students to do the exercise in parallel pairs. Circulate, monitor and assist where necessary.
- Call the class to order and elicit the answers.
- Get individual pairs to read the exchanges with feeling.

1 b **2** f **3** a **4** c **5** g **6** h **7** d **8** e

B

- Before the class, photocopy the prompts for the conversation. Make as many photocopies as there will be students. (All students see both sides of the conversation.)
- Ask the whole class to look again at the expressions in the Useful language box on page 11 of the Course Book and get them to read the expressions with the right intonation.
- Tell students they are networking at a trade fair. Allow students a minute or two to prepare the expressions they might use before doing the role play.
- Get students to do the role play in parallel pairs. Circulate, monitor and assist where necessary, noting down examples of language used and five or six points for correction, including pronunciation and intonation.
- Bring the class to order. Praise good language and intonation that you heard and go through points that need improvement, getting individual students to say the improved version.
- After this feedback, students may repeat the activity, swapping roles.
- With one-to-one students, take on one of the roles yourself. Then do the activity again, swapping roles.

Unit 2 Training

Clarifying and confirming

A

- Ask the whole class to look again at the expressions in the Useful language box on page 18 of the Course Book and practise the intonation of the phrases.
- Get students to read them with realistic intonation. Do this with the whole class, then repeat in individual pairs.
- Ask students to close their Course Books and work on this exercise.
- Go through the answers with the whole class, getting them to explain *why* particular answers are correct, rather than just calling them out and moving on to the next one. For example, with item 1, get someone to explain that *Would you mind* ... is always followed by the *-ing* form.
- Practise the intonation of the correct expressions.

1 Would you mind ~~to~~ repeating that for me again?
2 Would you mind going over ~~on~~ that?
3 Sorry, could I ask you to give ~~to~~ me that address again?
4 Could you clarify ~~out~~ what you meant by 'delocalisation'?
5 So that's three o'clock on Wednesday, ~~by~~ then.
6 Let me see if I ~~can~~ understand correctly.
7 Can I just check ~~up~~ that?
8 I'd ~~to~~ like to just confirm that.
9 Actually, ~~that~~ what I said was Tuesday, not Thursday.
10 What I meant ~~with~~ by 'delocalisation' was not what my colleagues usually mean by it.

B

- Before the class, make as many photocopies of the role cards as there are pairs in the class.
- Explain the scenario set out in the rubric. Divide the class into pairs and hand out the role cards.
- Begin the role play in parallel pairs. Go round the room and monitor the language being used. Note down strong points and points that need correction or improvement; this can include incorrect structures, vocabulary and pronunciation. Focus particularly on clarifying and confirming language. At this level, be very demanding in relation to appropriate language and intonation. Put items that need work on the board for later feedback.
- When most pairs have finished, bring the class to order and praise good language points used.
- Refer students to the board and work on the corrections together, getting students to provide the correct form, vocabulary and pronunciation if possible.
- If there is time, ask students to change roles and repeat the role play, integrating the corrections.

Unit 3 Energy

Decision-making

A

- Relate this exercise to the expressions in the Useful language box on page 26 of the Course Book. Then get students to close their Course Books.
- Get students, in pairs, to match the expressions and the functions.
- Circulate, monitor and assist where necessary.
- Bring the class together and go through the answers with the whole class.
- Practise the intonation of these phrases with the whole class.
- For further practice, students could use some of these phrases to make a short dialogue of their own in parallel pairs. Then get pairs to give 'performances' for the whole class.

1 d **2** b **3** a **4** b **5** c **6** a **7** c **8** d

- Ask the whole class to look again at the expressions on page 26 of the Course Book and in the previous exercise.
- Get students to work in groups of four or five. Tell them to read the problem and the possible budget cuts that they can make. Answer any questions.
- Circulate, monitor and assist while students discuss the problem and solutions. Make a note of the good expressions they use, as well as five or six language points for correction.
- Bring the class to order and go through the correction work with the whole class, asking students to say the expressions correctly.
- Ask one or two groups for feedback. What solutions did they come up with, and why?

Unit 4 Marketing

Making an impact in presentations

- Ask the whole class to look again at the Useful language box on page 40 of the Course Book. Then get students to close their Course Books and work in pairs on Exercise A.
- Circulate, monitor and assist, telling students to look for clues in relation to grammar and meaning.
- Bring the class to order. Work on any difficulties and get individual students to say complete sentences with the correct stress and intonation.
- Do Exercise B as a quick-fire whole-class activity, getting students to call out the correct answers.

1 c, iv **2** d, v **3** a, ii **4** b, iii **5** f, vi **6** e, i

C

- Give students time to prepare their presentations, or better, tell them to start now and finish preparation in time for the next class.
- Circulate, monitor and assist.
- When pairs are ready, get the presenters to give their presentations in parallel pairs. Circulate, monitor and assist.
- When most presenters have finished, bring the class to order. Praise good language and intonation that you heard and go through points that need improvement, getting individual students to say the improved version.
- You could then get one or two students to give their presentations, incorporating the improvements. If there is time and interest, get other students to give their presentations in later classes.

Unit 5 Employment trends

Resolving conflict

A

- Relate this exercise to the expressions in Exercise E on page 48 of the Course Book.
- Get students, in pairs, to read the sentences and replace the wrong word in each case.
- Circulate, monitor and help where necessary, pointing out where students have or haven't identified and replaced the word correctly and giving them an opportunity to look again if necessary.
- Remind students that each wrong word should be replaced by just one correct word.
- Bring the class together and go through the answers with the whole class.

1. Let me see if I **follow** you – you're saying that the premium is increasing by 40 per cent compared to last year's, right?
2. From our **point** of view, we have to remain competitive.
3. Can I just **check** that I understand the situation correctly?
4. I'm sorry, I didn't **get** that. Could you say it again, please?
5. I'm having trouble following you. Could you say that **once** more?
6. Please continue. I'm **interested** to know your side of the story.
7. I **fully** understand how you must be feeling.
8. I'm listening – please **continue**.
9. I sense that you're feeling **upset** about the situation.
10. This is how it looks to me from my **angle** – you were not to blame for the accident.

B

- Before the class, make as many photocopies of the role cards as there are pairs in the class.
- Explain the scenarios set out in the rubric. Divide the class into pairs and hand out the role cards for the first scenario.
- Begin the role play in parallel pairs. Go round the room and monitor the language being used. Note down strong points and points that need correction or improvement; this can include incorrect structures, vocabulary and pronunciation. Focus particularly on conflict-resolution language. Put items that need work on the board for later feedback.
- When most pairs have finished, bring the class to order and praise good language points used.
- Refer students to the board and work on the corrections together, getting students to say the correct thing.
- If there is time, ask students to change roles and repeat the role play, integrating the corrections.
- Then hand out the role cards for the second scenario and repeat the above procedure.

Unit 6 Ethics

Ethical problem-solving

- Relate this exercise to the expressions in the Useful language box on page 56 of the Course Book.
- Get students to read the sentences and find the errors. Circulate, monitor and help where necessary, pointing out where students have or haven't identified the incorrect word and giving them an opportunity to look again if necessary.
- Get students to compare their answers in pairs.
- Bring the class to order and go through the answers with them.
- Get individual students to read out the correct sentences.

1 **Another thing** you could do is to tell your boss.
2 You **might/may** like to think **about** the best time to speak to her.
3 The **important** thing is to do **what** is **morally** right.
4 You have to **weigh** up the **pros** and the **cons**.
5 **On** the **one** hand, developing countries need investment; on the **other** hand, they shouldn't be exploited.
6 **On balance,** I think that we are doing the right thing.
7 **What** I ***would*** **say** is that we should **certainly** think about this very carefully.
8 Are you **really sure** that you want to do that?

B

- Go through the oath (teach this word if necessary), getting individual students to read different parts. Work on any difficulties.
- Get students to work on the task in threes or fours. (If you have a class with students from different industries, it might be good to mix them so that they can compare what is appropriate in each industry.)
- Begin the discussion in parallel groups. Go round the room and monitor the language being used. Note down strong points and points that need correction or improvement; this can include incorrect structures, vocabulary and pronunciation. Focus particularly on ethics language. Put items that need work on the board for later feedback.
- When most groups have finished, bring the class to order and praise good language points used.
- Refer students to the board and work on the corrections together, getting students to say the correct thing.
- If there is time, get representatives of the groups to summarise their conclusions and explain any differences of opinion within their groups.

Unit 7 Finance

Managing questions

- Make the link with the expressions on page 71 of the Course Book and explain the situation.
- Get students to read them with realistic intonation. Do this with the whole class, then repeat individually.
- Ask students to close their Course Books and work on this exercise in pairs.
- Go through the answers with the whole class, getting them to explain why particular answers are correct.
- Practise the intonation of the correct expressions.

1 Do **you** think **you** could explain what you **were doing on** the yacht?
2 Would **you** mind **telling us** what **your** relationship **with** Mr Stanislavski **is exactly?**
3 I'**m wondering** if **you** realise **the** effect that **the**(**se**) pictures **will have** / **have had** / **are having**.
4 I'**m** certain we **would like to** hear why **you** have **such** a close **relationship with** Mr Stanislavski.
5 Let **me** put **it** another way. What **precisely were you discussing that** evening?
6 I'**ll rephrase the** question. **Did you talk** about **his** plans for **expansion in** this country?
7 With all **due respect**, you **haven't answered** / **did not answer** my question.
8 **Are you denying** / **Do you deny** that Mr Stanislavski will benefit **from this** / **the** meeting?
9 I'm not sure if **I entirely** understand your question. **Do you mean that** I **acted unethically**?
10 **If** I could just finish what I **was saying**, **your** accusations **are completely** unfounded.
11 If you'd just let **me** finish, you **have misunderstood my** actions.
12 Hang **on a** minute. You'**re jumping to** conclusions.

B

- Before the class, make photocopies of the role cards: one for Student A for each group, and three or four each of Student B for each small group into which the class will be divided.
- In the class, explain the scenario set out in the rubric. Divide the class into groups of four or five (one Student A (Vladimir Stanislavski) and three or four Student Bs (journalists) in each group) and hand out the role cards.
- Begin the role play in parallel groups. Go round the room and monitor the language being used. Note down strong points and points that need correction or improvement; this can include incorrect structures, vocabulary and pronunciation. Focus particularly on the language for managing questions. Put items that need work on the board for later feedback.
- When most groups have finished, bring the class to order and praise good language points used.
- Refer students to the board and work on the corrections together, getting students to provide the correct forms.
- If there is time, ask students in one of the groups to repeat the role play, or parts of it, for the whole class, integrating the corrections and improvements.

Unit 8 Consultants

Negotiating

- Get students to refer quickly to the expressions in the Useful language box on page 79, to refresh their memories.
- Tell students that the e-mail in the exercise follows on from situation 4 in the role plays in Exercise F on page 79 of the Course Book.
- Ask students to close their Course Books and work on this exercise individually or in pairs.
- Go through the answers with the whole class, getting them to explain why particular answers are correct, rather than just calling them out and moving on to the next one.

Dear Ms Aubusson

It was very nice meeting you this morning. I'm writing to confirm **what** we discussed re. our shampoo and sun-tan products. I'm **pleased** to confirm our offer of a unit price of €1.05 for our leading shampoo product, for an order of 250,000 units. I sensed you were more hesitant about the sun-tan lotion, which is why I'm prepared to go even further than I did this morning, when I **offered** you a unit price of €0.75. I've discussed this with my boss, and we are now prepared to offer you 50,000 units at €0.69 per unit for a firm sale, although not, unfortunately, on the **sale**-or-return basis that you requested.

As **for** payment and delivery, I'm sending you a copy of an outline sales agreement (attached), with our suggested payment terms and delivery schedule. Can you **please** confirm your order by email as soon as possible, as we will not be able to guarantee the above prices beyond the end of this week.

If you **need** any more information, please phone or email me. Looking forward to **doing** business with you.

Best **regards**

Belinda Tomasso

B

- Explain the situation and divide the class into pairs. (Students A and B see both sides of the conversation.)
- Begin the conversation in parallel pairs. Go round the room and monitor the language being used. Note down strong points and points that need correction or improvement; this can include incorrect structures, vocabulary and pronunciation. Focus particularly on conflict-resolution language. Put items that need work on the board for later feedback.
- When most pairs have finished, bring the class to order and praise good language points used.
- Refer students to the board and work on the corrections together, getting students to say the correct thing.
- If there is time, ask students to change roles and repeat the conversation, integrating the corrections.

Unit 9 Strategy

Brainstorming and creativity

- Ask the whole class to look again at the expressions in the Useful language box on page 86 of the Course Book and work on the intonation of the phrases.
- Get students to read and correct the expressions.
- Circulate, monitor and help where necessary. If extra help is needed, put the correct words on the board in random order.
- Bring the class together and go through the answers with everyone.
- Practise the intonation of any of the expressions which might be difficult for students.

1 Who'd like to get the ball rolling ~~on~~?
2 Let's just get the ideas ~~right~~ down at this stage.
3 That's a cool ~~off~~ idea!
4 Let's go around ~~about~~ the table once and then open the discussion up.
5 Here's what I'd add ~~on~~ to your suggestion.
6 You've taken the words right out ~~off~~ of my mouth.
7 I'd like to expand ~~widest~~ on that.
8 I was just ~~around~~ going to say that!
9 Let's try and suspend ~~up~~ judgement until later.
10 The rule is there are no ~~any~~ bad ideas.

B

- Depending on time available, etc., you could get different groups to work on one or more different brainstorming situations. Make as many photocopies as you will need and cut up the different brainstorming situations.
- Divide the class into groups of five or six and hand out the relevant brainstorming situation to members of each group. Appoint a student in each group to 'lead' the brainstorming, but remind them that this is not like chairing a meeting.
- Answer any remaining queries. Then get the brainstorming sessions to begin.
- Go round the room and monitor the language being used. Note down strong points and points that need correction or improvement; this can include incorrect structures, vocabulary and pronunciation. Focus particularly on brainstorming language. Put items that need work on the board for later feedback.
- When most groups have finished, bring the class to order and praise good language points used.
- Refer students to the board and work on the corrections together, getting students to say the correct thing.
- If there is time, ask students to repeat relevant parts of their respective brainstorming sessions, integrating the corrections.

Unit 10 Online business

Presentations: thinking on your feet

- Get students to look again at the expressions in the Useful language box on page 101 of the Course Book before doing this exercise.
- Get them to close their books and work on the exercise in pairs.
- Circulate, monitor and help where necessary.
- Bring the class together and go through the answers with the whole class.
- Practise pronunciation and intonation of the expressions.

1. **Funnily** enough, someone **asked** me the same question yesterday.
2. Could you just **repeat** that question because I don't think everyone **caught** it.
3. I'm **pleased/delighted** that you **raised** that point – it's an exceedingly interesting one.
4. I'm **afraid/sorry** that I don't have **that information / those details** to hand.
5. I'm **sorry**, but that's not really my **field/area** of **research**.
6. Can I **get** back **to** you on that one?
7. **Do** you mind if we **deal with** that later **on**?
8. I don't want to **get into** too **much** detail at this **stage/point**.
9. I'd be happy to discuss **this** with you after my **talk/presentation**.
10. **Actually**, I'll be **getting to** that later this afternoon.

B

- Explain the activity. Tell students that the utterances 1–8 are not models for them to copy!
- Divide the class into pairs and make sure that students know what they are going to talk about. (The subject doesn't matter – they could repeat parts of presentations that they have done in earlier classes if necessary.)
- When the situation is understood, get students to start the activity in parallel pairs. Go round the class and assist where necessary.
- Note down strong points and points that need correction or improvement. Focus particularly on polite/tactful language. Put items that need work on the board for later feedback.
- When students have finished, bring the class to order. When most groups have finished, bring the class to order and praise good language points used.
- Refer students to the board and work on the corrections together, getting students to say the correct version.
- If there is time, ask students to repeat relevant parts of their respective presentations, integrating the corrections.

Unit 11 New business

Chasing payment

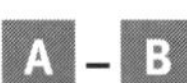

- Before the class, make as many photocopies as there will be pairs of students in the class. Cut up the sets of turns and be sure not to mix them up.
- Look again at the useful language for chasing payment on page 109 of the Course Book with your students and work on any difficulties.
- Divide students into pairs and get them to rearrange the turns into the first part of a logical phone conversation. Circulate, monitor and help where necessary.
- Bring the class to order and discuss the correct order of the turns with them.
- When you are sure that students have the correct order, get them to read the conversation in parallel pairs and to continue it as indicated in Exercise B. Circulate, monitor and assist.
- Bring the class together and get one or two of the pairs to say what solutions they found.

The conversation is in the correct order on the photocopiable sheet.

Unit 12 Project management

Teleconferencing

- Ask the whole class to look again at the expressions in the box on page 117 of the Course Book and practise the intonation of the phrases.
- Explain the activity and get students to match the two parts of the expressions in pairs, paying attention to clues related to grammar and meaning.
- Then get individual students to read out the complete expressions for the whole class, concentrating on stress and intonation.

1 c **2** a **3** e **4** h **5** f **6** g **7** b **8** d **9** j **10** i

B

- Before the class, photocopy the role cards for students, but do not cut them up. Make as many photocopies as there will be groups of four students. Also prepare small pieces of paper marked 'A', 'B', 'C' and 'D' and fold them so that the letters are not visible.
- In the class, explain the situation, pointing out that this role play is unusual in that they will not know which student has which role. One of the purposes of the activity is to guess this.
- Divide the class into groups of four. Hand out a sheet with all four role cards to each student. Then hand out one of the small pieces of paper marked 'A', 'B', 'C' or 'D' to each student in each group of four. Tell them that this letter refers to the role that they will take from among the four roles that they can see, but that they should not tell other students which role it is.
- Get students to unfold their piece of paper and check which letter is on it in a way that makes it impossible for others to see it.
- Allow students a minute or two to highlight or make a note of the expressions they might use before doing the teleconferencing role play.
- When students are ready, get them to start their teleconferences in parallel groups.
- Circulate and help where necessary during the role play, noting down examples of key language used and five or six points for correction, including pronunciation and intonation.
- Bring the class to order and get students to say who had each role in their group, and how they know this.
- Then go through the corrections and feedback from the role play with the whole class.

UNIT 1

First impressions

NETWORKING

A **Match the expressions and the responses between two people at a company's trade-fair stand.**

1 Excuse me, could you do me a favour and pass the juice?
2 That's a great calling card.
3 How's business in your part of the world?
4 I don't think you've met Dr Kay from R&D?
5 Have you been in Reykjavik recently?
6 I'll write down my details for you.
7 Do you mind me asking where you're from?
8 We should do lunch one day.

a) Could be worse – we've been through a bad patch, but it's picking up now.
b) Here you go.
c) I don't think I have. Hello. I'm Aysha Khan – I'm in marketing.
d) I've lived in Greece all my life, but actually I'm from Albania.
e) That would be nice.
f) Do you like it? Our internal design people did it.
g) I was there not long ago, actually.
h) Thanks – here's a pen.

B **Work in pairs. Role-play the conversation using the prompts below.**

Student A: You are working on your company's stand at a trade fair in Chicago.
Student B: You are a visitor to the trade fair.

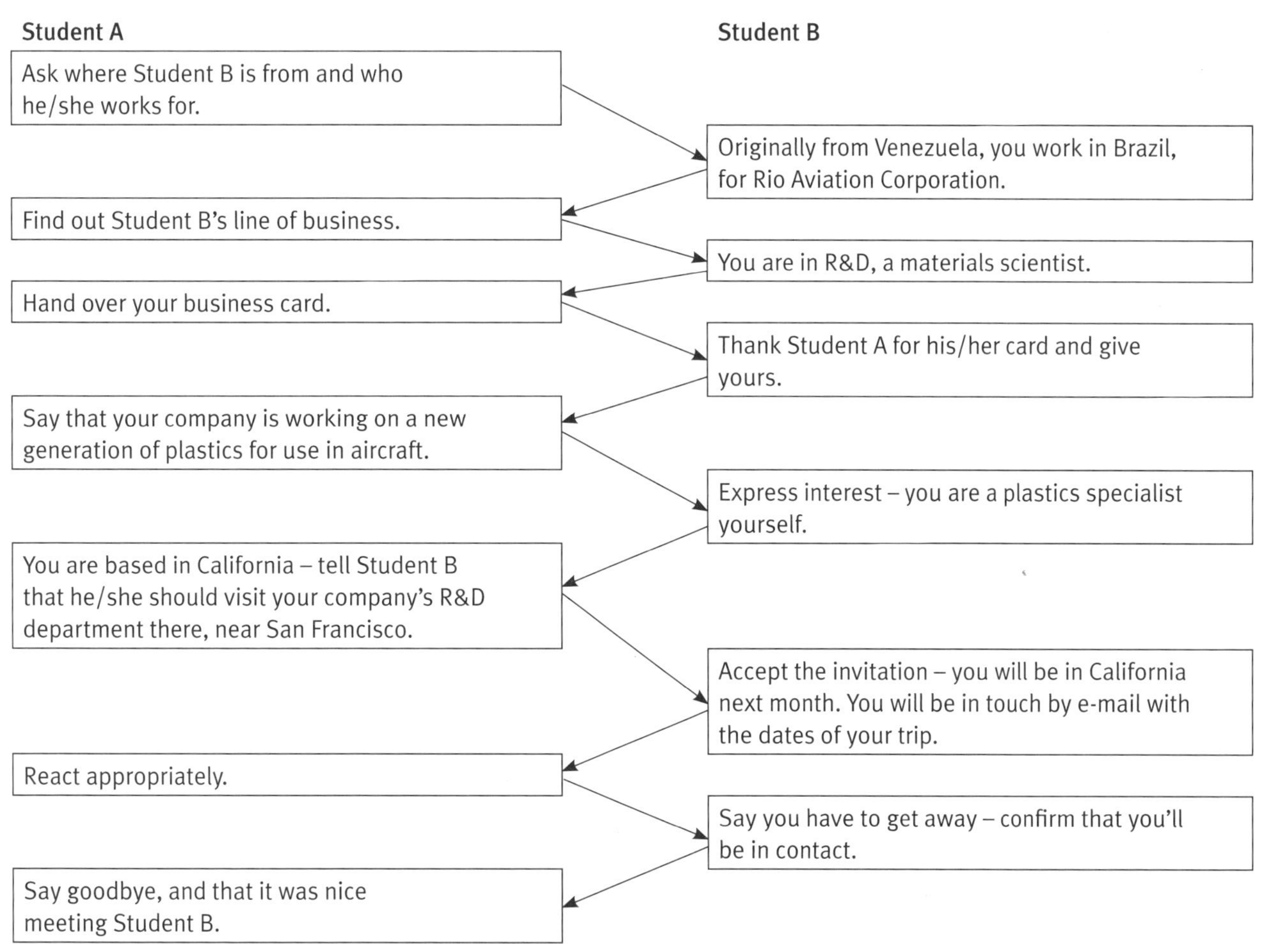

RESOURCE BANK – Speaking

UNIT 2

Training

CLARIFYING AND CONFIRMING

A **Cross out the unnecessary word in each of these expressions.**

1 Would you mind to repeating that for me again?
2 Would you mind going over on that?
3 Sorry, could I ask you to give to me that address again?
4 Could you clarify out what you meant by 'delocalisation'?
5 So that's three o'clock on Wednesday, by then.
6 Let me see if I can understand correctly.
7 Can I just check up that?
8 I'd to like to just confirm that.
9 Actually, that what I said was Tuesday, not Thursday.
10 What I meant with by 'delocalisation' was not what my colleagues usually mean by it.

B **Work in pairs. Student A phones Student B to clarify the arrangements.**

Student A: You have enrolled for a residential training course organised by your company, but you have only heard about the arrangements through a colleague.

Student B: You work in the Training Department of the company.

Student A

You have heard from your colleague that the course:

- is about controlling aggression;
- is to be held at the company's HQ in Brussels, with participants staying at a hotel nearby;
- will be on Wednesday to Friday next week;
- will be run by in-house trainers;
- is for mid-ranking managers only;
- doesn't require participants to bring any special clothes or equipment.

Student B

The course ...

- is on assertiveness training;
- is to be held at the Trianon Hotel in Versailles, outside Paris;
- will be held on Monday and Tuesday next week, with participants staying at the Trianon Hotel;
- will be run by an outside expert, Wilma Golgotha;
- is for mid-ranking managers and senior executives, including the CEO;
- requires participants to bring running kit and shoes for a run round the Versailles Palace park each evening after the training sessions. (This is obligatory.)

UNIT 3

Energy

DECISION-MAKING

A **Match the expressions (1–8) to the functions (a–d).**

1 Let's not rush into making decisions.
2 I'm not certain that I agree with you.
3 What if we were to drop Plan A and go ahead with Plan B?
4 You're right up to a point, but if you look at it from this angle, the problem looks completely different.
5 I really think it's essential to think about this carefully.
6 We should think about a more radical solution.
7 You're probably fed up with me banging on about this, but ...
8 On the one hand ... , on the other hand ... Let's leave it open for the time being.

a) putting forward proposals
b) disagreeing indirectly
c) emphasising a point
d) avoiding making decisions

B **You are city councillors (locally elected politicians). You have been instructed by central government to reduce the city's spending by €1 billion this year. Discuss these proposals and come up with a plan to make this cut. (Potential savings are shown in brackets.)**

- Close some schools and increase class sizes in the remaining schools by 15 per cent. (€400,000)
- Stop all council funding of arts and cultural activities. (€150,000)
- Abandon work on a new route for the city's tram network. (€550,000)
- Reduce household refuse collection from once a week to once every two weeks. (€100,000)
- Reduce by one-third the council's contribution to the overall police budget. (€250,000)
- Suspend road maintenance in the city for three years. (€200,000)
- Reduce the number of social workers by a third. (€300,000)
- Stop all maintenance at the city's parks. (€100,000)

UNIT 4

Marketing

MAKING AN IMPACT IN PRESENTATIONS

A **Match the two parts of these expressions.**

1 There's just one key idea that
2 There are three key factors in valuing real estate:
3 As Roosevelt said, 'We have nothing
4 Only by restoring consumer *confidence*
5 I'm sure you'll all agree with me when
6 In the state of Nevada, one in four

a) to fear but fear itself.'
b) can the government turn this situation round.
c) I'd like you all to take away with you today.
d) location, location and location, but not necessarily in that order.
e) real-estate loans have ended in foreclosure.
f) I say that things can't go on like this.

B **Match each of the expressions in Exercise A to its function (i–vi).**

i) Referring to surprising facts or figures
ii) Quoting someone
iii) Emphasising key words
iv) Calling for action
v) Building rapport with the audience by using humour
vi) Building rapport with the audience by inviting agreement

C **Work in pairs. Give a brief presentation about one of the topics below to your partner, using expressions relating to the functions in Exercise B. The listener's task is to identify the function each time the speaker uses one of them.**

- A country that you have visited
- A company or organisation that you are interested in
- A businessperson that you admire
- The market for a product that you have bought or are thinking of buying
- A demo/presentation of your mobile phone or laptop computer

Employment trends

RESOLVING CONFLICT

A **Replace the one wrong word in each of these expressions with the correct word.**

1 Let me see if I pursue you – you're saying that the premium is increasing by 40 per cent compared to last year's, right?

2 From our position of view, we have to remain competitive.

3 Can I just control that I understand the situation correctly?

4 I'm sorry, I didn't receive that. Could you say it again, please?

5 I'm having trouble following you. Could you say that one more?

6 Please continue. I'm interesting to know your side of the story.

7 I full understand how you must be feeling.

8 I'm listening – please continuate.

9 I sense that you're feeling upsetting about the situation.

10 This is how it looks to me from my orientation – you were not to blame for the accident.

B **Work in pairs. These role plays are based on a car-insurance company's call centre.**

Role play 1

Student A: You are a potential customer phoning about buying car insurance.

Student B: You are the agent who takes the call.

Role play 2 (six months later)

Student A: You are the agent.

Student B: You are the same customer as in Role play 1. You have had an accident and are making a claim.

Role play 1
Student A: Potezl customer

- You have a two-year-old Volvo XC60.
- You have been with your current insurer for 10 years and had one accident in that time, for which you did not claim, as it was the other driver's fault.
- You will be the only driver of the car.
- You want cover to start on 1 December.
- Your current insurer has given you a quote of €525 per year for comprehensive insurance, including a courtesy car while your car is being repaired after any accident.
- Continue or end the call suitably, in relation to what the agent says.

Role play 1
Student B: Agent

- Ask:
  - about the car make and model
  - the number of years with no claims
  - if the policy should cover other drivers
  - when the policy should start
  - what other quotes the customer has had and what the cover includes.
- Say that you will check on the computer system. Then give a quote for €490 for the same cover.
- Continue or end the call suitably, in relation to how the customer reacts.

Role play 2
Student A: Agent

- You want to reassure the customer after his/her stressful experience, as far as possible.
- Ask for full details of the accident.
- Sympathise, but in a professional way.
- Say that the car will be repaired in Budapest next week, but that there are no courtesy cars available, as the insurance company has no arrangements for this in Hungary.
- There is no arrangement for payment of customers' travel costs.
- Deal suitably with the customer's reactions.

Role play 2
Student B: Customer

- You are upset and want to be reassured.
- You were on a roundabout in Budapest and another car, that did not have right of way, hit you.
- You have to fly home urgently to Munich, and you want to know if the insurer will pay for this flight and the return flight to Budapest to pick up the car.
- You would like a courtesy car while you are back in Munich.
- React to what the agent says.
- End the call suitably.

UNIT 6

Ethics

ETHICAL PROBLEM-SOLVING

A **Correct the errors in these sentences related to giving advice about ethical problems, replacing the incorrect words with the same number of correct ones.**

1 Other something you could do is to tell your boss.
2 You should like to think around the best time to speak to her.
3 The significant thing is to do that is moral right.
4 You have to weight up the prose and the contras.
5 In the left hand, developing countries need investment; on the right hand, they shouldn't be exploited.
6 In equilibrium, I think that we are doing the right thing.
7 That I *may* tell is that we should certain think about this very carefully.
8 Are you truly ensured that you want to do that?

B **Read the MBA oath below developed by a number of business schools. Is it appropriate for using in your company or sector? Why? / Why not? Which points would you change, if any? What other points could you add?**

THE MBA OATH

As a business leader, I recognise my role in society.

- My purpose is to lead people and manage resources to create value that no single individual can create alone.
- My decisions affect the well-being of individuals inside and outside my enterprise, today and tomorrow.

Therefore, I promise that:

- I will manage my enterprise with loyalty and care, and will not advance my personal interests at the expense of my enterprise or society.
- I will understand and uphold, in letter and spirit, the laws and contracts governing my conduct and that of my enterprise.
- I will refrain from corruption, unfair competition or business practices harmful to society.
- I will protect the human rights and dignity of all people affected by my enterprise, and I will oppose discrimination and exploitation.
- I will protect the right of future generations to advance their standard of living and enjoy a healthy planet.
- I will report the performance and risks of my enterprise accurately and honestly.
- I will invest in developing myself and others, helping the management profession continue to advance and create sustainable and inclusive prosperity.

In exercising my professional duties according to these principles, I recognise that my behaviour must set an example of integrity, eliciting trust and esteem from those I serve. I will remain accountable to my peers and to society for my actions and for upholding these standards.

This oath I make freely, and upon my honour.

UNIT 7

Finance

MANAGING QUESTIONS

Vladimir Stanislavski owns TV channels and newspapers all over Europe and North America. Ian Stonehouse, the UK's Minister for Industry, has been pictured having drinks on Stanislavski's yacht by photographers with telescopic lenses. The minister is currently involved in drafting new competition laws for the media industry. Following critical articles in the press about his conduct, the minister has called a press conference.

A **Complete these utterances used at the press conference, by journalists (1–8) and the minister (9–12). Between one and three words are missing in each gap. Complete them using the words in brackets. Change the grammatical form where necessary.**

1 Do .... think .... could explain what you .... *(do)* .... the yacht?

2 Would .... mind .... *(tell)* .... *(we)* what .... relationship .... Mr Stanislavski .... *(be)* .... *(exact)*?

3 I .... *(be)* .... *(wonder)* if .... realise .... effect that .... pictures .... *(have)*.

4 I .... *(be)* certain we .... *(like)* .... hear why .... have .... a close .... *(relation)* .... Mr Stanislavski.

5 Let .... put .... another way. What .... *(precise)* .... *(discuss)* .... evening?

6 I .... *(rephrase)* .... question. .... *(talk)* about .... plans for .... *(expand)* .... this country?

7 With all .... *(respectful)*, you .... *(answer not)* my question.

8 .... *(deny)* that Mr Stanislavski will benefit .... meeting?

9 I'm not sure if .... *(entire)* understand your question. .... *(mean)* .... I .... *(act)* .... *(unethical)*?

10 .... I could just finish what I .... *(say)*, ... *(you)* accusations .... *(be)* .... *(complete)* unfounded.

11 If you'd just let .... *(I)* finish, you .... *(misunderstand)* .... actions.

12 Hang .... minute. You .... *(jump)* .... conclusions.

B **Vladimir Stanislavski has called a press conference of his own to 'clarify' the situation. Role-play the situation.**

Student A: Vladimir Stanislavski

You want to reassure journalists that there is no impropriety (unethical behaviour) between you and the Minister. You were just in the resort of Simi, on a Greek island, when you phoned Ian Stonehouse (only an acquaintance, not a friend) and happened to find that he was there too on holiday, by pure coincidence, and invited him to spend a couple of hours on your yacht.

Another British minister was also on your yacht at the same time, but you don't know if the journalists know this.
You have plans to buy a TV channel in the UK, but you don't think the fact that you know the minister is of any importance. Stonehouse told you that the government would not prevent you from buying the TV channel, but of course you will not mention this.

Use some of the expressions/techniques for managing questions when challenged by the journalists at the press conference.

Student B: Journalists

You want to find out:

- how well Vladimir Stanislavski (VS) knows Ian Stonehouse (IS);
- the circumstances in which he invited IS to the yacht;
- whether any other guests were on the yacht at the same time. (There are rumours that there were.);
- what they discussed, in particular whether they talked about VS's acquisition of a TV channel in the UK;
- what the UK government's attitude is to this acquisition, and whether they will allow it to go ahead.

In general, you want to give VS as hard a time as possible. Be insistent but polite in your questioning.

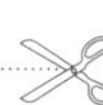

UNIT 8 Consultants

NEGOTIATING

A **Correct the nine mistakes in this e-mail from the sales rep of a toiletries company to the buyer for a low-cost supermarket chain following the negotiation in situation 4, Exercise F, on page 79 of the Course Book.**

To: aude.aubusson@trendtoiletries.com

From: b.tomasso@zieglersupermarkets.com

Subject: Confirmation

Dear Ms Aubusson

It was very nice meeting you this morning. I'm writing to confirm that we discussed re. our shampoo and sun-tan products. I'm please to confirm our offer of a unit price of €1.05 for our leading shampoo product, for an order of 250,000 units. I sensed you were more hesitant about the sun-tan lotion, which is why I'm prepared to go even further than I did this morning, when I offer you a unit price of €0.75. I've discussed this with my boss, and we are now prepared to offer you 50,000 units at €0.69 per unit for a firm sale, although not, unfortunately, on the sell-or-return basis that you requested.

As of payment and delivery, I'm sending you a copy of an outline sales agreement (attached), with our suggested payment terms and delivery schedule. Can you pleased confirm your order by e-mail as soon as possible, as we will not be able to guarantee the above prices beyond the end of this week.

If you needed any more information, please phone or e-mail me. Looking forward to do business with you.

Best regard

Belinda Tomasso

B **Aude Aubusson phones Belinda Tomasso the next day. Role-play their conversation using these prompts and appropriate negotiations language.**

Student A: Aude Aubusson	Student B: Belinda Tomasso
Say hello and identify yourself.	
	Say hello. Ask if Aude would like to place an order now.
You want to place a firm order for the shampoo for the quantity and price (confirm these) in Belinda's e-mail.	
	Thank Aude. Ask if she wants to order the sun-tan lotion.
Say you will order 25,000 units of the lotion at the price mentioned, but only on a sale-or-return basis.	
	This is not possible – your company's policy is only to accept firm sales, as the lotion has a sell-by date just three months from now.
Agree to buy the lotion on a firm sale basis if the price is lower.	
	Offer a slightly lower unit price.
Agree to this price.	
	Thank Aude. You will send a revised sale agreement by e-mail.
Say you look forward to receiving it.	
	Close the conversation suitably.
Reply suitably.	

UNIT 9

Strategy

BRAINSTORMING AND CREATIVITY

A **Cross out the unnecessary word in each of these expressions.**

1 Who'd like to get the ball rolling on?
2 Let's just get the ideas right down at this stage.
3 That's a cool off idea!
4 Let's go around about the table once and then open the discussion up.
5 Here's what I'd add on to your suggestion.
6 You've taken the words right out off of my mouth.
7 I'd like to expand widest on that.
8 I was just around going to say that!
9 Let's try and suspend up judgement until later.
10 The rule is there are no any bad ideas.

B **Brainstorm the problem that your teacher gives you in groups of five or six.**

Company centenary
A consumer-goods company that makes cleaning products, washing powder, etc. is celebrating its 100th anniversary next year. Brainstorm ways of using this event to boost the company's brands. Try to come up with five promotional activities specifically related to the anniversary.

Charity fundraising
A charity that raises money for projects in the developing world wants to increase its income from sponsored events in which people participate to raise funds for it. An example of one of its recent events was a sponsored climb of Mount Kilimanjaro in East Africa – fundraisers got friends and family to promise to donate a particular amount if the sponsored participant reached the top. Think of more possible sponsored events like this.

Annoying neighbours
The head of the management company of an apartment block (10 flats) wants to reduce the increasing number of problems associated with the building. She lives in the building herself, and has had complaints about:

- loud parties that go on all night, organised by the teenage daughter of one of the flat owners while her parents are away. (The latest party was announced on Facebook, and dozens of people unknown to the daughter turned up and ruined the flat.)
- families with children leaving pushchairs and bicycles cluttering the hall and staircases.
- people leaving out rubbish for collection in front of the building several days before the collection day – it looks untidy and smells, and the management company has been warned that it could be fined by the city authorities for this.
- people who run their washing machines at two o'clock in the morning, with noise heard throughout the building.

The head of the management company would like to find voluntary solutions to these issues in a brainstorming session with fellow flat owners.

UNIT 10 Online business

PRESENTATIONS: THINKING ON YOUR FEET

A **Correct the errors in these utterances, replacing the incorrect words with the same number of correct ones.**

1 Funny enough, someone interrogated me the same question yesterday.
2 Could you just resay that question because I don't think everyone catched it.
3 I'm ecstatic that you elevated that point – it's an exceedingly interesting one.
4 I'm fearful that I don't have those informations to hand.
5 I'm apologetic, but that's not really my terrain of researches.
6 Can I return back for you on that one?
7 Are you mind if we dealing about that later in?
8 I don't want to got onto too excessive detail at this state.
9 I'd be happy to discuss about with you after my talking.
10 Factually, I'll be arriving at that later this afternoon.

B **Work in pairs. Student A prepares and starts to give a two-minute presentation on a subject of his/her choice. After one minute, Student B interjects with an interruption, question, etc. Student A must respond appropriately, using a polite and tactful expression, corresponding to one of the 'inner thoughts' (1–8) below. Student B must then guess which 'inner thought' Student A was thinking.**

1 That's irrelevant.
2 I talked about that earlier. Weren't you listening?
3 Isn't it obvious I was going to cover that point later?
4 That's not my area, and my colleagues are too ignorant to know, because they aren't interested in anything outside their own little area. So there's no point in asking them, but I'll lie and say that I'll ask them.
5 I don't really want to go to the trouble of contacting you later about this, but I suppose I must show willing.
6 We'll deal with that later, if you insist, but in five minutes you'll probably forget you mentioned it at all.
7 I can't be bothered to go into any more detail, either now or later.
8 We could talk about this after my talk, but it'd better be quick, as I have a train to catch. I want to be back home in time for dinner.

UNIT 11

New business

CHASING PAYMENT

A **Look again at the useful language for chasing payment on page 109 of the Course Book and rearrange the 'turns' that your teacher will give you into the first part of a logical phone conversation.**

FP: Ziegler Supermarkets Accounts Payable, good morning. Fred Polidori speaking.

SO: Hello Fred. This is Trend Toiletries. My name's Stig Olsson. I'm phoning from the Accounts Department here about an outstanding invoice. Payment is now way overdue.

FP: Could you give me the invoice number, Stig?

SO: It's GH9324U/D/39271-0911-FL/963.

FP: Sorry, could you say the last part again, please, from the 'D' onwards?

SO: Yes, it's D ... 392 ... 71 ... hyphen 0911 hyphen ... FL slash 963.

FP: Right, got it. I've found it on the system.

SO: Good! You can probably see on the screen that it's for shampoo and sun-tan lotion.

FP: Yes, it's been a good summer – we sold tons of sun-tan lotion. But I think I see the problem.

SO: Problem? We need the money badly, I can tell you. Three hundred thousand-odd euros is a serious amount!

FP: Yes, but it's the payment terms. Your invoice is dated 15th July, and our payment terms are 90 days, and it's only mid-September.We won't be paying this till the end of October.

SO: That's not possible, Fred. When we negotiated the order with your toiletries buyer, Aude Aubusson, she agreed to credit terms of 30 days, and I have the e-mail to prove it.

FP: Aude didn't have the authority to change our usual payment terms, which are 90 days. She's always trying to do this – her boss should have a word with her.

SO: I'm sorry, but under the circumstances, we would really appreciate payment soon.

FP: I'm afraid that's not possible. The payments system is set up in a particular way, and there's no procedure for exceptions.

SO: Given the situation, we'll have to consider withdrawing credit terms if this invoice isn't settled within seven days.

B **Continue the conversation. (Fred says he has no authority to change the payment terms, but might be persuaded to make an exception. Stig must suggest alternative solutions. For example, he could ask to talk to the Head of Ziegler's Accounts Payable Department, pay part of the amount due now and part later ... Think of others.)**

UNIT 12 Project management

TELECONFERENCING

A **Match the two parts of these expressions used in a teleconference.**

1 Alessandra here. Let's
2 We've only got half an hour, so
3 There's a lot to
4 Can we hear first
5 Hi, Alessandra. This is Tom. I
6 I'd like to
7 Rick, here. Can
8 Let's summarise
9 Can I just check
10 Let's go over the action

a) let's make a start.
b) I comment at this stage?
c) go over the agenda.
d) what we've said so far.
e) get through today.
f) have a question for you.
g) add to what Tom has just said.
h) from Tom in Oslo, and then from Rick in Vancouver, and finally we'll go over to Harriet in Kuala Lumpur.
i) points before we finish.
j) who's doing what and by when?

B **Role-play this situation.**

The engineering design company that you work for has decided to move its headquarters from London to one of the locations abroad where it already has regional offices.

Each participant in the teleconference is speaking from the regional office of the city that he/she wants to recommend. Reasons for moving could include lower company tax, weather, lifestyle, transport, infrastructure, good schools and universities. Choose a city that you have visited or that you know about.

Your teacher will give you role cards for this situation, but you will not know who has each role card. The objectives are to:

- further practise teleconferencing language
- guess who has which role card.

Student A

You are not necessarily the host, but you want to hurry things along at a good pace, as you have another teleconference immediately after this one. Despite this, you do not want to seem rude. You do not really mind where the company moves to as long as the city is not far from good beaches. (Your partner was insistent on this when you told him/her about the move.)
However, you hide this and pretend that you have more 'serious' reasons for your choice.

Student B

You have never travelled outside Europe, but you have lots of ideas, sometimes pretending to have knowledge that you do not really possess.
You want to show you are contributing positively the whole time to the teleconference (this is your first one). You are younger than the other participants (you are only 23) and this is your first job.
You want to avoid interrupting when other people are speaking, and you apologise profusely if this happens.

Student C

You think of yourself as well travelled, and you have a number of suggestions, but you make clear quite early on which one your favourite is, and for what reason(s). You have teenage children who would benefit from time abroad, and you do not hide this, but you make clear what the benefits would be for the company as a whole.
You are quite impatient with other participants, especially those you consider less knowledgeable than yourself.

Student D

You do not really want the HQ to move from London at all. You are happy working in the regional office where you are. You are a senior regional manager who enjoys trips to London for business meetings because you can combine them with going to football matches, but you don't mention this. (You support Arsenal.)
You want to sound enthusiastic about doing what's best for the company, but your 'hidden agenda' is to stay exactly where you are.

UNIT 1

First impressions

ANNELIESE GUÉRIN-LETENDRE, INTERCULTURAL COMMUNICATIONS EXPERT, COMMUNICAID

A CD1.1 **Listen to the first part of the interview and match the verbs (1–6) with the expressions that they relate to (a–e). (One of the expressions relates to two verbs.)**

1 make	a) an image
2 break down	b) impressions
3 take in	c) that vital first impression
4 put together	d) these messages
5 view	e) a composite picture
6 build up	

B **Match the adverbs (1–6) from the first part of the interview with expressions that could replace them (a–e), keeping the same meaning. (Two of the adverbs can be replaced by the same expression.)**

1 usually	a) normally
2 really	b) swiftly
3 quickly	c) separately from each other
4 independently	d) definitely
5 certainly	e) in fact
6 actually	

C CD1.1 **Listen to the first part of the interview again and put the adverbs in Exercise B into the order that you hear them. (One occurs three times, one occurs twice and the others once each.)**

D CD1.2 **Listen to the second part of the interview and find expressions that mean the following.**

1 stiff
2 to free
3 how you look at people, how long you look at them each time, etc.
4 look round a room
5 the way that you change your voice
6 the way that you change the pitch of your voice
7 movements of body, especially hands and arms
8 repeated movements of the body, ways of speaking, etc. that can be irritating to others
9 irritating movements of the body, perhaps 'playing' with one's clothes, jewellery, etc.
10 something that prevents you from concentrating on something

UNIT 2

Training

DR BERND ATENSTAEDT, CHIEF EXECUTIVE, GERMAN INDUSTRY-UK

A CD1.6 **Listen to the first part of the interview and identify:**

1 three types of workplace.
2 an expression for people who work for an organisation under a long-term contract.
3 a word referring to the feeling of belonging to an organisation.
4 an expression referring to the fact of having a main interest or activity to occupy you.
5 an expression used to talk about an apprentice's pay and how often they receive it.
6 an expression to say that an activity is a good idea.

B CD1.7 **Listen to Dr Atenstaedt's answers to the first question in the second part of the interview and choose the correct alternative to replace each expression in *italic*.**

1 And about 60 per cent of all school leavers, aged 16, become apprentices. The rest goes into higher education either into colleges or into universities, so *the majority* become apprentices.
a) more of b) most c) the most
2 Most of them want to go into *well-known* companies like BMW, Mercedes, Siemens.
a) famous b) aware c) recognised
3 ... they then sign an *employment contract*, which tells them how many hours they have to work ...
a) job undertaking b) position agreement c) work agreement
4 ... you can *extend* to three and a half years.
a) expand b) explode c) take as much as
5 And then it *sets down* how much allowance[s] the company pays them.
a) puts up b) sets out c) sets off
6 And they spend usually three to four days in the company and one to two days in a *vocational school*, which is usually in the same place, town or city.
a) training centre b) educational school c) pedagogical centre

C CD1.7 **Listen to Dr Atenstaedt's answer to the second question in the second part of the interview and decide whether these statements are true (T) or false (F).**

1 There is a national scheme for apprenticeships in the UK.
2 There is a national scheme for apprenticeships in Germany.
3 Apprentices in Germany only work in factories.
4 Dr Atenstaedt mentions three 'labels'.
5 Dr Atenstaedt's organisation is working with the British government to introduce a similar scheme in the UK.

UNIT 3 Energy

ANGUS McCRONE, CHIEF EDITOR, BLOOMBERG NEW ENERGY FINANCE

A CD1.18 **Listen to the first part of the interview and decide whether these statements about expressions as they are used in the interview are true (T) or false (F).**

1 *News* is a plural noun: you can say *The news are good*, for example.
2 *Data* is the plural of *datum*, but *datum* is hardly ever used.
3 *Analysis* is here used as an uncountable noun, but when it is used as a countable noun, its plural is *analyses*.
4 The prefix *mega-* means 'one thousand'.
5 *Carbon capture* can be used in a plural form.
6 *Enables* could be replaced by *allows* and the meaning would be the same.
7 *Renewable* also exists as a countable noun.

B **Complete this table with expressions from the first part of the interview, and related expressions.**

verb	noun
provide	..........[1]
..........[2] (usual British English spelling) ....[3] (American English spelling)	analysis
..........[4]	capture
..........[5]	storage
calculate	..........[6]
deter	.........., ...[7]
affect	..........[8]

C CD1.19 **Listen to the second part of the interview and replace the eight changes in this audio script with what Angus McCrone actually says.**

Well, right now, the most developed of the *main* clean energy sectors is wind because the technologies have basically been homogenised for 20, 25, 30 years, through bladed turbine. And people know exactly how much it costs to produce power with that technology. They know where the best geographical locations are to base wind farms, so it's considered as a mature technology and often an alternative to things like gas and coal. But I think in the long term, solar is the clean energy technology [that] will probably get the biggest uptake, both putting plants in places like deserts and in very sunny areas, taking advantage of land that hasn't got a lot of other potential. But also micro-generation, people putting solar panels on roofs. Once the technology comes down enough, it's not there yet, but once it comes down enough, then it'll be something that people do all the time as a way of actually dealing with some of their power needs during the course of the year. And solar panels will have a vast market for that.

D **Look again at the changes in the audio script in Exercise C. Is each of them possible a) grammatically, and b) so as to keep the same meaning?**

UNIT 4

Marketing

DR JONATHAN REYNOLDS, ACADEMIC DIRECTOR, OXFORD INSTITUTE OF RETAIL MANAGEMENT, AND LECTURER, SAÏD BUSINESS SCHOOL

A CD1.28 **Listen to the first part of the interview, and choose the correct alternative to replace the expression in *italic*, keeping the same meaning.**

1 Customer relationship management, or CRM as it's known *for short*, ...

a) briefly b) shortly c) by its initials

2 In some people's minds, CRM has been *associated* with software, ...

a) created b) identified c) collaborated

3 But increasingly, I think we need to think about customer relationship management as being a much *broader* set of responsibilities for organisations; ...

a) wider b) taller c) deeper

4 ... creating, if you like, customer-centric businesses where the customer is at the *heart* of everything that an organisation thinks and feels about its market.

a) brains b) threshold c) centre

5 *Certainly*, systematising the way in we think about customers might be thought of as a little mechanical.

a) Undecidedly b) Undoubtedly c) Unhopefully

6 When you're dealing with a mass market ... using some kind of *systematic* piece of CRM software, it's very important to ...

a) methodical b) organised c) structured

7 ... provide a *consistent service* to the customer.

a) service that does not vary b) service that does not relate c) service that does not improve

B CD1.29 **Listen to the second part and complete these statements with appropriate forms of expressions used in the interview.**

If a retailer ...

1 persuades people to continue buying its products, it .... them.

2 encourages customers to continue to buy its products, it encourages their ....

3 develops particular programmes for the customers in question 2 above, it invests in ....

4 studies which products particular customers buy, when they buy them, etc., it studies their ....

5 collects information about customers as in question 4 above, it .... about them.

6 designs offers for particular types of customers, it .... for them.

7 invests in ...., it lowers prices.

C CD1.30 **Listen to the third part and complete this table with expressions used in the interview, and related expressions.**

noun	adjective/*-ing* form
..........1	private
relevance	2
..........3	concerning
glass	4
indifference	5
..........6	unaware

RESOURCE BANK – Listening

UNIT 5

Employment trends

IAN BRINKLEY, DIRECTOR OF THE KNOWLEDGE ECONOMY PROGRAMME FOR THE WORK FOUNDATION

A CD2.9 **Listen to the first part of the interview and identify:**

1 an uncountable noun related to the verb *employ*.
2 an adjective meaning *going on all the time*.
3 a multiword verb meaning *happen* or *appear*.
4 a compound adjective that in this context means *adding a lot of profit*.
5 a compound adjective that means *advanced*.
6 an adjective relating to a type of job that involves one's imagination.
7 a noun that usually refers to machines producing electricity, used here to mean something completely different.
8 a multiword verb to say that something is becoming bigger.

B CD2.9 **Listen to the first part again. How many times does Ian Brinkley use each of these verb tenses, and where does he use them?**

1 first conditional
2 present perfect
3 past simple
4 present continuous
5 past continuous

C CD2.10 **Listen to the second part of the interview. Which alternative *cannot* be used to replace the expression in *italic*, keeping a similar meaning, because it is not grammatical and/or because it makes no sense?**

1 ... it's made things much *faster*, ...
a) quicker b) speedier c) rapider

2 ... so the *response times* of businesses and individuals, ...
a) reaction times b) answer times c) turnaround times

3 ... people are expected now to work at a much faster *pace* than they did in the past.
a) speed b) rate c) flow

4 Secondly, it's *placed* a big emphasis on communication skills.
a) put b) built c) meant

5 If you think about all the changes in new technology, most of them are *related* to communications in some way or another.
a) linked b) connected c) stringed

6 And so, businesses and individuals who *have* good communication skills, ...
a) possess b) behave c) display

7 ... these are the ones which we've seen *develop* most.
a) transform b) change c) evolve

D CD2.11 **Listen to the third part of the interview. Complete the audio script below using the alternative expressions (a–f) in the correct places, keeping the same meaning.**

a) skill and experience b) essential c) experts with a narrow focus d) range e) field f) criterion

I think the most ....[1] thing is to get the widest set of skills and experiences that you possibly can. Most employers now are not looking for ....[2], they want people who can work across a wide ....[3] of tasks within the workplace. So particularly, communication skills, the ability to get on with other people, and work in a team, as well as some technical ....[4]. But the most important ....[5] is to make sure that you have got a wide set of skills, rather than just skills in a very, very narrow ....[6].

RESOURCE BANK – Listening

UNIT 6 Ethics

PHILIPPA FOSTER BACK, DIRECTOR OF THE INSTITUTE OF BUSINESS ETHICS

A CD2.20 **Listen to the first part of the interview and decide whether these statements about expressions used are true (T) or false (F).**

1 A *sea change* relates to changes happening in the oceans.
2 *Throughout the world* means 'in the whole world'.
3 *Extract* here refers to removing oil and gas from the ground, but it can also refer to removing teeth.
4 *Level of awareness* could be replaced by *degree of awareness*, with no change in meaning.
5 *Significantly* could be replaced by *importantly*, with no change in meaning.
6 If someone is *brought to account*, they are made to pay a sum of money.
7 *Environmental* could be replaced by *ecological*, with no change in meaning.
8 If something is *exposed*, it is revealed.

B CD2.21 **Listen to the second part of the interview and replace the 10 mistakes in this audio script with what Philippa Foster Back actually says.**

I think they've changed in the sense that in the old days when they were family-owned companies – and I'm going back now a hundred years – there was a great deal of *trust* in the way that the companies were being managed. Companies were quite paternalistic, so there was an attitude of 'Don't worry, we'll look after you', both of the customers, clearly, but also of workers. And that model, that business model, I would call a *trust* model.

And that carried on for many, many years, and it's really only until the 1980s, 1990s when there were some quite big corporate scandals that caused people to doubt this. And, linked with what the growing media attention on how companies were behaving, the growing attention around environmental issues – back in the oil and gas industry – led again to this increase in awareness, so much that companies thought, 'Mm, maybe this isn't the model any more.' And certainly from their customers and people interested in business they said, 'No, we don't trust you. Please involve us.' So we moved to more of a paradigm of, 'Involve us in how you do your business. We would like to help you to do it better.'

C CD2.22 **Listen to the third part of the interview and identify:**

1 a noun used to refer to everyone with an interest in how a company is run.
2 an adjective meaning *relating to companies*, but that is not grammatically related to the word *company*.
3 an expression meaning *as well as*.
4 a name for the yearly financial information that companies publish.
5 three names for the non-financial reports that companies have been producing.
6 an adjective meaning *more*.
7 a verb meaning *apply* in the context of law.

UNIT 7

Finance

CHARLES MIDDLETON, UK MANAGING DIRECTOR, TRIODOS BANK

A CD2.30 **Listen to the first part of the interview and complete this table with words used by Charles Middleton, and related words.**

verb	noun
award	..........[1]
..........[2]	presentation
mix	.........., ...[3]
focus	..........[4]
..........[5]	impact
..........[6]	delivery
expose	..........[7]
	repercussion

B **Match the nouns from Exercise A to these statements about them.**

This noun can also be used to refer to ...

1 a collision.
2 taking goods to a customer.
3 a combination of more than two things.
4 a talk.
5 being able to see clearly.
6 a compensation payment.
7 a positive effect, but it usually refers to negative ones.
8 the effects of extreme cold.

C CD2.31 **Listen to the second part of the interview and replace the expressions in *italic* with grammatically related forms of the words in brackets, adding any other necessary words.**

1 ... they *are all focused on* making a difference in a social and environmental way ... (concentrate)
2 ... we're lending to some of the major renewable energy *providers* in the UK. (supply)
3 ... we're *financing* some of the big providers of social housing in the UK, such as Mencap and their subsidiaries. (funds)
4 ... Café Direct, who are the ... *major* hot-drinks fair-trade provider in the UK. (importance)
5 ... the *return for us is merely* the interest that we are paid on the loan. (profitable, we, only)

D CD2.32 **Listen to the third part of the interview and complete these statements with correct forms of expressions used by Charles Middleton.**

1 If x is not directly associated with y, it's .... from y.
2 A .... is an idea or theory, sometimes a false or illusory one.
3 The two possible forms for the past participle of *prove* are *proved* and ....
4 If you have dealings with an organisation, you .... with it: there is .... with it on your part.
5 Unusual activities that few people understand are ....
6 Something simple and uncomplicated is ....
7 Something that is unsuitable for a particular situation is ....

RESOURCE BANK – Listening

UNIT 8

Consultants

PETER SIRMAN, HEAD OF OPERATIONS CONSULTING, PA CONSULTING GROUP

A CD2.41 **Listen to the first part of the interview and identify:**

1. a verb that can also be used to talk about giving the meanings of words in dictionaries. (Give the infinitive.)
2. a noun that is also an old-fashioned way of referring to an area of land owned by someone.
3. an adverb that means *in fact*.
4. a noun that can also be used to talk about the way actors act and sportspeople play sport.
5. a noun referring to a general understanding of something.
6. a verb relating to customers that can also be used in the context of restaurants. (Give the infinitive.)
7. a plural noun that can also be used to talk about the appearance of a person.
8. an adjective that can also be used to talk about the width of objects.

B CD2.42 **Listen to the second part of the interview and replace the eight mistakes in this audio script with what Peter Sirman actually says.**

The second point is that we then want to understand the work that the company is doing to deliver those services and products. We use a technique called 'value stream mapping' – that many people will know about – but it looks at the complete process, at all of the activities needed to deliver the service or product, connected together so that we can see how the whole organisation is working together to deliver those services.

We then start to examine the work in more detail: we're interested in the amount of time that each step takes; we're interested in levels of quality at each step of the process; we want to know where things go wrong; why they go wrong; we look at all of the work that's done in that process and we ask 'is this work of value to the customer? Is this merely internal bureaucracy? Are we doing things twice or three times and not adding value to the customer?' So that we have a real understanding of the efficacy with which services are delivered in terms of the quality, the cost and the delivery effectiveness of those services.

C CD2.43 **Listen to the third part of the interview and correct these statements where necessary with accurate forms of expressions used by Peter Sirman, and related expressions. One of the statements is correct.**

1. If you change the design of something, you redesignate it.
2. Finding the cause of something is a process of diagnosis; the related noun for the study of this is *diagnostics*.
3. If you have a new idea, you throw up with it.
4. Inventive new methods, approaches, etc. can be described as *creationist*.
5. The ideas that someone contributes to a project, etc. is their feed-in.
6. The time between an order and its delivery is the leading time.
7. If you lay on a particular target, you decide what it will be.

D CD2.44 **Listen to the final part of the interview. Which of these subjects does Peter Sirman *not* mention?**

1. outsourcing
2. restructuring
3. site consolidation
4. just-in-time delivery
5. management systems
6. consensus building
7. case studies
8. client consultation

RESOURCE BANK – Listening

UNIT 9

Strategy

MARJORIE SCARDINO, CEO, PEARSON

A CD3.1 **Listen to the beginning of the first part of the interview and replace the seven mistakes in this audio script with what Marjorie Scardino actually says.**

We decided a long time ago, maybe 10 years ago, that, as a publishing company, we were dedicated to content, to high-quality content, but content was never going to be enough by itself. We decided that we had to add services to that content to make it more helpful to users. So we added technology in most cases. We added different ways for our customers to exploit that content. If you are a child learning math, we added new kinds of interactive tools, for instance. Those kinds of things have changed our strategy. And now, much of what we sell is digital, or digitally facilitated in some way.

B CD3.1 **Listen to Marjorie Scardino's answer later in the first part of the interview and choose the correct alternative to replace each expression in *italic*.**

1 We start with the idea that you *have to* communicate more than strategy.
a) might b) would c) must

2 You have to first communicate what the company's *goals* are and what its values are.
a) objectives b) objects c) objections

3 So we have tried to communicate our ... goals first, and then our strategy for *achieving* those goals.
a) retaining b) constraining c) attaining

4 I think I have to communicate directly with everybody. ... But I *try* to, ...
a) endeavour b) reach c) look

5 ... and the Internet *allows me* to do that, so I try to write letters to everybody every time I think there's something important to say.
a) lets me to b) lets me c) let me

6 And the people who run different parts of our company try to do *the very* same, to communicate directly with the people they work with.
a) absolutely the b) totally the c) exactly the

7 ... we try to communicate in a colourful way ... so that everyone feels that we're all *on the* same *plain*.
a) on the same ship b) on the same level c) on the same planet

C CD3.2 **Listen to the second part of the interview. What do the expressions in *italic* refer to in these statements summarising Marjorie's opinions? Choose the correct alternative.**

1 *They* will be enabled in their quest to make progress in their lives.
a) strategies b) individuals

2 *They* aren't at the micro-level, they're at the macro-level.
a) bigger-thinking strategies b) how you change the world

3 *It* is something that people can go beyond themselves to reach.
a) something larger than themselves b) progress

4 *They* are one way of reaching large numbers of people.
a) textbooks b) large schools

5 *This* allows people to learn at their own pace.
a) delivering education in a way that teaches every person in their own way, in their own time
b) allowing everyone to get out of bed ready to do something bigger than themselves

6 *It* is propelled by this strategy.
a) education in general b) our education company (i.e. Pearson)

UNIT **10**

Online business

DAVID BOWEN, SENIOR CONSULTANT, BOWEN CRAGGS & CO.

A CD3.22 **Listen to the first part of the interview. Which of these things does David Bowen *not* mention?**

1 social networking
2 booksellers
3 corporate purchasing
4 local plumbers
5 online dating
6 auction sites

B CD3.23 **Listen to the second part of the interview and identify:**

1 an expression for Internet sites designed to be accessed from all over the world.
2 a noun referring to something not being simple.
3 an expression referring to the fact that things are not all in the same place.
4 four nouns relating to 'audiences' for websites.
5 three nouns used to talk about the ease or otherwise of using websites.
6 an adverb that increases the strength of the adjective that follows it.
7 an *-ing* form used to talk about the identity of a company.
8 a verb that could be replaced by *binds*, with no change in meaning.

C CD3.24 **Listen to the third part of the interview and decide whether these statements about expressions used there are true (T) or false (F).**

If ...

1 there is *subtle use* of something, it is done in a sophisticated way.
2 something is *engaging*, it is tedious.
3 a story *gets out*, it becomes known.
4 you have been *traditionally used to* something, this is the way that you used to do it.
5 you *counter* an idea, argument, etc., you agree with it.
6 a story *goes around*, it comes back to the person who started it.
7 you *put out* a story, you hide it.
8 you *put out* a fire, you extinguish it.

D CD3.25 **Listen to the final part and identify:**

1 six uses of the present simple.
2 four uses of the present continuous.
3 four uses of *will*, including those in its contracted and negative forms.
4 four uses of *going to*.

UNIT 11

New business

MIKE SOUTHON, AN EXPERT ON STARTING NEW BUSINESSES

A CD3.28 **Listen to the first part of the interview and replace the seven mistakes in this audio script with what Mike Southon actually says.**

Well, really there's two kinds of start-ups which people do these days. One is something that solves a problem in a local area. So, for example, there's a local entrepreneur and sees there's a problem, so may start a plumbing company, or an accountancy company, or just something that brings services to the local region that aren't there already, so that's some kind of physical business, usually a services business. And the other one, of course, are Internet businesses, where anybody in principle can have a website and send people to there and then sell things from it. It could be selling information, it could be selling products. So I'd say there are two types: there's local businesses and Internet businesses.

B CD3.29 **Listen to the second part of the interview and find these expressions and related expressions.**

1 a noun that refers to providing goods or services (Is it countable or uncountable in this sense?)
2 a multiword verb that means *restrain*
3 a noun that can also refer to a classical legend
4 a noun of French origin referring to the skills and activities involved in starting new companies
5 an adjective to describe someone who does things on their own (What related noun refers to a musician who plays on their own?)
6 an expression that could refer to a sport like football or hockey
7 an adjective to describe someone with potential, also used to describe plants
8 a word for someone who has a different perspective from you, giving you a better understanding of a situation
9 a word for someone who is not outgoing (What is the related noun for the characteristics of people like this?)
10 the opposite of 9 above, and its related noun

C CD3.30 **Listen to the third part of the interview and identify the five Ps that Mike Southon refers to.**

D **Match each of these utterances to one of the Ps in Exercise C.**

1 I couldn't imagine going back to being a salary slave. And I want to make a lot of money.
2 People can watch the video on our website – we stick this car to a wall – it's incredible.
3 We can manufacture these fixings and make a fortune.
4 I've invented this great new product for fixing objects to walls without nails or screws.
5 We make a great team – our competitors are just a bunch of losers.

UNIT 12 Project management

TOM TAYLOR, VICE-PRESIDENT, ASSOCIATION FOR PROJECT MANAGEMENT

A CD3.36 **Listen to the first part of the interview. Which of these project stakeholders does Tom Taylor refer to using pronouns (*we*, *they*, etc.)?**

1 bride
2 groom
3 guests
4 employees
5 clients
6 stakeholders
7 suppliers
8 neighbours

B CD3.37 **Listen to the second part of the interview. Which expressions in *italic* could you use *the* in front of?**

I think it's mainly about *change*[1]. *Projects*[2] are about *change*[3]. *Society*[4] wants *change*[5].

The best use of *technology*[6], *technology*[7] appropriate to the project ...

There's an interest everywhere in *sustainability*[8], the environment and *green issues*[9]. A lot of that is appearing in projects, to make *things*[10] better, to overcome some of the problems and *damage*[11] that has occurred in the world, er, that's, that's an important issue for *people*[12].

C CD3.37 **Complete this table with words from the second part of the interview, and related expressions.**

verb	noun	adjective (but not *-ing* or *-ed* forms)
change	change	changeable
challenge	..........[1]	
..........[2]	..........[3]	tight
..........[4]	.........., ...[5]	appropriate
	capability	..........[6]
sustain	..........[7]	..........[8]
damage	..........[9]	

D **Look at the completed table in Exercise C and answer these questions.**

1 Which verbs can be **a)** only transitive, **b)** only intransitive, **c)** both?
2 Which verb has a very different sense from the noun and adjective forms?
3 Which nouns can only ever be used in their uncountable forms?
4 Which noun and adjective could lose their first three letters and still have almost the same meaning?

RESOURCE BANK – Listening

RESOURCE BANK LISTENING KEY

Unit 1

A

1 c 2 c 3 b 4 e 5 d 6 a

B

1 a 2 e 3 b 4 c 5 d 6 e

C

actually, really, certainly, really, usually, independently, usually, quickly, really

D

1 rigid 2 liberate 3 eye contact 4 scan 5 modulation 6 intonation 7 gestures 8 mannerisms 9 fidgeting 10 a distraction

Unit 2

A

1 office, factory, warehouse 2 permanent employees 3 loyalty 4 focus in life 5 monthly allowance 6 worthwhile exercise

B

1 b 2 a 3 c 4 c 5 b 6 a

C

1 F (There's no training programme for all apprentices right across the UK.)
2 T
3 F (They also work in offices.)
4 F (He mentions two: 'Trained in Germany' and 'Made in Germany'.)
5 T

Unit 3

A

1 F (It's always singular: 'The news is good.')
2 T
3 T
4 F (It means 'one million'.)
5 F (It's always singular and uncountable.)
6 T
7 T

B

1 provision 2 analyse 3 analyze 4 capture 5 store 6 calculation 7 deterrent/detterence 8 effect

C

Well, right now, the most **mature** of the *main* clean energy sectors is wind because the technologies have basically been **standardised** for 20, 25, 30 years, through bladed turbine. And people know exactly how much it costs to **generate** power with that technology. They know where the best geographical locations are to base wind farms, so it's **regarded** as a mature technology and often an alternative to things like gas and coal. But I think in the long term, solar is the clean energy technology [that] will probably get the **widest** uptake, both putting plants in places like deserts and in very sunny areas, taking advantage of land that hasn't got a lot of other **use**. But also micro-generation, people putting solar panels on roofs. Once the technology comes down enough, it's not there yet, but once it comes down enough, then it'll be something that people do **routinely** as a way of actually dealing with some of their power needs during the course of the year. And solar panels will have a **huge** market for that.

D

All the changes are possible, both grammatically and so as to keep the same meaning.

Unit 4

A

1 c 2 b 3 a 4 c 5 b 6 c 7 a

B

1 retains
2 loyalty
3 loyalty marketing schemes
4 buying behaviour
5 gathers intelligence
6 creates promotions
7 price promotion activity

C

1 privacy 2 relevant 3 concern 4 glass 5 indifferent 6 awareness

Unit 5

A

1 employment 2 constant 3 come through 4 high-value 5 hi-tech 6 creative 7 generators 8 open up

B

1 once: ***If you look*** *at the increases in employment, they****'re*** *all for jobs with high levels of skills.*
2 six times: *... jobs* ***have become*** *much more skilled.*
The second big change ***has been*** *the industries. The new jobs* ***have come through*** *in service industries, and they****'ve come through*** *...*
And these ***have been*** *the big generators of new jobs ...*
*And a third thing we****'ve noticed*** *...*
3 not used at all
4 four times: *... a lot of this job growth* ***is taking place*** *in major cities, and in particular, we****'re seeing*** *a big gap open up ...*
... the new jobs ***are occurring*** *only in certain parts of the country ...*
*... they****'re*** *really* ***seeing*** *little benefit from this job growth.*
5 twice: *... a big gap open up between those cities that* ***were doing*** *well, and those cities [that were]* ***doing*** *badly.*

C

1 c 2 b 3 c 4 b 5 c 6 b 7 a

D

1 b 2 c 3 d 4 a 5 f 6 e

Unit 6

A

1 F (It refers to a very big transformational change.)
2 T
3 T
4 T
5 F (*Importantly* is not possible here.)
6 F (They are punished for doing something wrong.)
7 T
8 T

B

I think they've changed in the sense that in the old days when they were family-**run** companies – and I'm going back now a hundred years – there was a great deal of *trust* **around** the way that the companies were being **run**. Companies were quite paternalistic, so there was an attitude of 'Don't worry, we'll look after you', both of the customers, **obviously**, but also of **employees**. And that model, that business model, I would call a *trust* model.
And that carried on for many, many years, and it's really only until the 1980s, 1990s when there were some quite **significant** corporate scandals that caused people to doubt this. And, **married** with what the growing media attention on how companies were behaving, the growing attention around environmental issues – back in the oil and gas industry – led again to this **raising of** awareness, **to the extent** that companies thought, 'Mm, maybe this isn't the model any more.' And certainly from their customers and people interested in business they said, 'No, we don't trust you. Please involve us.' So we moved to more of a **model** of, 'Involve us in how you do your business. We would like to help you to do it better.'

C

1 stakeholders
2 corporate
3 in addition to
4 annual report accounts
5 social responsibility reports, corporate responsibility reports, sustainability reports
6 further
7 enforce

Unit 7

A

1 award 2 present 3 mix, mixture 4 focus 5 impact
6 deliver 7 exposure

B

1 impact 2 delivery 3 mix/mixture 4 presentation
5 focus 6 award 7 repercussion 8 exposure

C

1 ... they **all concentrate on** making a difference in a social and environmental way.
2 ... we're lending to some of the major renewable energy **suppliers** in the UK.
3 ... we're **funding** some of the big providers of social housing in the UK, such as Mencap and their subsidiaries.
4 ... Café Direct, who are the ... **most important** hot-drinks fair-trade provider in the UK.
5 ... the **profit for us is only** the interest that we are paid on the loan.

D

1 several places removed
2 notion
3 proven
4 engage; engagement
5 esoteric
6 straightforward
7 inappropriate

Unit 8

A

1 define 2 domain 3 actually 4 technique
5 overview 6 serve 7 features 8 broad

B

The second point is that we then want to understand the work that the company is doing to deliver those services and products. We use a technique called 'value stream mapping' – that many people will **be familiar with** – but it looks at the complete process, at all of the activities **required** to deliver the service or product, **linked** together so that we can see how the whole organisation is working together to deliver those services.
We then start to **analyse** the work in more detail: we're interested in the amount of time that each step takes; we're interested in levels of quality at each **stage** of the process; we want to know where things go wrong; why they go wrong; we look at all of the work that's done in that process and we ask 'is this work **valuable** to the customer? Is this **just** internal bureaucracy? Are we doing things twice or three times and not adding value to the customer?' So that we have a real understanding of the **efficiency** with which services are delivered in terms of the quality, the cost, and the delivery effectiveness of those services.

C

1 If you change the design of something, you **redesign** it.
2 *correct*
3 If you have a new idea, you **come** up with it.
4 Inventive new methods, approaches, etc. can be described as **creative**.
5 The ideas that someone contributes to a project, etc. is their **input**.
6 The time between an order and its delivery is the **lead** time.
7 If you lay **down** a particular target, you decide what it will be.

D

4, 7

Unit 9

We decided a long time ago, maybe 10 years ago, that, as a **media** company, we were **devoted** to content, to high-quality content, but content was never going to be enough **on its own**. We **felt** that we had to add services to that content to make it more helpful to users. So we added technology in most cases. We added different ways for our customers to **use** that content. If you are a child **studying** math, we added new kinds of interactive tools, for instance. Those kinds of things have changed our strategy. And now, much of what we sell is digital, or digitally **enabled** in some way.

B

1 c 2 a 3 c 4 a 5 b 6 c 7 b

C

1 b 2 a 3 a 4 b 5 a 6 b

Unit 10

A

1, 5

B

1 global websites
2 complexity
3 geographically dispersed
4 customers, shareholders, journalists, governments
5 signposting, navigation, usability
6 extremely
7 branding
8 pulls

C

1 T
2 F (It is interesting.)
3 T
4 F (It is what you are accustomed to.)
5 F (You challenge it.)
6 F (It circulates among people.)
7 F (You make it known.)
8 T

D

1 Well, I **think** the developments ...
... no longer necessarily **listen** to what a company **says** to them.
It**'s** something that**'s** ...
I **think** we're going to ...
I **think** that's going to ...

2 ... that **are** already **starting** where companies **are having** to be ...
It's something that**'s happening** ...
... whether you**'re using** a television or a computer.

3 They**'ll go** and ask ...
... so we**'ll get** quite a lot more ...
... you really **won't notice** ...
They **will be** the same thing.

4 ... that's **going to develop** enormously.
... we're **going to get** 3D ...
... that's **going to become** quite big ...
... we're **going to get** the convergence of ...

Unit 11

Well, really there's two **types** of start-ups which people do **nowadays**. One is something that solves a problem in a local area. So, for example, there's a local entrepreneur and **notices** there's a problem, so may start a plumbing company, or an **accounting** company, or just something that brings services to the local **area** that aren't there already, so that's some kind of physical business, usually a services business. And the other one, of course, are Internet businesses, where anybody in **theory** can have a website and **drive** people to there and then sell things from it. It could be selling information, it could be selling products. So I'd say there are two types: there's local businesses and Internet businesses.

B

1 delivery (uncountable in this sense)
2 hold back
3 myth
4 entrepreneurship
5 solo (soloist)
6 team game
7 budding
8 foil
9 introvert (introversion)
10 extrovert, extroversion

C

Pain, premise, people, proof, purpose

D

1 purpose 2 proof 3 premise 4 pain 5 people

Unit 12

A

1, 2, 3, 6

B

7, 11

C

1 challenge 2 tighten 3 tightness 4 appropriate
5 appropriateness, appropriacy 6 capable
7 sustainability 8 sustainable 9 damage

D

1 **a)** challenge, appropriate, sustain, damage
b) none of them
c) change, tighten
2 appropriate
3 tightness, appropriateness, appropriacy, sustainability
4 capability, capable

UNIT 1

First impressions

CASE STUDY WRITING TASK: MODEL ANSWER

Dear Ms de la Tour

Logistaid's Managing Director, Ed Kaminsky, has asked me, as the organisation's Press Officer, to write to thank you so much for attending our Gala Dinner. I'm sure you will be pleased to hear that Logistaid raised $350,000 at the event.

We are extremely grateful to you for agreeing to promote our new educational programme. Logistaid will shortly be announcing a series of summer schools in different locations around the world, where renowned experts will be giving seminars and courses on a range of development issues. We would be very pleased if you could help us raise awareness of these events.

With this in mind, Ed Kaminsky would like to invite you to a meeting at Logistaid's headquarters here in London sometime in the next month to discuss the promotion of these events in more detail. He suggests one of the following dates: 3rd, 12th or 20th November. I'd be grateful if you could let me know which would be most suitable for you.

We look forward to hearing from you, and thank you again for agreeing to become an 'ambassador' for Logistaid.

Yours sincerely,

R. Orr

Rona Orr

Press Officer, Logistaid

(See the Writing file, Course Book page 142, for the format of formal letters.)

A **Write a letter from Amy de la Tour to Logistaid's Press Officer, with these points. Say that you ...**

- enjoyed the Gala Dinner enormously, especially Ed Kaminsky's speech
- are pleased that Logistaid raised so much money from the dinner
- are happy to accept the role of promoting Logistaid's educational programme
- would be glad to attend a meeting in London on 12th November in the afternoon
- look forward to discussing ways in which you can help promote Logistaid's summer schools.
- End suitably.

B **You are Amy de la Tour's PA (personal assistant). It's 10th November. Write an e-mail to Rona Orr, Logistaid's Press Officer.**

- Say that Amy de la Tour will be unable to come to the meeting on 12th November because of a family crisis. (Invent details.)
- Suggest three other possible dates later in November.
- Say that Amy looks forward to working with Logistaid, and apologises for having to change the date of the meeting.
- End suitably.

UNIT 2

Training

CASE STUDY WRITING TASK: MODEL ANSWER

Hi everyone

This is to thank you all for your input into our recent discussions about training needs here. There was a consensus that some of our training programmes are excellent, especially those for our graduate recruits. However, we agreed that training for those who have been in the company for longer needs to be upgraded, both in the areas of sales training, including 'soft' skills such as organisational and leadership skills, and assertiveness training. Training in the new IT applications will also be given.

Please find attached a detailed training programme that combines training from a) peers, b) line managers, c) the IT department, and d) external training companies. This programme will hopefully give excellent value for money following the recent figures showing that retailers' brands have begun to eat into our market share in a serious way, and the resulting cut in the training budget.

However, I'm sure you'll agree that this training is more urgent than ever, and I count on you all to help us deliver the best training package ever for our sales people. If you have any queries or comments, please do not hesitate to contact me.

Best

Jane

A **Look at the audio scripts for the four salespeople in the Case study (CD1.14–1.17) on page 169 of the Course Book. Choose one of the salespeople: Amy Cheng, Charlie Turner, Kamal Satinder or Jessica Armstrong.**
Write an e-mail from that person to C&R's Sales Director, explaining what sort of training you would like to be able to follow in the new training programme, and why. (If you write an e-mail from Charlie Turner, say why you do not want to follow any of the courses.)

B **The person you chose in Exercise A has now followed the course(s) that they requested. (Even Charlie Turner was 'persuaded' to go on one.) Write another e-mail from the person you chose in Exercise A, this time to a friend of theirs in another company, saying what the course was like and if it was useful. Talk about:**

- the subject of the course
- duration (too long/short?)
- the trainer
- the other participants (cooperative, motivated ...)
- the sorts of activities on the course (role plays, case studies ...)
- whether the course was useful or not for your work.
- End suitably.

Energy

CASE STUDY WRITING TASK: MODEL ANSWER

Tumalet Energy Project Team

FAO: Joanne Hopper

Introduction

As you know, the Energy Project Team recently met in order to consider the options for energy saving and carbon-footprint reduction at the company.

Findings

We came up with the following:

1 **Ways of involving staff in energy efficiency:** We agreed to encourage staff to work virtually from home so as to decrease office occupancy and release more office space as the company grows. Videoconferences rather than face-to-face meetings will become the norm. This also has the advantage of reducing pressure on office equipment such as printers. (However, employees will continue to be encouraged not to print things unless they really need to.)
Similarly, staff will be encouraged to suggest 'virtual' meetings with clients and suppliers. This will reduce CO_2 emissions and travel costs.
These two measures will in themselves involve employees more in the energy-cutting process, and employees will understand better the purpose and impact of the other measures outlined below.

2 **Options for reducing and offsetting CO_2 emissions:** In addition to the two measures above, we should go ahead with installation of solar panels on the roof of our building, as well as planting grass and other plants on the roof to act as natural insulation and to reduce heating bills. We decided on this measure, rather than painting the roof white. However, we will paint internal walls white to increase luminosity and reduce the need for lighting, which will be centrally controlled. Reducing energy consumption in this way in turn reduces CO_2 emissions, of course. In terms of offsetting, we recommended contributing money to carbon-offset projects – such as planting trees – so that the company can compensate for its CO_2 emissions.

3 **Feasible sources of renewable energy and benefits:** We agreed to look further into the question of obtaining energy from solar energy and wind power, which will also reduce our carbon footprint. We hope to get rebates from our energy supplier if we go down this route.

4 **Other measures for our sustainable business strategy:** We also agreed to other measures at every stage of our production process, such as water conservation, greener product packaging, transportation of goods and waste management.

Conclusion/Recommendations

It was agreed that we should go ahead immediately with the ideas on involving staff in our energy-efficiency measures – see point 1 above – with the measures in point 2 put into place in the first quarter of next year.
This will prepare the way for other measures to be introduced over the next five years. The meeting recommended that a specific task force should be set up to look further into energy efficiency and reduction of CO_2 emissions next year under points 3 and 4 above. The first meeting of this task force is scheduled for December 15th.

(See the Writing file, Course Book pages 146–147, for the format of reports. The format there has been adapted for the above report.)

Write an e-mail from a supplier of solar roof panels to Joanne Hopper, with the following points. Say that ...

- you have heard that Tumalet are looking to install solar panels on the roof of its office building
- can offer a very good deal on solar panels and their installation
- you can carry on the installation within a week of receiving Tumalet's order.
- End suitably.

UNIT 4

Marketing

CASE STUDY WRITING TASK: MODEL ANSWER

Press Presse Prensa

Home2u: Eddie Velázquez endorsement

FOR IMMEDIATE RELEASE

For the general and trade press

July 6, 9.00 a.m.

For additional information, visit our website www.home2u.com/press
or contact Silvia Flores at our Miami press office (305) 555 9244

Home2u is delighted to announce a brand-new marketing campaign featuring endorsement by Eddie Velázquez—a hero and role model to young people, not only rap fans, all over the U.S. and Mexico. Eddie will be appearing in our exciting new campaign of English- and Spanish-language ads on radio, TV, and the Internet.

Eddie's concerts in the U.S. and Mexico will also be an integral, energizing part of our new campaign—the concerts will be streamed to our website and feed content to Facebook, appealing to our young Hispanic demographic.

Publicity and promotional material will focus on Eddie's concert appearances, and appearances at special in-store events and store openings. These concerts and events will be trailed on social media. For upcoming concerts, click here.

About us: Founded by Mexican-American Carla Salinas in 1985, Home2u has over 2,000 stores selling innovative furnishings throughout the United States, Puerto Rico, Mexico, and Canada.

(See the Writing file, Course Book page 148, for the format of press releases.)

A **Write a letter from Home2u's Marketing Department to Eddie Velázquez's agent, written before the above agreement was announced.**

- Give a brief outline of your marketing plans involving Eddie (as in the press release above).
- Ask about his availability in relation to other endorsement deals he may have.
- Ask about the feasibility of tie-ins between concerts and use of content on Home2u's website and on social networking sites.
- Suggest a meeting to discuss possibilities.
- End suitably.

B **Write a letter from Eddie Velázquez's agent in response to the letter you wrote in Exercise A, agreeing to a meeting to discuss possibilities and asking for further details about what the endorsement campaign would involve.**

Employment trends

CASE STUDY WRITING TASK: MODEL ANSWER

Subject: Monthly performance

Hi Tricia

As part of Delaney's efforts to improve conditions for staff, we have been looking at the performance of all our agents.

Unfortunately, for the second month running, you have not been able to meet your target. We all know that it's sometimes difficult to keep to the limit of five minutes per call, but we would really like everyone to achieve this. Your average call duration has been slightly higher – I hope you'll be able to reduce this over the coming months.

We've also been having a look at your absence and sickness records. It's difficult to discuss what may be perfectly valid reasons for lateness in an ongoing exchange of e-mails, so I suggest we meet face to face to discuss these issues, and anything else you'd like to bring up. I suggest one evening at the end of your day shift – please let me know which day would be suitable.

Looking forward to hearing from you.

Regards

A **You are the Call Centre Operations Manager for a UK bank – the Southshires Bank. You have just opened a new call centre, to replace three regional call centres. Write a press release from Southshires Bank's PR firm to announce this news. Include this information:**

- There is now one centralised call centre in a state-of-the-art building in Edinburgh.
- It offers 24-hour operation – shifts with 300 agents during the day and 50 at night.
- Southshires has been developing best practices for the employment and working conditions, which it will be implementing at the new centre to make it the most attractive call centre in the UK to work in.
- Facilities will include an on-site gym and crèche.
- There will be personal mentoring for all staff, so as to prevent the onset of stress.

(See the Writing file, Course Book page 148, for the format of press releases.)

B **Write a letter of application to work in the new call centre in Exercise A, saying what attracts you about working there.**

Ethics

CASE STUDY WRITING TASK: MODEL ANSWER

Press Presse Prensa

Daybreak
FOR IMMEDIATE RELEASE
For the general and trade press
14 October, 15:00

For additional information, visit our website www.daybreak.co.uk/cerealupdate or contact Jemima Robertson at our UK press office +44 (0) 161 732 4777

Following widespread concern about sugar and salt levels in our products, Daybreak would like to apologise for mistakes we have made in the past as a consequence of not listening carefully enough to our customers. We realise that parents are rightly concerned about the nutritional aspects of the foods that their children eat. We also apologise to nutritionists whose concerns we did not take sufficiently seriously.

Earlier this year, we reduced the amount of sugar and salt in all our cereals by 30 per cent, and we are committed to further reductions over the next five years. We have now taken the decision to improve the labelling of our products, showing nutritional information per 100g as well as per 30g serving. (The typeface used will also be clearer and easier to read.)

We will also be carrying out a full audit of all our products, from sourcing of ingredients, processing and packaging through to distribution. We will be looking to become the industry leader in the ethical production and marketing of all our products. Further announcements will be made about specific changes introduced following the audit.

About us: Daybreak is a leading manufacturer of breakfast cereals and a proud member of the UK food industry since 1910.

(See the Writing file, Course Book page 148, for the format of press releases.)

A **One of Paradise Cruises' ships has caught fire in the Caribbean. All passengers and crew were lifted to safety on military helicopters. This is the second such fire on Paradise Cruises' ships in the space of a month. Write the press release issued by Paradise Cruises, including the following points:**

- Give brief details of the cause of the fire, the number of passengers and crew lifted off the liner, and their situation now – passengers are being put up in hotels in Kingston, Jamaica. They will then be flown home on aircraft chartered by Paradise, at the company's expense.
- All passengers will be given a full refund, and a free cruise in the future.
- You are cancelling all your company's cruises until further notice so that safety inspections can be carried out of the company's five cruise ships. Passengers with bookings will be able to choose between a full refund, or delaying their cruise until a later date.

B **You have a booking on one of Paradise's cruises later this year. Write a letter to the company, including the following points:**

- Say that you have seen on the news that Paradise are cancelling their upcoming cruises.
- Specify the cruise that you were on, and who you were going to be travelling with. (Invent details including dates, itinerary, etc.)
- Ask for a refund or to transfer your cruise to a later date – specify the date next year that you would like.
- End suitably.

Finance

CASE STUDY WRITING TASK: MODEL ANSWER

To: tina@d&a.com
From: jim@d&a.com
Subject: Last week's speed-funding

Hi Tina

A pity you missed the speed-funding event and the three entrepreneurs that we might invest in. Here's a run-down:

Evan Griffiths
Evan was very sure of himself, almost arrogant. He says he has an 18% share of the e-book market – I don't know how he does it with competitors like Amazon and Apple iBooks. He now wants to start selling an e-reader – like Kindle, but smaller. I don't think he stands a chance in the face of Kindle, iPad and all the other tablet computers that are coming through from computer manufacturers, so I don't recommend investing in him. What's more, he wanted £400 to £500k, which is a lot of money for such a big gamble.

The McQueen sisters
They want £100 to £125k to remodel their production activities along 'green' lines and to expand their business. Agnes McQueen was very eloquent and made a very good pitch, but I wasn't convinced it's for us – I had a taste of their cheese and it's very nice, but there's something about goat's cheese that doesn't inspire me. I'm sure they will continue to do well, with or without investment from us.

Troels McClintock
A very passionate guy! He wants £45 to £55 million to develop his solar-powered plane. He understood that we don't have this kind of money, but suggested that we put money in along with other investors – he has Edinburgh University lined up, as well as aircraft and ship manufacturers in the US. He's an aeronautical engineer and seems to know what he's talking about.

Recommendation
I suggest we go with Troels and his plane. I think he's right when he says that we've reached a tipping point for alternative energy. We need to talk more to him about how the technology used in his plane can be applied elsewhere. We could use his plane as a promotional vehicle (literally!) for some of the other ventures we've been investing in recently. The free global news coverage that we get will catapult us into the top division of investment angels. So let's go for a bold level of investment – £500k, or about a 1% stake in the overall cost of the plane. I think we can easily envisage a 25% return on investment, but we must work closely with him (and his other investors) to a) maximise the promotional power of the plane, and b) exploit to the full the spin-off effects of his solar technology for application in other areas. No 'sleeping' partnership here!

Looking forward to getting your reactions,

Best,
Jim

A **You are one of the investors in the D&A team. Write an e-mail to Troels McClintock:**

- outlining the terms of the deal that you are offering, using the information in the model answer above and adding your own ideas where necessary
- suggesting ways in which to collaborate with him and other investors on maximising the commercial and technological potential of the plane (applications to other products, etc.).

B **Write a tactful e-mail to one of the two entrepreneurs whose project you don't want to invest in, giving your reasons.**

Consultants

CASE STUDY WRITING TASK: MODEL ANSWER

Dear Mr Bajaj

Following our various discussions re setting up a Bajaj-tel mobile phone network in South Africa, I am writing to confirm what we have agreed so far.

Reports

Firstly, we understand your request, considering the complexity of this project, to work with senior consultants at Heitinga T-com, and I hereby confirm that, from now on, either Andrew Heitinga or I will report to you in person on the project's progress. (We will also recruit a new consultant with specific, extensive experience of mobile-phone network roll-outs, but Mr Heitinga and I will be your direct contacts.)

Schedule

As you'll understand, I'm sure, 12 months is a demanding lead time for a complex project like this, and we agreed that the 12-month period will run from the date we receive regulatory approval from the government, which we will endeavour to obtain as soon as possible.

Implementation

We will provide you with fortnightly updates on key milestones reached during the project itself, including technical reports on the ordering and installation of the infrastructure (phone masts, computer servers, payment systems, etc.) and progress with the pre-launch marketing campaign.

Commercial issues

We will do a more detailed analysis of the South African mobile-phone market, including competitors' profitability and probable costs. This will help us to suggest the correct pricing structures for users. We agreed that your initial customer base will probably be 80 per cent pay-as-you-go users, but that it would be advisable to transform these users into contract customers as time goes on.

Fees

We are charging the equivalent of 160 USD per hour for the feasibility study. You agreed to increase this to 200 USD per hour from now on, considering the level of expertise that will be applied to your project.

If you can agree to the above, and as time is of the essence, we suggest moving as soon as possible to signature of contract for this consultancy project.

Best regards

Jeff Carstens
Senior Consultant, Heitinga T-com Consulting

A **Write an e-mail from Mr Bajaj in response to the model above, following one of these three possible outlines.**

- Agree to the conditions offered by Jeff Carstens and say that your lawyers will be in touch soon to suggest clauses in the consultancy contract, following your company's experience in other countries; or
- Ask for further clarifications and explanations, saying that you will sign the consultancy contracts once these points have been finalised; or
- Say, politely, that you are withdrawing completely from working with Heitinga T-com, giving reasons (absence of Andrew Heitinga, showing lack of commitment to this key project, lack of experience of mobile-phone network installation and commercialisation, unsatisfactory suggested lead-times ...).

B **It's 12 months later, and Bajaj-tel's South African mobile-phone operation is on the point of being inaugurated by its new subsidiary there. Write a mission statement for this company, bearing in mind Mr Bajaj's low-cost approach and adding other points in relation to the subsidiary's customers and employees in South Africa, and its social responsibilities there more generally.**

CASE STUDY WRITING TASK: MODEL ANSWER

Stella/Victoria Jets joint venture

Marketing campaign brainstorming meeting – summary of key ideas

These are the key points that emerged from our meeting.

Strategy

The main thrust of this will be to advertise low fares, but to actually charge fares on most flights that are more or less the same as those of regular airlines. We will introduce some LCC (low-cost carrier) methods to our long-haul routes – for example charging for all baggage, for priority boarding of planes, meals, etc. – but the meals will be imaginative and worth the money! There will be charging for all entertainment: films, music, video games, etc. We will reduce the number of cabin staff per aircraft to the regulatory minimum, to reduce costs. We will emphasise ease of booking on the website, and the possibility of making changes to flights without it costing too much.

Corporate identity

To underline our low-cost approach, uniforms of ground staff and cabin crew will have a simple but modern look. The company logo will be no-nonsense but forward-looking. The appearance of the website and all advertising will be homogenous.

Name

There was a lot of discussion about a name for the alliance. Talking about a new name in this way was perhaps putting the cart before the horse. We need to think about the name further in relation to strategy, when we have finalised one.

A **It's one year later, and the joint-venture airline has launched. Write a press release for the national press to announce the launch of the airline (choose a name) and give key information about the new airline and its services.**

(See the Writing file, Course Book page 148, for the format of press releases.)

B **There were various problems in the airline's first week of operations, described as 'teething troubles' by the new airline's operations manager. Write a (reasonably good-tempered!) blog entry on a travel discussion website by one of the airline's first passengers. You could write about:**

- the airline's website and booking system
- the check-in process
- punctuality
- food
- entertainment

or a number of these things. (Use your own flying experiences as inspiration.)

UNIT **10** # Online business

CASE STUDY WRITING TASK: MODEL ANSWER

Meerza Tailoring Fashions

Internet strategy meeting **10 October**

Summary of key points

We invited two respected consultants to present their ideas to us on how we can better manage our online presence. Both agree that in an era of social networking and blogging, companies have less control over what is said about them than before. Following their presentations, we adopted the following ideas:

- **Recruit a Social Media Manager (SMM)** to follow what is being said about us on Facebook, Twitter and in blogs. However, the most important part of their remit will be to control the content of 'Friends of Meerza' on Facebook, i.e. the photos, text, etc. that we provide will dominate the site. For Twitter and blogs, the SMM will track what is being said about us and provide instant rebuttals of false accusations, e.g. that we employ sweatshop labour. We also have to be upfront about the fact that our clothes are not all made in Paris.
- **Concentrate on building our website** and abandon personal fitting sessions for clothes ordered on our website, as these are time consuming and limit our potential clientele. To help us become the best online clothing retailer in the world, we will commission a web-design consultancy to improve the customer experience on the website with better photos, advice on measurement-taking, fabric selection and so on, with how-to videos. Our goal should be to make the ordering process on our site even better than the ultra-smooth experience found on sites like Amazon.
- **Improve logistics** so that after ordering, we follow through with perfect execution – making the clothes, packaging, delivery and returns. We will be calling in representatives from courier companies such as FedEx and DHL to discuss the delivery/returns issues, to make this part of the customer service as hassle-free as possible. We will then make our final choice of 'delivery partner'.

Conclusions

Hopefully, the improved customer experience will feed through to positive customer feedback on our site and elsewhere, but it will be the SMM's job to manage this communication in the best possible way for us. We envisage that recruitment of the SMM will be followed by other, lower-level recruitments to carefully track our 'online image' and rectify it where necessary.

A A director of Meerza Tailoring Fashions has asked a sales representative from European Express Couriers (EEC) to make a 20-minute presentation on how the logistics process can be made as efficient as possible for delivery of Meerza's products within Europe. Prepare about 10 PowerPoint slides to show how this can be done. (If you don't have PowerPoint, draw them on paper.) The presentation should cover:

- pick-up of packages from Meerza's suppliers in Paris, London and Frankfurt
- transport to EEC's distribution centres near these cities
- overnight transport (by road and/or air) to courier's local distribution centres throughout Europe
- deliveries
- arrangements for returning goods (wrong size, colour, etc.)
- terms and conditions for invoicing and payment by EEC.

B It is six months later. Meerza has implemented the strategy outlined in the model answer above, with varying results for its image and reputation. Write (on paper) six 'tweets' from different people – Meerza customers and others – that you might find on Twitter, some positive, some negative, in response to the Twitter prompt 'What's happening?'. (A tweet can contain up to 140 characters, i.e. letters or spaces.) One is given here as an example.

What's happening?
Have just received my Meerza suit – it's fantastic – beautiful fabric and it fits perfectly.

UNIT 11 New business

CASE STUDY WRITING TASK: MODEL ANSWER

Dear Emily

Following the recent discussions at OTC about our future growth strategy, this is to let you have our latest thinking on the subject.

We don't want to spread ourselves too much, so we have decided to concentrate on European markets for the time being. We will find ways of getting our products more available for self-service from shelves and counters. OTC will keep its production in Copenhagen for the foreseeable future.

We will also look in the mid-term at the emerging markets in the developing world, such as India, where increasing prosperity will mean burgeoning demand for our products. We won't try to get into the US – the regulatory approval process there is too expensive and time consuming.

OTC will also look at e-commerce in Europe. Initially, it might be good to develop this channel for our existing customers – people who know us and are making repeat orders with us.

We will look at our product range to see if we can extend it to high- and low-tech items, but we will only introduce new products where we have a clear cost or quality advantage over competitors' products. Product development will need collaboration of some kind with universities and medical schools – we will appoint a research director, perhaps someone with an academic background, to develop these contacts.

Finally, we are considering entering into a distribution agreement with a major chain of pharmacy stores ('chemists') in the UK, a key market. I'm attaching their proposal for the agreement, which I think is rather complicated from our point of view. If you could advise us on how to proceed, we would be very grateful.

Best regards

Anders Larsen

Chief Executive, OTC

A The two OTC directors have had another meeting with Emily Brookes, the outside consultant, to discuss the practical arrangements for proceeding with the points in the model answer above. Continue the action minutes for this meeting shown below. (Feel free to invent further information.)

OTC strategy meeting: action minutes

Date: 30 November

Venue: OTC, Copenhagen

Present: Anders Larsen (Chief Executive), Ulla Hofmann (Chief Scientist), Emily Brookes (Senior Consultant, Omega Consulting)

	Action	By
1 **Target market: Europe** Develop fair and equitable distribution agreements in the 'Big Five' countries – France, Germany, Spain, Italy, UK – with self-service availability a key criterion.	EB	15 Jan

(See the Writing file, Course Book page 144, for the format of action minutes.)

B It's five years later. Anders and Ulla have changed their minds and think the time is now right to exploit the potential of the US market. Write an e-mail from Anders to the director of the Danish Chamber of Commerce in New York. Give some brief information about OTC and ask for:

- background information about the distribution of medical equipment and devices in the US
- the names of retailers in the US who might be interested in retailing OTC's products
- general advice about getting into the US market.
- End suitably.

Project management

CASE STUDY WRITING TASK: MODEL ANSWER

Report on Raghavan Port Development Project

To: All senior managers, Blake–Martins consortium; Director, Gujarati Ports Authority; Minister for Infrastructure, Gujarat state government

Re: Teleconference, 3 March

Background to the project

As you know, the Gujarat state government selected the Blake–Martins consortium to carry out the project to construct a world-class port at Raghavan, with the consortium as the major shareholders, and the Port Authority and State Ministry each having a 15-per-cent stake.

Reasons for this review

As we all are too well aware, there have been severe delays, cost increases and communication breakdowns on the project. Also, the original layout and design for the project were radically altered after it commenced.

Key findings

The change in the initial plans and the monsoon weather have caused problems, but the teleconference participants agreed that communication breakdown has been the most important contributing factor to the delays and cost overruns. Completing the first phase on time, or at least reducing the current slippage, should be our main priority.

Recommendations

All those present agreed (or were persuaded) that the Internet application has to be the main means of communication and source of information for the project. It will be upgraded to take account of criticisms that it has not been completely suitable. E-mails, faxes and other forms of unapproved communication will be forbidden. Despite protests from some managers, it was felt that the teleconferences are not ideal for the project, given the time differences involved. The information previously expressed orally at these conferences (and often not noted down) will now be exchanged and recorded in writing on the website. However, there will also be more onsite meetings between the project managers and our lead contractor, with the outcomes noted on the website application. Teleconferences will now take place once a month, rather than once a week.

Requests from managers for authorisation to spend more on machinery, materials, overtime, morale-boosting incentives, workers' accommodation and buses, etc. will be dealt with on a case-by-case basis by the project manager.

Immediate action plans

The project website will be upgraded as a matter of urgency. Video training in the form of a virtual guided tour will be available on the website itself so that people know how to use it to its full potential.

Requests for additional resources to the project manager by individual managers should be submitted on the website by next Friday evening.

And, following a request from our Dutch colleagues, there will be a party for all on-site managers so that people can get to know each other better! (Date to be confirmed.)

It's a few months later. The project manager has been able to partially make up the delays, but the first phase of the project will still be delivered three months late. Write a formal letter from the project manager to the Director of the Gujarati state government's Ministry for Infrastructure. Make the following points:

- The six-month delay was largely caused by changes in the plans demanded by the Gujarat government and port authorities. (Be very tactful about this and mention some of the other factors, too.)
- However, you have increased your spending on machinery, overtime, etc. to make up the delay, and this has partly succeeded. (Slippage at one point of six months has been reduced to three.) However, the cost of the first phase has increased by 15 per cent.
- The contract for the project specifies that cost overruns should be shared 50/50 between the Gujarati authorities and the project partners.
- Say, politely, that the project's Finance Director will soon be in touch with a breakdown of these extra costs, and a suggestion about how the costs should be shared in this case, given that they are largely due to changes in the initial plans made by the authorities.
- Say that the next phase is going well. Lessons have been learned – there should be no more delays or cost overruns.
- End suitably.

(See the Writing file, Course Book page 143, for advice on breaking bad news.)

Pearson Education Limited
Edinburgh Gate
Harlow
Essex CM20 2JE
England
and Associated Companies throughout the world.

www.pearsonlongman.com

First published 2006
This edition 2011

ISBN: 978-1-4082-6802-5

Set in MetaPlus 9.5/12pt

Printed and bound by Graficas Estella, Spain

Acknowledgements
We are grateful to the following for permission to reproduce copyright material:

Text
Extract 3.2 from 'You have had the credit crisis – next it will be oil', *The Financial Times*, 09/06/2010 (Jeremy Leggett), copyright © Jeremy Leggett; Extract 5.1 adapted from 'Winds of change head for the workplace', *The Financial Times*, 25/07/2010 (Lynda Gratton), copyright © Lynda Gratton; Extract 5.2 abridged 'Time to work on the jobs of the future', *The Financial Times*, 24/08/2010 (Luke Johnson), copyright © Luke Johnson; Extract 6.2 adapted from 'Ethics teaching asks the wrong questions', *The Financial Times*, 13/09/2010 (Mary C. Gentile), copyright © Mary C. Gentile; Extract 8.2 from 'Tips for when the tide turns', *The Financial Times*, 16/11/2009 (Dave Ulrich), copyright © Dave Ulrich; and Extract in Resource Bank Speaking 6.b from 'The MBA Oath', www.MBAoath.org. Reproduced with permission.

The Financial Times
Extract 1.1 abridged from 'Businesses urged to keep interview standards high', *The Financial Times*, 04/10/2007 (Willman, J.), copyright © The Financial Times Ltd; Extract 2.1 from 'Ivory Coast turns to HEC', *The Financial Times*, 10/01/2010 (Bleby, M.), copyright © The Financial Times Ltd; Extract 2.2 adapted from 'Analysis: Flexibility and reach draw ever greater numbers', *The Financial Times*, 15/03/2010 (Clarke, C.), copyright © The Financi Times Ltd; Extract 4.1 from 'Social media: Tarnish the brand or build an aspirational following?', *The Financial Times*, 14/06/201 (Gelles, D.), copyright © The Financial Times Ltd; Extract 4.2 from 'Marketing Marketing to minorities', *The Financial Times*, 07/09/2010 (Garrahan, M.), copyright © The Financial Times Ltd; Extract 7.1 from 'Fayed goes out in style as Harrods leaps 40 per cent', *The Financial Times*, 02/10/2010 (Jacobs, R.), copyright © The Financial Times Ltd; Extract 7.2 from 'What happens to marke when numbers don't add up', *The Financial Times*, 16/04/2010 (Tett, G.), copyright © The Financial Times Ltd; Extract 8.1 from 'Candidates in some sectors need a little coercing', *The Financial Times*, 16/09/2010 (Parslow, N.), copyright © The Financial Times Ltd; Extract 9.1 abridged from 'The job of business secretary is to put the future first', *The Financial Times*, 28/09/2010 (Kay, J.), copyright © The Financial Times Ltd; Extract 10.2 abridged from 'Valley that thrives on hope of the next big online fad', *The Financi Times*, 29/09/2010 (Waters, R.), copyright © The Financial Times Ltd; and Extract 11.1 from 'Fledgling ventures flock to London for seed funding', *The Financial Times*, 17/09/2010 (Moules, J. and Bradshaw, T.), copyright © The Financial Times Ltd

In some instances we have been unable to trace the owners of copyright material, and we would appreciate any information that would enable us to do so.

Project managed by Chris Hartley